APHIC NOVEL

ndants of Darkness

Yami no Matsuei

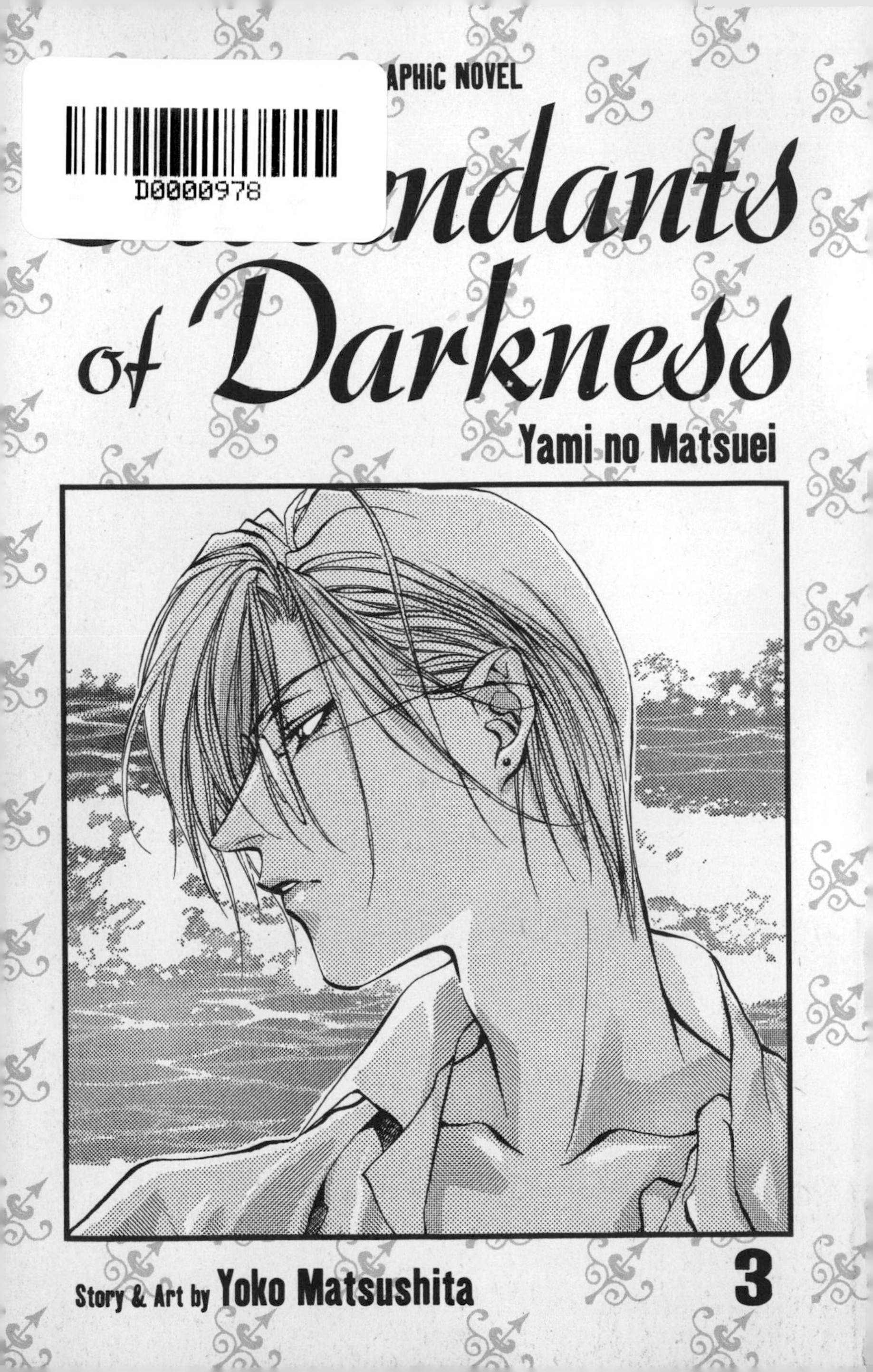

3

Story & Art by Yoko Matsushita

Descendants of Darkness
Yami no Matsuei

Vol. 3
Shôjo Edition

Story & Art by
Yoko Matsushita

English Adaptation/Kelly Sue DeConnick
Translation/David Ury
Touch-Up & Lettering/Gia Cam Luc
Graphics & Cover Design/Hidemi Sahara
Editor/Pancha Diaz

Editor in Chief, Books/Alvin Lu
Editor in Chief, Magazines/Marc Weidenbaum
VP, Publishing Licensing/Rika Inouye
VP, Sales & Product Marketing/Gonzalo Ferreyra
VP, Creative/Linda Espinosa
Publisher/Hyoe Narita

Yami no Matsuei by Yoko Matsushita © Yoko Matsushita 1997. All rights reserved. First published in Japan in 1998 by HAKUSENSHA, Inc., Tokyo. English language translation rights arranged with HAKUSENSHA, Inc., Tokyo.

Printed in the U.S.A.

Published by VIZ Media, LLC
P.O. Box 77064
San Francisco, CA 94107

Shôjo Edition
10 9 8 7 6 5 4 3
First printing, December 2004
Third printing, August 2008

www.viz.com   store.viz.com

Table of Contents

The Sword of K

Chapter 1.................. 3

Chapter 2.................. 45

Chapter 3.................. 77

Chapter 4.................. 107

Chapter 5.................. 135

Chapter 6.................. 165

The Ministry of Hades:
Basic Course............ 197

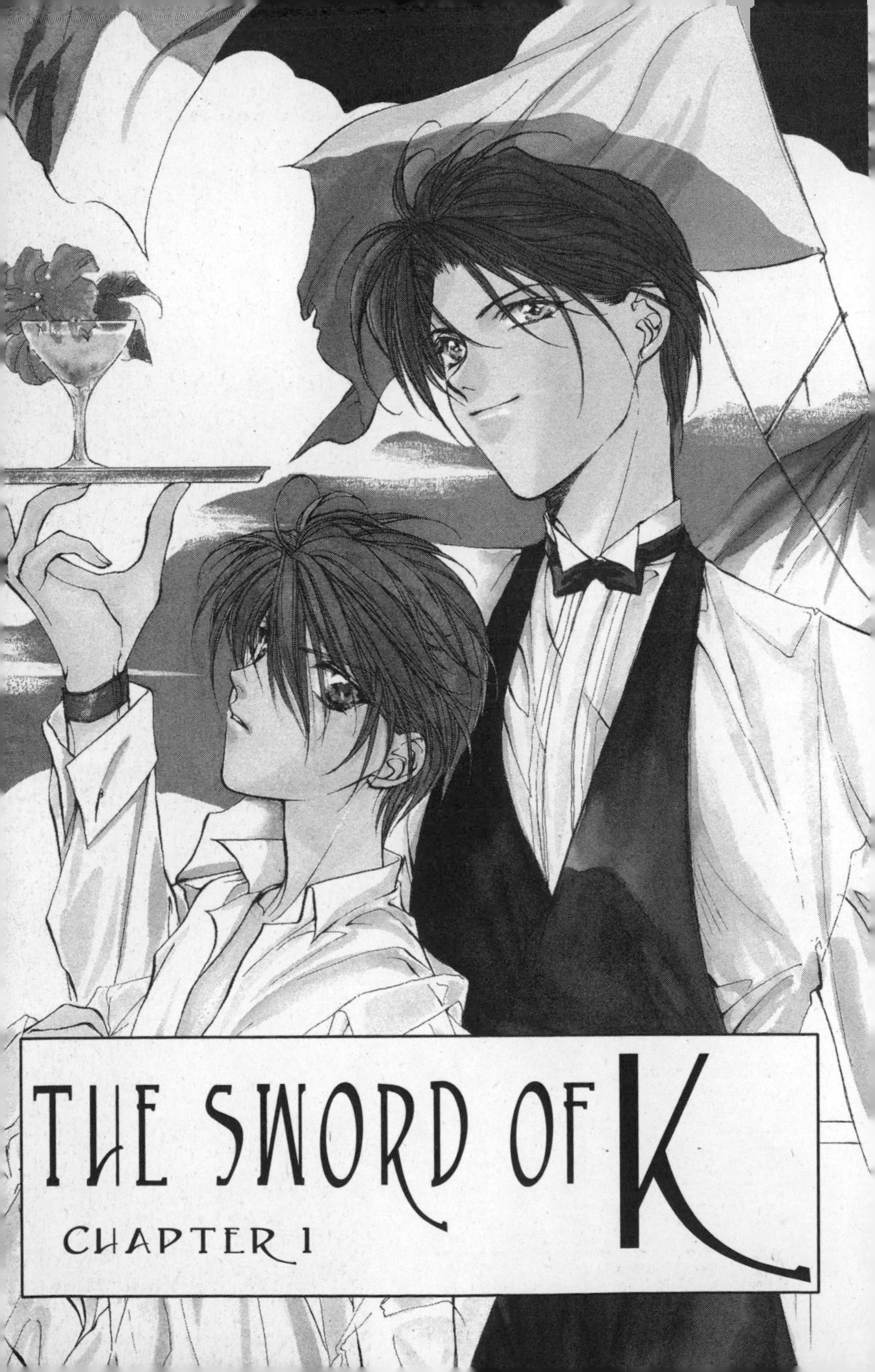
THE SWORD OF K
CHAPTER 1

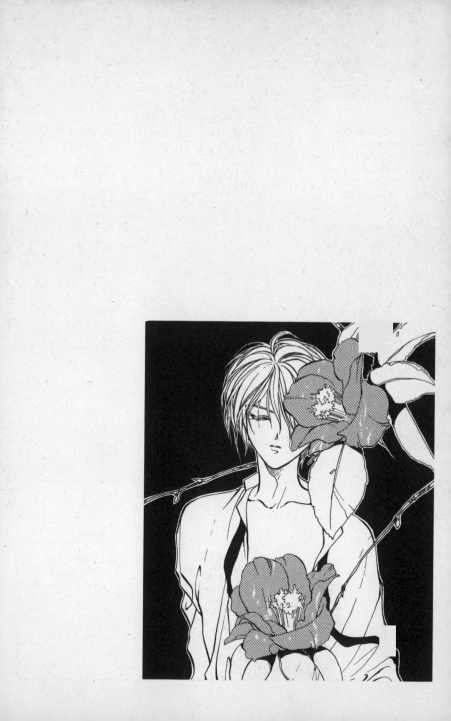

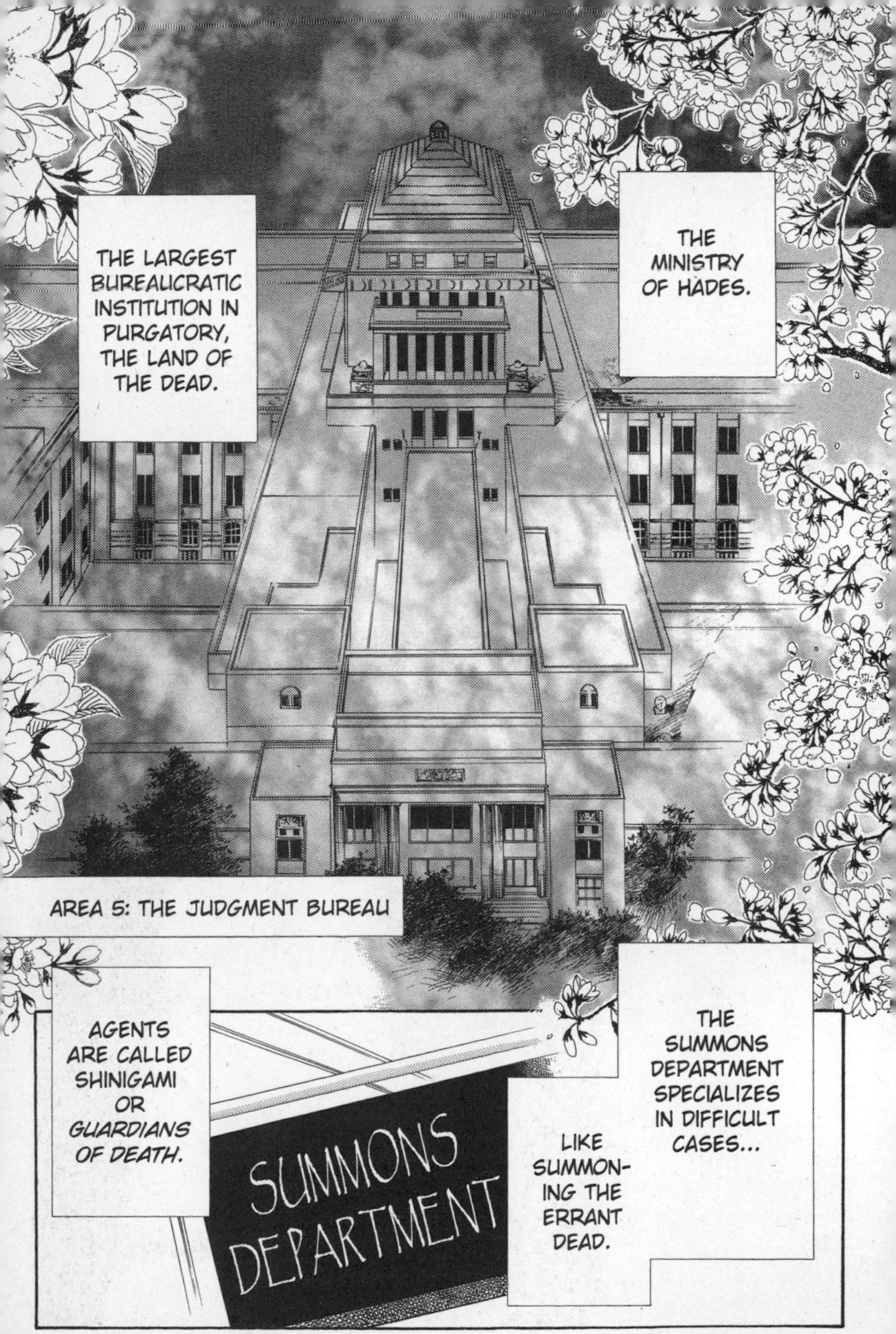
THE MINISTRY OF HADES.
THE LARGEST BUREAUCRATIC INSTITUTION IN PURGATORY, THE LAND OF THE DEAD.
AREA 5: THE JUDGMENT BUREAU
THE SUMMONS DEPARTMENT SPECIALIZES IN DIFFICULT CASES...
LIKE SUMMONING THE ERRANT DEAD.
SUMMONS DEPARTMENT
AGENTS ARE CALLED SHINIGAMI OR *GUARDIANS OF DEATH.*

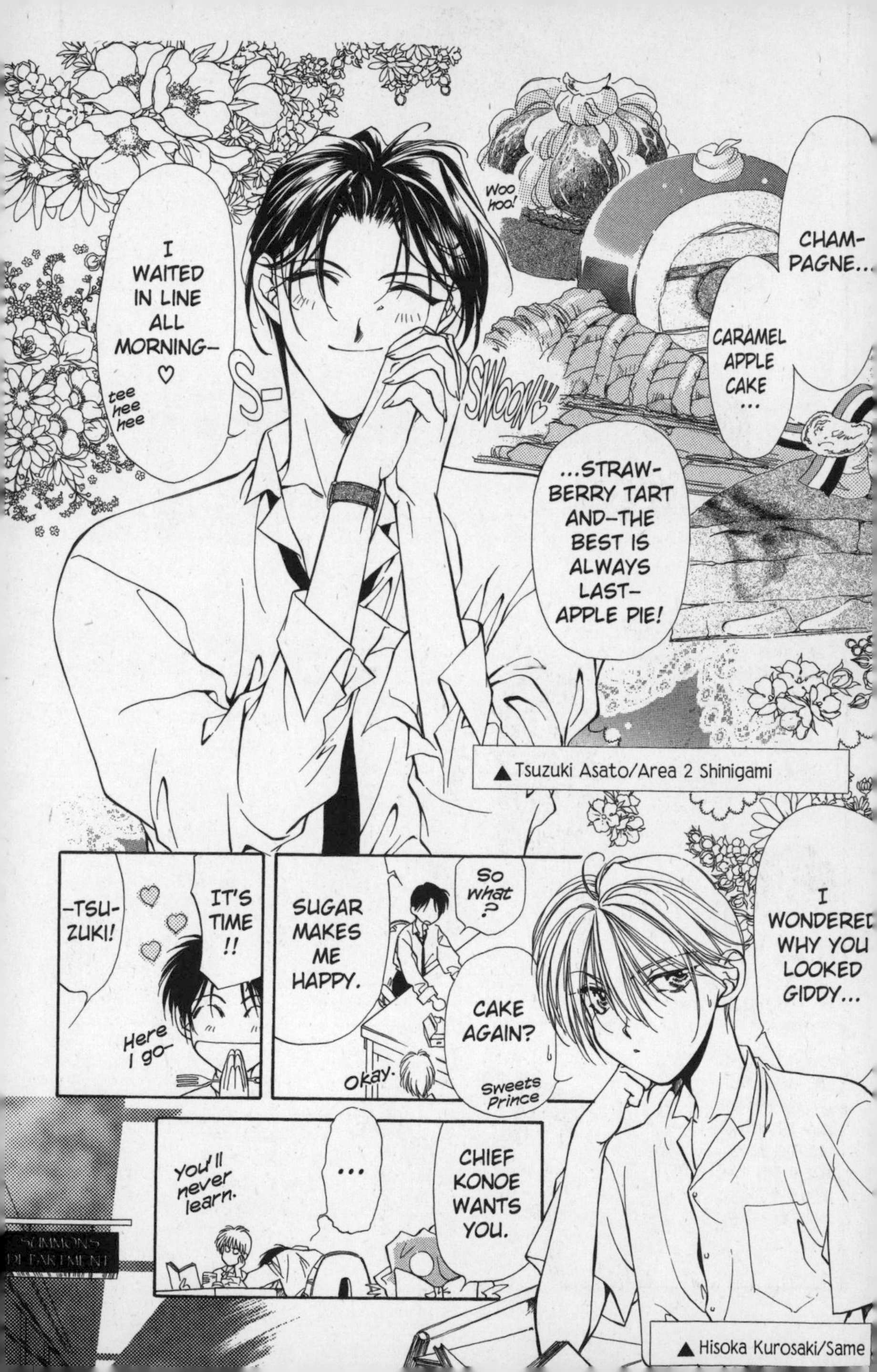
CHAMPAGNE...
CARAMEL APPLE CAKE...
...STRAWBERRY TART AND—THE BEST IS ALWAYS LAST—APPLE PIE!
Woo hoo!
SWOON♡!!
I WAITED IN LINE ALL MORNING—♡
tee hee hee
S—
▲Tsuzuki Asato/Area 2 Shinigami
I WONDERED WHY YOU LOOKED GIDDY...
CAKE AGAIN?
Sweets Prince
▲Hisoka Kurosaki/Same
So what?
SUGAR MAKES ME HAPPY.
Okay.
IT'S TIME!!
—TSUZUKI!
Here I go—
CHIEF KONOE WANTS YOU.
...
You'll never learn.
SUMMONS DEPARTMENT

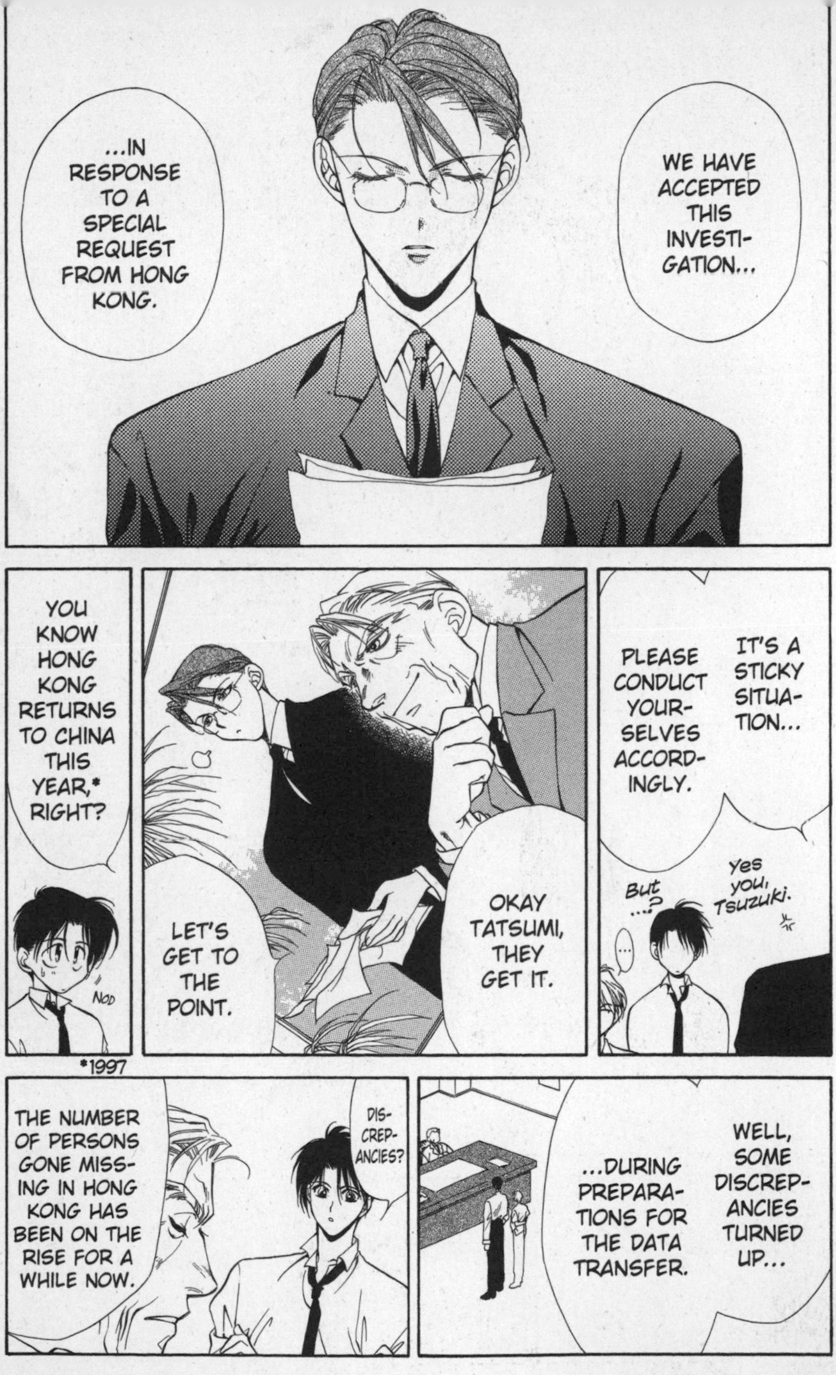
WE HAVE ACCEPTED THIS INVESTIGATION...
...IN RESPONSE TO A SPECIAL REQUEST FROM HONG KONG.
IT'S A STICKY SITUATION...
PLEASE CONDUCT YOURSELVES ACCORDINGLY.
Yes you, Tsuzuki.
But ...?
...
OKAY TATSUMI, THEY GET IT.
LET'S GET TO THE POINT.
YOU KNOW HONG KONG RETURNS TO CHINA THIS YEAR,* RIGHT?
NOD
*1997
WELL, SOME DISCREPANCIES TURNED UP...
...DURING PREPARATIONS FOR THE DATA TRANSFER.
DISCREPANCIES?
THE NUMBER OF PERSONS GONE MISSING IN HONG KONG HAS BEEN ON THE RISE FOR A WHILE NOW.

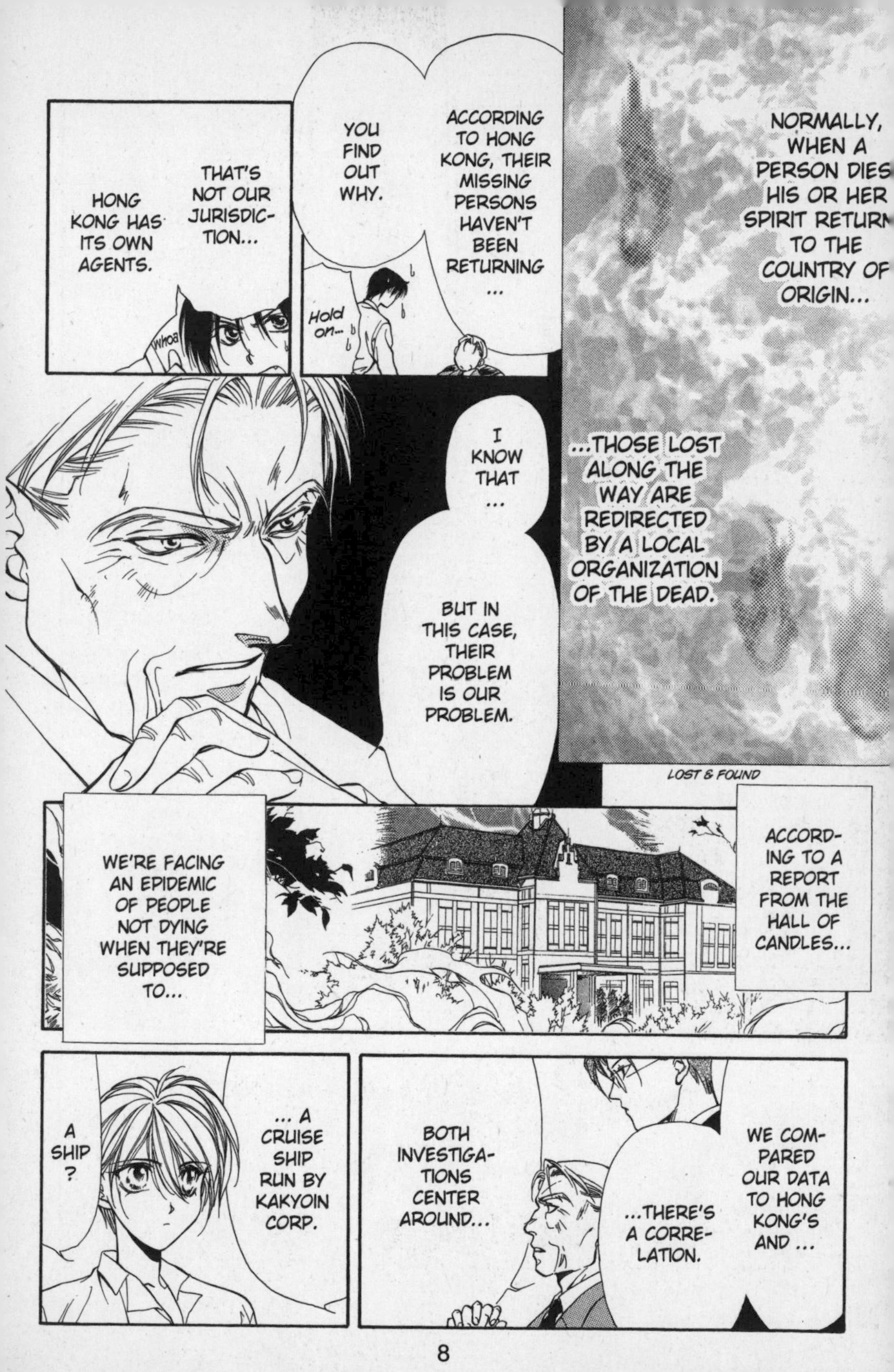
NORMALLY, WHEN A PERSON DIES HIS OR HER SPIRIT RETURN TO THE COUNTRY OF ORIGIN...
...THOSE LOST ALONG THE WAY ARE REDIRECTED BY A LOCAL ORGANIZATION OF THE DEAD.
ACCORDING TO HONG KONG, THEIR MISSING PERSONS HAVEN'T BEEN RETURNING ...
YOU FIND OUT WHY.
Hold on...
THAT'S NOT OUR JURISDICTION...
HONG KONG HAS ITS OWN AGENTS.
whoa
I KNOW THAT ...
BUT IN THIS CASE, THEIR PROBLEM IS OUR PROBLEM.
LOST & FOUND
ACCORDING TO A REPORT FROM THE HALL OF CANDLES...
WE'RE FACING AN EPIDEMIC OF PEOPLE NOT DYING WHEN THEY'RE SUPPOSED TO...
WE COMPARED OUR DATA TO HONG KONG'S AND ...
...THERE'S A CORRELATION.
BOTH INVESTIGATIONS CENTER AROUND...
... A CRUISE SHIP RUN BY KAKYOIN CORP.
A SHIP ?

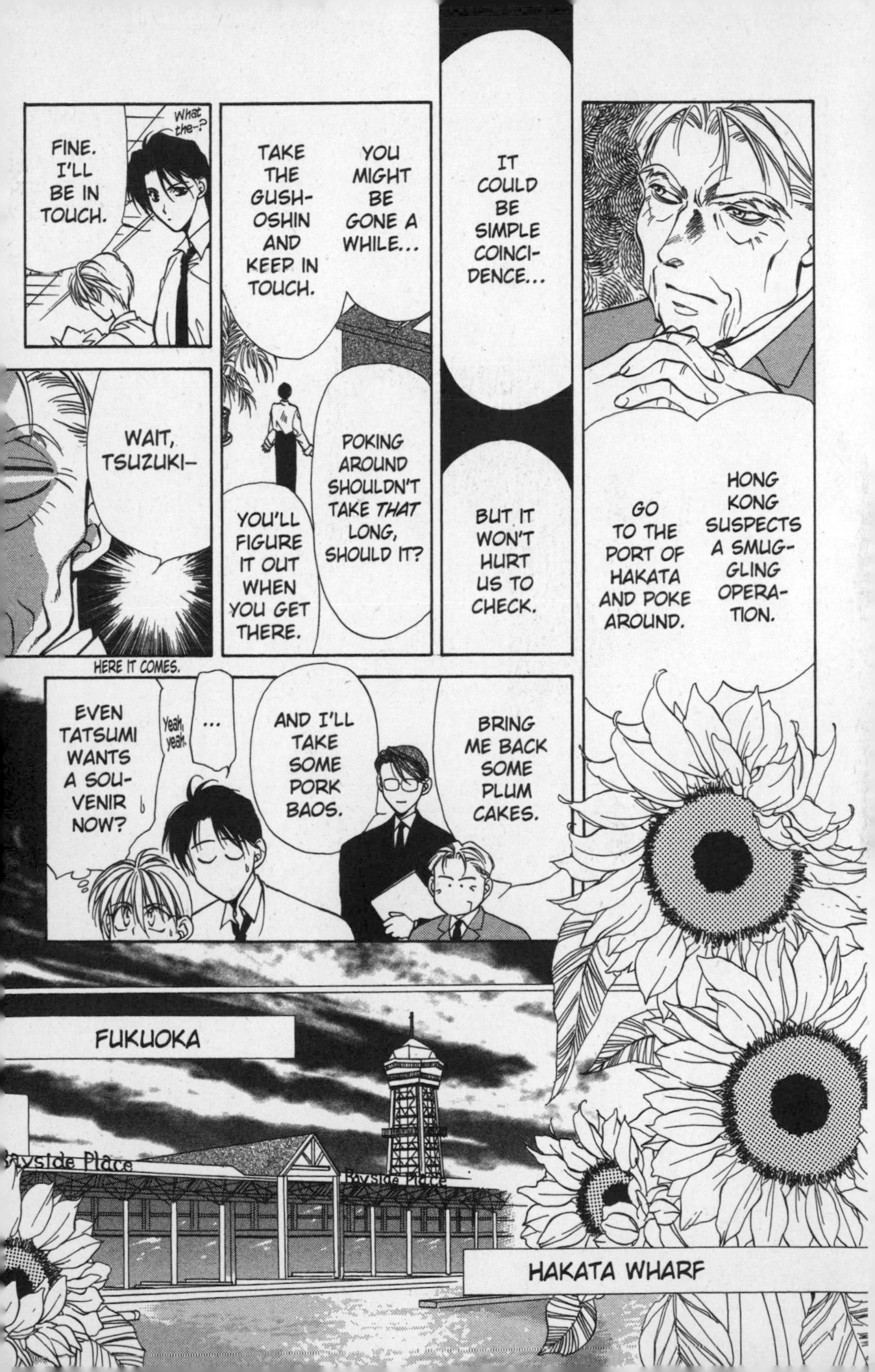
HONG KONG SUSPECTS A SMUG-GLING OPERA-TION.
GO TO THE PORT OF HAKATA AND POKE AROUND.
IT COULD BE SIMPLE COINCI-DENCE...
BUT IT WON'T HURT US TO CHECK.
YOU MIGHT BE GONE A WHILE...
TAKE THE GUSH-OSHIN AND KEEP IN TOUCH.
POKING AROUND SHOULDN'T TAKE THAT LONG, SHOULD IT?
YOU'LL FIGURE IT OUT WHEN YOU GET THERE.
What the-?
FINE. I'LL BE IN TOUCH.
WAIT, TSUZUKI–
HERE IT COMES.
BRING ME BACK SOME PLUM CAKES.
AND I'LL TAKE SOME PORK BAOS.
...
Yeah, yeah.
EVEN TATSUMI WANTS A SOU-VENIR NOW?
FUKUOKA
Bayside Place
Bayside Place
HAKATA WHARF

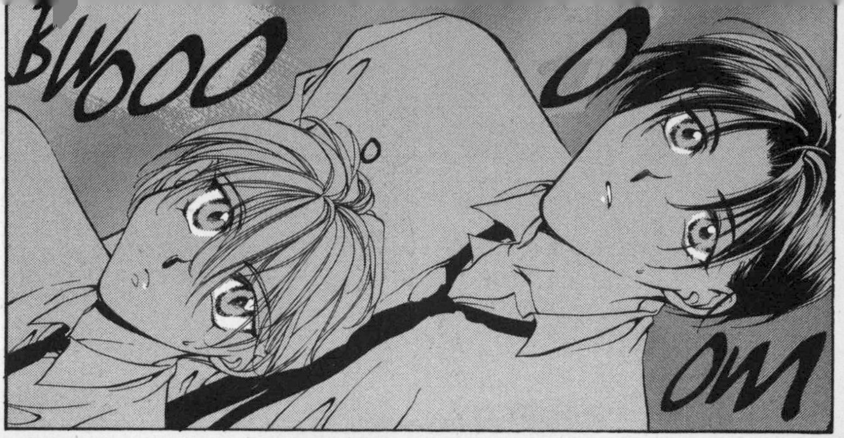
BWOOOOOM

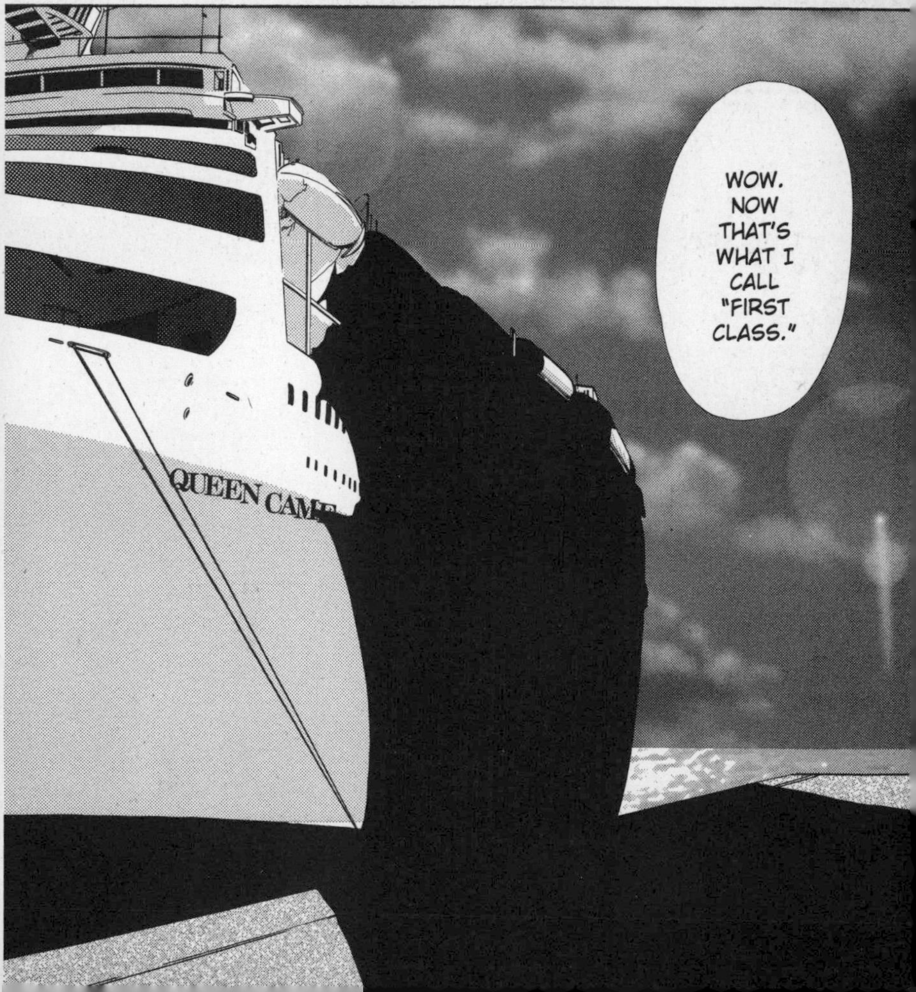
QUEEN CAME
WOW. NOW THAT'S WHAT I CALL "FIRST CLASS."

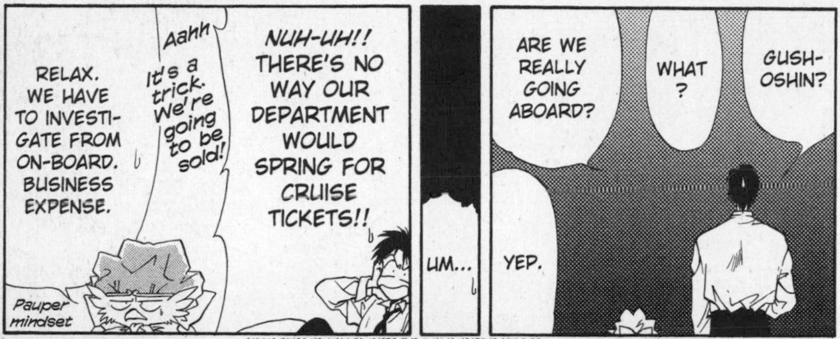
GUSH-OSHIN?
WHAT?
ARE WE REALLY GOING ABOARD?
YEP.
UM...
NUH-UH!! THERE'S NO WAY OUR DEPARTMENT WOULD SPRING FOR CRUISE TICKETS!!
Aahh
It's a trick. We're going to be sold!
RELAX. WE HAVE TO INVESTIGATE FROM ON-BOARD. BUSINESS EXPENSE.
Pauper mindset

SAILING TAKES ME AWAY TO WHERE I'VE ALWAYS HEARD IT COULD BE

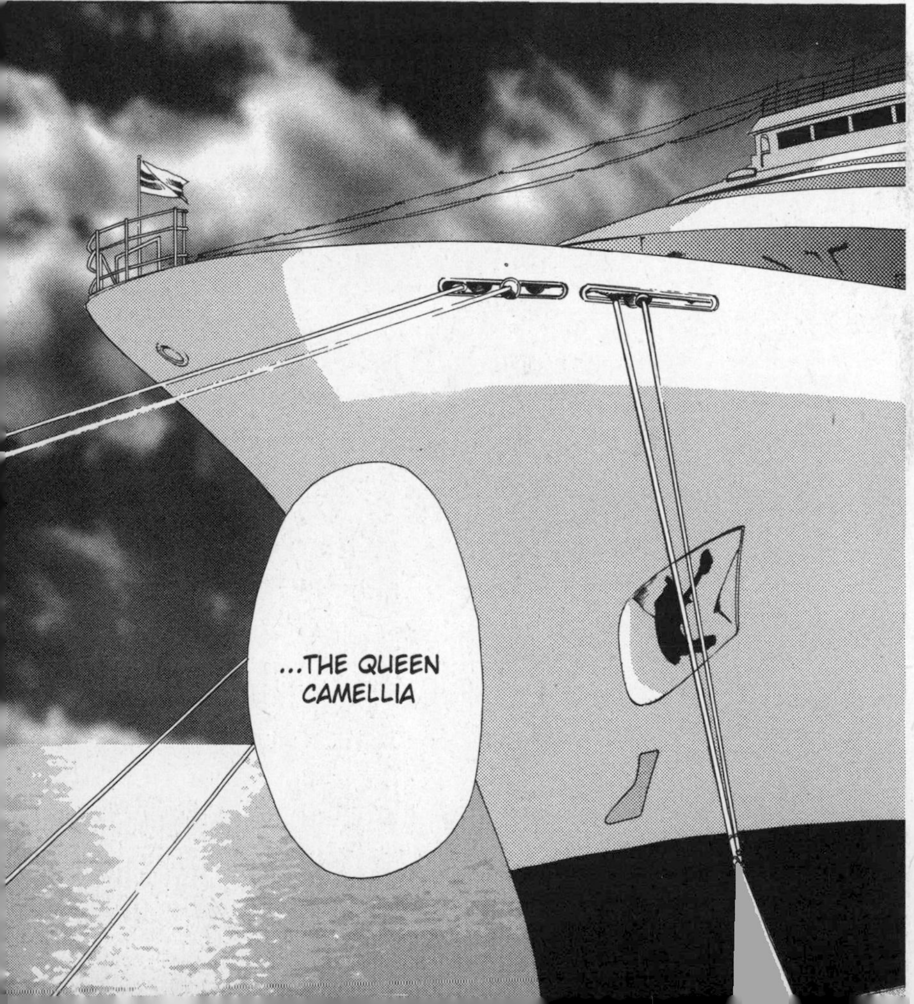
...THE QUEEN CAMELLIA

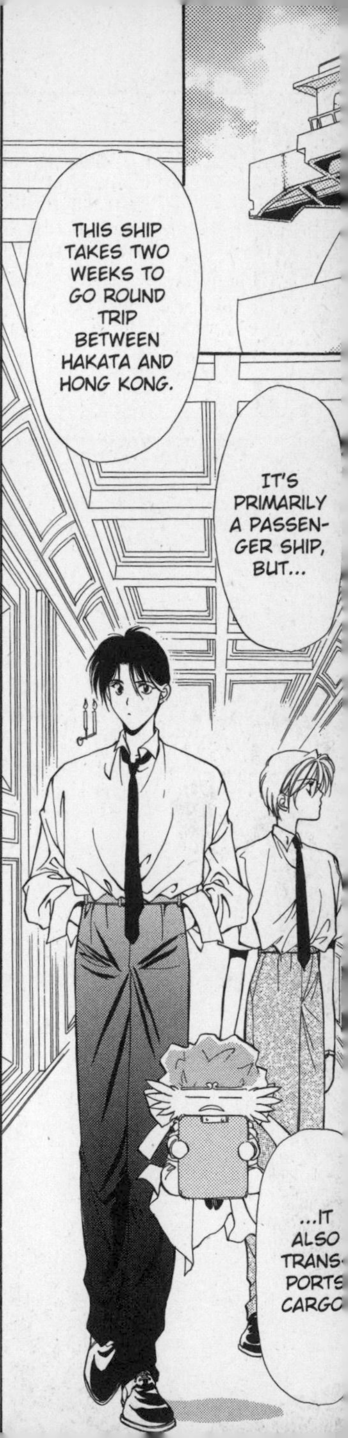
THIS SHIP TAKES TWO WEEKS TO GO ROUND TRIP BETWEEN HAKATA AND HONG KONG.
IT'S PRIMARILY A PASSENGER SHIP, BUT...
...IT ALSO TRANS-PORTS CARGO

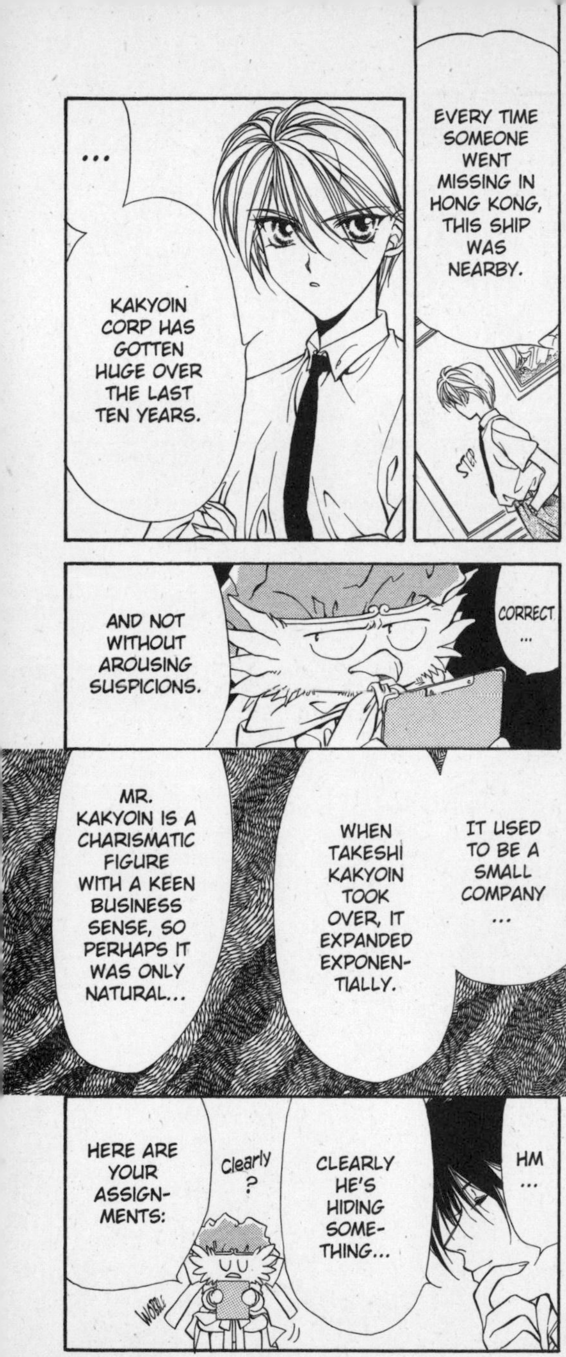
EVERY TIME SOMEONE WENT MISSING IN HONG KONG, THIS SHIP WAS NEARBY.
...
KAKYOIN CORP HAS GOTTEN HUGE OVER THE LAST TEN YEARS.
CORRECT...
AND NOT WITHOUT AROUSING SUSPICIONS.
IT USED TO BE A SMALL COMPANY...
WHEN TAKESHI KAKYOIN TOOK OVER, IT EXPANDED EXPONEN-TIALLY.
MR. KAKYOIN IS A CHARISMATIC FIGURE WITH A KEEN BUSINESS SENSE, SO PERHAPS IT WAS ONLY NATURAL...
HM...
CLEARLY HE'S HIDING SOME-THING...
Clearly?
HERE ARE YOUR ASSIGN-MENTS:

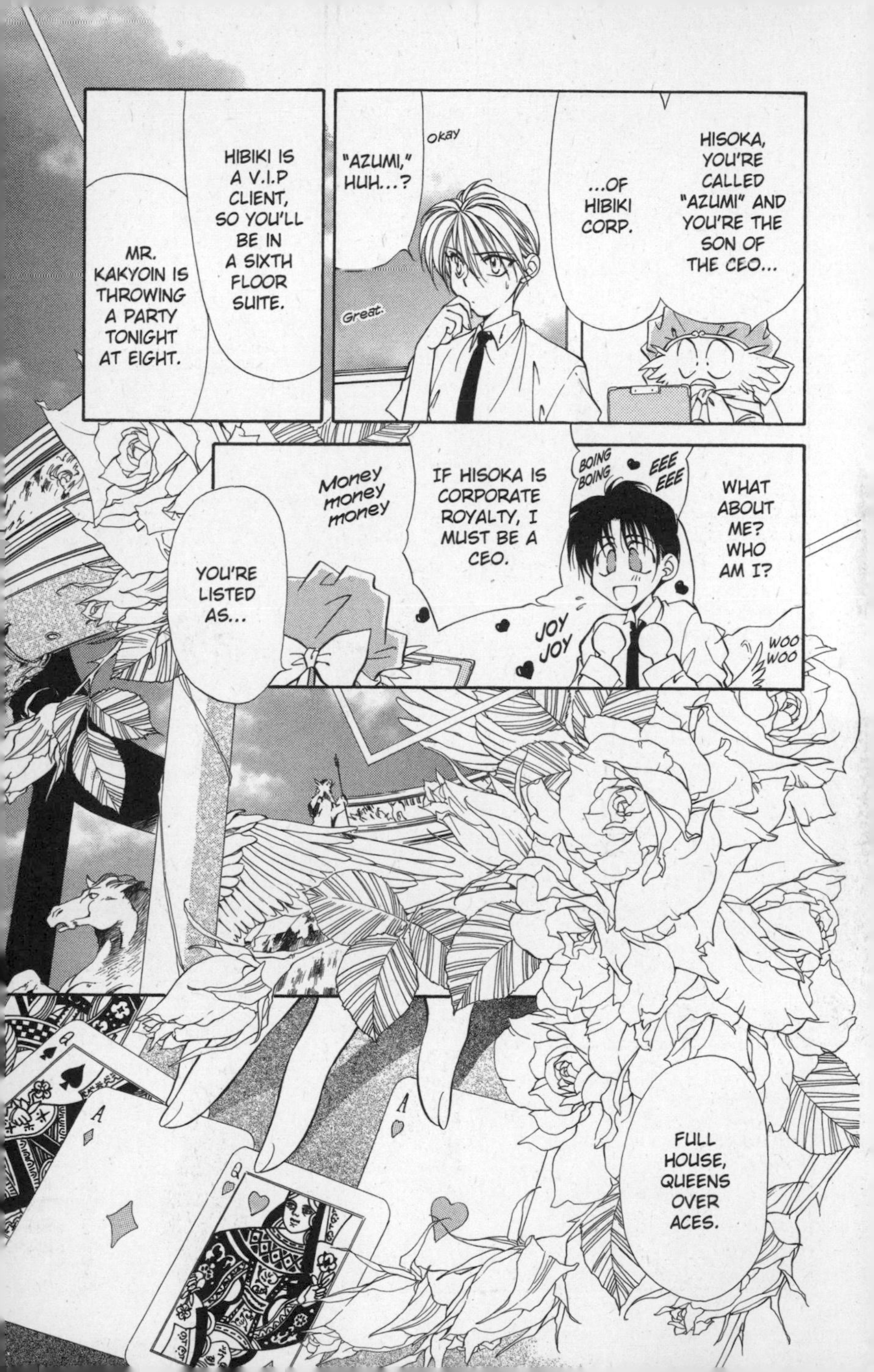
HISOKA, YOU'RE CALLED "AZUMI" AND YOU'RE THE SON OF THE CEO...
...OF HIBIKI CORP.
"AZUMI," HUH...?
Okay
Great.
HIBIKI IS A V.I.P CLIENT, SO YOU'LL BE IN A SIXTH FLOOR SUITE.
MR. KAKYOIN IS THROWING A PARTY TONIGHT AT EIGHT.
WHAT ABOUT ME? WHO AM I?
WOO WOO
BOING BOING
EEE EEE
JOY JOY
IF HISOKA IS CORPORATE ROYALTY, I MUST BE A CEO.
Money money money
YOU'RE LISTED AS...
FULL HOUSE, QUEENS OVER ACES.

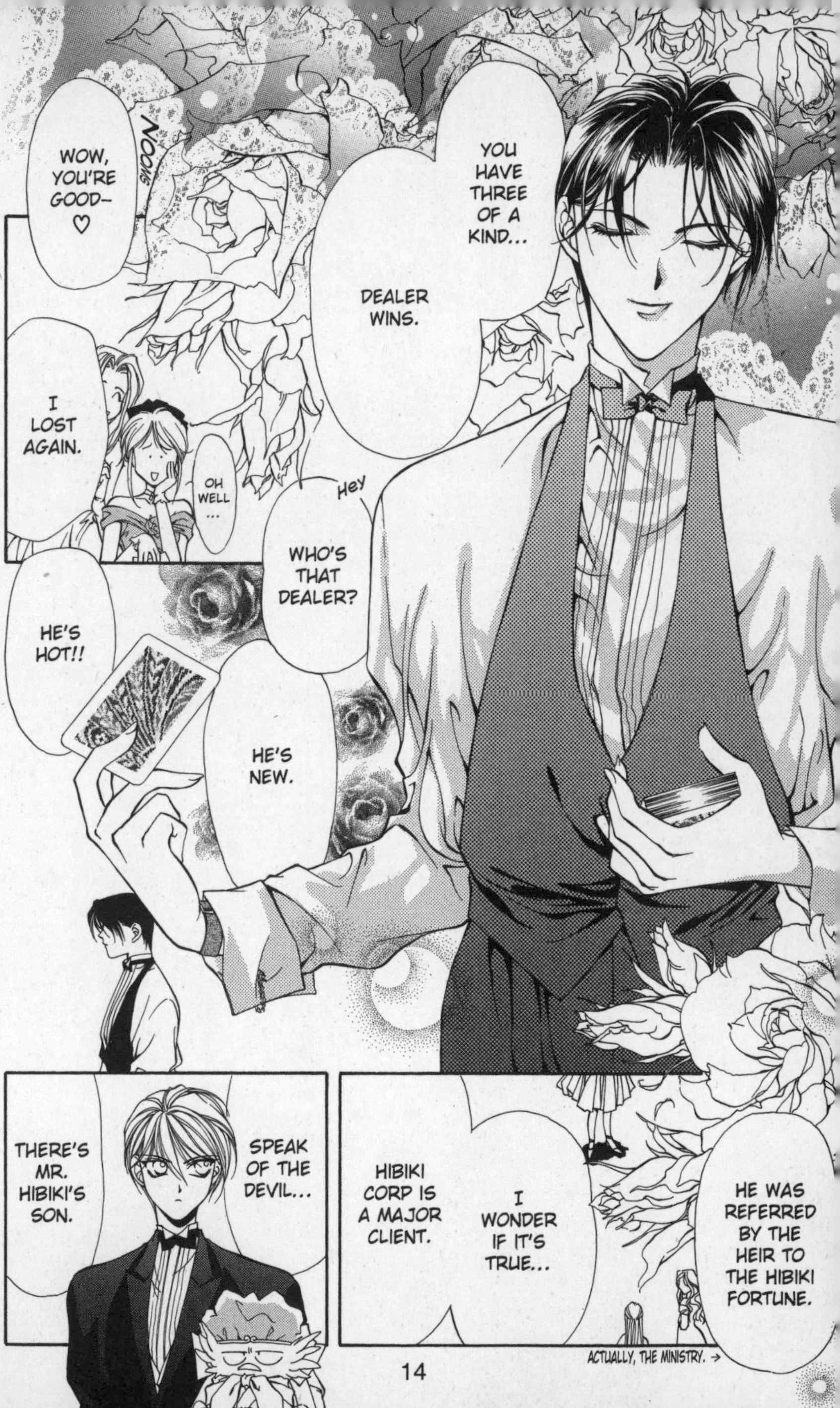
YOU HAVE THREE OF A KIND...
DEALER WINS.
WOW, YOU'RE GOOD-♡
SWOON
OH WELL...
I LOST AGAIN.
Hey
WHO'S THAT DEALER?
HE'S NEW.
HE'S HOT!!
HE WAS REFERRED BY THE HEIR TO THE HIBIKI FORTUNE.
I WONDER IF IT'S TRUE...
HIBIKI CORP IS A MAJOR CLIENT.
SPEAK OF THE DEVIL...
THERE'S MR. HIBIKI'S SON.
ACTUALLY, THE MINISTRY. →

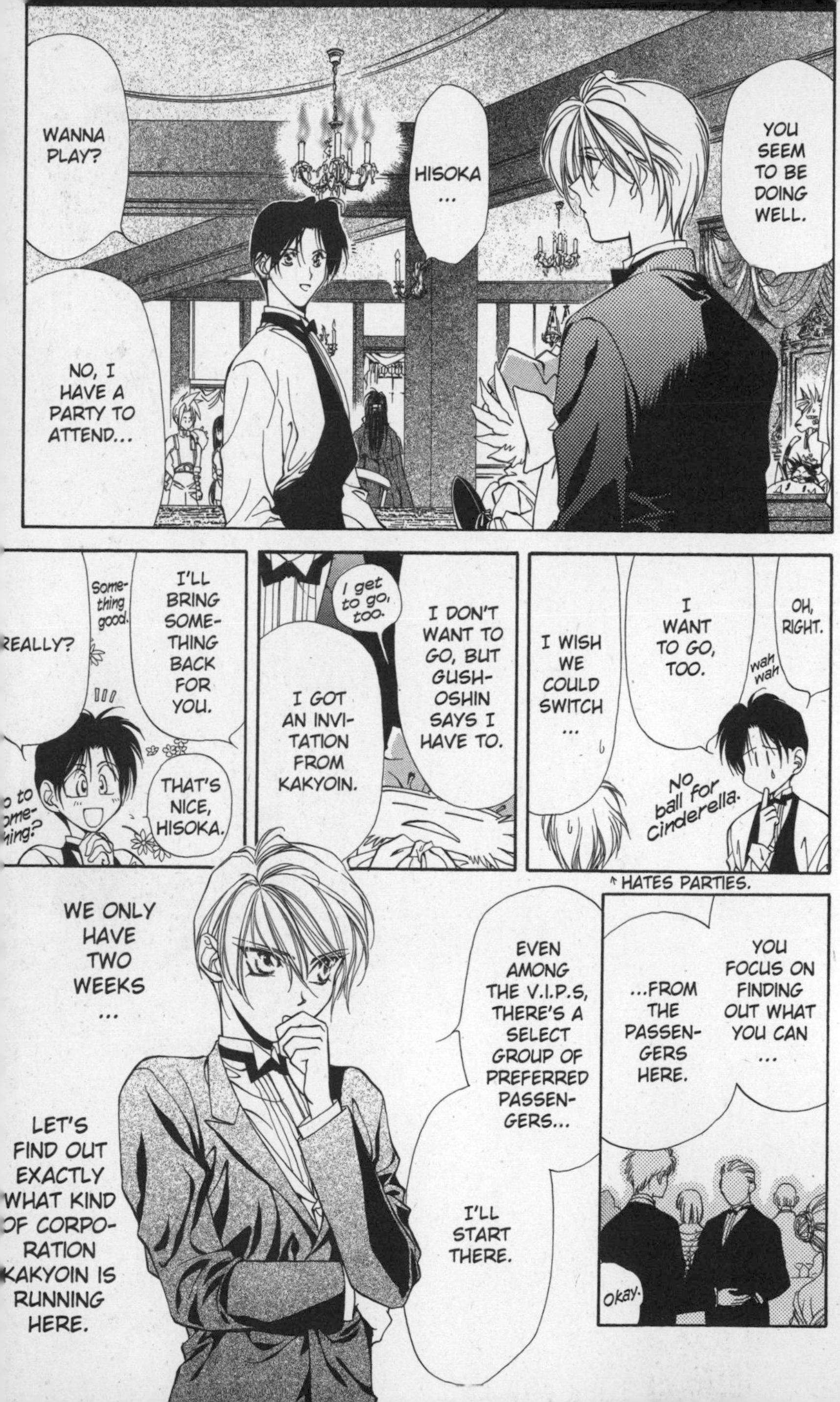
YOU SEEM TO BE DOING WELL.
HISOKA...
WANNA PLAY?
NO, I HAVE A PARTY TO ATTEND...
OH, RIGHT.
wah wah
I WANT TO GO, TOO.
I WISH WE COULD SWITCH...
No ball for Cinderella.
↑HATES PARTIES.
I get to go, too.
I DON'T WANT TO GO, BUT GUSH-OSHIN SAYS I HAVE TO.
I GOT AN INVITATION FROM KAKYOIN.
I'LL BRING SOME-THING BACK FOR YOU.
Some-thing good.
REALLY?
THAT'S NICE, HISOKA.
YOU FOCUS ON FINDING OUT WHAT YOU CAN...
...FROM THE PASSEN-GERS HERE.
Okay.
EVEN AMONG THE V.I.P.S, THERE'S A SELECT GROUP OF PREFERRED PASSEN-GERS...
I'LL START THERE.
WE ONLY HAVE TWO WEEKS...
LET'S FIND OUT EXACTLY WHAT KIND OF CORPO-RATION KAKYOIN IS RUNNING HERE.

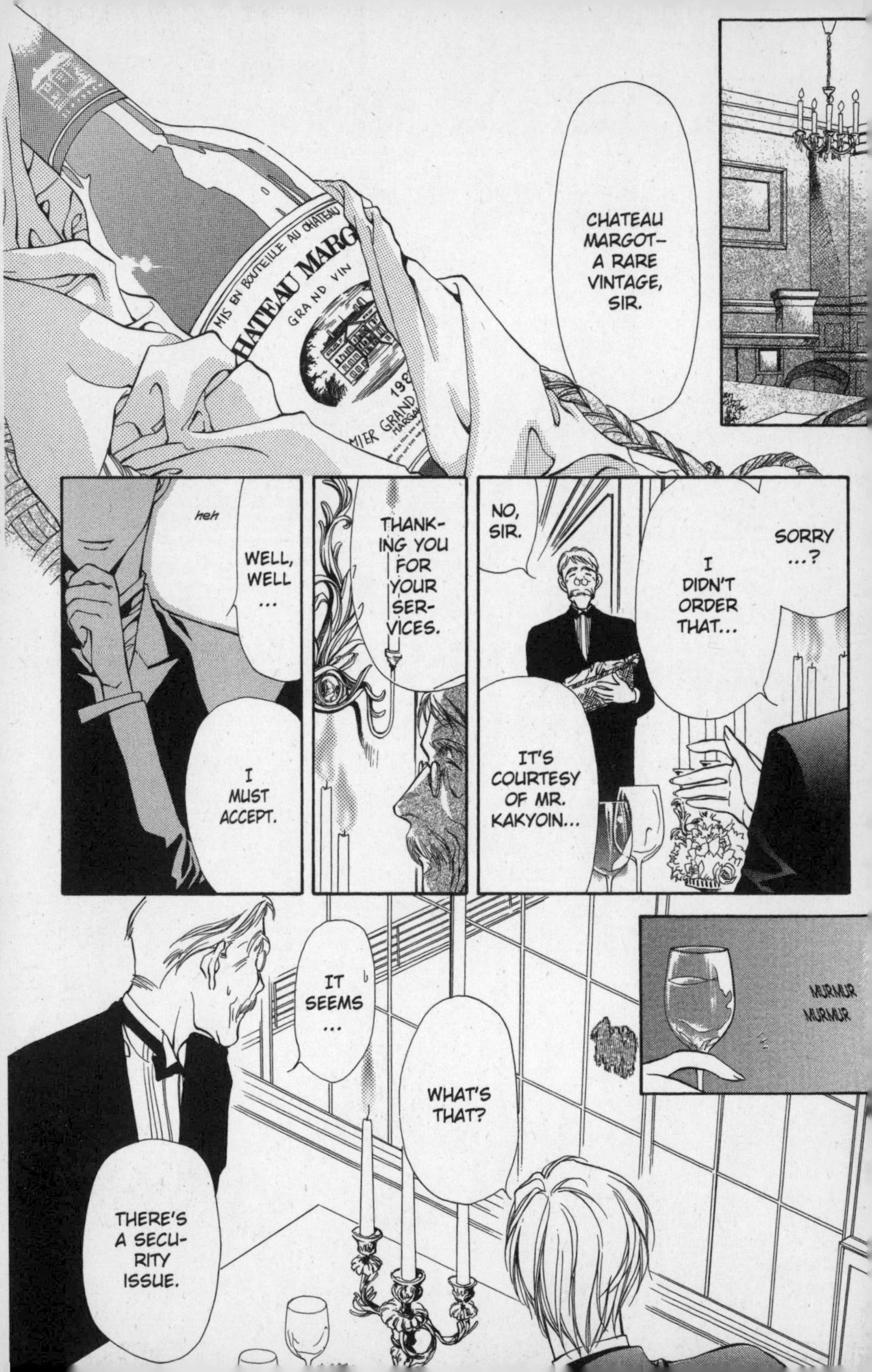
CHATEAU MARGOT– A RARE VINTAGE, SIR.
MIS EN BOUTEILLE AU CHATEAU
GRAND VIN
SORRY …?
I DIDN'T ORDER THAT…
NO, SIR.
IT'S COURTESY OF MR. KAKYOIN…
THANKING YOU FOR YOUR SERVICES.
heh
WELL, WELL …
I MUST ACCEPT.
MURMUR MURMUR
WHAT'S THAT?
IT SEEMS …
THERE'S A SECURITY ISSUE.

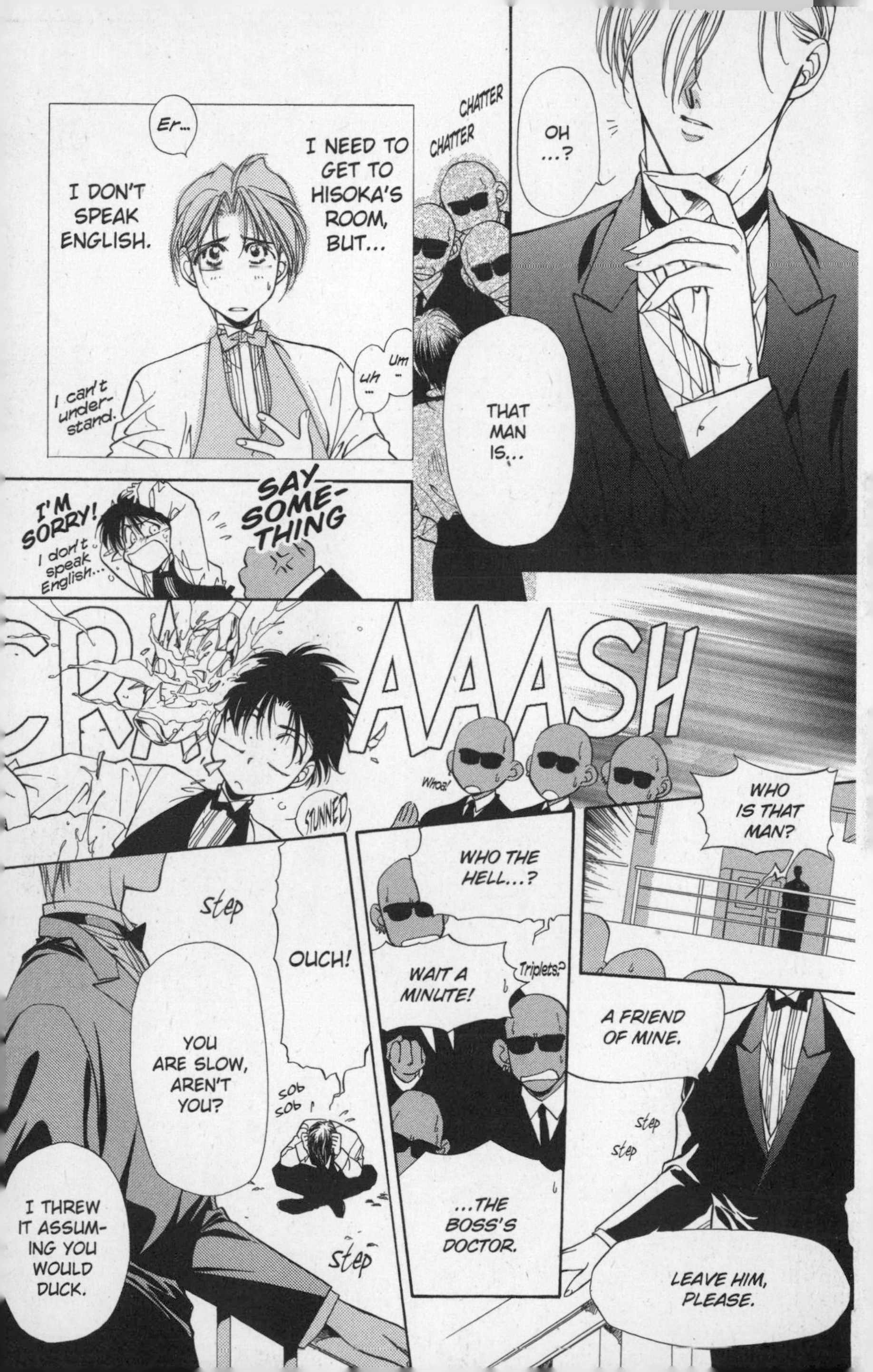
OH ...?
THAT MAN IS...
CHATTER
CHATTER
Er...
I NEED TO GET TO HISOKA'S ROOM, BUT...
I DON'T SPEAK ENGLISH.
Um ...
uh ...
I can't under-stand.
SAY SOME-THING
I'M SORRY!
I don't speak English...
AAASH
Whoa!
STUNNED
WHO IS THAT MAN?
A FRIEND OF MINE.
step
step
LEAVE HIM, PLEASE.
WHO THE HELL...?
Triplets?
WAIT A MINUTE!
...THE BOSS'S DOCTOR.
sob sob
step
OUCH!
YOU ARE SLOW, AREN'T YOU?
I THREW IT ASSUMING YOU WOULD DUCK.
step

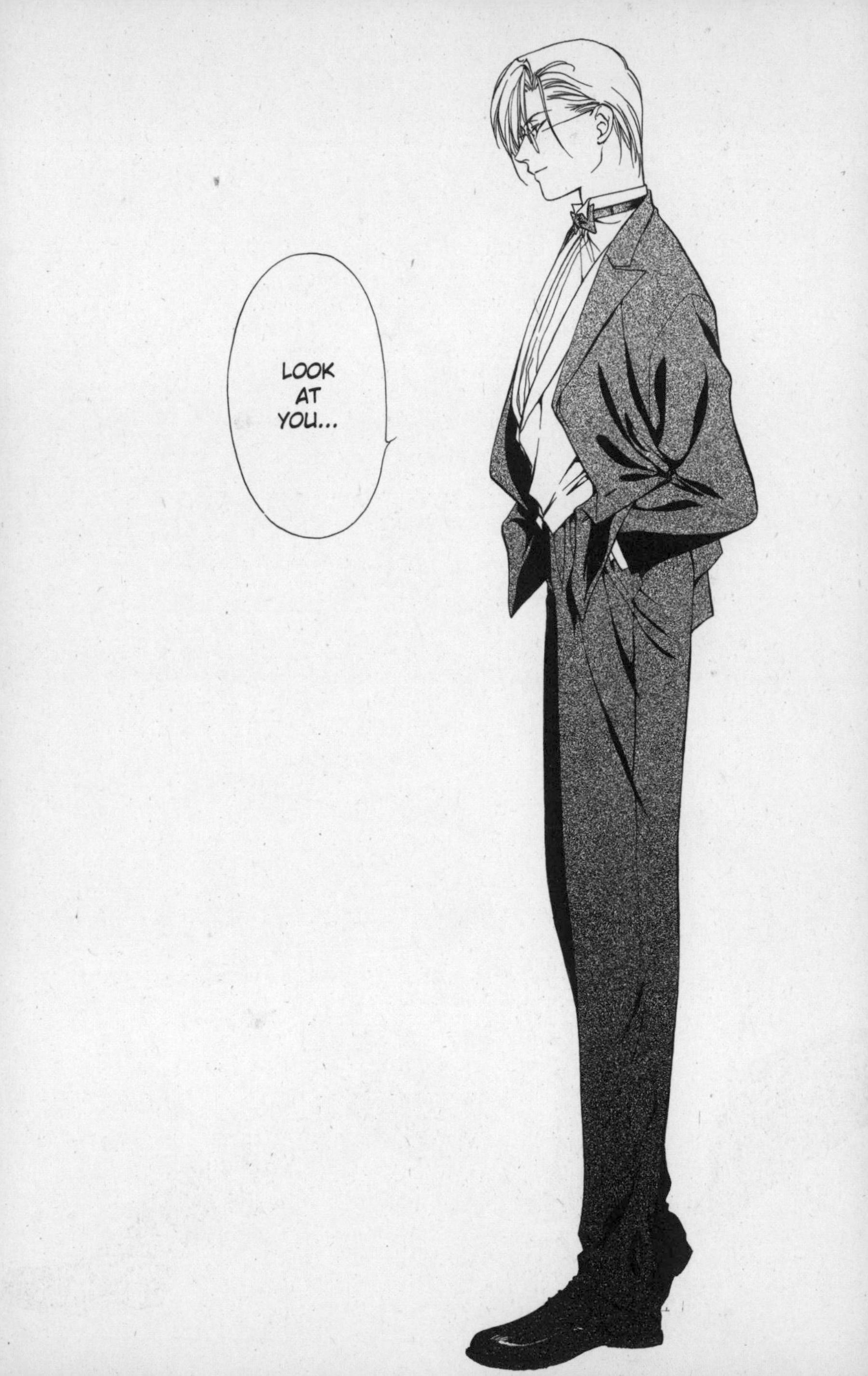
LOOK AT YOU...

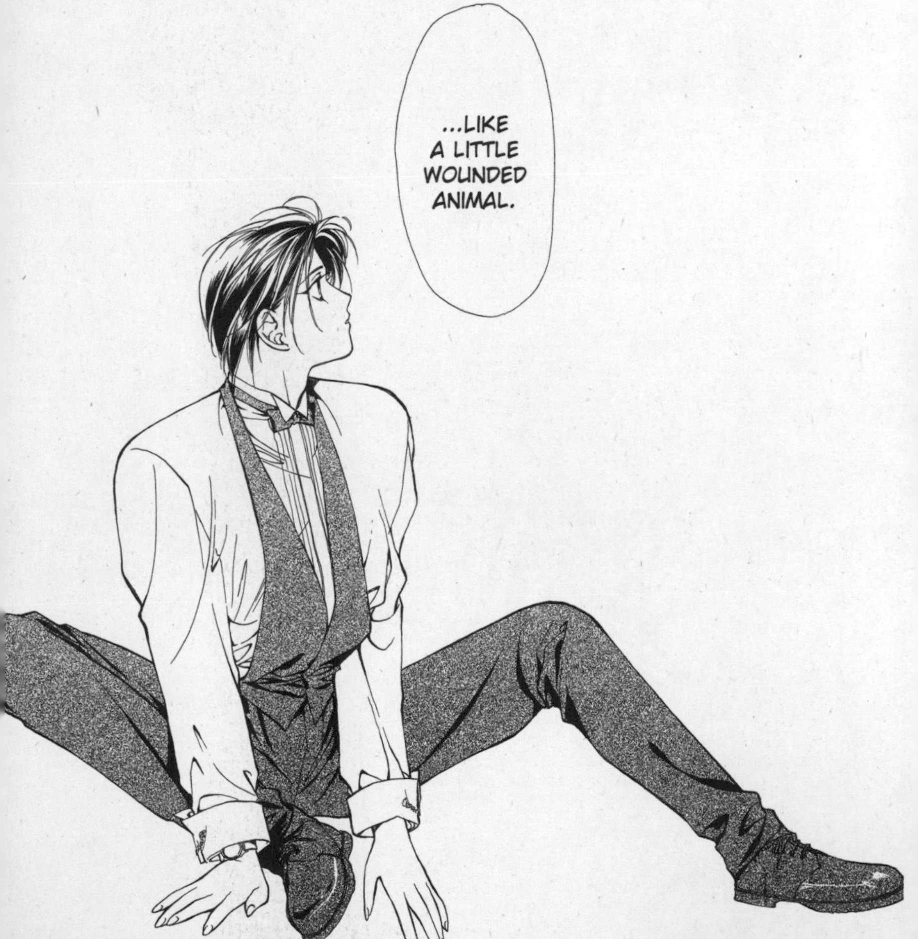
...LIKE A LITTLE WOUNDED ANIMAL.

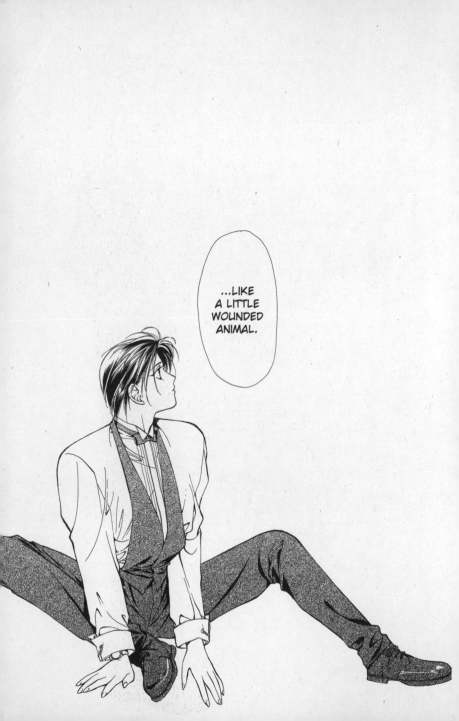

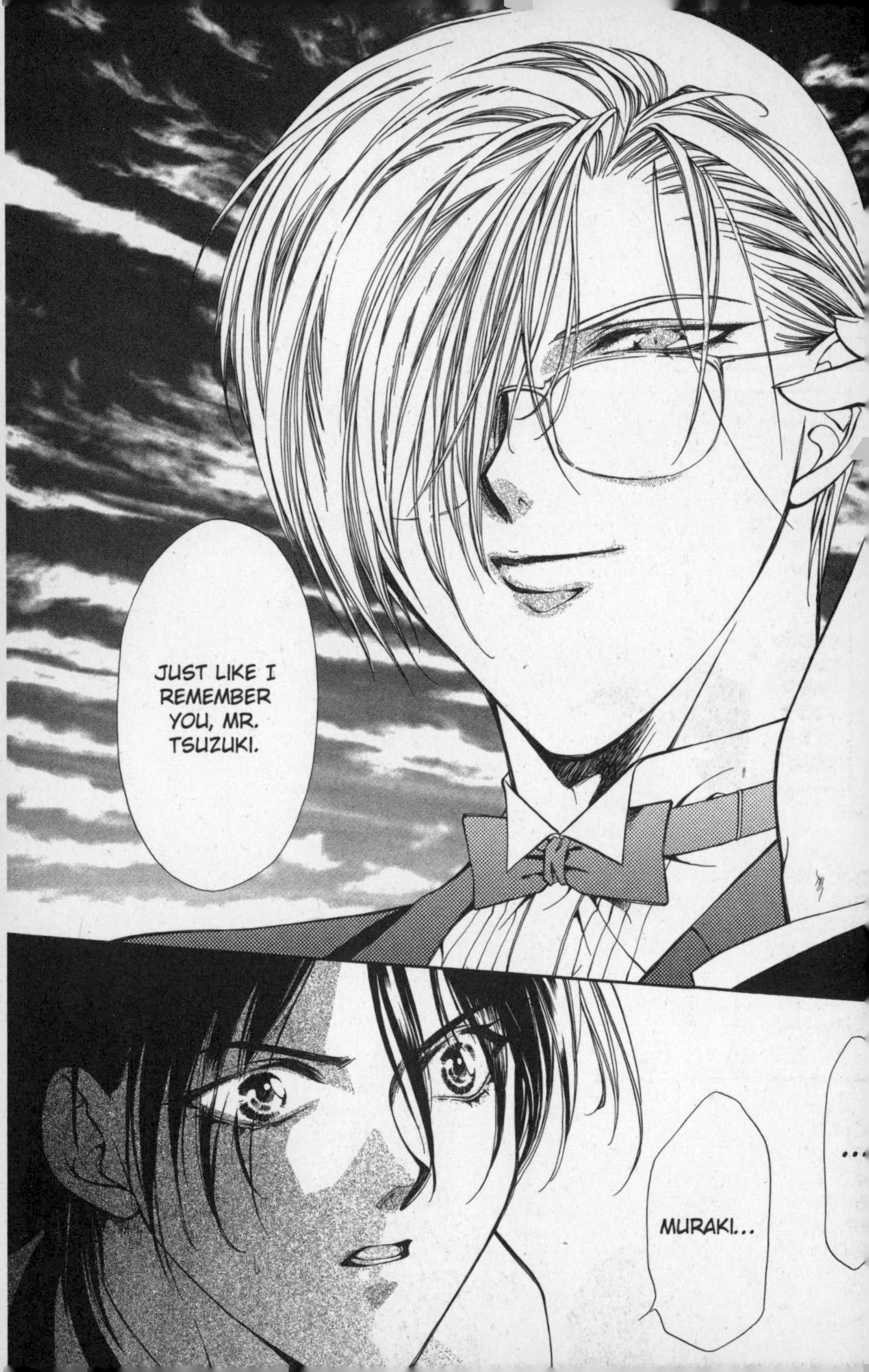
JUST LIKE I REMEMBER YOU, MR. TSUZUKI.
...
MURAKI...

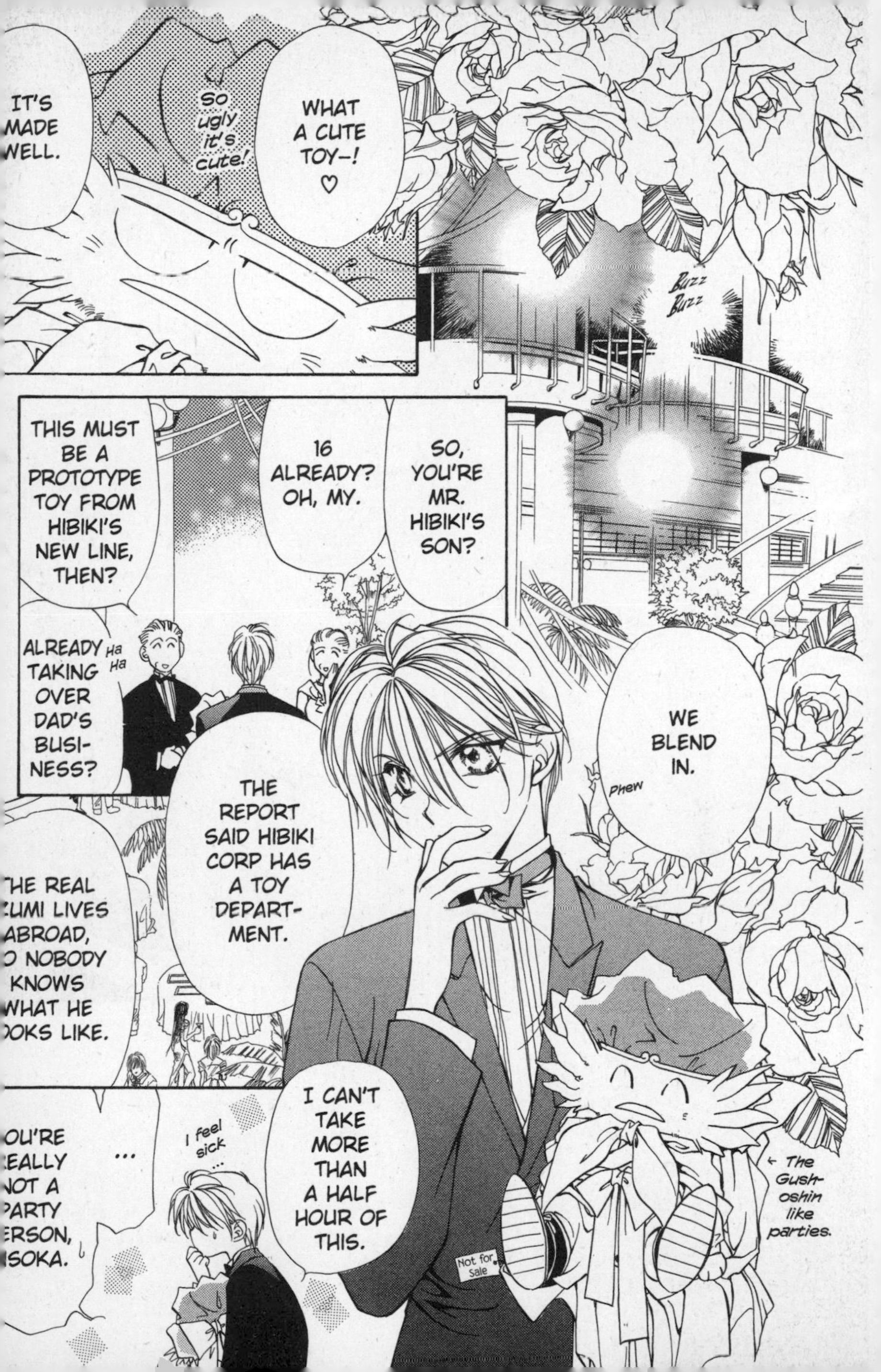
Buzz Buzz
WHAT A CUTE TOY–! ♡
So ugly it's cute!
IT'S MADE WELL.
SO, YOU'RE MR. HIBIKI'S SON?
16 ALREADY? OH, MY.
THIS MUST BE A PROTOTYPE TOY FROM HIBIKI'S NEW LINE, THEN?
ALREADY TAKING OVER DAD'S BUSI-NESS?
Ha Ha
WE BLEND IN.
Phew
THE REPORT SAID HIBIKI CORP HAS A TOY DEPART-MENT.
HE REAL UMI LIVES ABROAD, O NOBODY KNOWS WHAT HE OOKS LIKE.
← The Gush-oshin like parties.
Not for Sale
I CAN'T TAKE MORE THAN A HALF HOUR OF THIS.
...
I feel sick ...
OU'RE EALLY NOT A PARTY ERSON, SOKA.

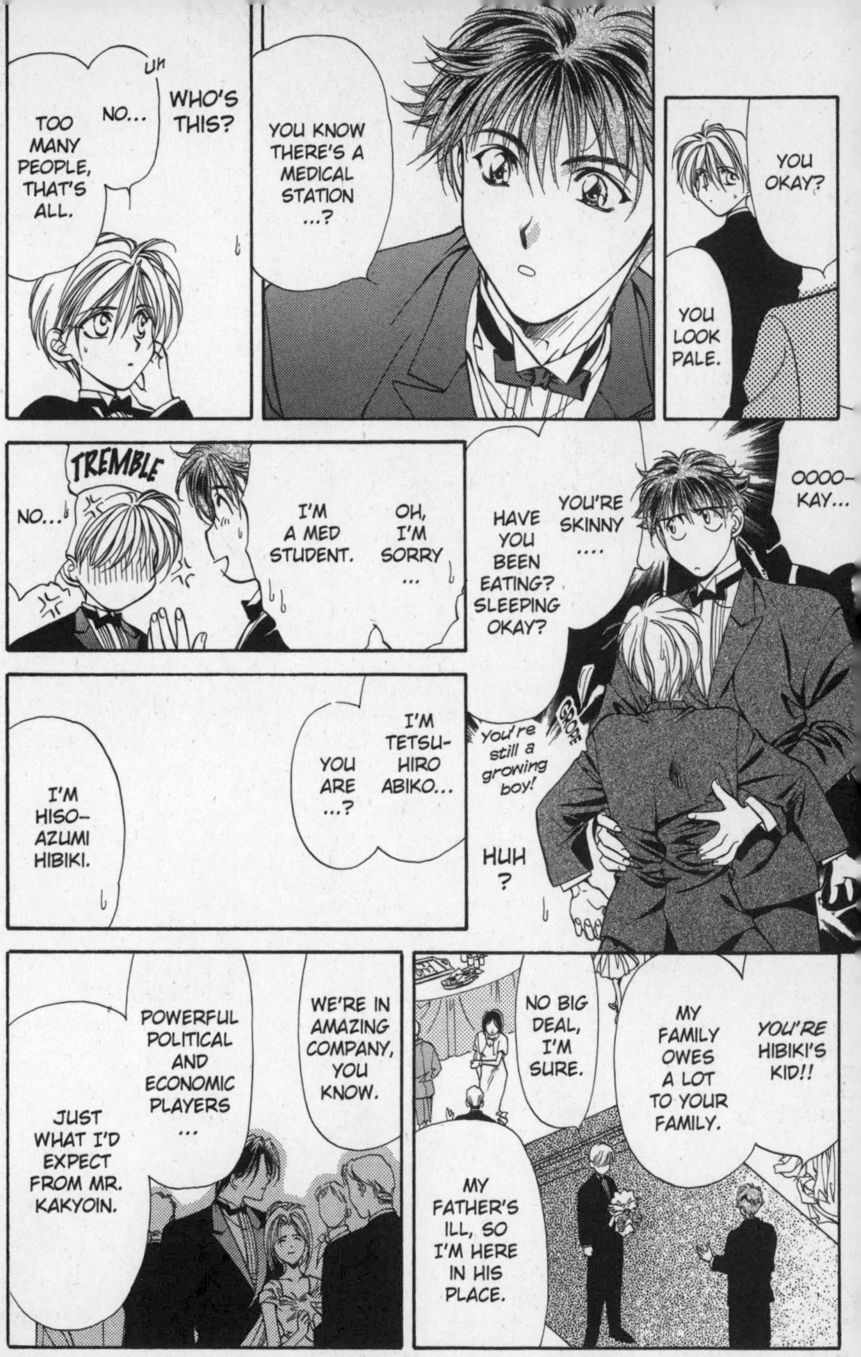
YOU OKAY?
YOU LOOK PALE.
YOU KNOW THERE'S A MEDICAL STATION ...?
WHO'S THIS?
UH
NO...
TOO MANY PEOPLE, THAT'S ALL.
OOOO-KAY...
YOU'RE SKINNY ....
HAVE YOU BEEN EATING? SLEEPING OKAY?
GROPE
You're still a growing boy!
HUH ?
OH, I'M SORRY ...
I'M A MED STUDENT.
TREMBLE
NO...
I'M TETSU-HIRO ABIKO...
YOU ARE ...?
I'M HISO-AZUMI HIBIKI.
YOU'RE HIBIKI'S KID!!
MY FAMILY OWES A LOT TO YOUR FAMILY.
NO BIG DEAL, I'M SURE.
MY FATHER'S ILL, SO I'M HERE IN HIS PLACE.
WE'RE IN AMAZING COMPANY, YOU KNOW.
POWERFUL POLITICAL AND ECONOMIC PLAYERS ...
JUST WHAT I'D EXPECT FROM MR. KAKYOIN.

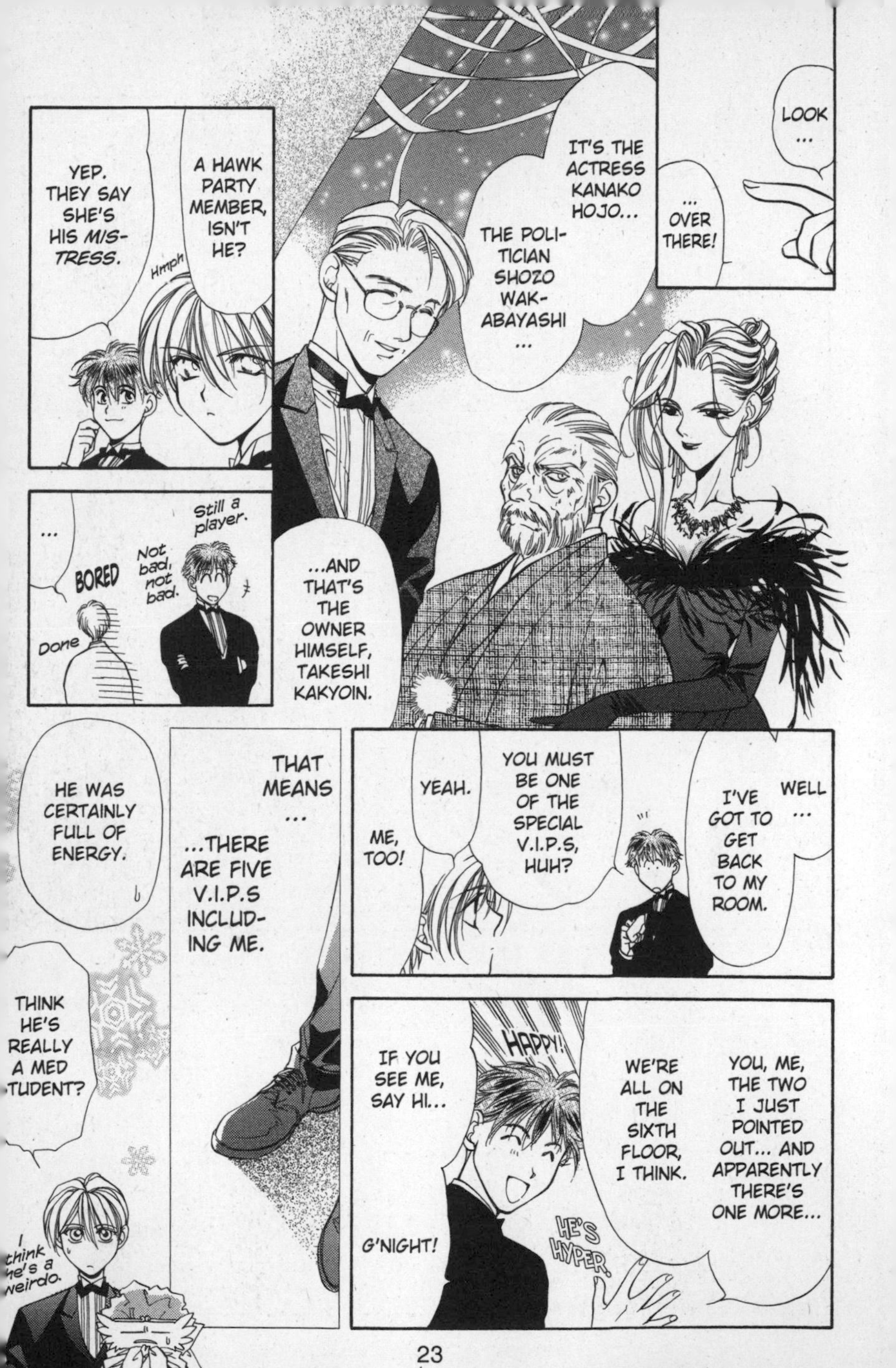
LOOK...
...OVER THERE!
IT'S THE ACTRESS KANAKO HOJO...
THE POLITICIAN SHOZO WAKABAYASHI...
...AND THAT'S THE OWNER HIMSELF, TAKESHI KAKYOIN.
A HAWK PARTY MEMBER, ISN'T HE?
Hmph
YEP. THEY SAY SHE'S HIS MISTRESS.
Still a player.
Not bad, not bad.
BORED
...
Done
WELL...
I'VE GOT TO GET BACK TO MY ROOM.
YOU MUST BE ONE OF THE SPECIAL V.I.P.S, HUH?
YEAH.
ME, TOO!
YOU, ME, THE TWO I JUST POINTED OUT... AND APPARENTLY THERE'S ONE MORE...
WE'RE ALL ON THE SIXTH FLOOR, I THINK.
HAPPY!
IF YOU SEE ME, SAY HI...
G'NIGHT!
HE'S HYPER.
THAT MEANS...
...THERE ARE FIVE V.I.P.S INCLUDING ME.
HE WAS CERTAINLY FULL OF ENERGY.
THINK HE'S REALLY A MED STUDENT?
I think he's a weirdo.

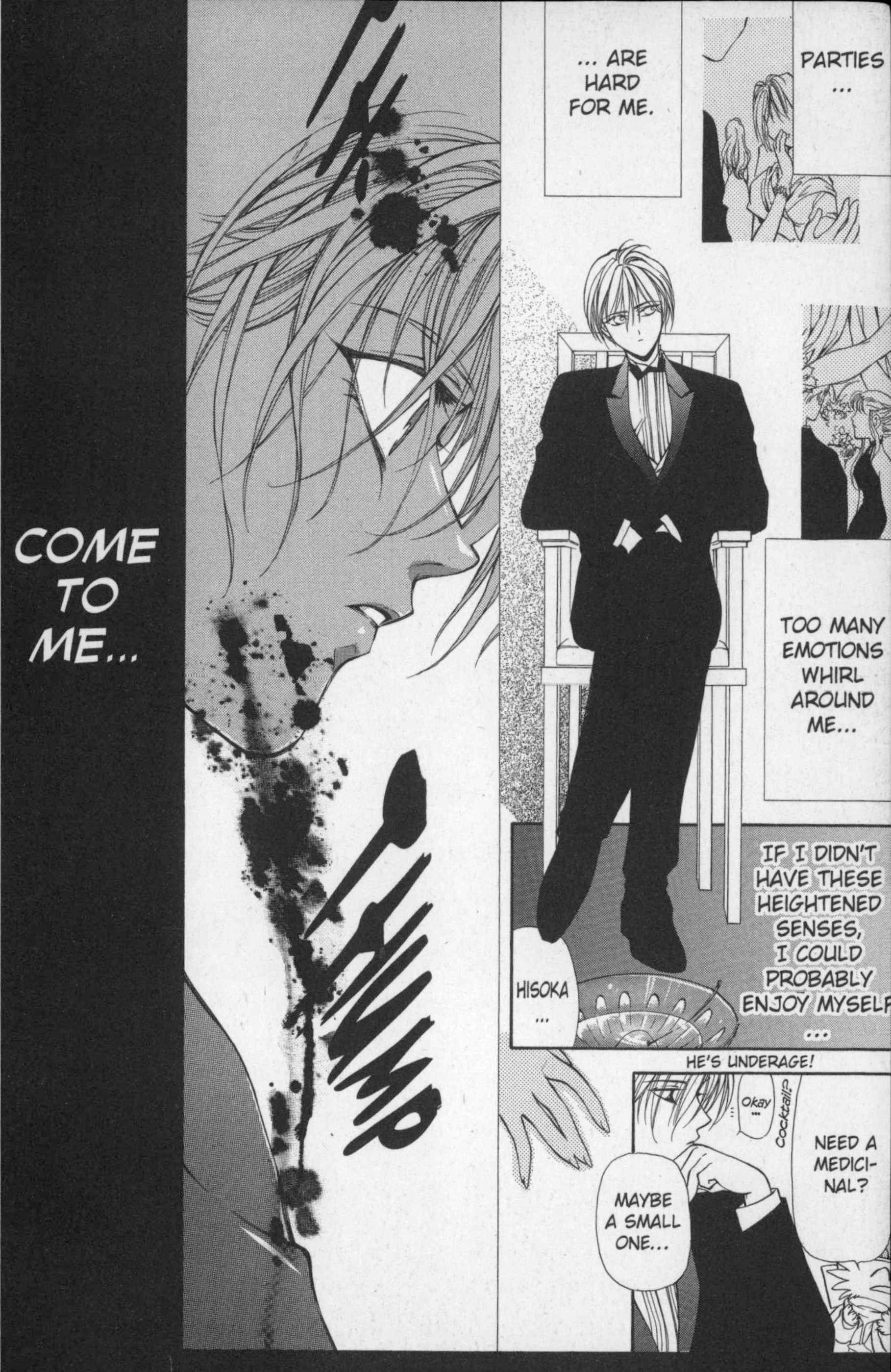
PARTIES ...
... ARE HARD FOR ME.
TOO MANY EMOTIONS WHIRL AROUND ME...
IF I DIDN'T HAVE THESE HEIGHTENED SENSES, I COULD PROBABLY ENJOY MYSELF ...
HISOKA ...
HE'S UNDERAGE!
NEED A MEDICINAL?
Cocktail?
Okay ...
MAYBE A SMALL ONE...
THUMP
COME TO ME...

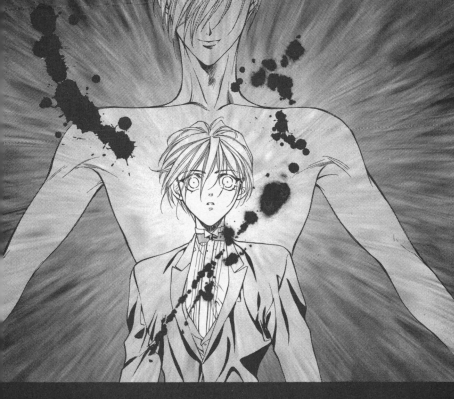

COME TO ME...

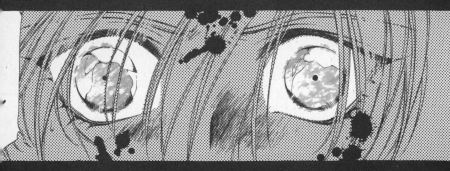

...MY POPPET.

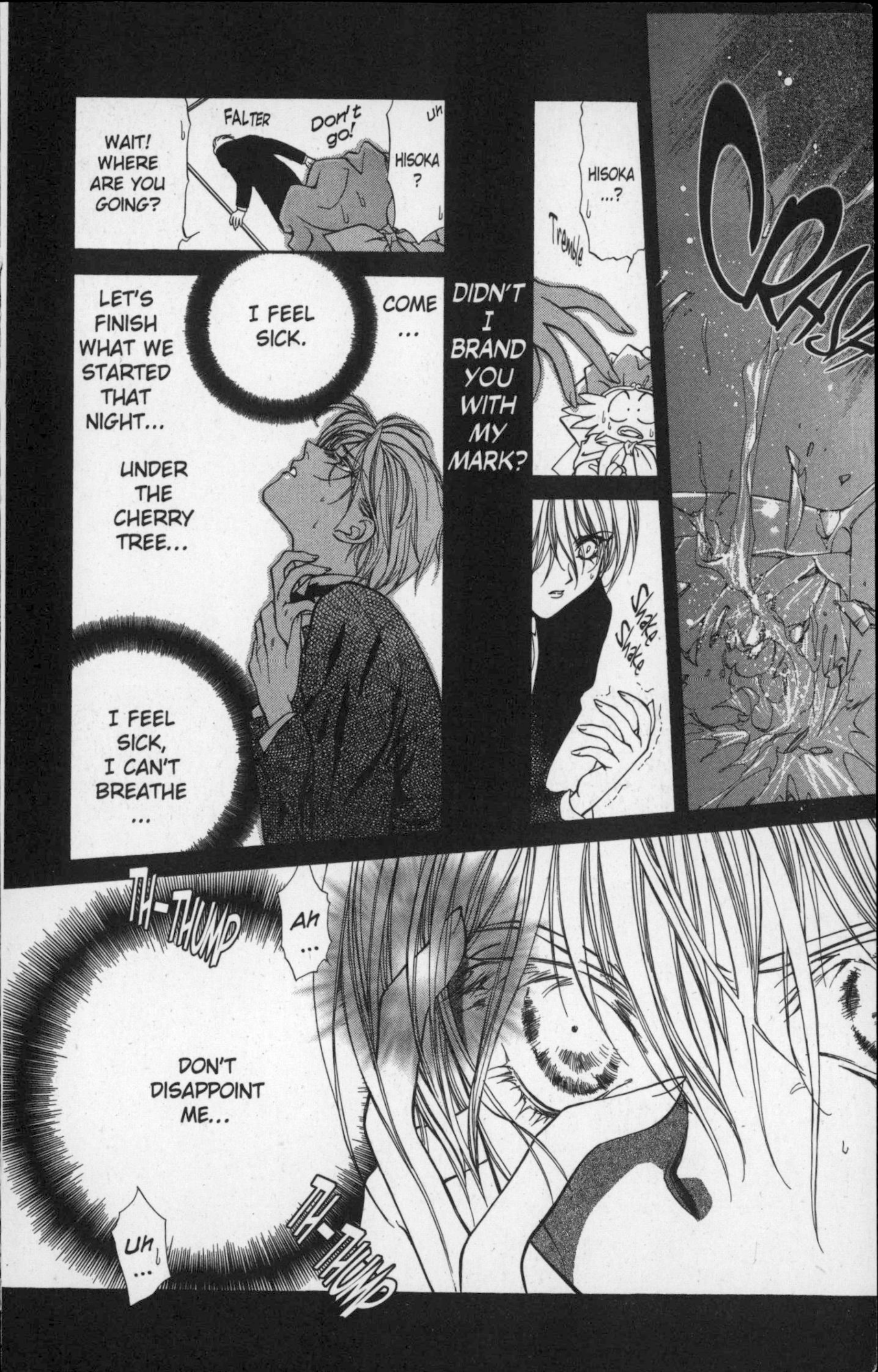
CRAS
HISOKA ...?
Tremble
DIDN'T I BRAND YOU WITH MY MARK?
Shake Shake
Uh
HISOKA ?
Don't go!
FALTER
WAIT! WHERE ARE YOU GOING?
COME ...
I FEEL SICK.
LET'S FINISH WHAT WE STARTED THAT NIGHT...
UNDER THE CHERRY TREE...
I FEEL SICK, I CAN'T BREATHE ...
Ah ...
TH-THUMP
DON'T DISAPPOINT ME...
TH-THUMP
Uh ...

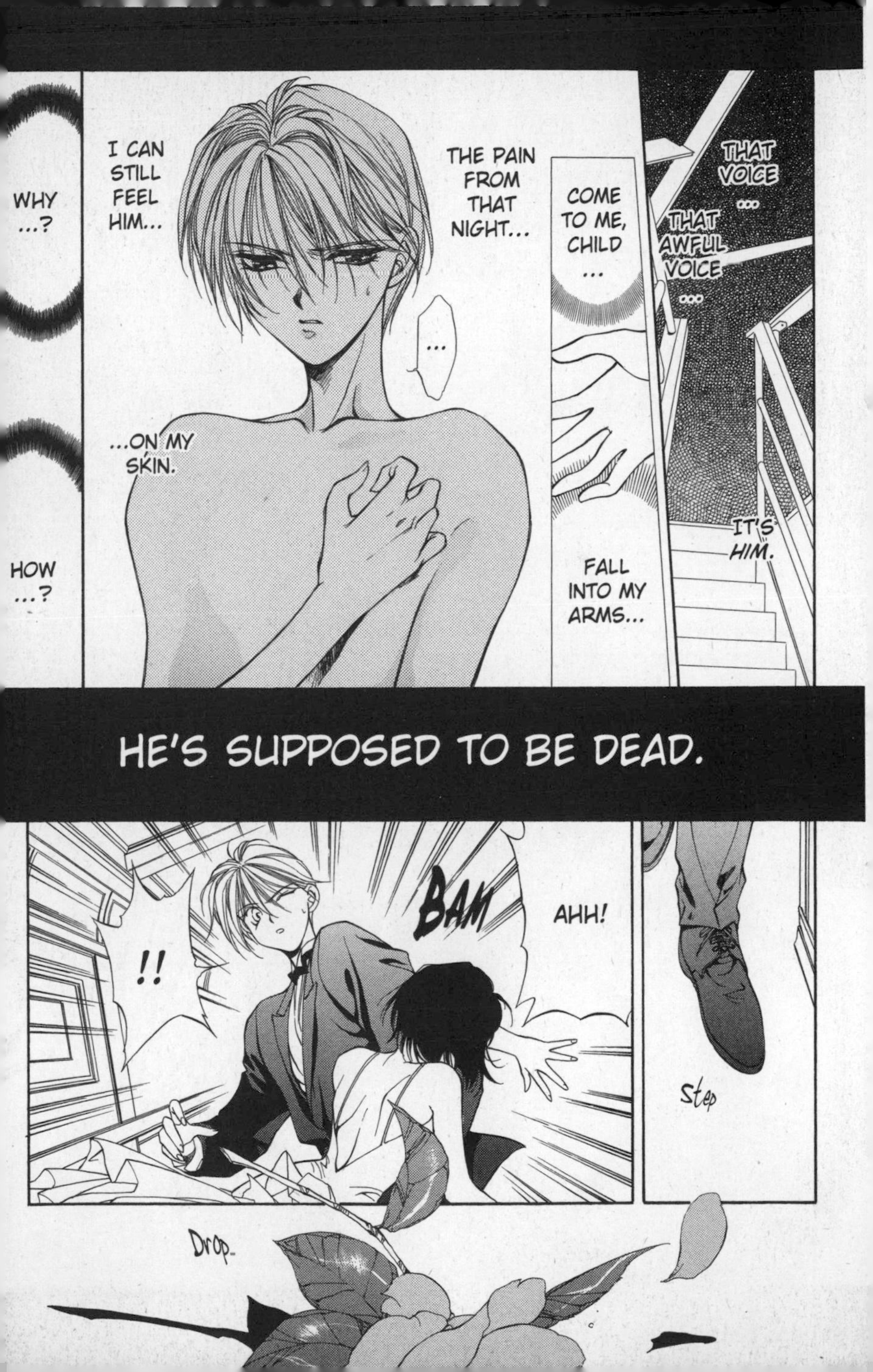
THAT VOICE ...
THAT AWFUL VOICE ...
IT'S HIM.
COME TO ME, CHILD ...
FALL INTO MY ARMS...
THE PAIN FROM THAT NIGHT...
I CAN STILL FEEL HIM...
...
...ON MY SKIN.
WHY ...?
HOW ...?
HE'S SUPPOSED TO BE DEAD.
Step
AHH!
BAM
!!
Drop...

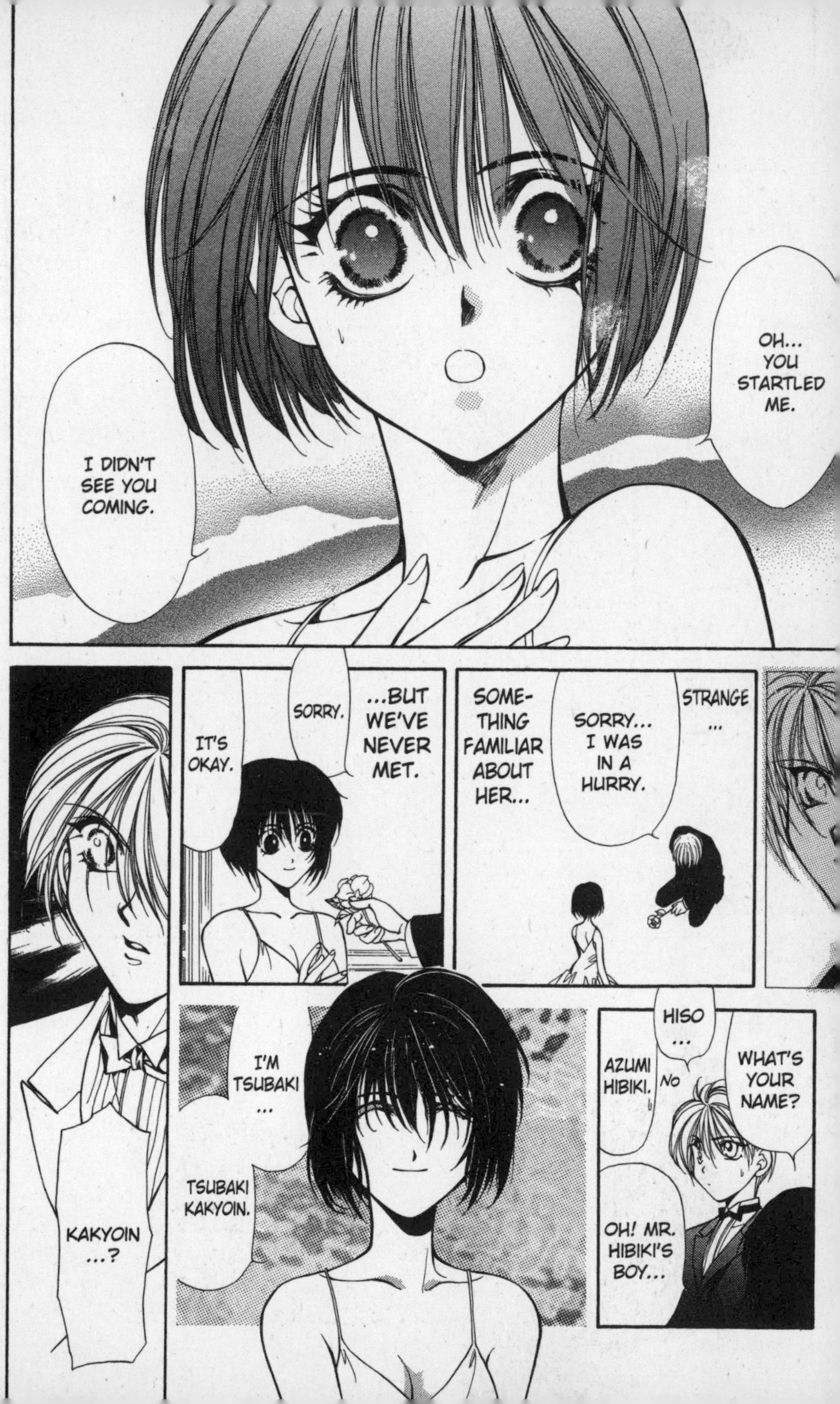
OH... YOU STARTLED ME.
I DIDN'T SEE YOU COMING.
STRANGE ...
SORRY... I WAS IN A HURRY.
SOME-THING FAMILIAR ABOUT HER...
...BUT WE'VE NEVER MET.
SORRY.
IT'S OKAY.
WHAT'S YOUR NAME?
HISO ...
NO
AZUMI HIBIKI.
OH! MR. HIBIKI'S BOY...
I'M TSUBAKI ...
TSUBAKI KAKYOIN.
KAKYOIN ...?

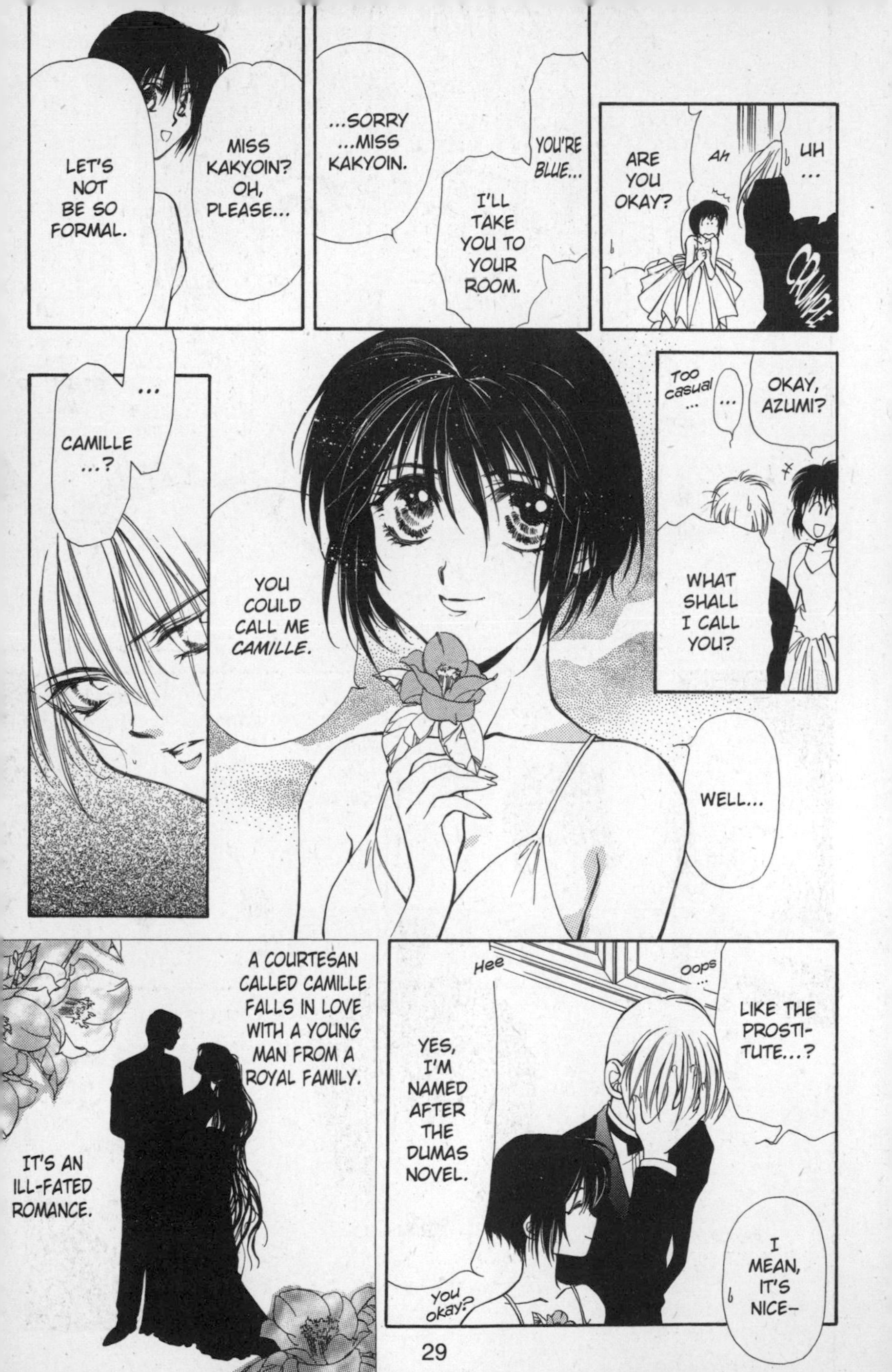
UH ...
Ah
ARE YOU OKAY?
CRUMPLE
YOU'RE BLUE...
I'LL TAKE YOU TO YOUR ROOM.
...SORRY ...MISS KAKYOIN.
MISS KAKYOIN? OH, PLEASE...
LET'S NOT BE SO FORMAL.
OKAY, AZUMI?
...
Too casual ...
WHAT SHALL I CALL YOU?
WELL...
YOU COULD CALL ME CAMILLE.
...
CAMILLE ...?
Oops ...
LIKE THE PROSTITUTE...?
Hee
YES, I'M NAMED AFTER THE DUMAS NOVEL.
I MEAN, IT'S NICE—
You okay?
A COURTESAN CALLED CAMILLE FALLS IN LOVE WITH A YOUNG MAN FROM A ROYAL FAMILY.
IT'S AN ILL-FATED ROMANCE.

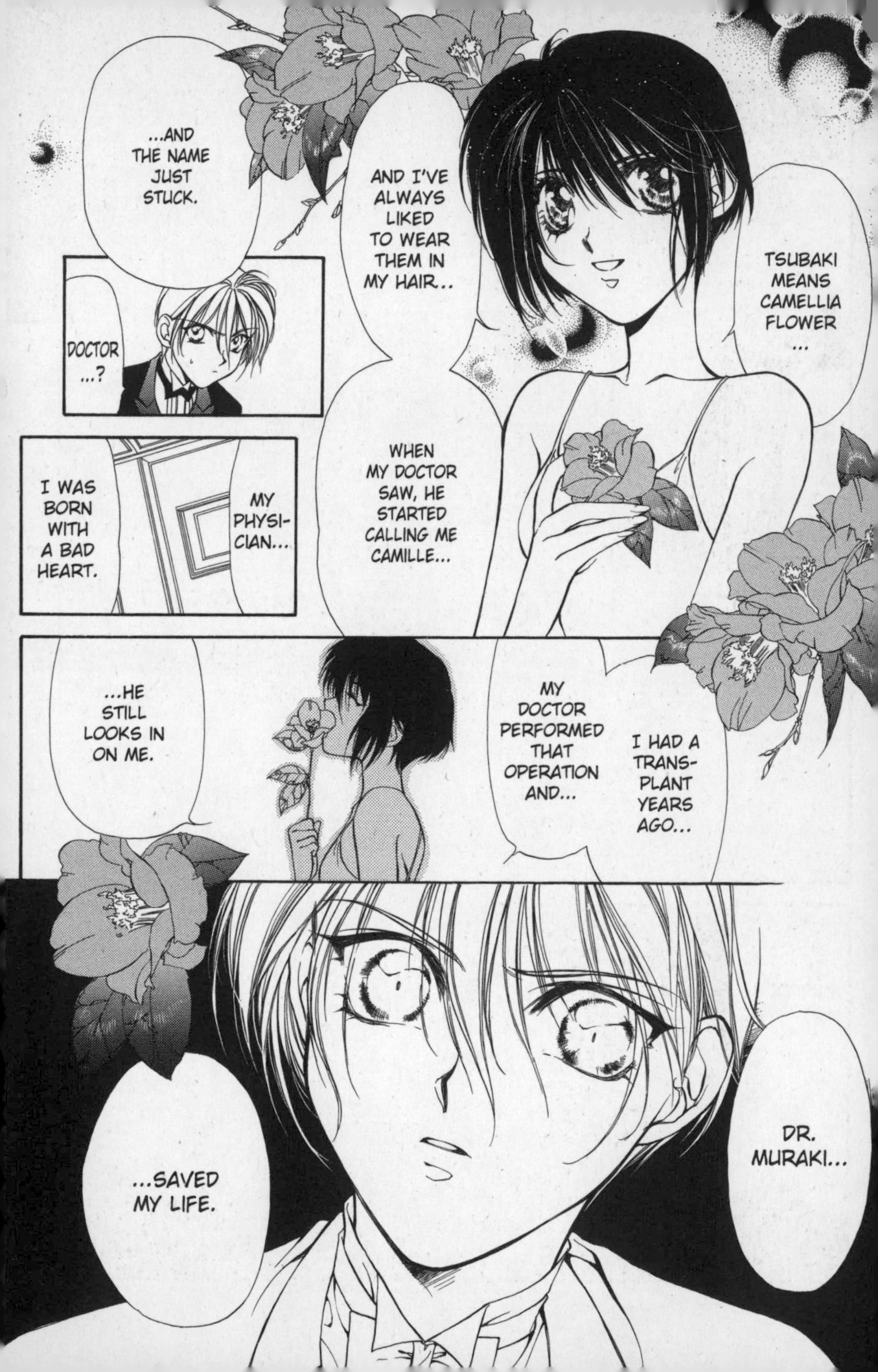
TSUBAKI MEANS CAMELLIA FLOWER...
AND I'VE ALWAYS LIKED TO WEAR THEM IN MY HAIR...
WHEN MY DOCTOR SAW, HE STARTED CALLING ME CAMILLE...
...AND THE NAME JUST STUCK.
DOCTOR...?
MY PHYSICIAN...
I WAS BORN WITH A BAD HEART.
I HAD A TRANS-PLANT YEARS AGO...
MY DOCTOR PERFORMED THAT OPERATION AND...
...HE STILL LOOKS IN ON ME.
DR. MURAKI...
...SAVED MY LIFE.

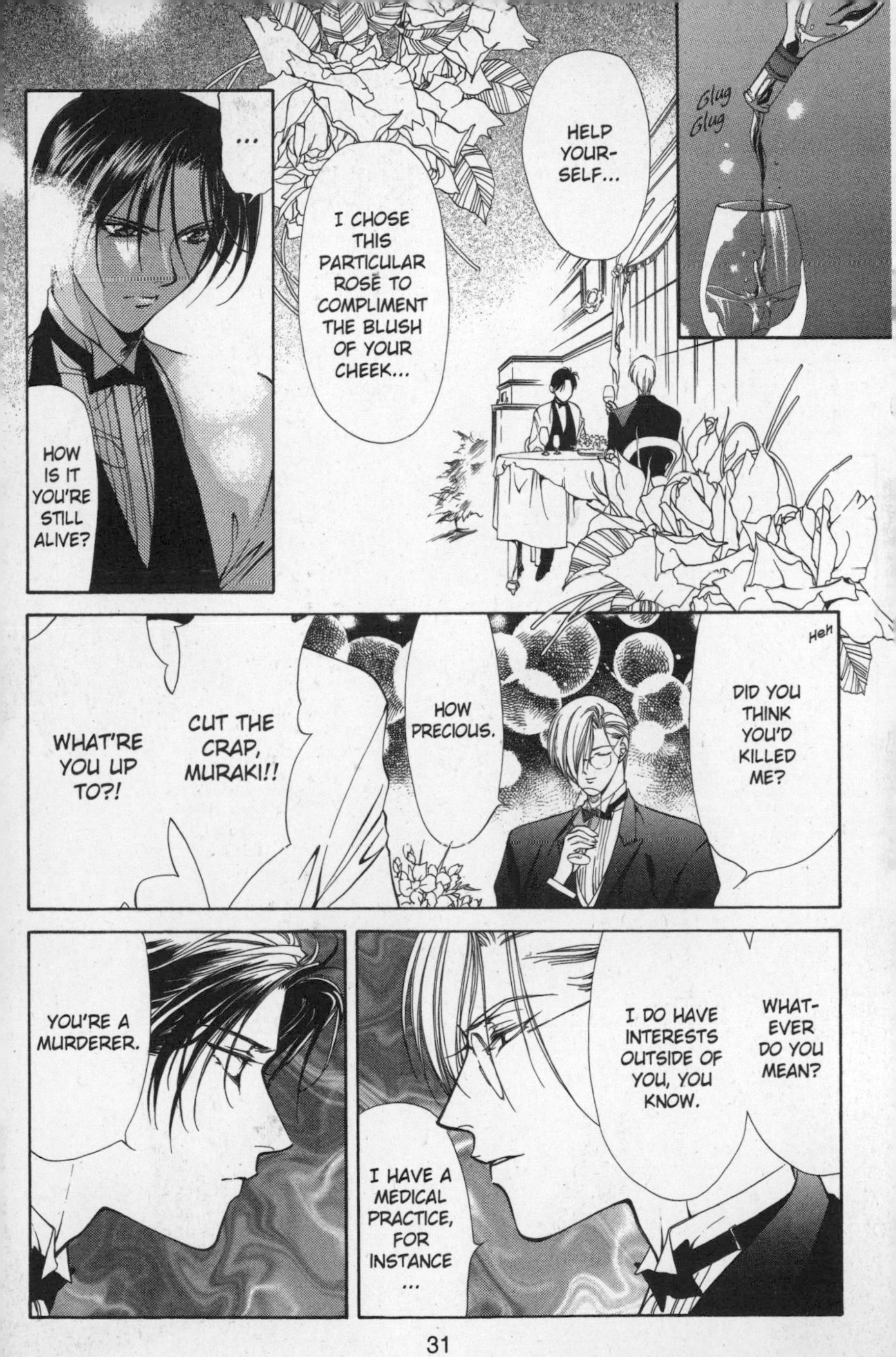
Glug Glug
HELP YOURSELF...
I CHOSE THIS PARTICULAR ROSE TO COMPLIMENT THE BLUSH OF YOUR CHEEK...
...
HOW IS IT YOU'RE STILL ALIVE?
Heh
DID YOU THINK YOU'D KILLED ME?
HOW PRECIOUS.
CUT THE CRAP, MURAKI!!
WHAT'RE YOU UP TO?!
WHATEVER DO YOU MEAN?
I DO HAVE INTERESTS OUTSIDE OF YOU, YOU KNOW.
I HAVE A MEDICAL PRACTICE, FOR INSTANCE ...
YOU'RE A MURDERER.

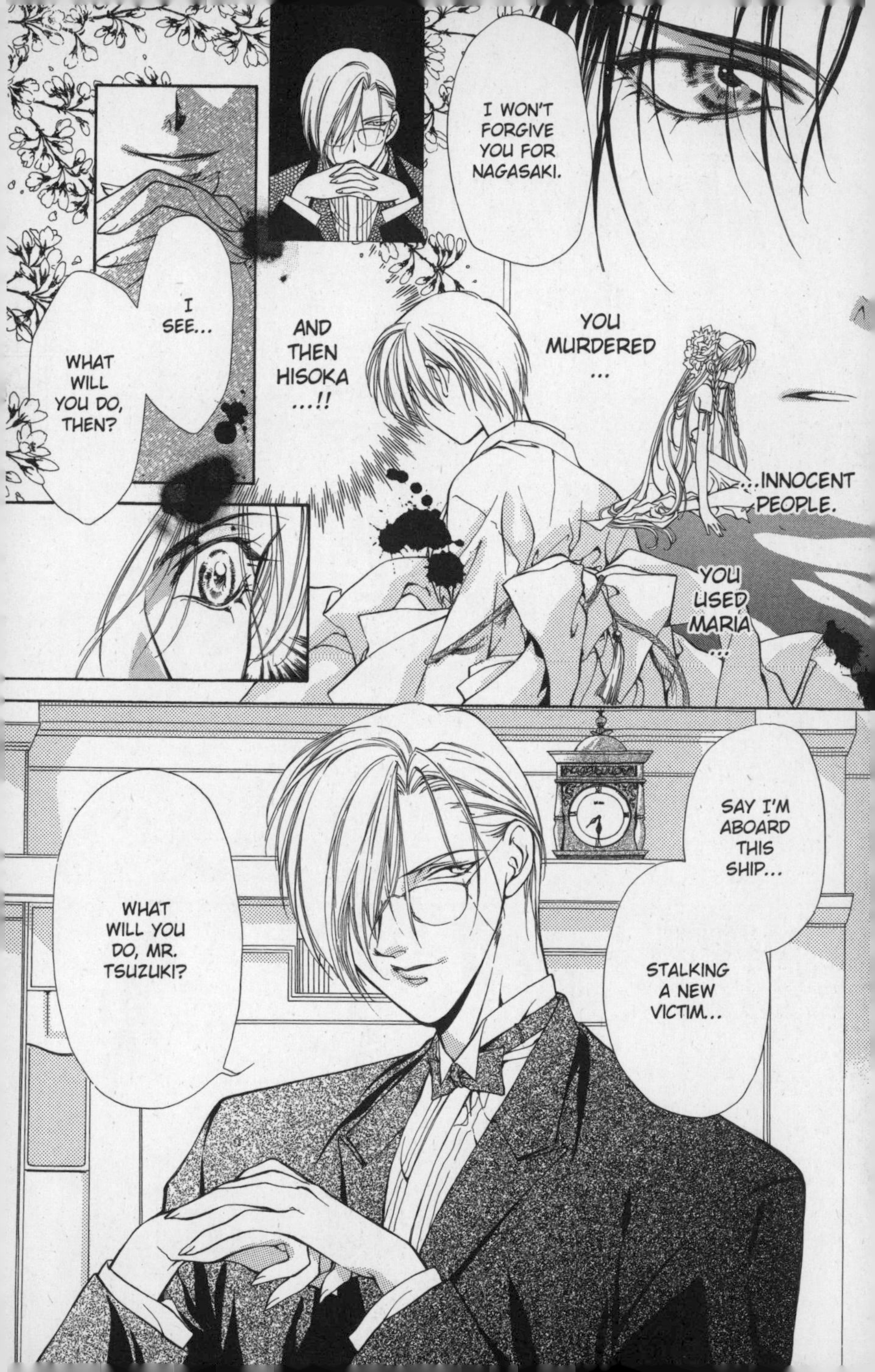

I WON'T FORGIVE YOU FOR NAGASAKI.
YOU MURDERED ...
...INNOCENT PEOPLE.
YOU USED MARIA ...
AND THEN HISOKA ...!!
I SEE...
WHAT WILL YOU DO, THEN?
SAY I'M ABOARD THIS SHIP...
STALKING A NEW VICTIM...
WHAT WILL YOU DO, MR. TSUZUKI?

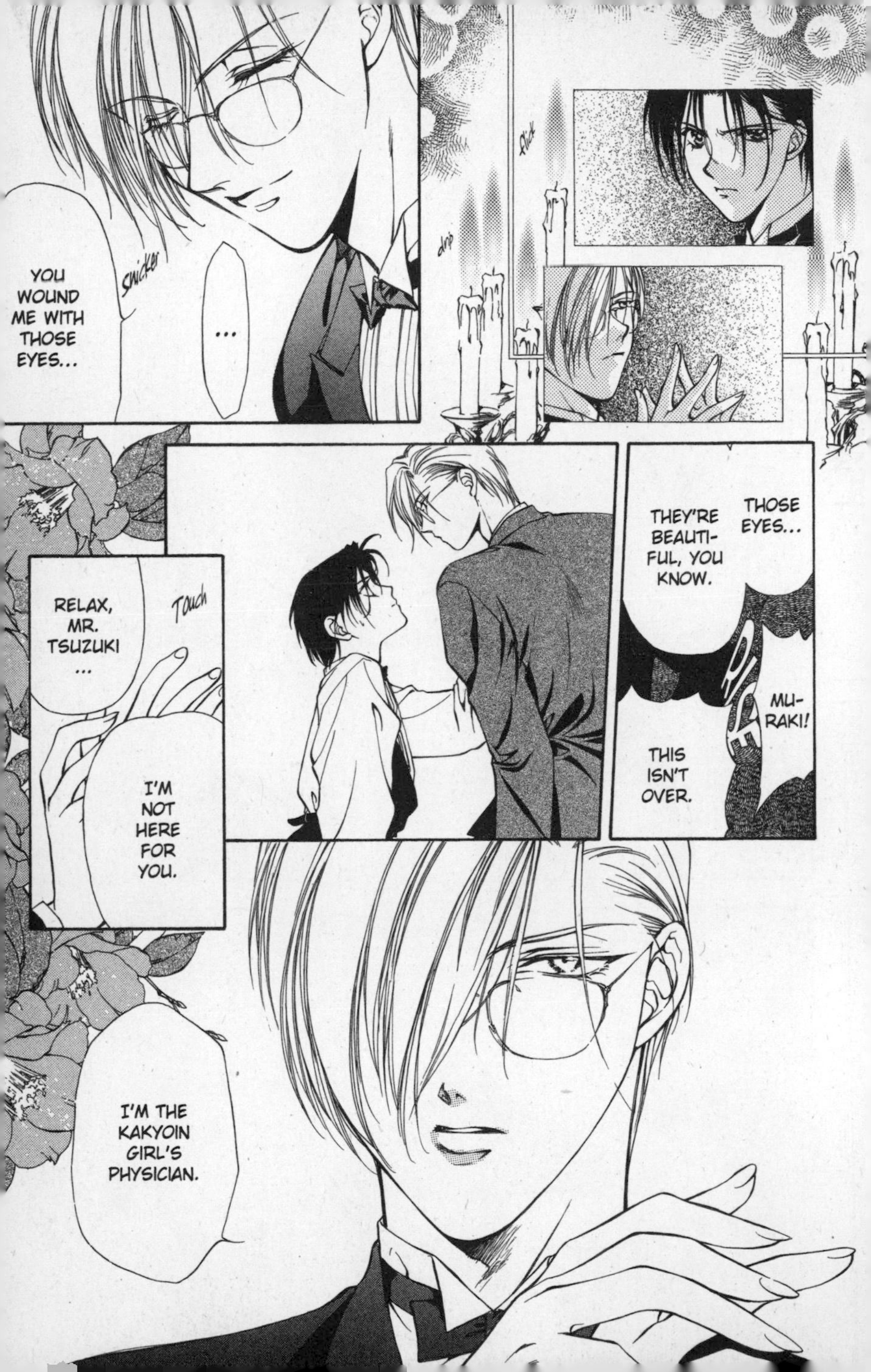
flick
drip
snicker
...
YOU WOUND ME WITH THOSE EYES...
THOSE EYES...
THEY'RE BEAUTIFUL, YOU KNOW.
MU-RAKI!
THIS ISN'T OVER.
Touch
RELAX, MR. TSUZUKI...
I'M NOT HERE FOR YOU.
I'M THE KAKYOIN GIRL'S PHYSICIAN.

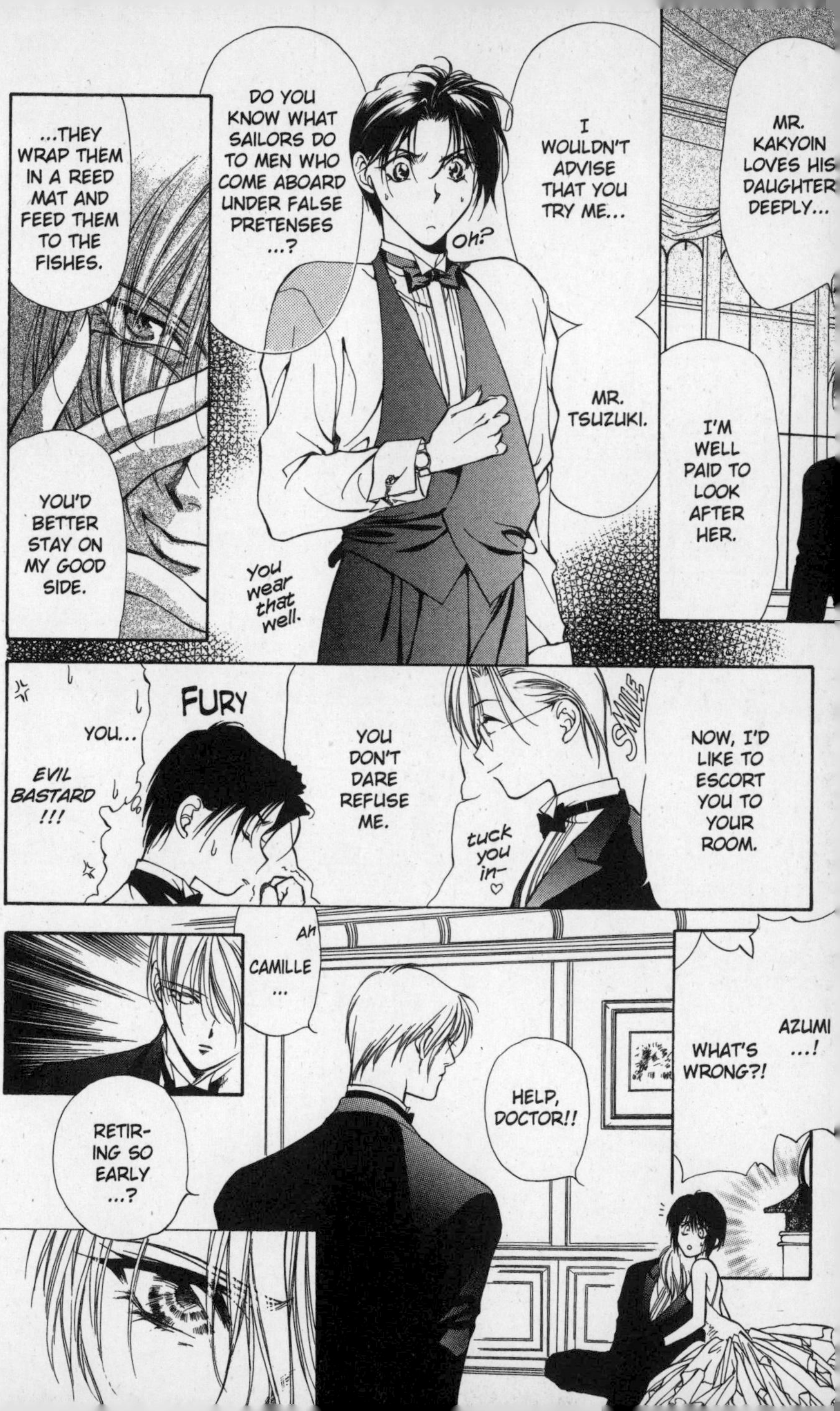
MR. KAKYOIN LOVES HIS DAUGHTER DEEPLY...
I'M WELL PAID TO LOOK AFTER HER.
I WOULDN'T ADVISE THAT YOU TRY ME...
MR. TSUZUKI.
Oh?
DO YOU KNOW WHAT SAILORS DO TO MEN WHO COME ABOARD UNDER FALSE PRETENSES ...?
You wear that well.
...THEY WRAP THEM IN A REED MAT AND FEED THEM TO THE FISHES.
YOU'D BETTER STAY ON MY GOOD SIDE.
NOW, I'D LIKE TO ESCORT YOU TO YOUR ROOM.
SMILE
tuck you in♥
YOU DON'T DARE REFUSE ME.
FURY
YOU...
EVIL BASTARD!!!
AZUMI ...!
WHAT'S WRONG?!
HELP, DOCTOR!!
Ah
CAMILLE ...
RETIR-ING SO EARLY ...?

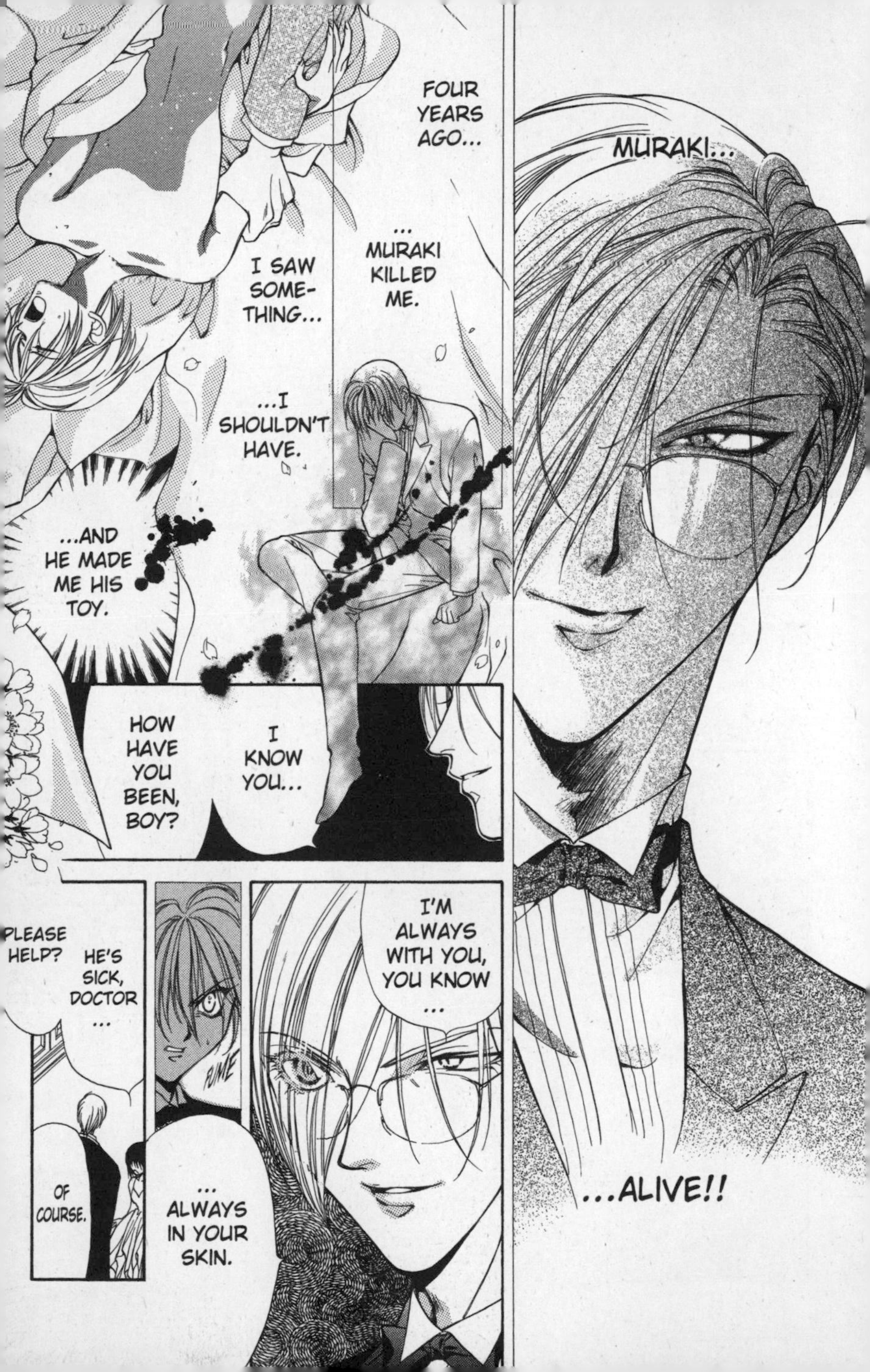
MURAKI...
...ALIVE!!
FOUR YEARS AGO...
...MURAKI KILLED ME.
I SAW SOME-THING...
...I SHOULDN'T HAVE.
...AND HE MADE ME HIS TOY.
I KNOW YOU...
HOW HAVE YOU BEEN, BOY?
I'M ALWAYS WITH YOU, YOU KNOW...
...ALWAYS IN YOUR SKIN.
HE'S SICK, DOCTOR...
PLEASE HELP?
OF COURSE.

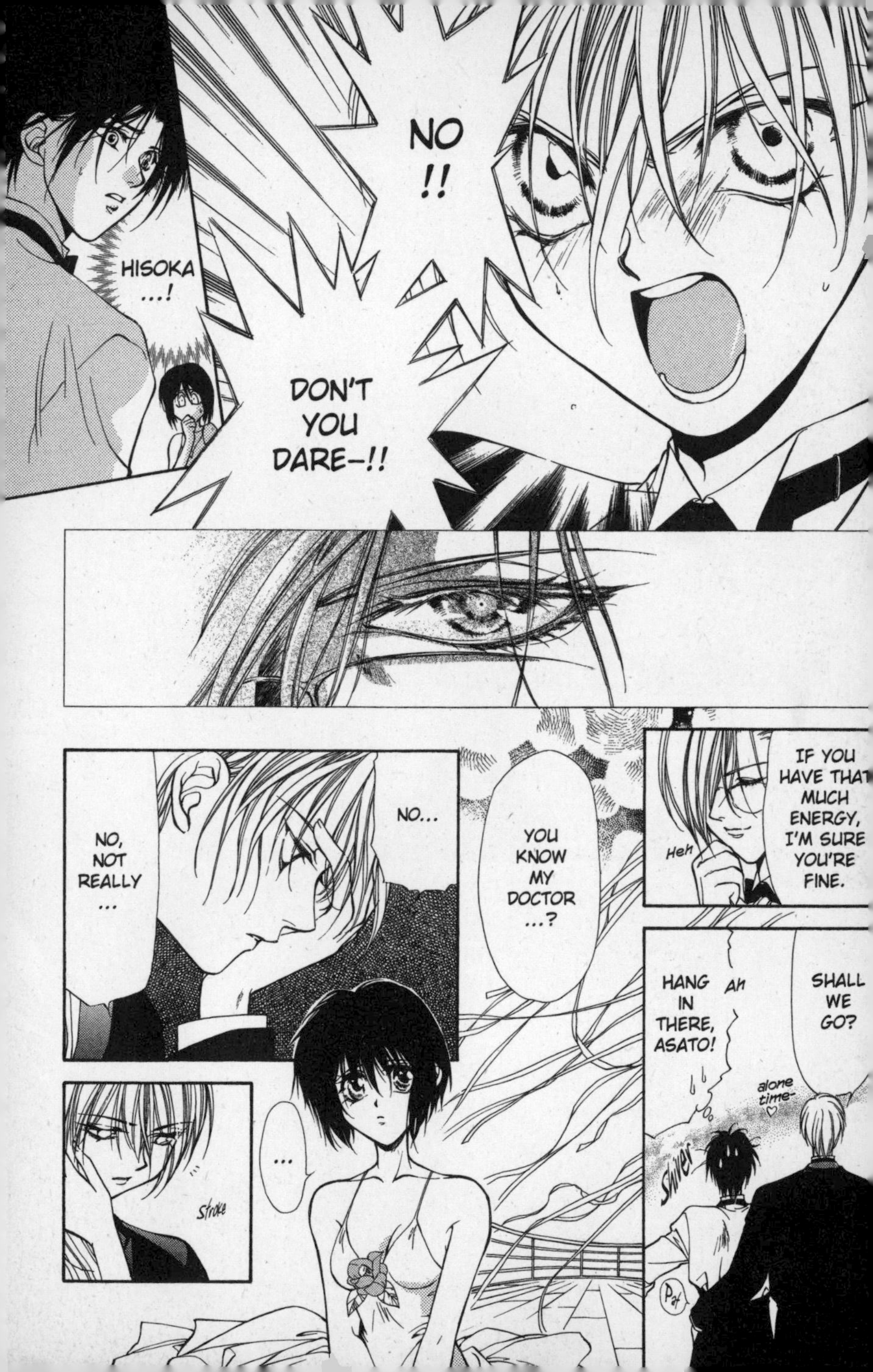
NO !!
DON'T YOU DARE-!!
HISOKA ...!
IF YOU HAVE THAT MUCH ENERGY, I'M SURE YOU'RE FINE.
Heh
YOU KNOW MY DOCTOR ...?
NO...
NO, NOT REALLY ...
SHALL WE GO?
alone time-♡
Ah
HANG IN THERE, ASATO!
Shiver
Pat
...
Stroke

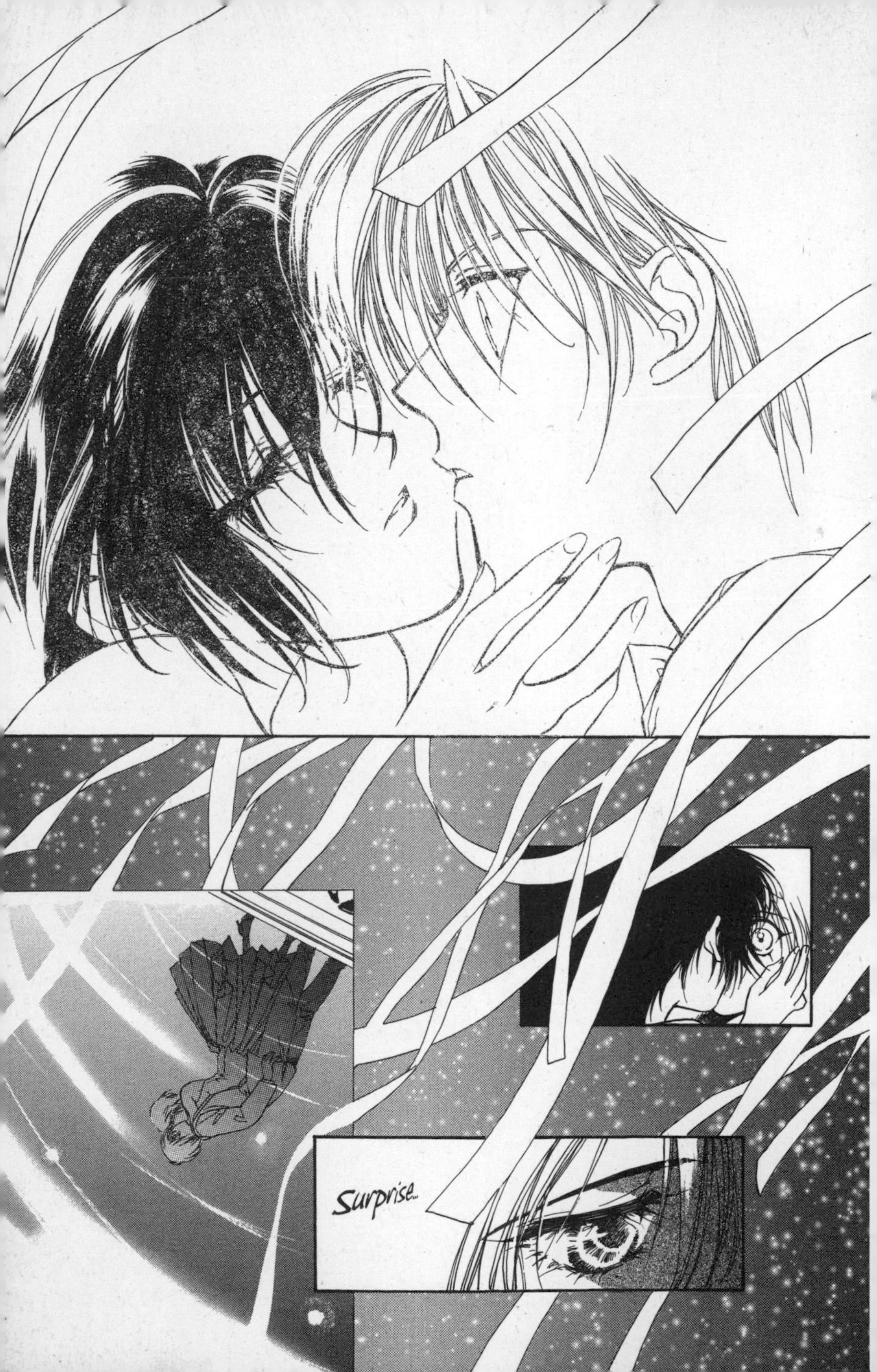
Surprise...

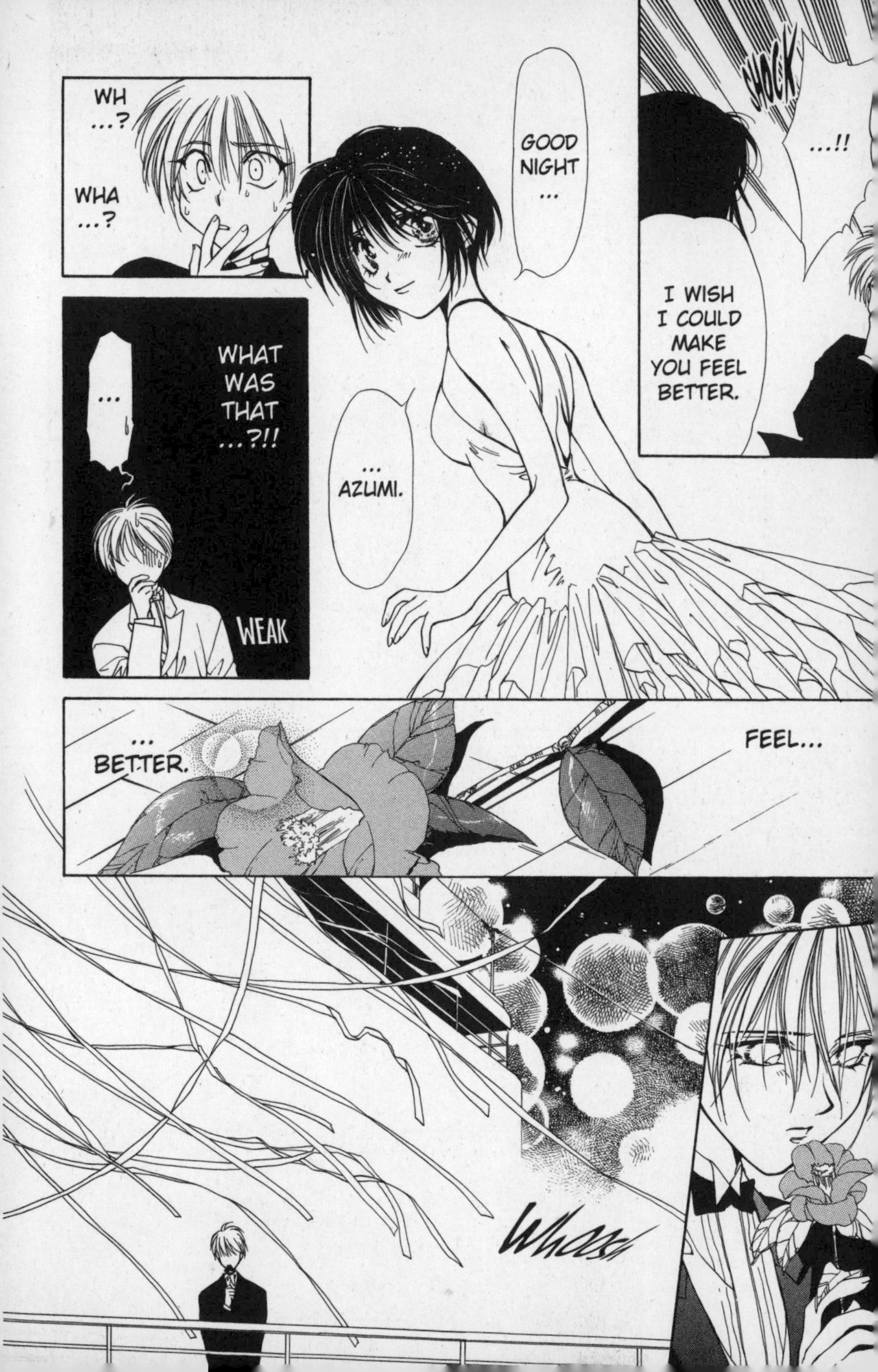
SHOCK
...!!
I WISH I COULD MAKE YOU FEEL BETTER.
GOOD NIGHT ...
... AZUMI.
WH ...?
WHA ...?
...
WHAT WAS THAT ...?!!
WEAK
FEEL...
... BETTER.
Whoosh

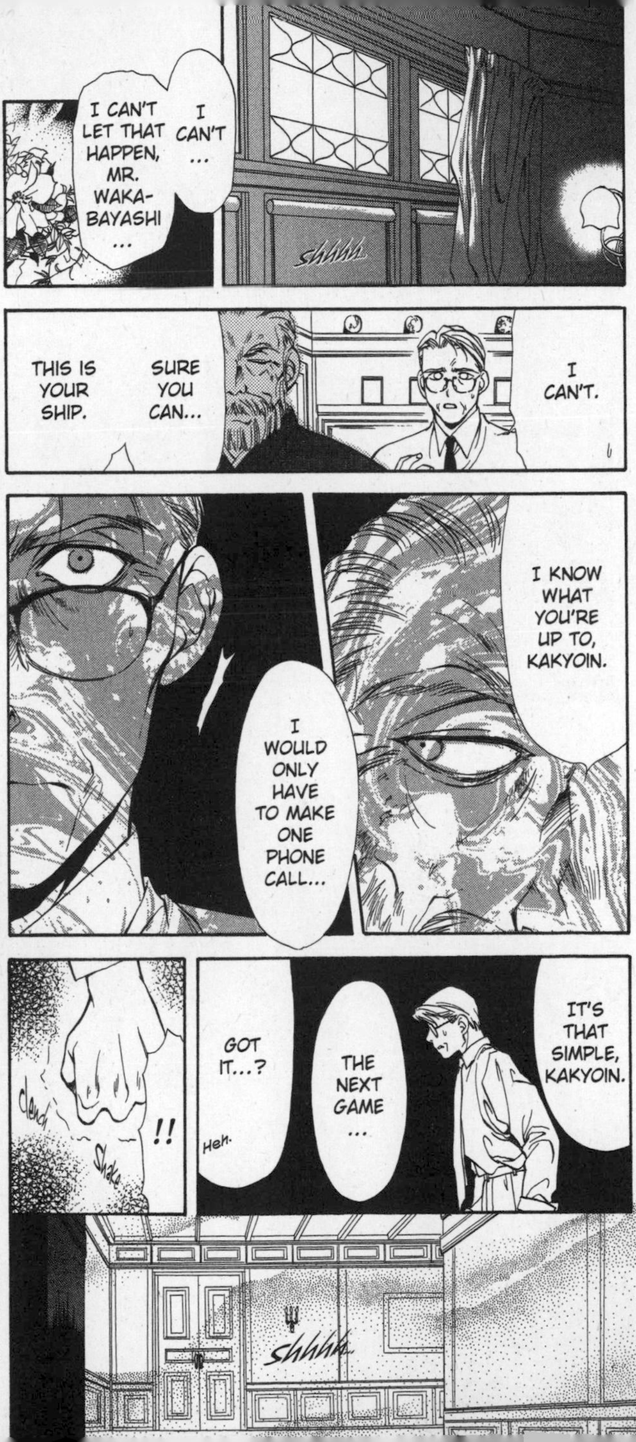
shhhh
I CAN'T ...
I CAN'T LET THAT HAPPEN, MR. WAKA-BAYASHI ...
I CAN'T.
SURE YOU CAN...
THIS IS YOUR SHIP.
I KNOW WHAT YOU'RE UP TO, KAKYOIN.
I WOULD ONLY HAVE TO MAKE ONE PHONE CALL...
IT'S THAT SIMPLE, KAKYOIN.
THE NEXT GAME ...
GOT IT...?
Heh.
!!
clench
Shake
shhhh

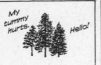

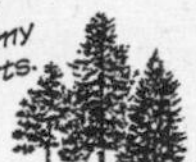
My tummy hurts.
Hello!

Hello there! My name is Matsushita, and I work s-l-o-w. (Just in case anyone was wondering, I guess.) So, welcome to Vol. 3! This story takes place on a casino liner at sea. (A poor artist like me could never afford a vacation like that!) Here we meet the evil Doctor Muraki again, who we last saw in Nagasaki. He must be doing all right for himself if he can afford to throw bottles of wine around!

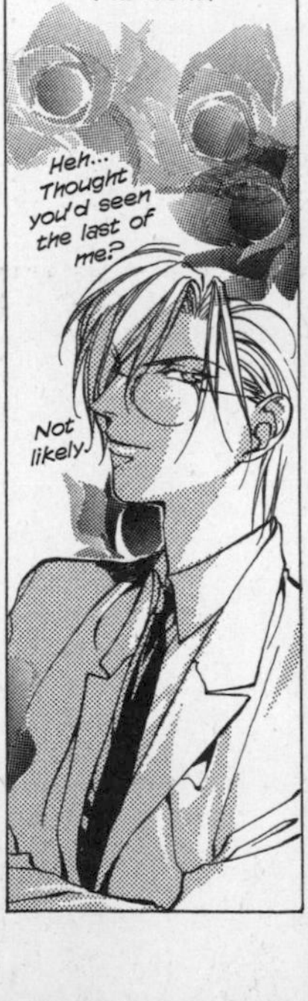
Heh... Thought you'd seen the last of me?
Not likely.

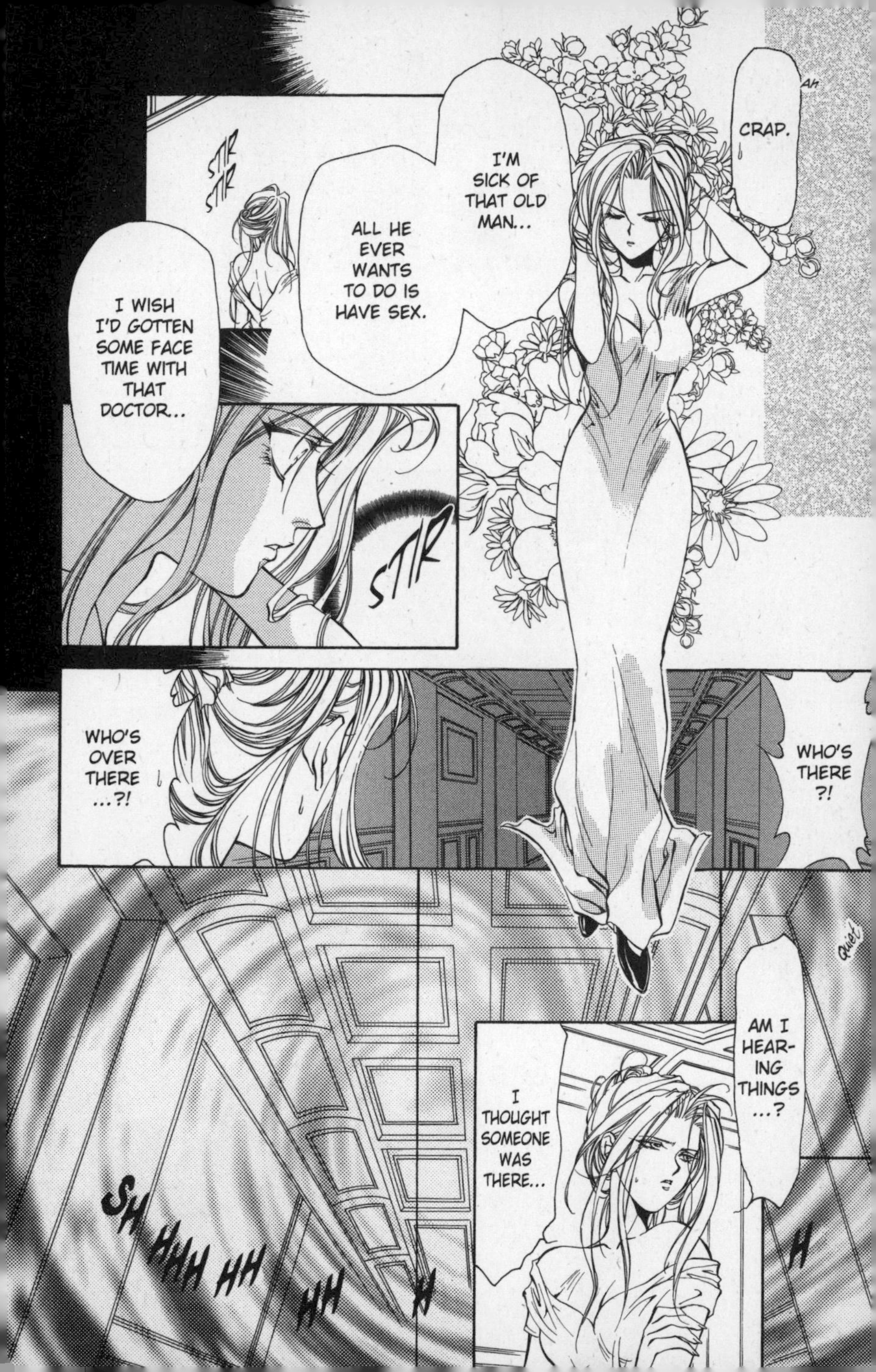
Ah
CRAP.
I'M SICK OF THAT OLD MAN...
ALL HE EVER WANTS TO DO IS HAVE SEX.
STIR STIR
I WISH I'D GOTTEN SOME FACE TIME WITH THAT DOCTOR...
STIR
WHO'S THERE ?!
WHO'S OVER THERE ...?!
Quiet
AM I HEAR-ING THINGS ...?
I THOUGHT SOMEONE WAS THERE...
SH HHH HH HH H H

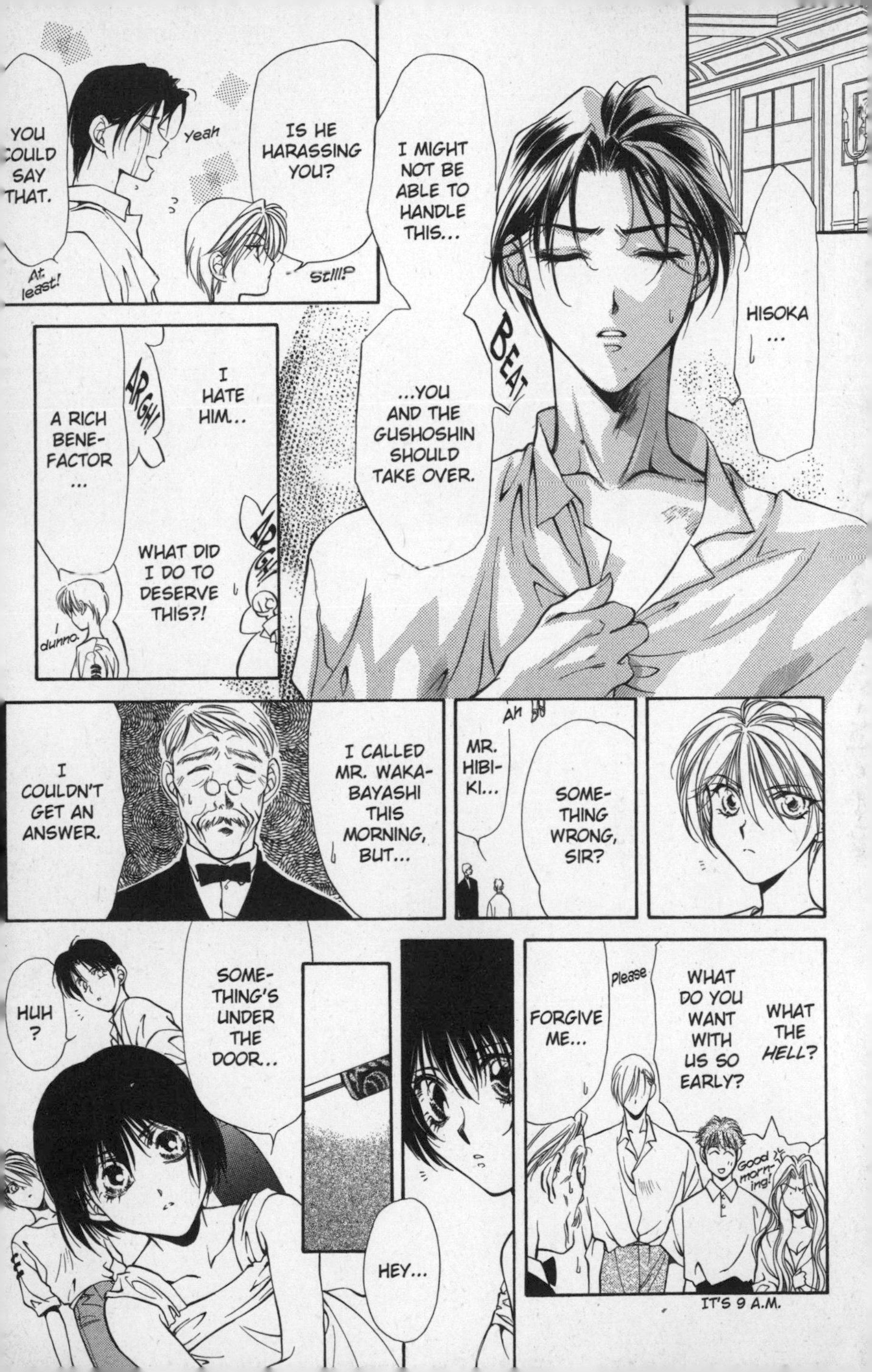
HISOKA...
I MIGHT NOT BE ABLE TO HANDLE THIS...
BEAT
...YOU AND THE GUSHOSHIN SHOULD TAKE OVER.
IS HE HARASSING YOU?
Still!?
Yeah
YOU COULD SAY THAT.
At least!
I HATE HIM...
ARGH!
A RICH BENE-FACTOR...
ARGH!
WHAT DID I DO TO DESERVE THIS?!
I dunno.
SOME-THING WRONG, SIR?
Ah
MR. HIBIKI...
I CALLED MR. WAKA-BAYASHI THIS MORNING, BUT...
I COULDN'T GET AN ANSWER.
WHAT THE HELL?
Good morning!
WHAT DO YOU WANT WITH US SO EARLY?
Please
FORGIVE ME...
IT'S 9 A.M.
HEY...
SOME-THING'S UNDER THE DOOR...
HUH?

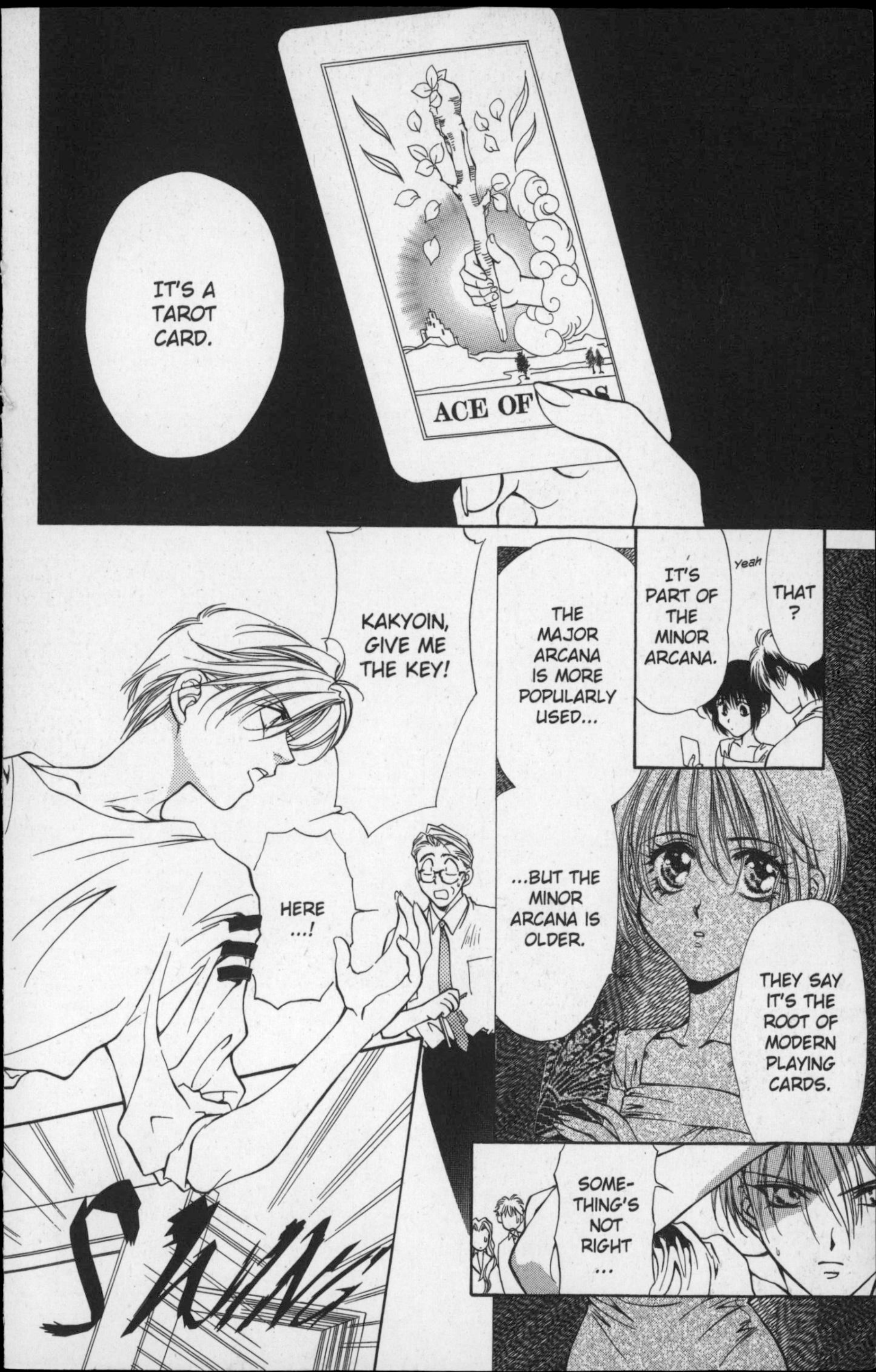
IT'S A TAROT CARD.
ACE OF
THAT?
Yeah
IT'S PART OF THE MINOR ARCANA.
THE MAJOR ARCANA IS MORE POPULARLY USED...
...BUT THE MINOR ARCANA IS OLDER.
THEY SAY IT'S THE ROOT OF MODERN PLAYING CARDS.
SOME-THING'S NOT RIGHT...
KAKYOIN, GIVE ME THE KEY!
HERE...!
SHING

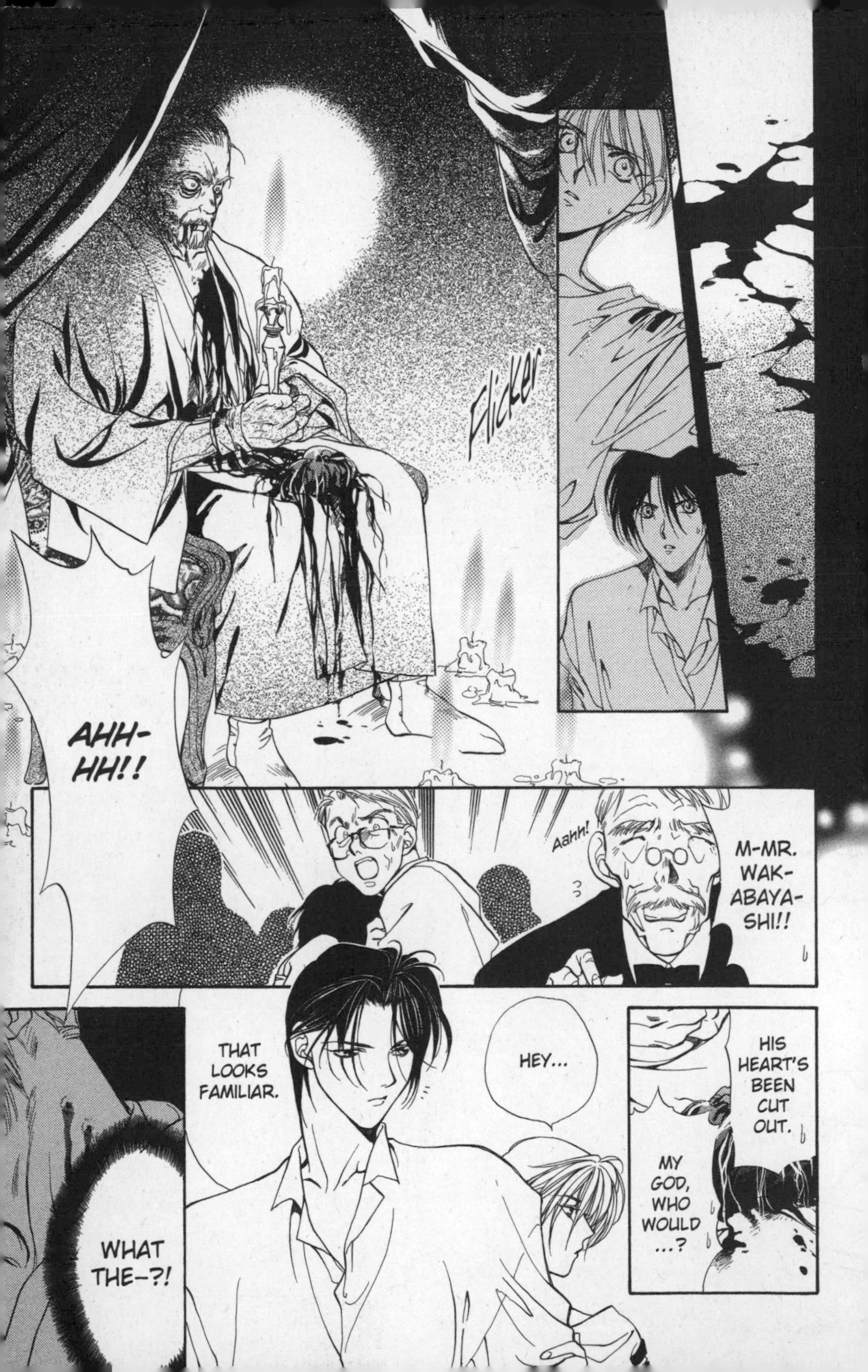
Flicker
AHH-HH!!
M-MR. WAK-ABAYA-SHI!!
Aahh!
HIS HEART'S BEEN CUT OUT.
MY GOD, WHO WOULD ...?
HEY...
THAT LOOKS FAMILIAR.
WHAT THE–?!

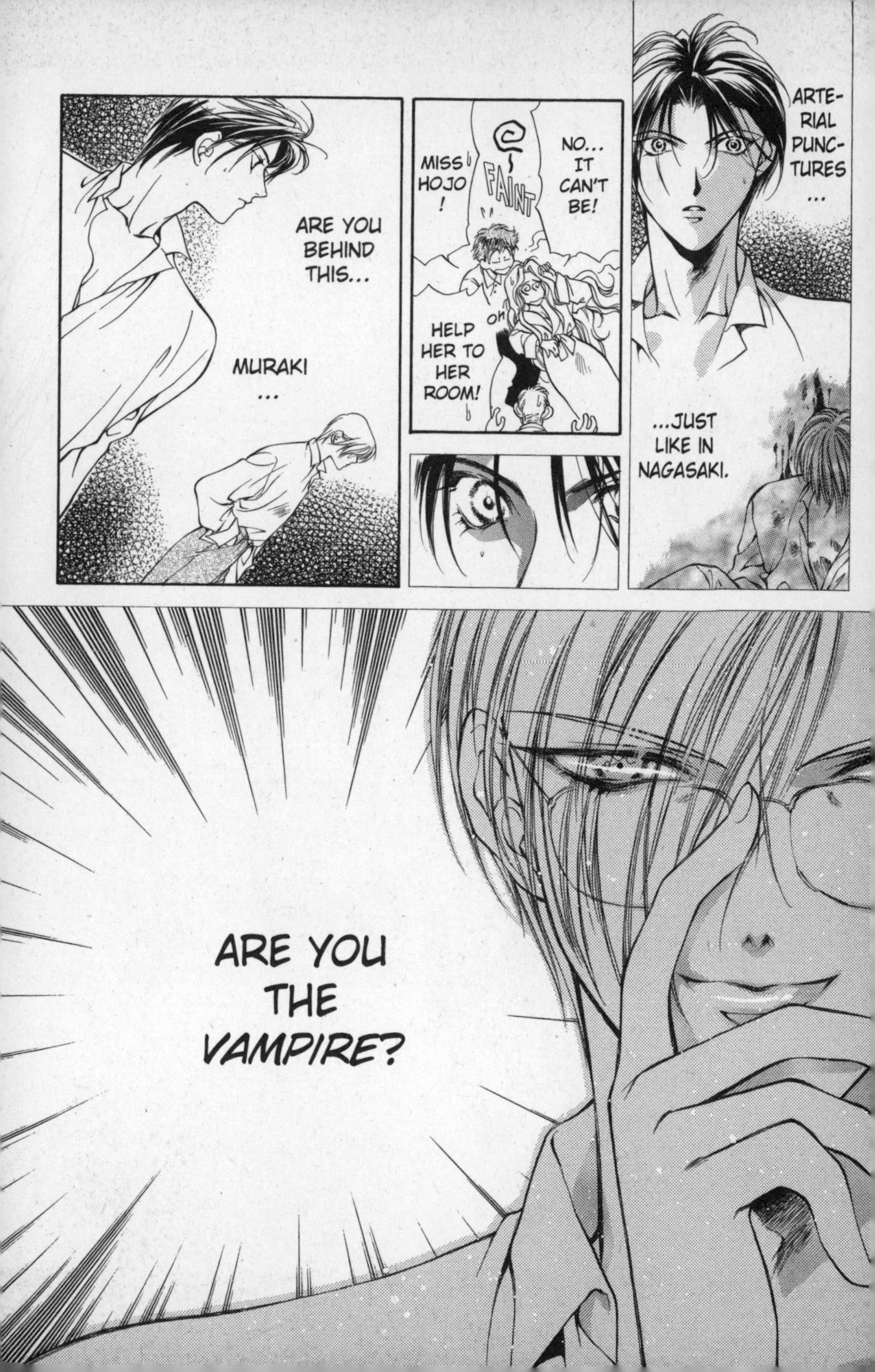
ARTE-RIAL PUNC-TURES ...
...JUST LIKE IN NAGASAKI.
NO... IT CAN'T BE!
FAINT
MISS HOJO!
oh
HELP HER TO HER ROOM!
ARE YOU BEHIND THIS...
MURAKI ...
ARE YOU THE VAMPIRE?

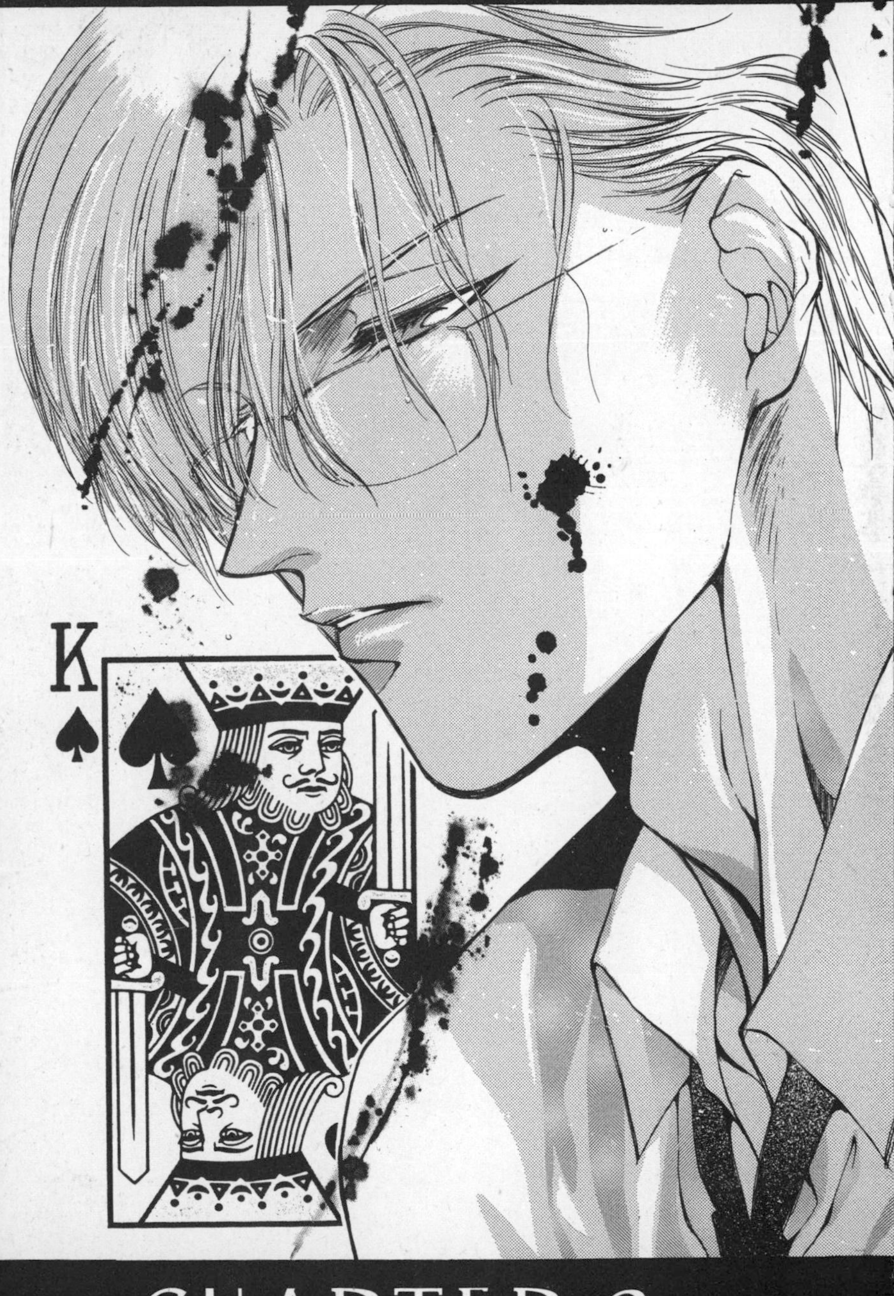
K

CHAPTER 2

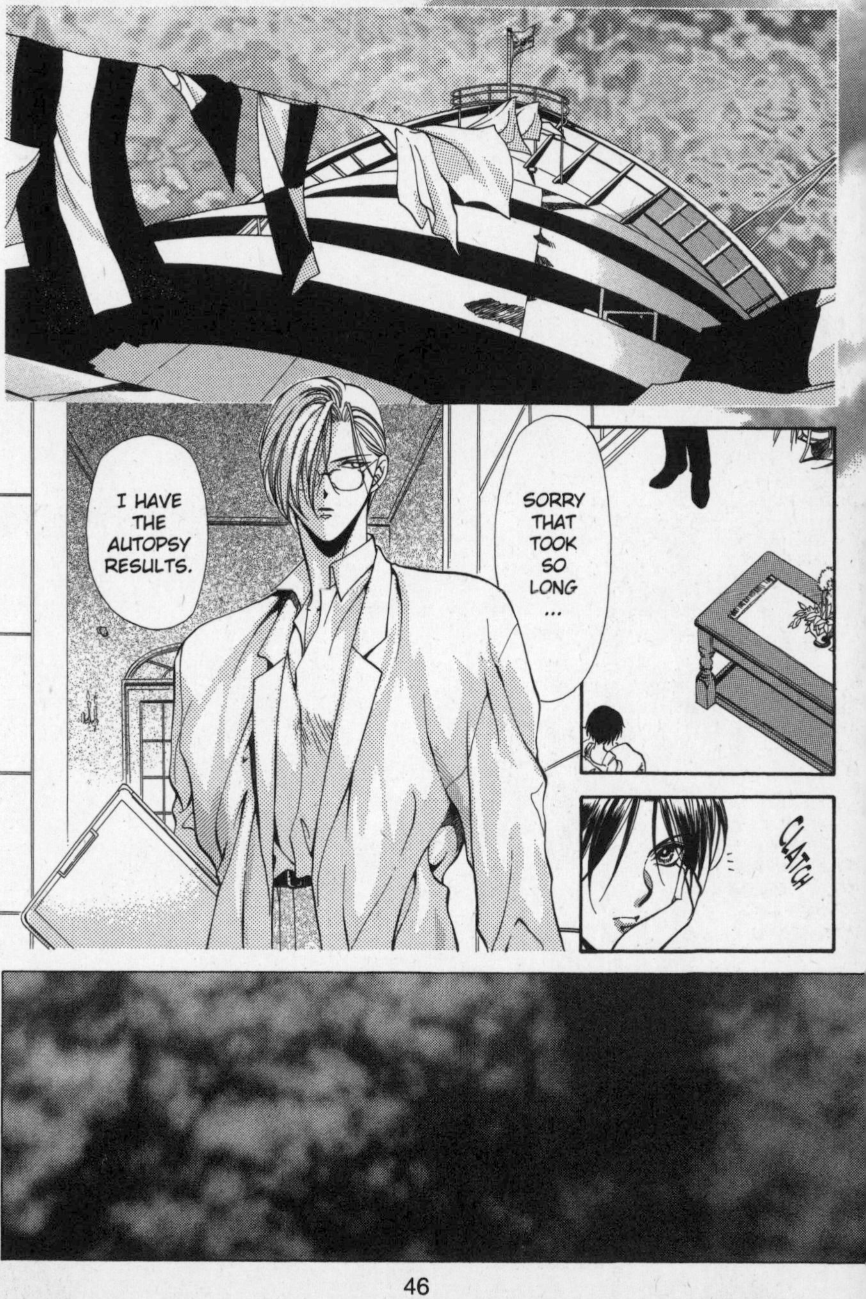
CLATCH
SORRY THAT TOOK SO LONG ...
I HAVE THE AUTOPSY RESULTS.

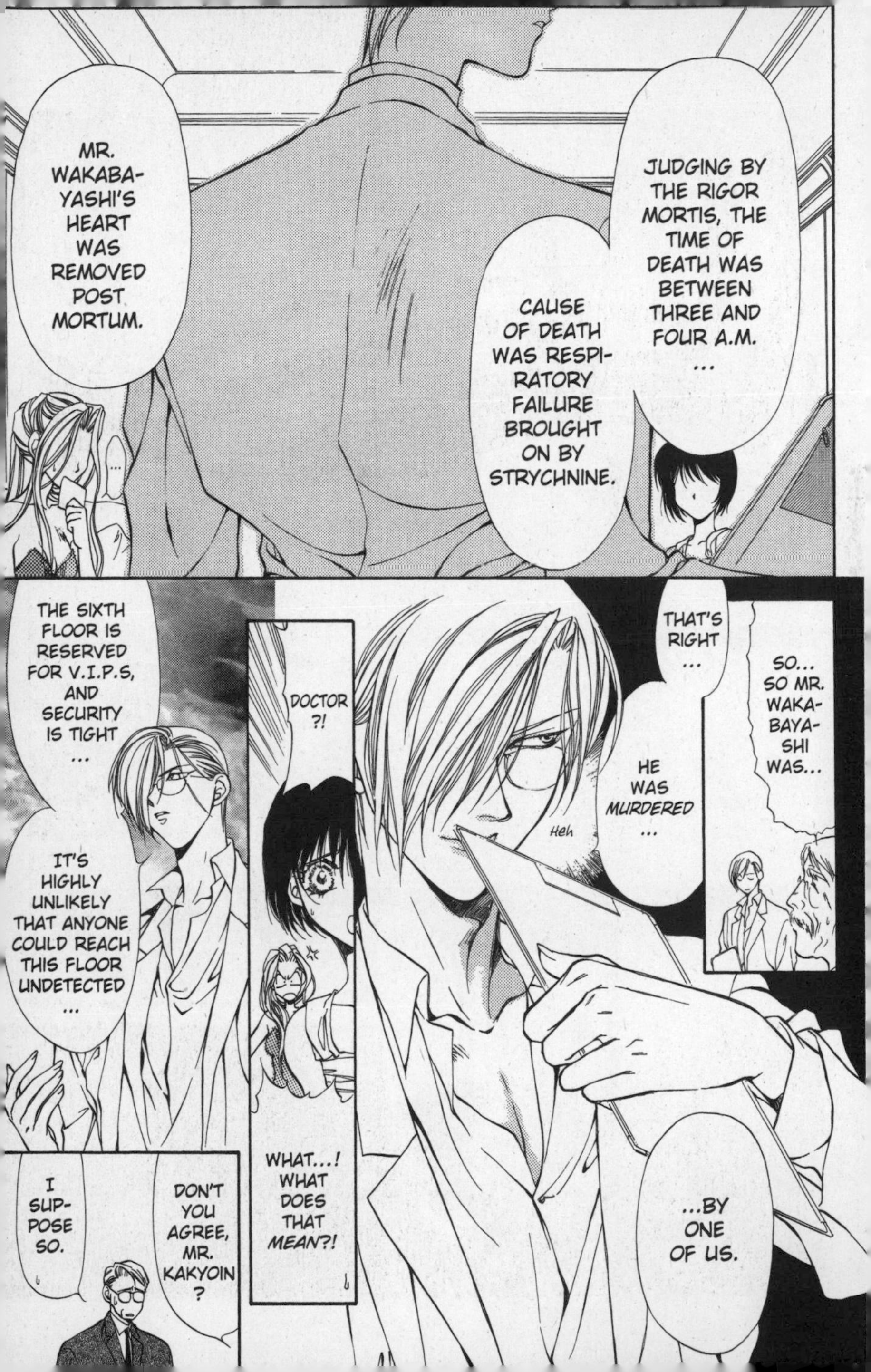
JUDGING BY THE RIGOR MORTIS, THE TIME OF DEATH WAS BETWEEN THREE AND FOUR A.M. ...
CAUSE OF DEATH WAS RESPI-RATORY FAILURE BROUGHT ON BY STRYCHNINE.
MR. WAKABA-YASHI'S HEART WAS REMOVED POST MORTUM.
...
SO... SO MR. WAKA-BAYA-SHI WAS...
THAT'S RIGHT ...
HE WAS *MURDERED* ...
Heh
...BY ONE OF US.
DOCTOR ?!
WHAT...! WHAT DOES THAT *MEAN*?!
THE SIXTH FLOOR IS RESERVED FOR V.I.P.S, AND SECURITY IS TIGHT ...
IT'S HIGHLY UNLIKELY THAT ANYONE COULD REACH THIS FLOOR UNDETECTED ...
DON'T YOU AGREE, MR. KAKYOIN ?
I SUP-POSE SO.

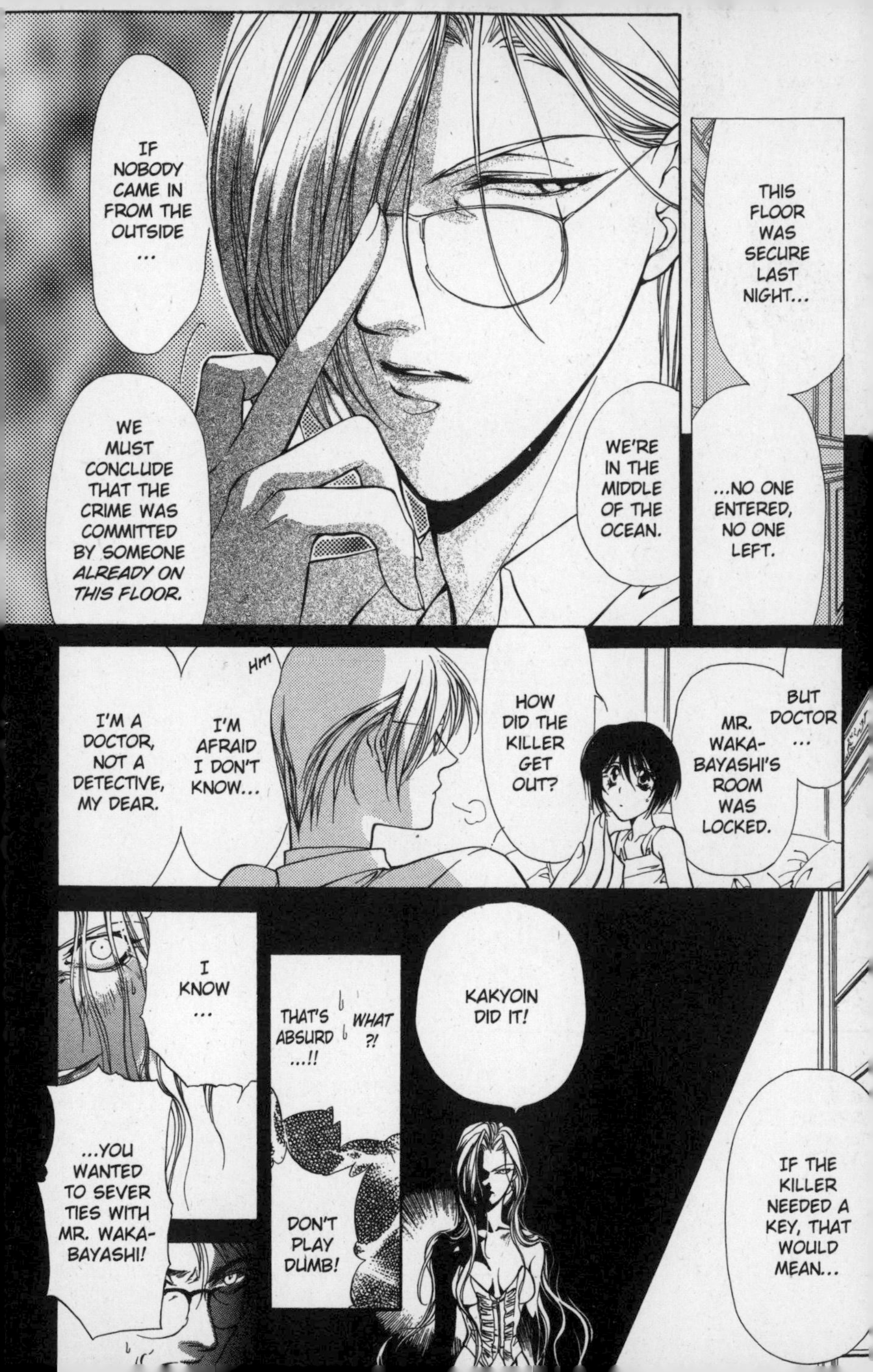
THIS FLOOR WAS SECURE LAST NIGHT...
...NO ONE ENTERED, NO ONE LEFT.
WE'RE IN THE MIDDLE OF THE OCEAN.
IF NOBODY CAME IN FROM THE OUTSIDE ...
WE MUST CONCLUDE THAT THE CRIME WAS COMMITTED BY SOMEONE *ALREADY ON THIS FLOOR.*
BUT DOCTOR ...
MR. WAKA-BAYASHI'S ROOM WAS LOCKED.
HOW DID THE KILLER GET OUT?
HM
I'M AFRAID I DON'T KNOW...
I'M A DOCTOR, NOT A DETECTIVE, MY DEAR.
IF THE KILLER NEEDED A KEY, THAT WOULD MEAN...
KAKYOIN DID IT!
WHAT ?!
THAT'S ABSURD ...!!
DON'T PLAY DUMB!
I KNOW ...
...YOU WANTED TO SEVER TIES WITH MR. WAKA-BAYASHI!

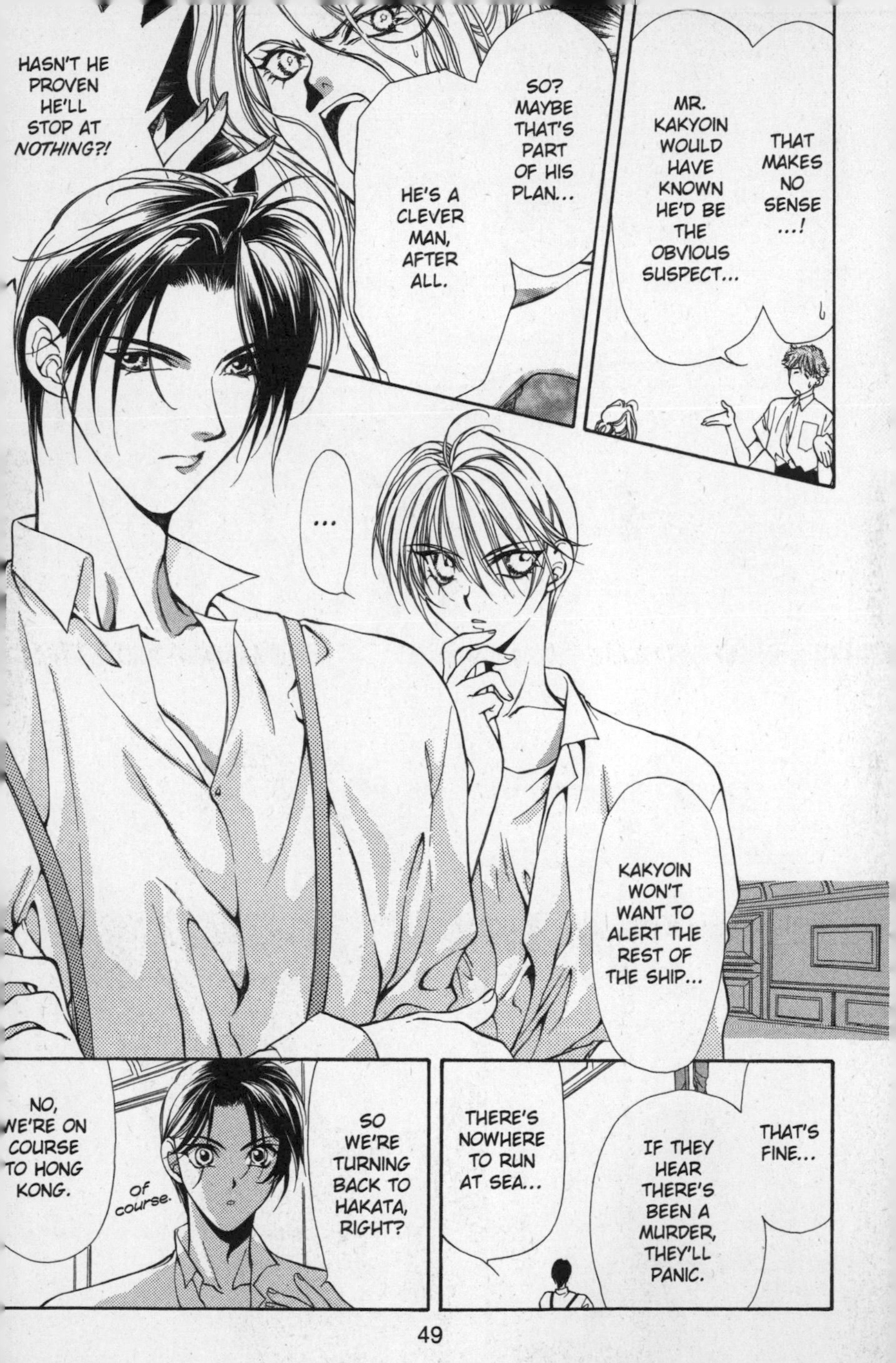
THAT MAKES NO SENSE ...!
MR. KAKYOIN WOULD HAVE KNOWN HE'D BE THE OBVIOUS SUSPECT...
SO? MAYBE THAT'S PART OF HIS PLAN...
HE'S A CLEVER MAN, AFTER ALL.
HASN'T HE PROVEN HE'LL STOP AT *NOTHING?!*
...
KAKYOIN WON'T WANT TO ALERT THE REST OF THE SHIP...
THAT'S FINE...
IF THEY HEAR THERE'S BEEN A MURDER, THEY'LL PANIC.
THERE'S NOWHERE TO RUN AT SEA...
SO WE'RE TURNING BACK TO HAKATA, RIGHT?
Of course.
NO, WE'RE ON COURSE TO HONG KONG.

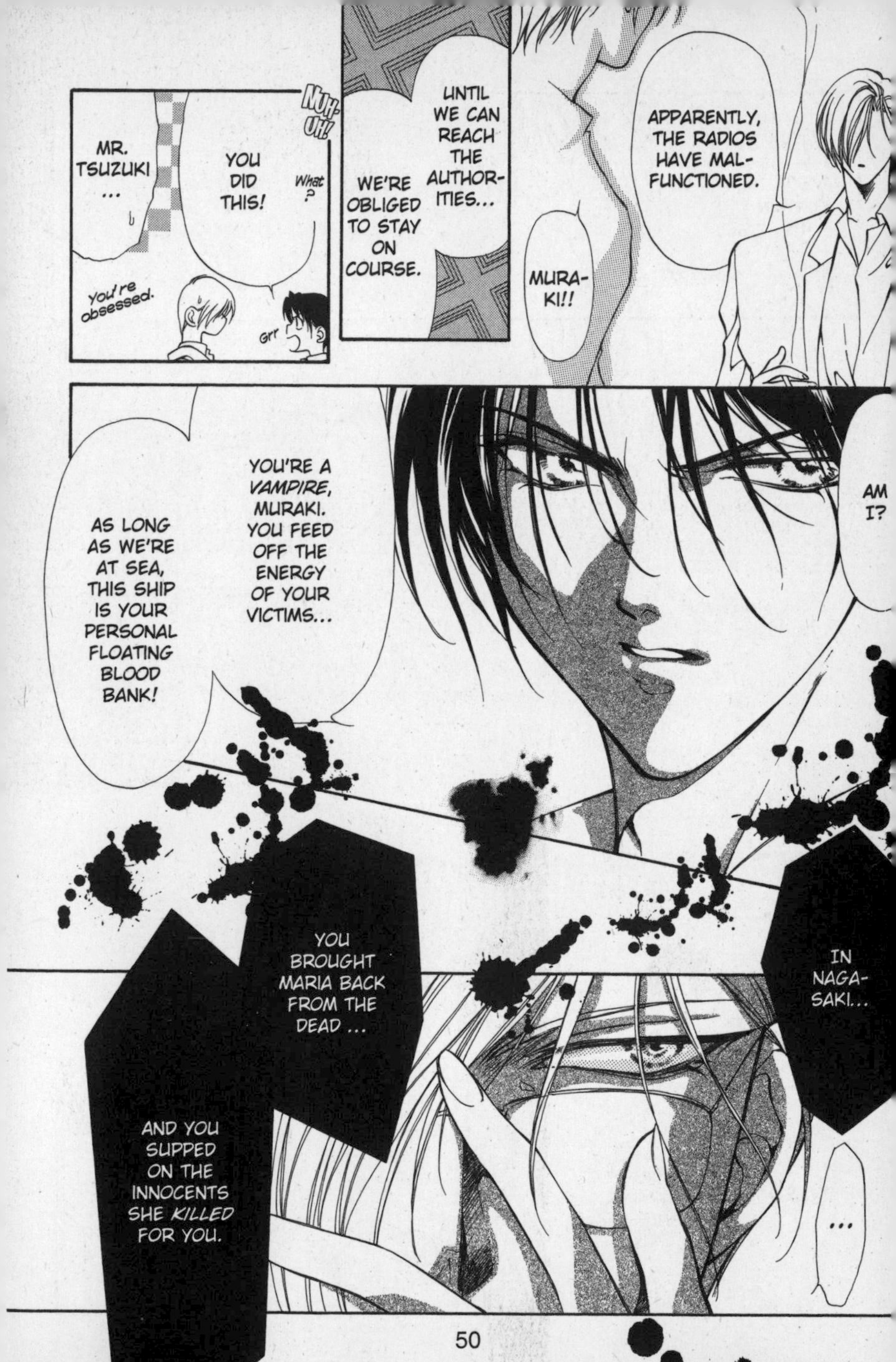
APPARENTLY, THE RADIOS HAVE MAL-FUNCTIONED.
MURA-KI!!
UNTIL WE CAN REACH THE AUTHOR-ITIES...
WE'RE OBLIGED TO STAY ON COURSE.
MUH-UH!
What?
YOU DID THIS!
MR. TSUZUKI ...
You're obsessed.
Grr
AM I?
YOU'RE A *VAMPIRE*, MURAKI. YOU FEED OFF THE ENERGY OF YOUR VICTIMS...
AS LONG AS WE'RE AT SEA, THIS SHIP IS YOUR PERSONAL FLOATING BLOOD BANK!
IN NAGA-SAKI...
YOU BROUGHT MARIA BACK FROM THE DEAD ...
AND YOU SUPPED ON THE INNOCENTS SHE *KILLED* FOR YOU.
...

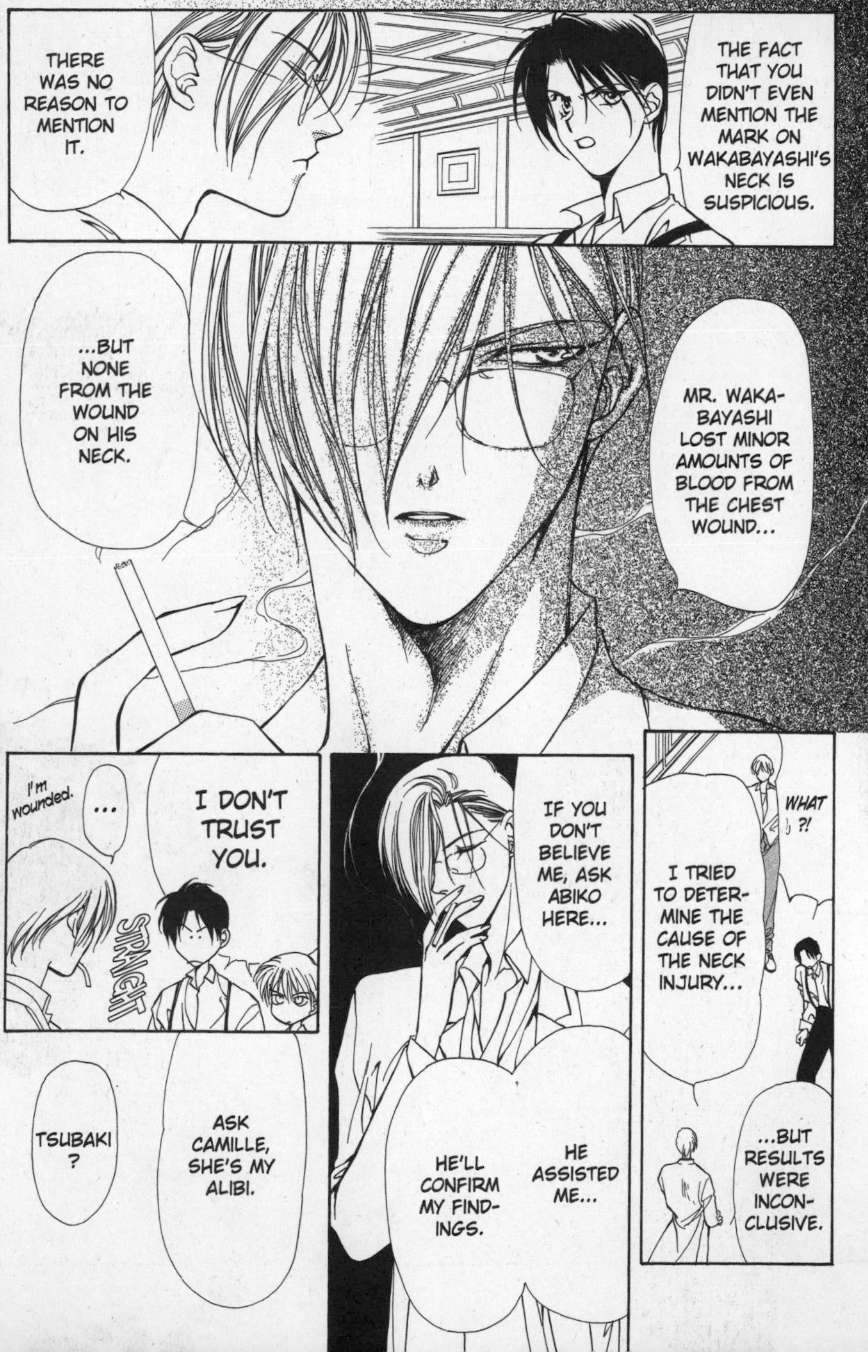
THE FACT THAT YOU DIDN'T EVEN MENTION THE MARK ON WAKABAYASHI'S NECK IS SUSPICIOUS.
THERE WAS NO REASON TO MENTION IT.
MR. WAKA-BAYASHI LOST MINOR AMOUNTS OF BLOOD FROM THE CHEST WOUND...
...BUT NONE FROM THE WOUND ON HIS NECK.
WHAT ?!
I TRIED TO DETER-MINE THE CAUSE OF THE NECK INJURY...
...BUT RESULTS WERE INCON-CLUSIVE.
IF YOU DON'T BELIEVE ME, ASK ABIKO HERE...
HE ASSISTED ME...
HE'LL CONFIRM MY FIND-INGS.
I DON'T TRUST YOU.
...
I'm wounded.
STRAIGHT
ASK CAMILLE, SHE'S MY ALIBI.
TSUBAKI ?

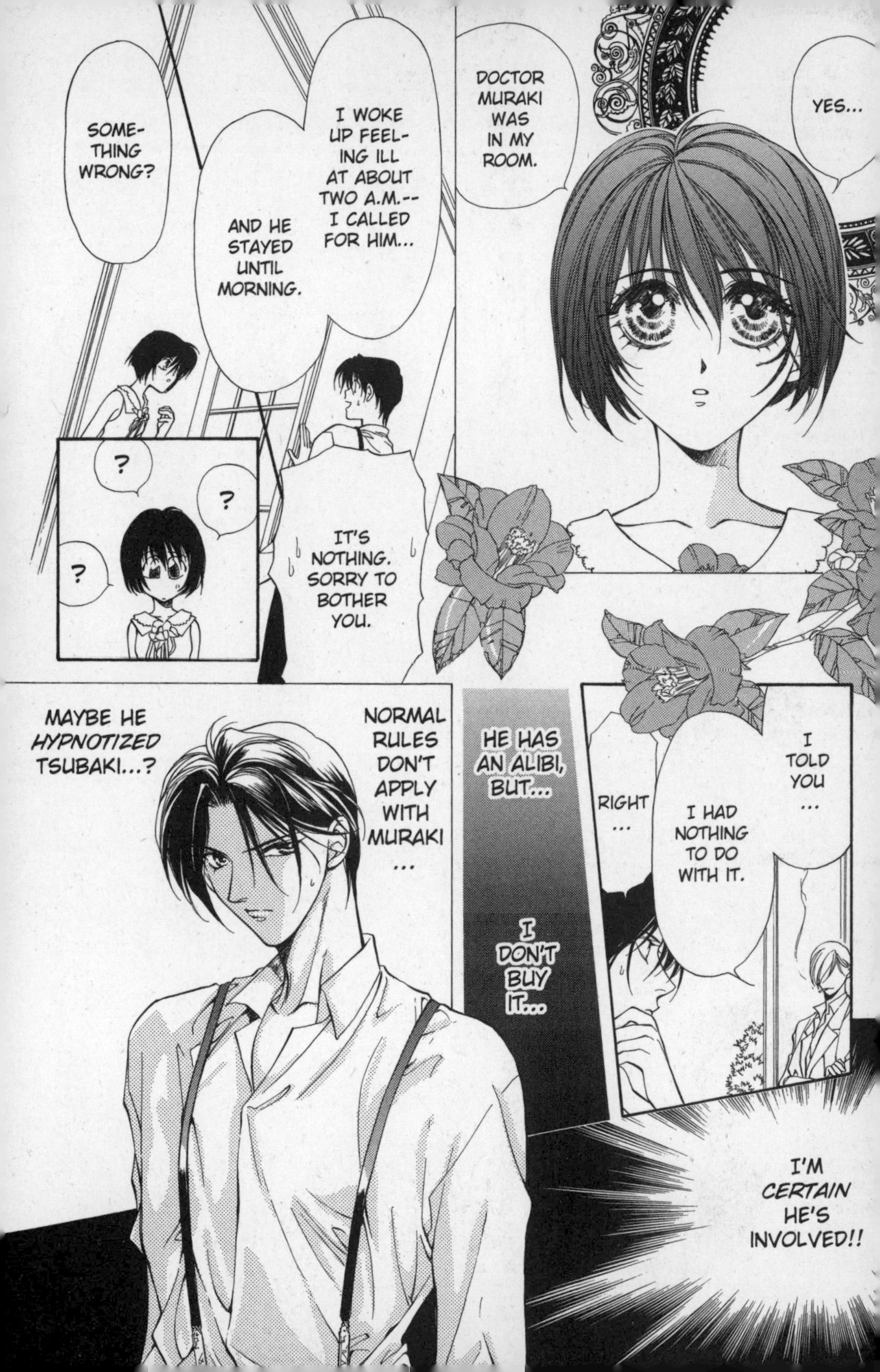
YES...
DOCTOR MURAKI WAS IN MY ROOM.
I WOKE UP FEELING ILL AT ABOUT TWO A.M.-- I CALLED FOR HIM...
AND HE STAYED UNTIL MORNING.
SOMETHING WRONG?
IT'S NOTHING. SORRY TO BOTHER YOU.
?
?
?
I TOLD YOU ...
I HAD NOTHING TO DO WITH IT.
RIGHT ...
HE HAS AN ALIBI, BUT...
I DON'T BUY IT...
NORMAL RULES DON'T APPLY WITH MURAKI ...
MAYBE HE *HYPNOTIZED* TSUBAKI...?
I'M *CERTAIN* HE'S INVOLVED!!

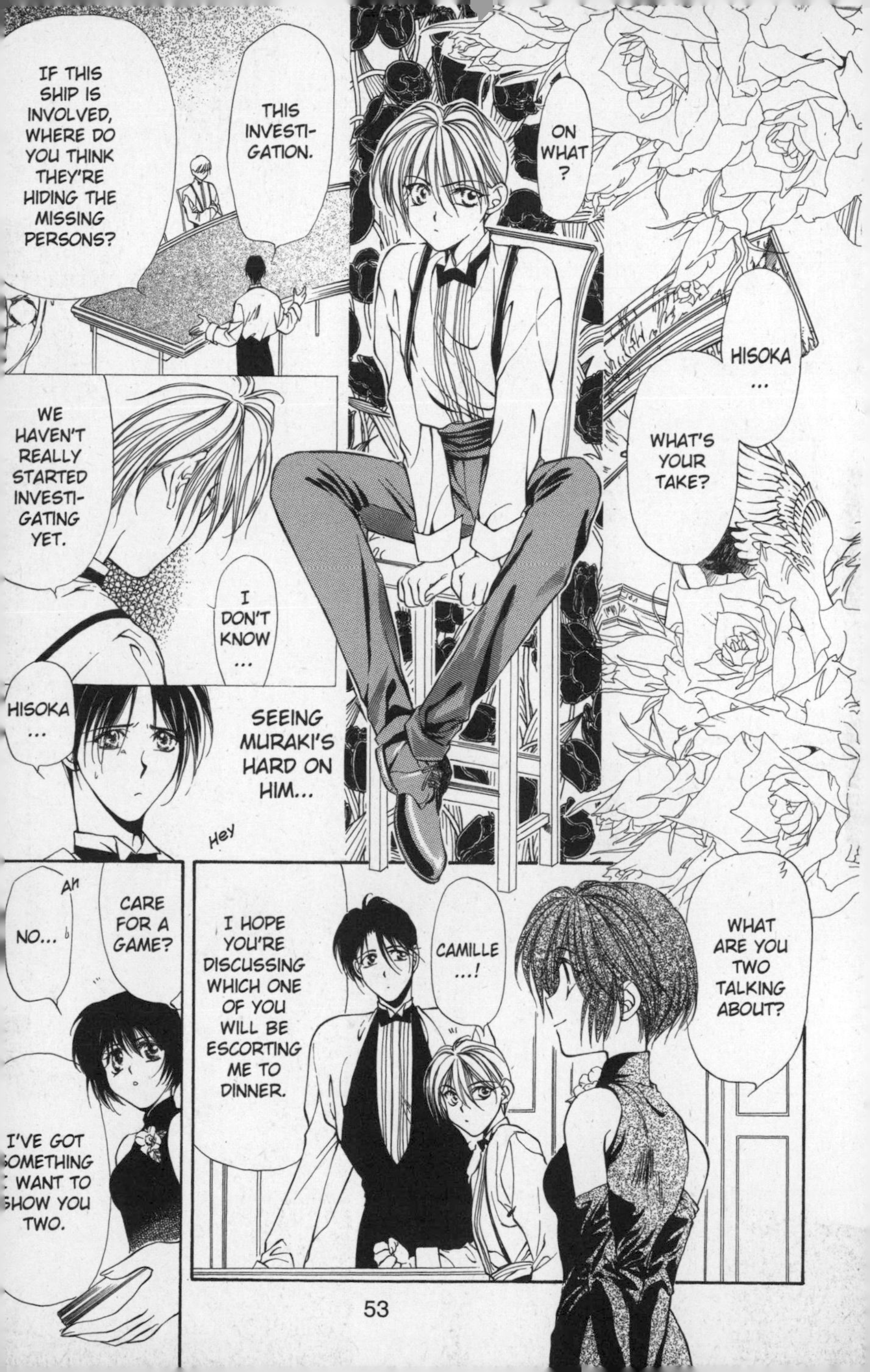
HISOKA ...
WHAT'S YOUR TAKE?
ON WHAT ?
THIS INVESTI-GATION.
IF THIS SHIP IS INVOLVED, WHERE DO YOU THINK THEY'RE HIDING THE MISSING PERSONS?
WE HAVEN'T REALLY STARTED INVESTI-GATING YET.
I DON'T KNOW ...
HISOKA ...
SEEING MURAKI'S HARD ON HIM...
Hey
WHAT ARE YOU TWO TALKING ABOUT?
CAMILLE ...!
I HOPE YOU'RE DISCUSSING WHICH ONE OF YOU WILL BE ESCORTING ME TO DINNER.
CARE FOR A GAME?
Ah
NO...
I'VE GOT SOMETHING I WANT TO SHOW YOU TWO.

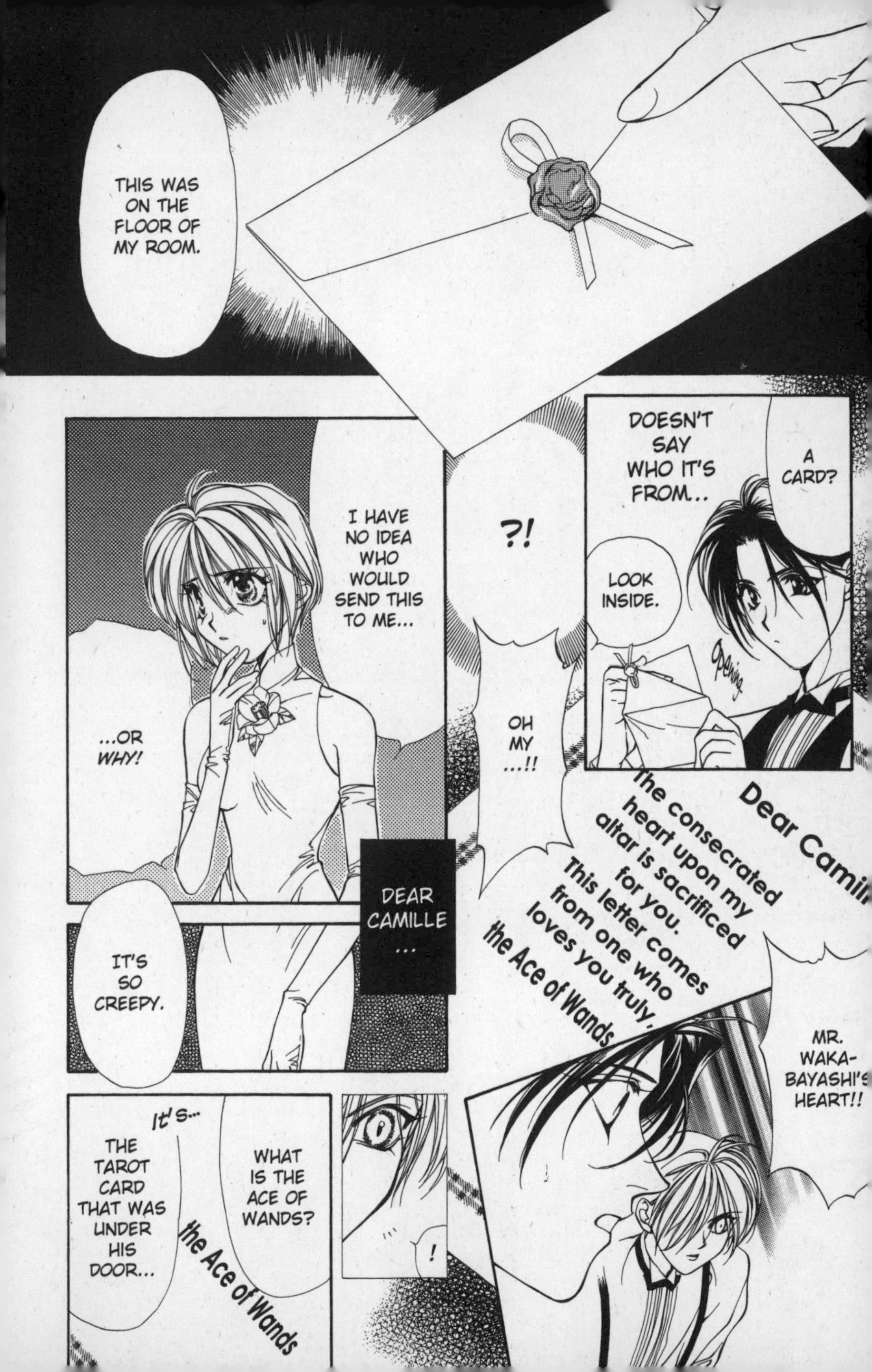
THIS WAS ON THE FLOOR OF MY ROOM.
A CARD?
DOESN'T SAY WHO IT'S FROM...
LOOK INSIDE.
Opening
?!
OH MY ...!!
Dear Camil
the consecrated heart upon my altar is sacrificed for you. This letter comes from one who loves you truly.
the Ace of Wands
I HAVE NO IDEA WHO WOULD SEND THIS TO ME...
...OR WHY!
DEAR CAMILLE ...
IT'S SO CREEPY.
MR. WAKA-BAYASHI'S HEART!!
!
WHAT IS THE ACE OF WANDS?
It's...
THE TAROT CARD THAT WAS UNDER HIS DOOR...
the Ace of Wands

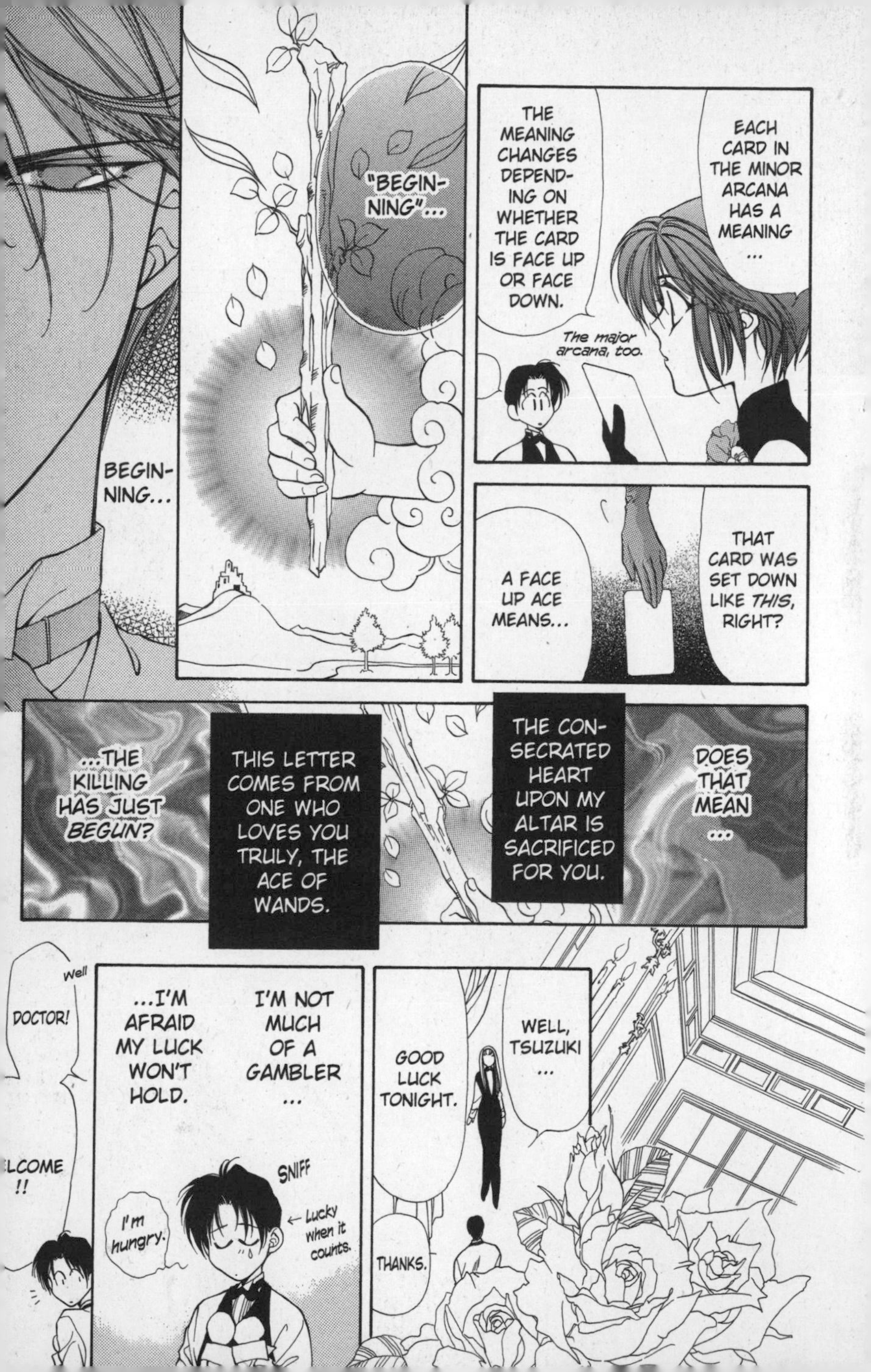
EACH CARD IN THE MINOR ARCANA HAS A MEANING ...
THE MEANING CHANGES DEPEND-ING ON WHETHER THE CARD IS FACE UP OR FACE DOWN.
The major arcana, too.
THAT CARD WAS SET DOWN LIKE *THIS*, RIGHT?
A FACE UP ACE MEANS...
"BEGIN-NING"...
BEGIN-NING...
DOES THAT MEAN ...
THE CON-SECRATED HEART UPON MY ALTAR IS SACRIFICED FOR YOU.
THIS LETTER COMES FROM ONE WHO LOVES YOU TRULY, THE ACE OF WANDS.
...THE KILLING HAS JUST *BEGUN*?
WELL, TSUZUKI ...
GOOD LUCK TONIGHT.
THANKS.
I'M NOT MUCH OF A GAMBLER ...
...I'M AFRAID MY LUCK WON'T HOLD.
SNIFF
Lucky when it counts.
I'm hungry.
Well
DOCTOR!
ELCOME !!

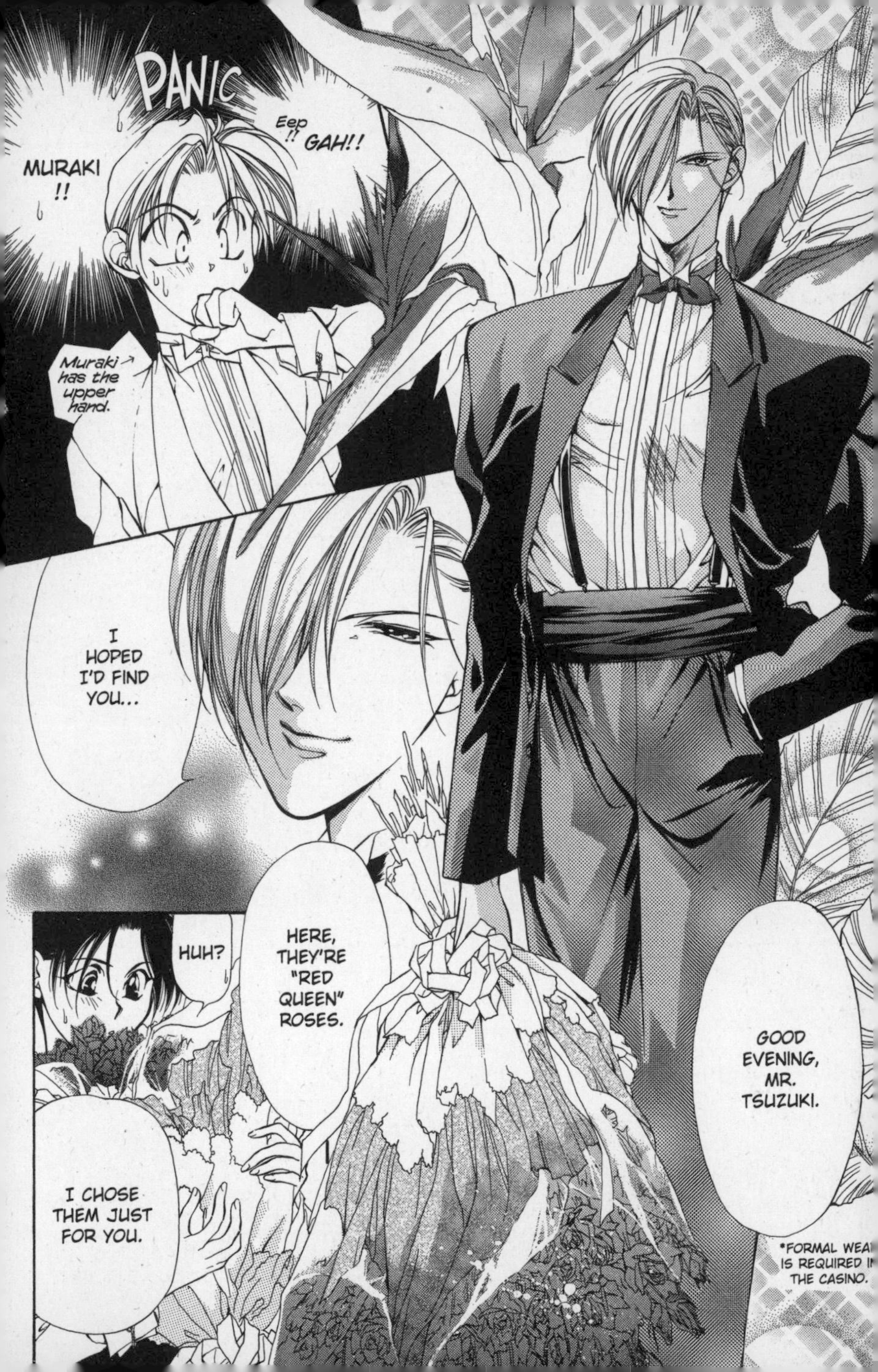
GOOD EVENING, MR. TSUZUKI.
*FORMAL WEA IS REQUIRED I THE CASINO.
PANIC
Eep!! GAH!!
MURAKI!!
Muraki has the upper hand.
I HOPED I'D FIND YOU...
HERE, THEY'RE "RED QUEEN" ROSES.
HUH?
I CHOSE THEM JUST FOR YOU.

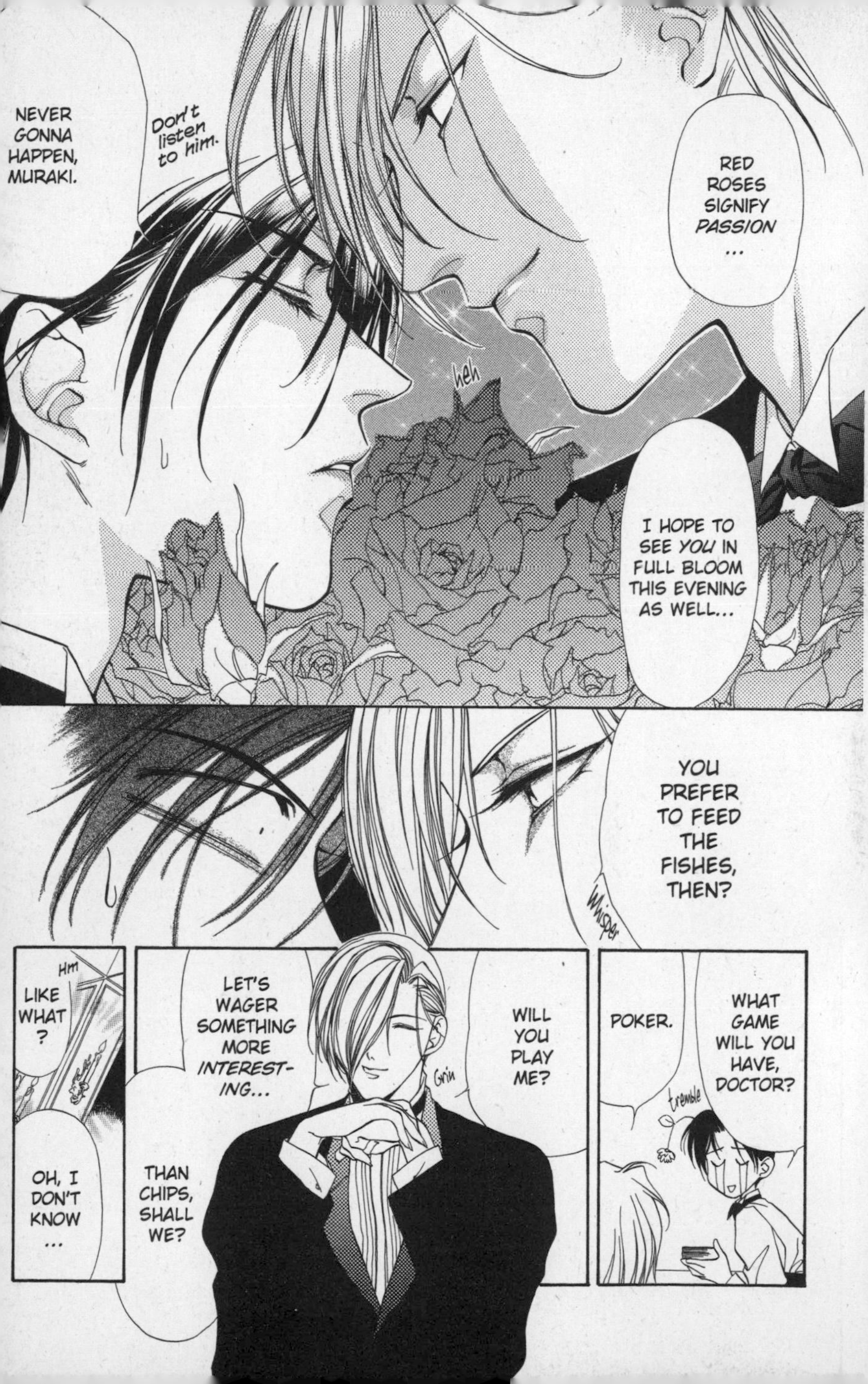
RED ROSES SIGNIFY *PASSION* ...
I HOPE TO SEE *YOU* IN FULL BLOOM THIS EVENING AS WELL...
heh
Don't listen to him.
NEVER GONNA HAPPEN, MURAKI.
YOU PREFER TO FEED THE FISHES, THEN?
Whisper
WHAT GAME WILL YOU HAVE, DOCTOR?
POKER.
tremble
WILL YOU PLAY ME?
Grin
LET'S WAGER SOMETHING MORE *INTEREST-ING*...
THAN CHIPS, SHALL WE?
Hm
LIKE WHAT?
OH, I DON'T KNOW ...

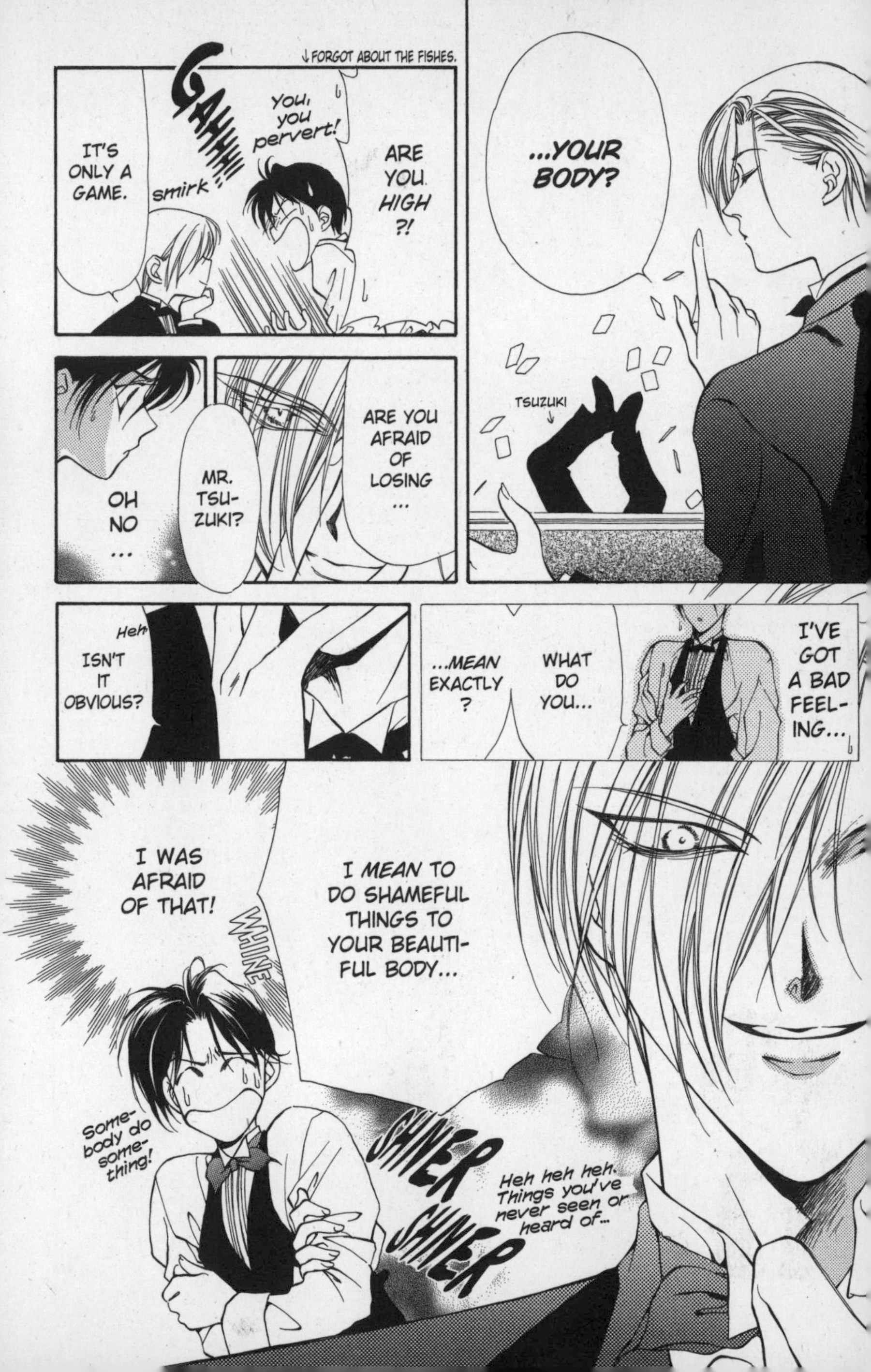
...YOUR BODY?
TSUZUKI
↓FORGOT ABOUT THE FISHES.
You, you pervert!
ARE YOU HIGH ?!
GAHHH!!
smirk
IT'S ONLY A GAME.
ARE YOU AFRAID OF LOSING ...
MR. TSU-ZUKI?
OH NO ...
I'VE GOT A BAD FEEL-ING...
WHAT DO YOU...
...MEAN EXACTLY ?
Heh
ISN'T IT OBVIOUS?
I MEAN TO DO SHAMEFUL THINGS TO YOUR BEAUTI-FUL BODY...
Heh heh heh. Things you've never seen or heard of...
SHIVER SHIVER
I WAS AFRAID OF THAT!
WHINE
Some-body do some-thing!

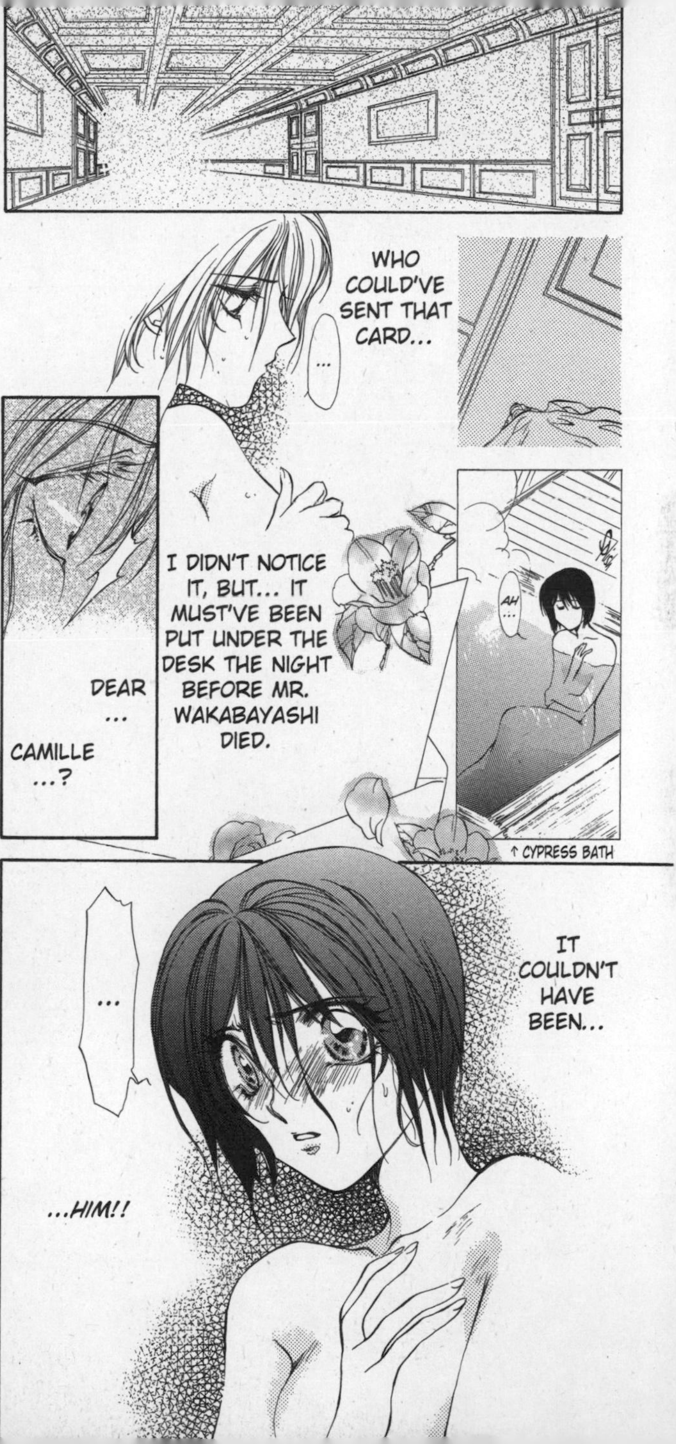
WHO COULD'VE SENT THAT CARD...
...
AH ...
↑ CYPRESS BATH
I DIDN'T NOTICE IT, BUT... IT MUST'VE BEEN PUT UNDER THE DESK THE NIGHT BEFORE MR. WAKABAYASHI DIED.
DEAR ...
CAMILLE ...?
IT COULDN'T HAVE BEEN...
...
...HIM!!

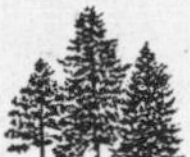

I like dealers' uniforms. I wrote this story just so I could draw one (ha ha). It looks good on Tsuzuki, huh? And...this is obvious, I know, but... that doctor is totally crazy. He won't let anything stop him from getting what he wants...(tee hee). That's okay. All that matters is that he's having fun. That's the way his character is, so why fight it? *?

People have been writing in to ask me if Doctor Muraki is gay. The answer is: not exclusively. He likes both boys and girls. If he's interested in someone, he doesn't care what gender they are. In other words, he's a dirty little slut! Little known fact: Muraki has a long-time girlfriend. They grew up together! ...I don't understand that guy.

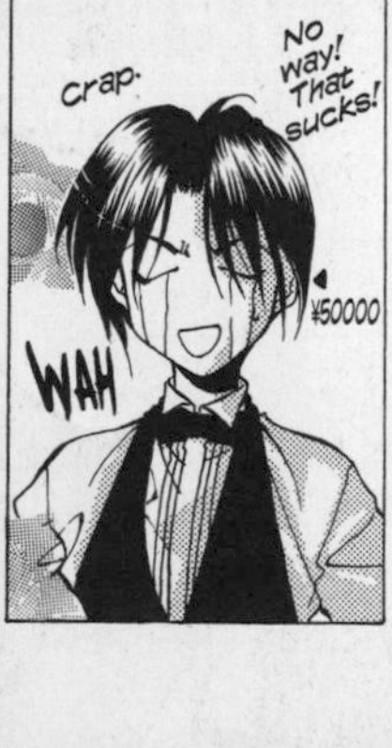
Crap.
No way! That sucks!
¥50000
WAH

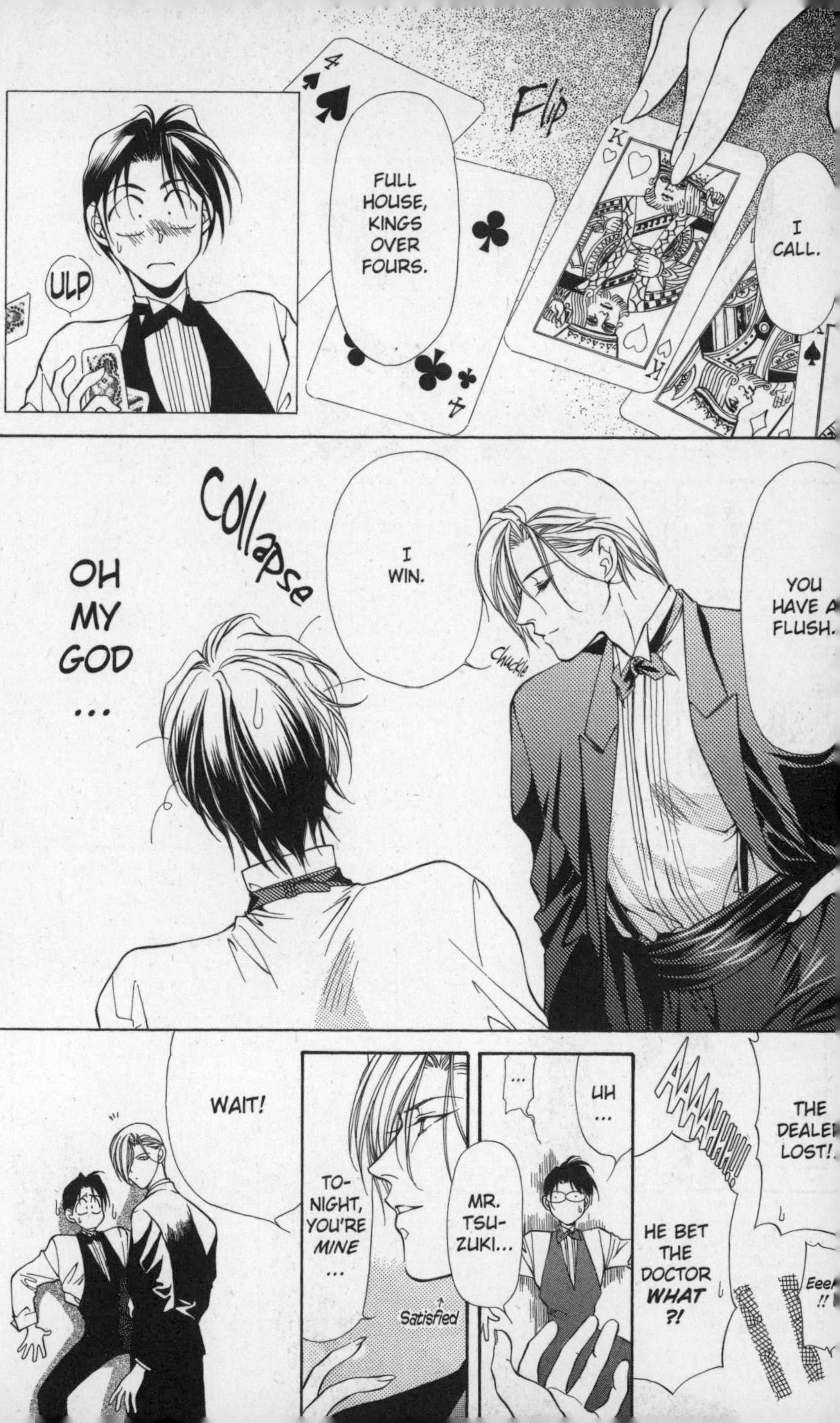
I CALL.
Flip
FULL HOUSE, KINGS OVER FOURS.
ULP
YOU HAVE A FLUSH.
Chuckle
I WIN.
Collapse
OH MY GOD ...
THE DEALE LOST!
AAAAHH!!
Eee !!
HE BET THE DOCTOR WHAT?!
...
UH ...
MR. TSUZUKI...
TONIGHT, YOU'RE MINE ...
Satisfied
WAIT!

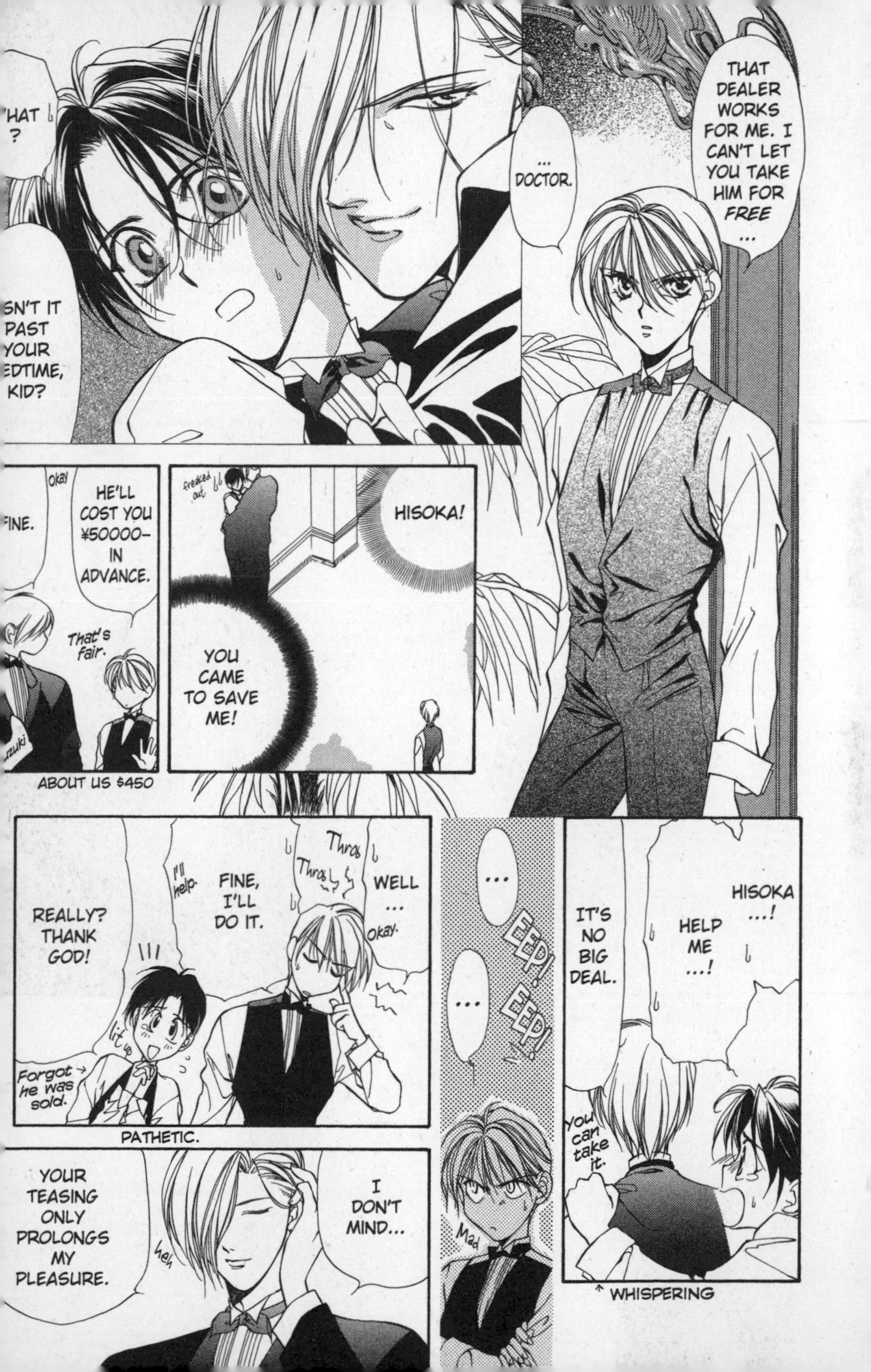
THAT DEALER WORKS FOR ME. I CAN'T LET YOU TAKE HIM FOR FREE ...
... DOCTOR.
HAT ?
SN'T IT PAST YOUR EDTIME, KID?
freaked out
HISOKA!
YOU CAME TO SAVE ME!
HE'LL COST YOU ¥50000— IN ADVANCE.
Okay
FINE.
That's fair.
ABOUT US $450
HISOKA ...!
HELP ME ...!
IT'S NO BIG DEAL.
You can take it.
WHISPERING
...
...
EEP! EEP!
Mad
WELL ...
Okay.
FINE, I'LL DO IT.
I'll help.
REALLY? THANK GOD!
Forgot he was sold.
PATHETIC.
I DON'T MIND...
heh
YOUR TEASING ONLY PROLONGS MY PLEASURE.

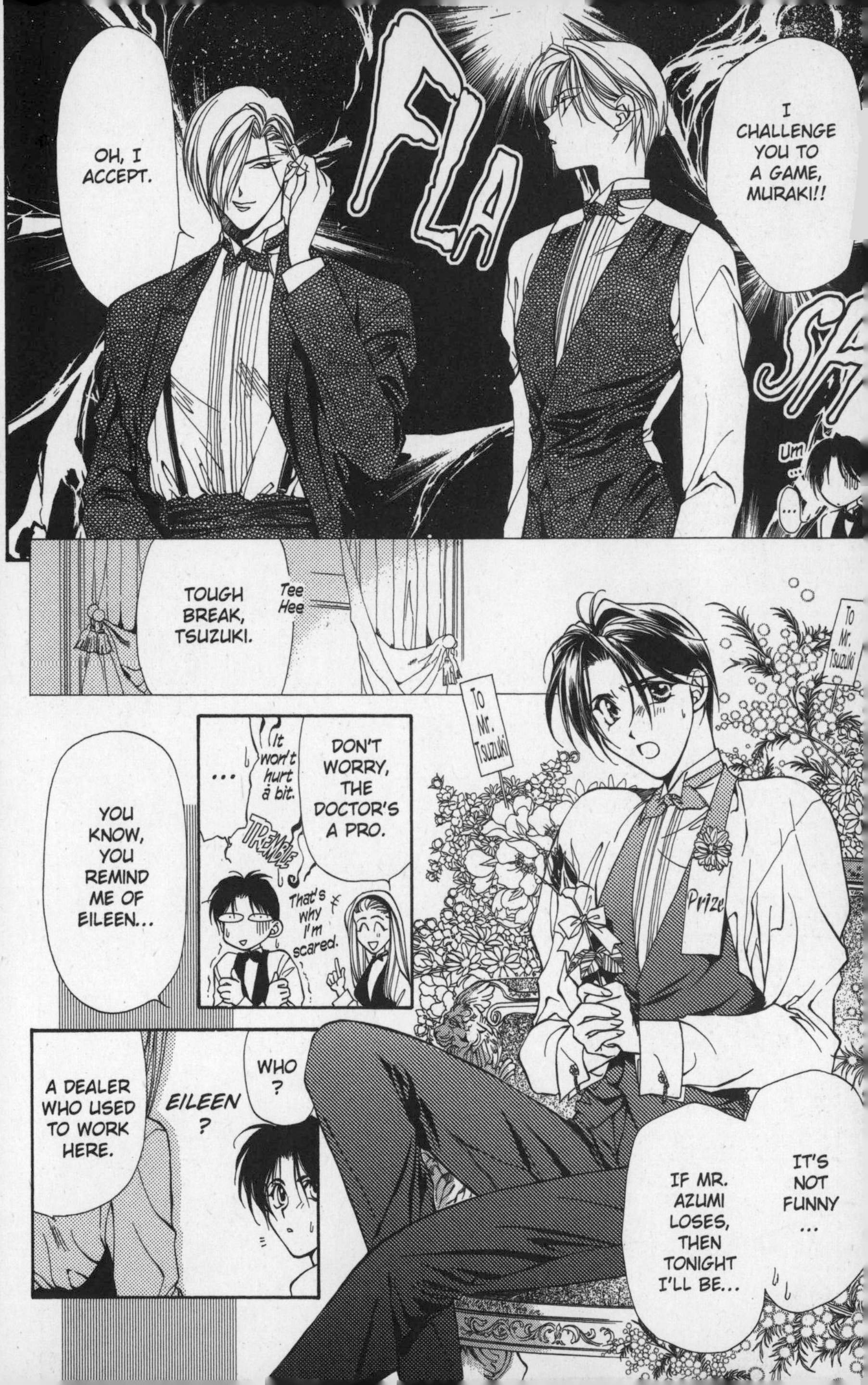
I CHALLENGE YOU TO A GAME, MURAKI!!
FLA
SH
Um...
...
OH, I ACCEPT.
To Mr. Tsuzuki
To Mr. Tsuzuki
Prize
IT'S NOT FUNNY...
IF MR. AZUMI LOSES, THEN TONIGHT I'LL BE...
TOUGH BREAK, TSUZUKI.
Tee Hee
DON'T WORRY, THE DOCTOR'S A PRO.
It won't hurt a bit.
...
TREMBLE
That's why I'm scared.
YOU KNOW, YOU REMIND ME OF EILEEN...
WHO?
EILEEN?
A DEALER WHO USED TO WORK HERE.

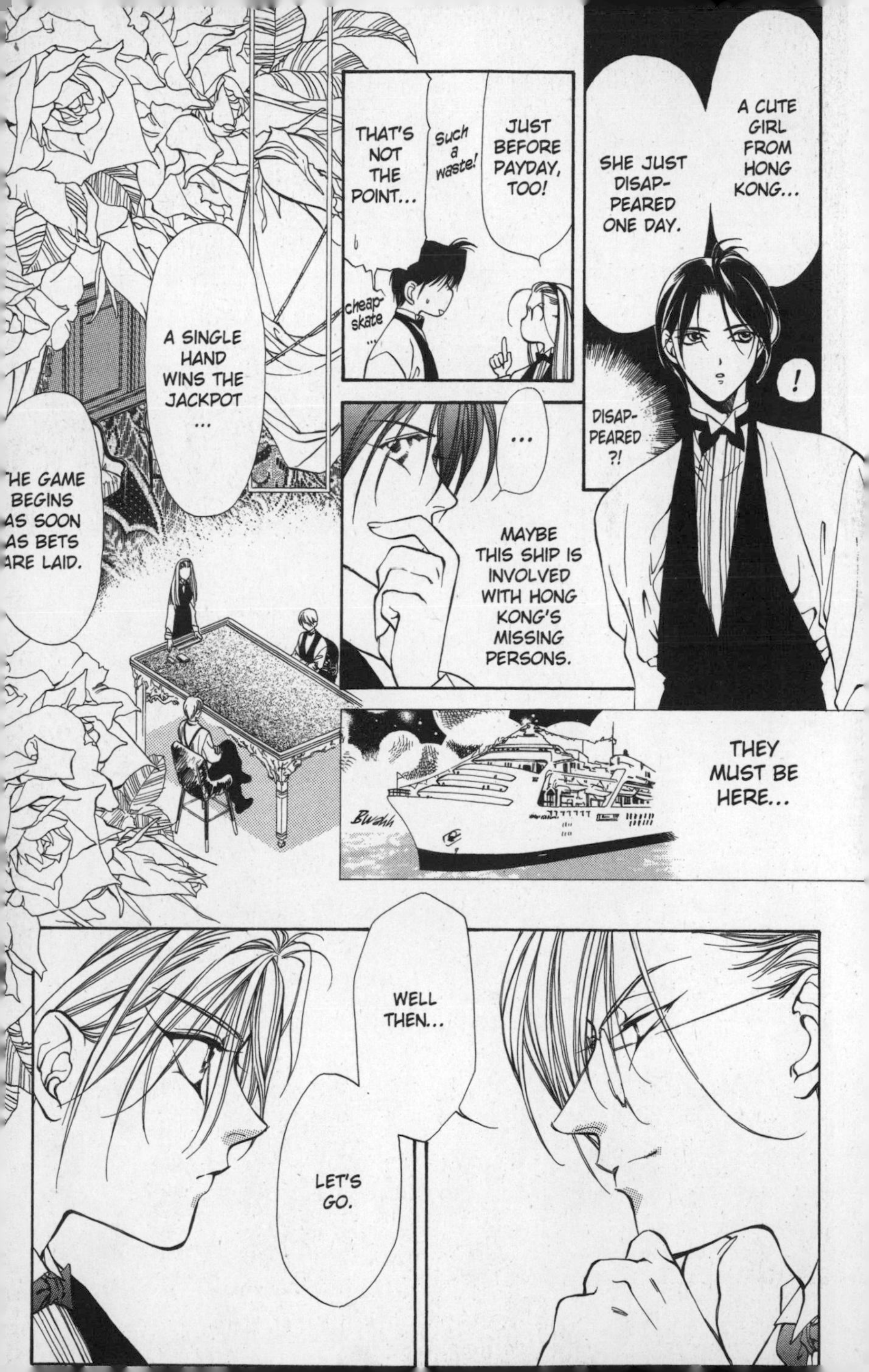
A CUTE GIRL FROM HONG KONG...
SHE JUST DISAP-PEARED ONE DAY.
!
DISAP-PEARED ?!
JUST BEFORE PAYDAY, TOO!
Such a waste!
THAT'S NOT THE POINT...
cheap-skate ...
...
MAYBE THIS SHIP IS INVOLVED WITH HONG KONG'S MISSING PERSONS.
THEY MUST BE HERE...
Bwahh
A SINGLE HAND WINS THE JACKPOT ...
THE GAME BEGINS AS SOON AS BETS ARE LAID.
WELL THEN...
LET'S GO.

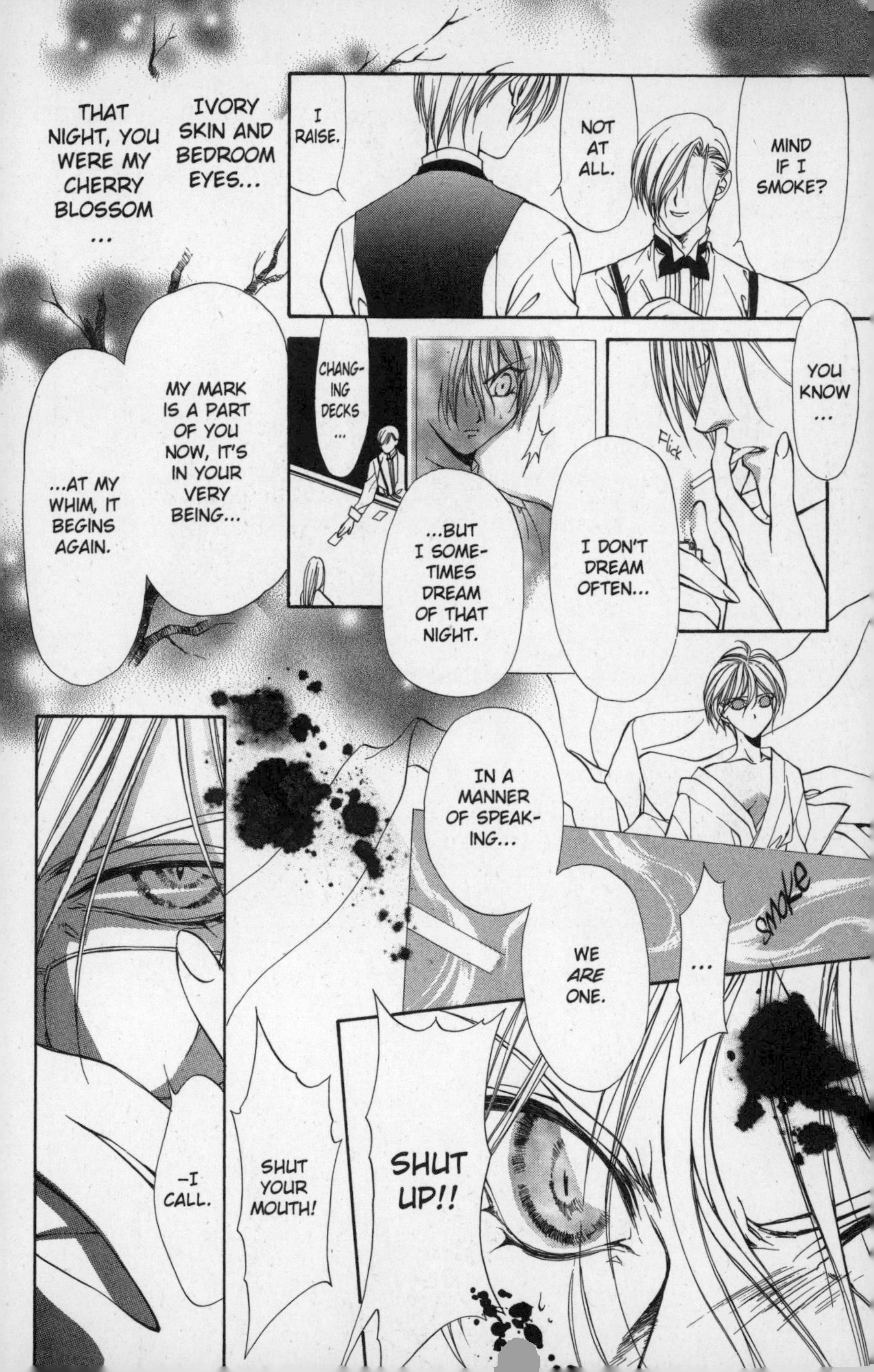
MIND IF I SMOKE?
NOT AT ALL.
I RAISE.
IVORY SKIN AND BEDROOM EYES...
THAT NIGHT, YOU WERE MY CHERRY BLOSSOM ...
YOU KNOW ...
Flick
I DON'T DREAM OFTEN...
...BUT I SOME-TIMES DREAM OF THAT NIGHT.
CHANG-ING DECKS ...
MY MARK IS A PART OF YOU NOW, IT'S IN YOUR VERY BEING...
...AT MY WHIM, IT BEGINS AGAIN.
IN A MANNER OF SPEAK-ING...
smoke
...
WE ARE ONE.
SHUT UP!!
SHUT YOUR MOUTH!
–I CALL.

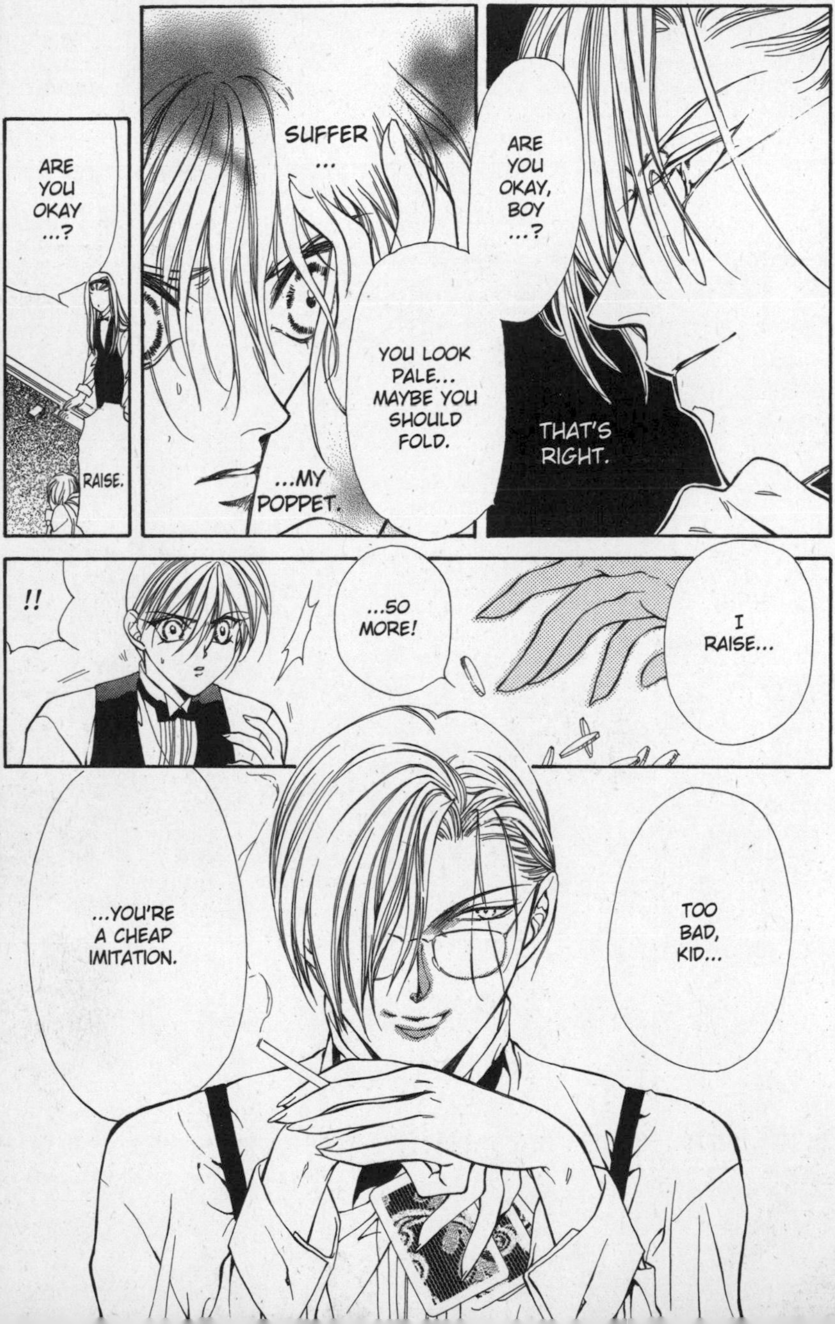
ARE YOU OKAY, BOY ...?
YOU LOOK PALE... MAYBE YOU SHOULD FOLD.
THAT'S RIGHT.
SUFFER ...
...MY POPPET.
ARE YOU OKAY ...?
RAISE.
I RAISE...
...50 MORE!
!!
TOO BAD, KID...
...YOU'RE A CHEAP IMITATION.

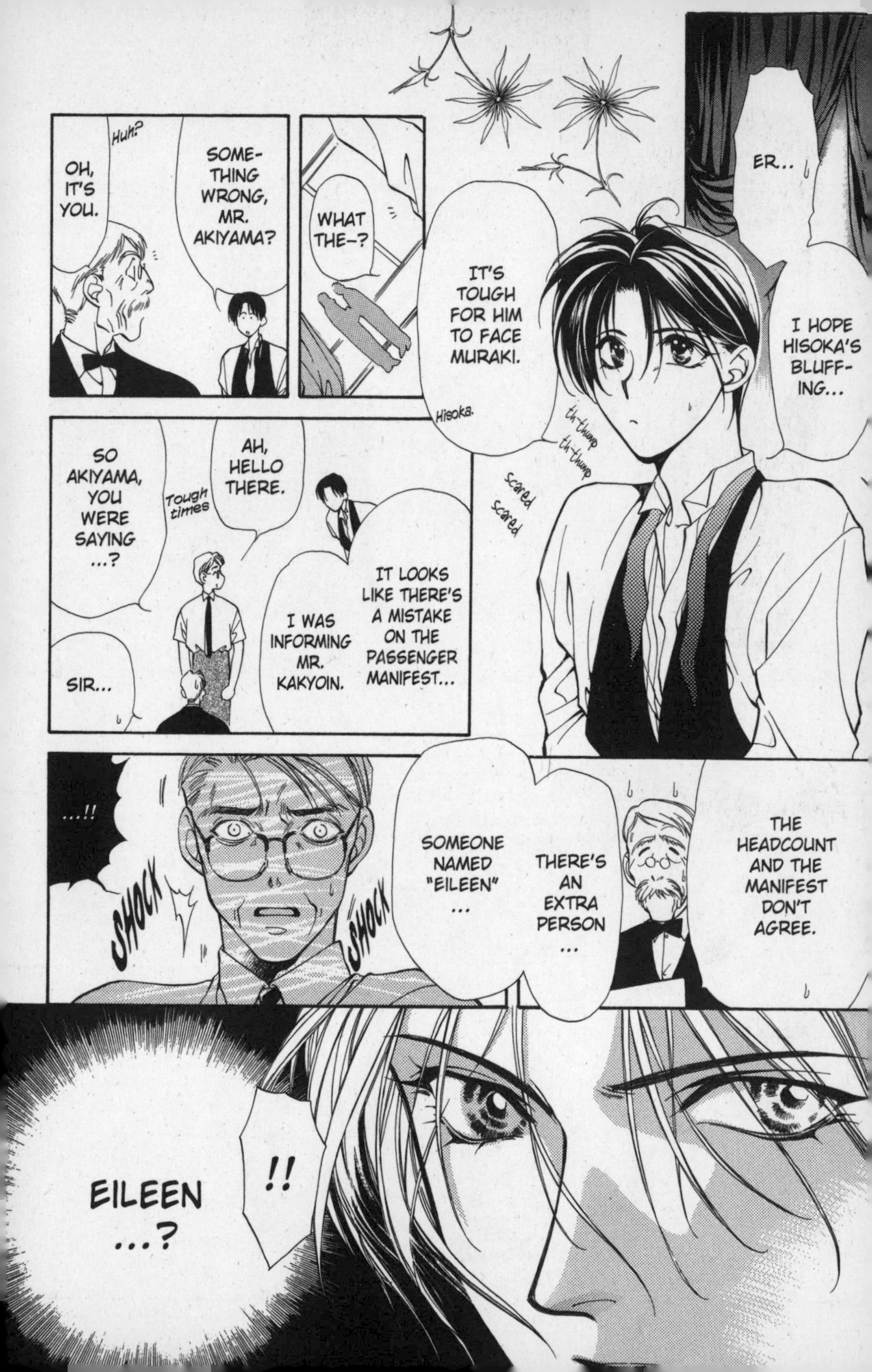
ER...
I HOPE HISOKA'S BLUFFING...
IT'S TOUGH FOR HIM TO FACE MURAKI.
Hisoka.
th-thump th-thump
scared scared
WHAT THE-?
SOMETHING WRONG, MR. AKIYAMA?
Huh?
OH, IT'S YOU.
AH, HELLO THERE.
Tough times
SO AKIYAMA, YOU WERE SAYING...?
SIR...
IT LOOKS LIKE THERE'S A MISTAKE ON THE PASSENGER MANIFEST...
I WAS INFORMING MR. KAKYOIN.
THE HEADCOUNT AND THE MANIFEST DON'T AGREE.
THERE'S AN EXTRA PERSON...
SOMEONE NAMED "EILEEN"...
...!!
SHOCK
SHOCK
!!
EILEEN ...?

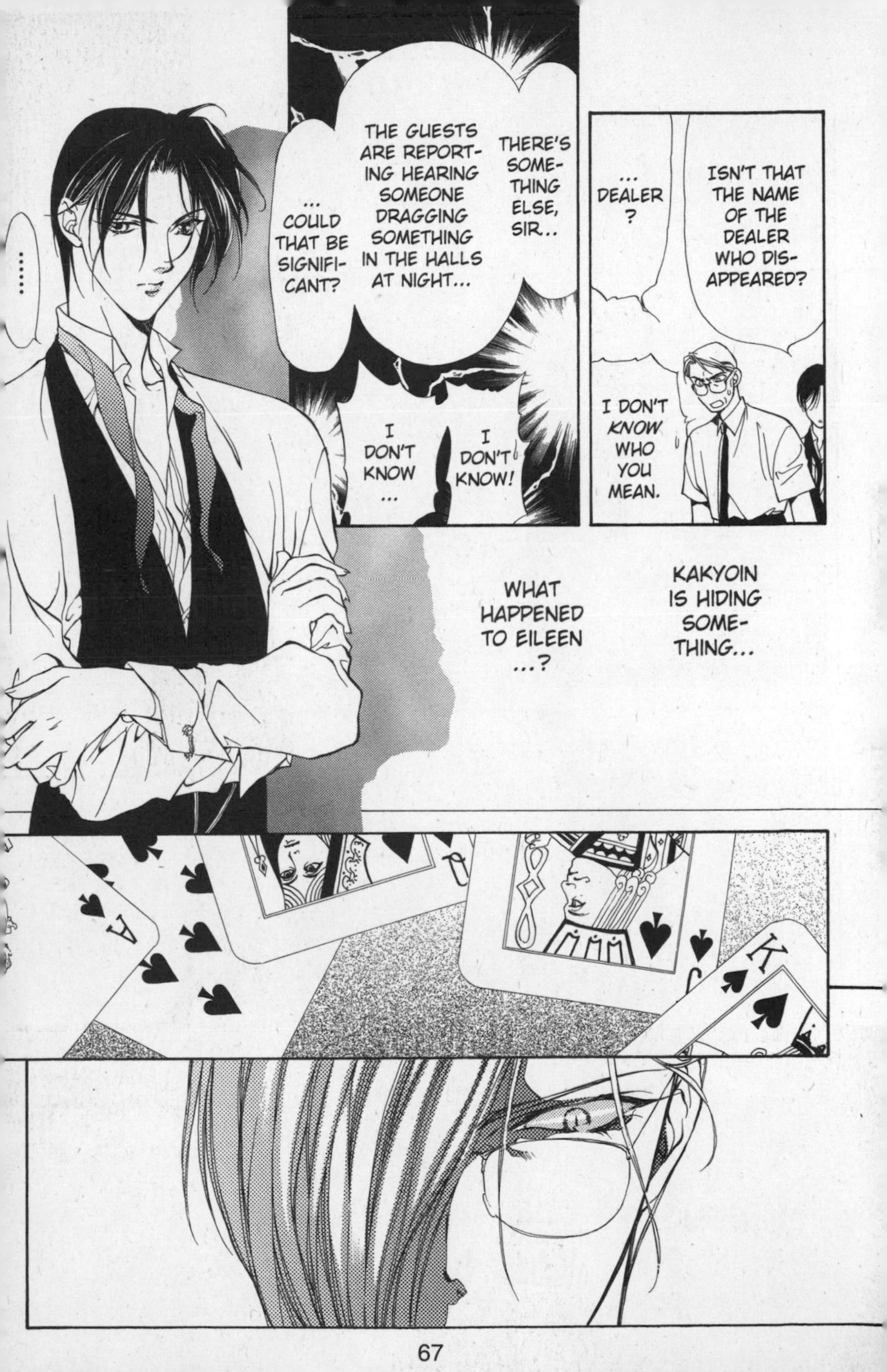
ISN'T THAT THE NAME OF THE DEALER WHO DIS-APPEARED?
... DEALER ?
I DON'T KNOW WHO YOU MEAN.
THERE'S SOME-THING ELSE, SIR...
THE GUESTS ARE REPORT-ING HEARING SOMEONE DRAGGING SOMETHING IN THE HALLS AT NIGHT...
... COULD THAT BE SIGNIFI-CANT?
I DON'T KNOW!
I DON'T KNOW ...
......
KAKYOIN IS HIDING SOME-THING...
WHAT HAPPENED TO EILEEN ...?

A ROYAL FLUSH IS THE BEST POSSIBLE.

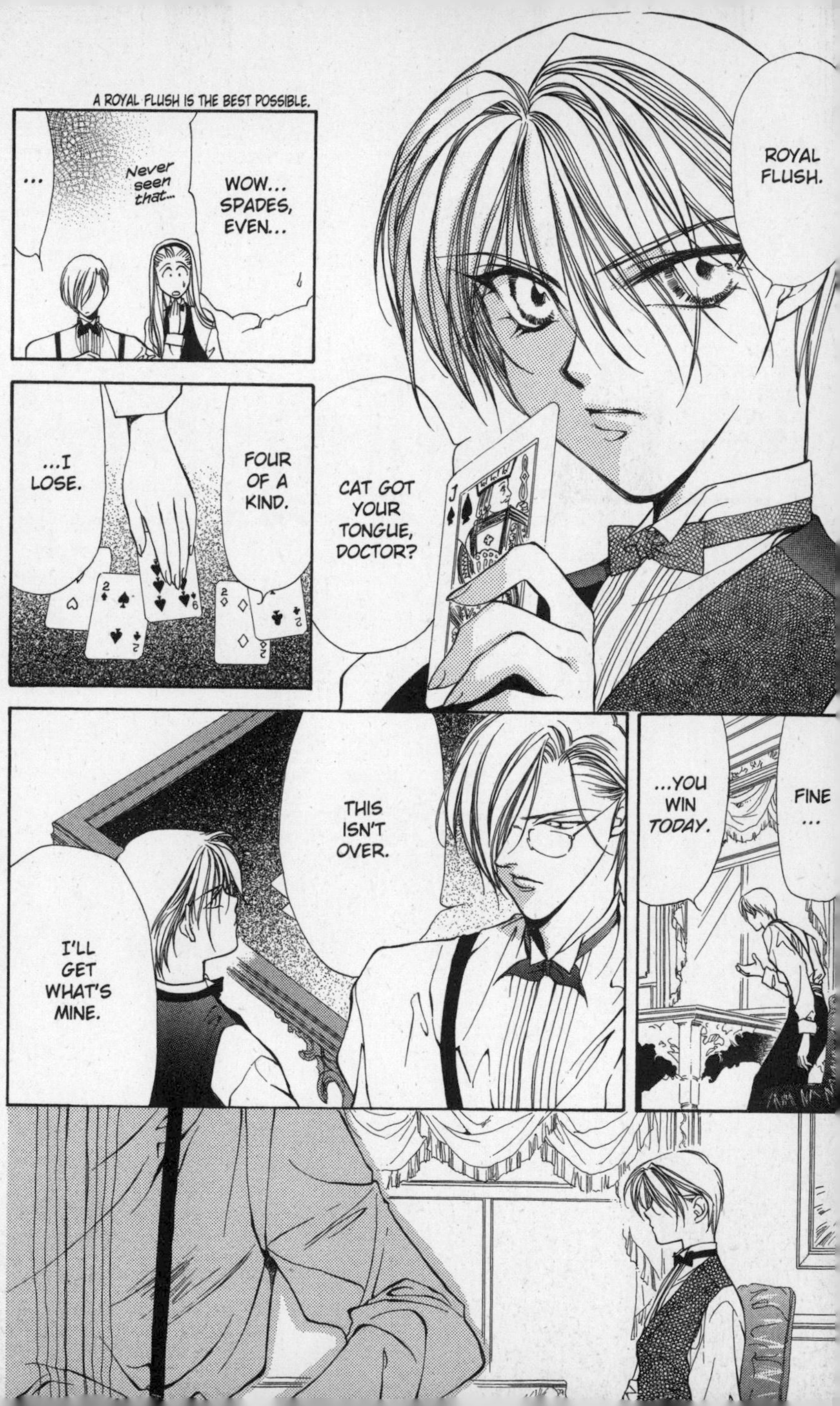
ROYAL FLUSH.
CAT GOT YOUR TONGUE, DOCTOR?
WOW... SPADES, EVEN...
Never seen that...
...
FOUR OF A KIND.
...I LOSE.
FINE ...
...YOU WIN TODAY.
THIS ISN'T OVER.
I'LL GET WHAT'S MINE.

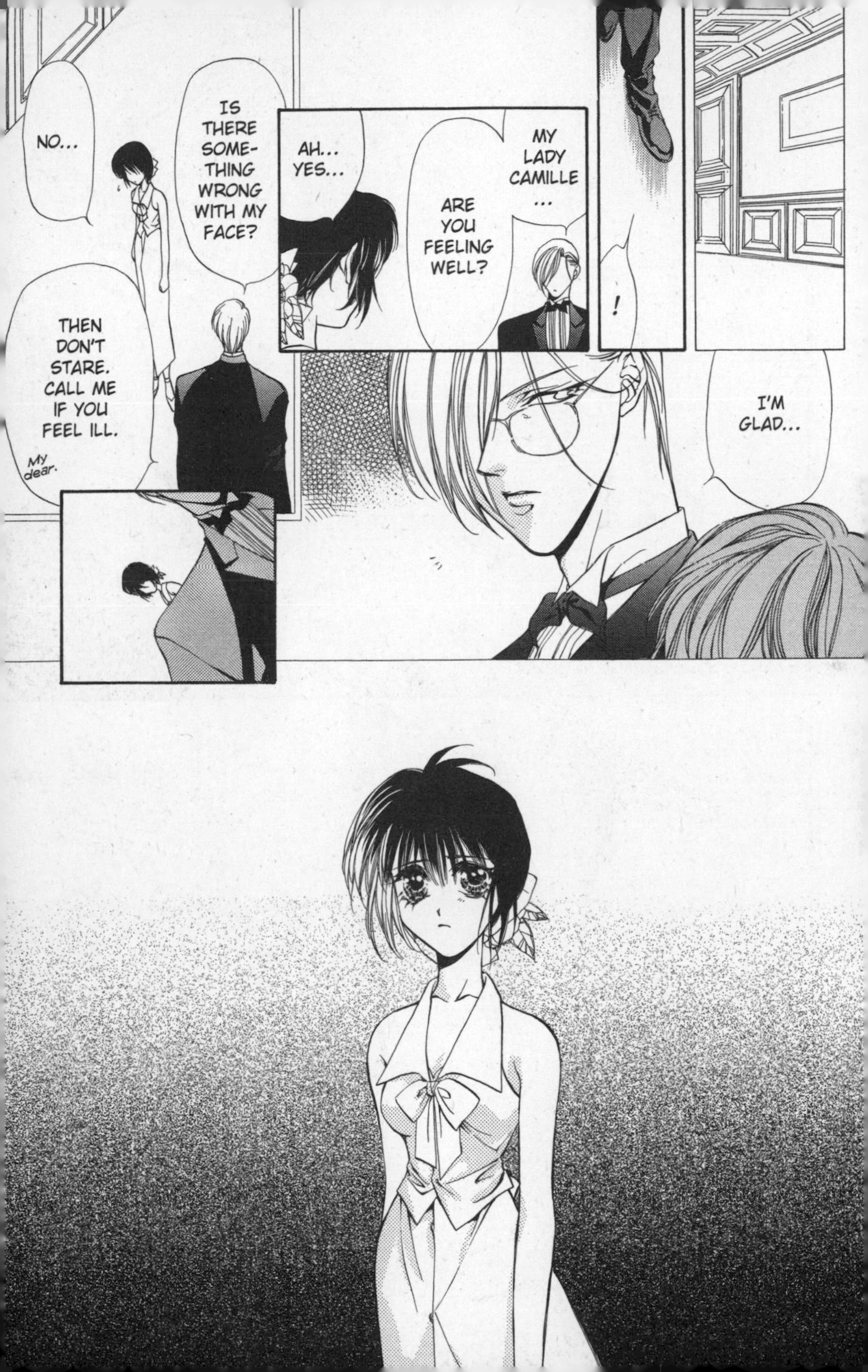
!
MY LADY CAMILLE...
ARE YOU FEELING WELL?
AH... YES...
IS THERE SOMETHING WRONG WITH MY FACE?
NO...
THEN DON'T STARE. CALL ME IF YOU FEEL ILL.
My dear.
I'M GLAD...

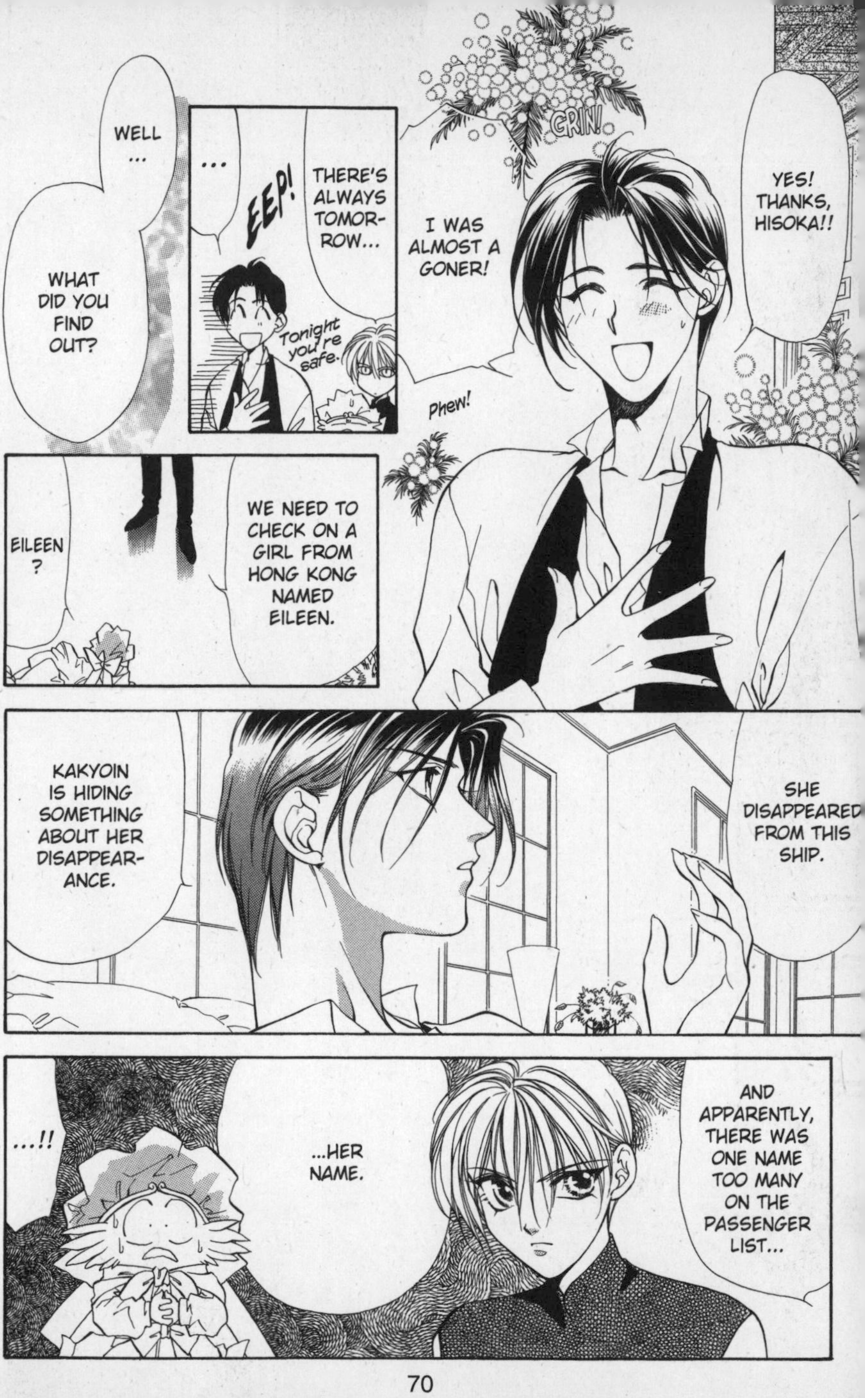
GRIN!
YES! THANKS, HISOKA!!
I WAS ALMOST A GONER!
Phew!
THERE'S ALWAYS TOMORROW...
EEP!
...
Tonight you're safe.
WELL ...
WHAT DID YOU FIND OUT?
WE NEED TO CHECK ON A GIRL FROM HONG KONG NAMED EILEEN.
EILEEN ?
SHE DISAPPEARED FROM THIS SHIP.
KAKYOIN IS HIDING SOMETHING ABOUT HER DISAPPEARANCE.
AND APPARENTLY, THERE WAS ONE NAME TOO MANY ON THE PASSENGER LIST...
...HER NAME.
...!!

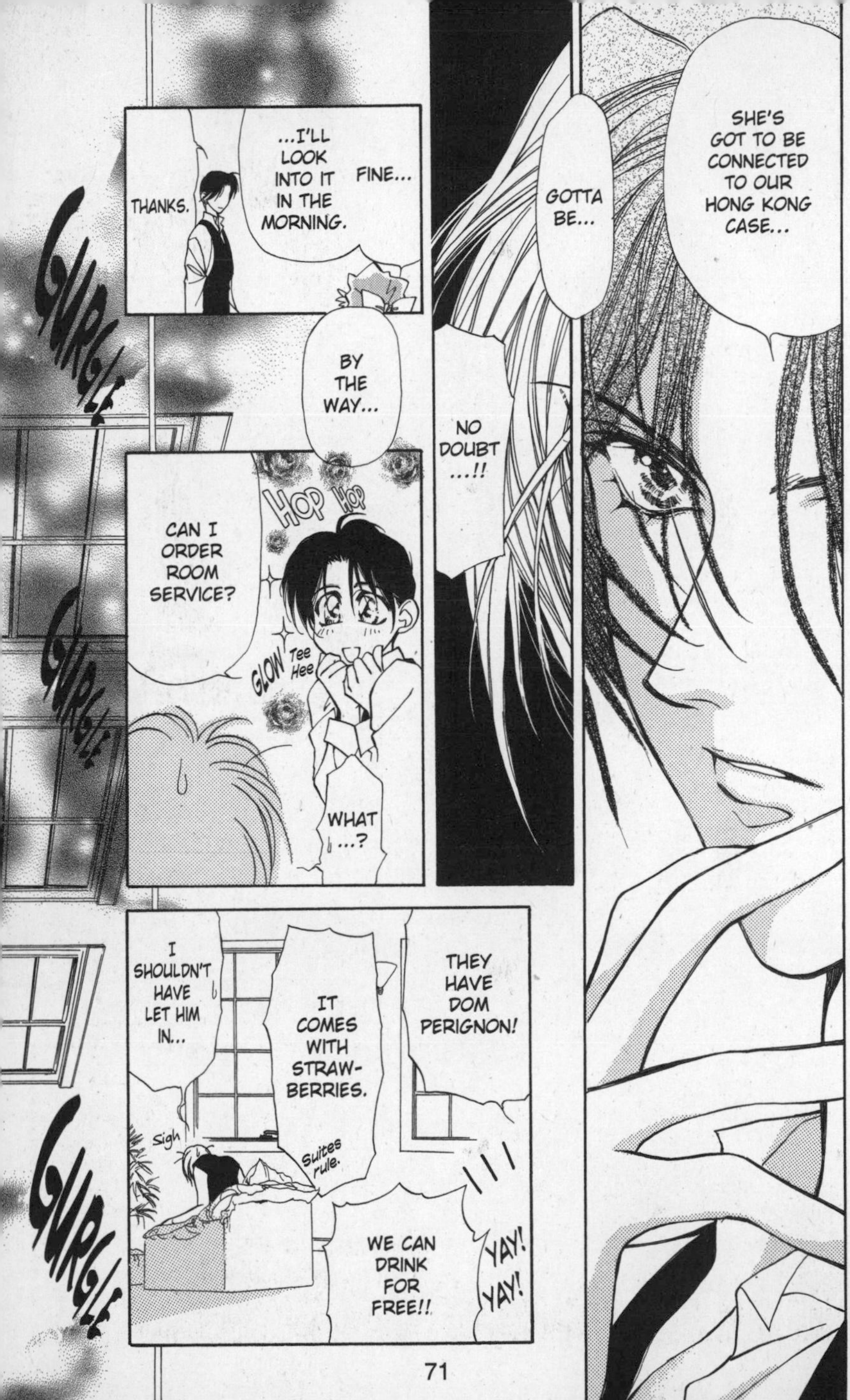
SHE'S GOT TO BE CONNECTED TO OUR HONG KONG CASE...
GOTTA BE...
NO DOUBT ...!!
FINE...
...I'LL LOOK INTO IT IN THE MORNING.
THANKS.
BY THE WAY...
HOP HOP
CAN I ORDER ROOM SERVICE?
GLOW Tee Hee
WHAT ...?
THEY HAVE DOM PERIGNON!
IT COMES WITH STRAW-BERRIES.
I SHOULDN'T HAVE LET HIM IN...
Sigh
Suites rule.
YAY! YAY!
WE CAN DRINK FOR FREE!!
GURGLE GURGLE GURGLE GURGLE

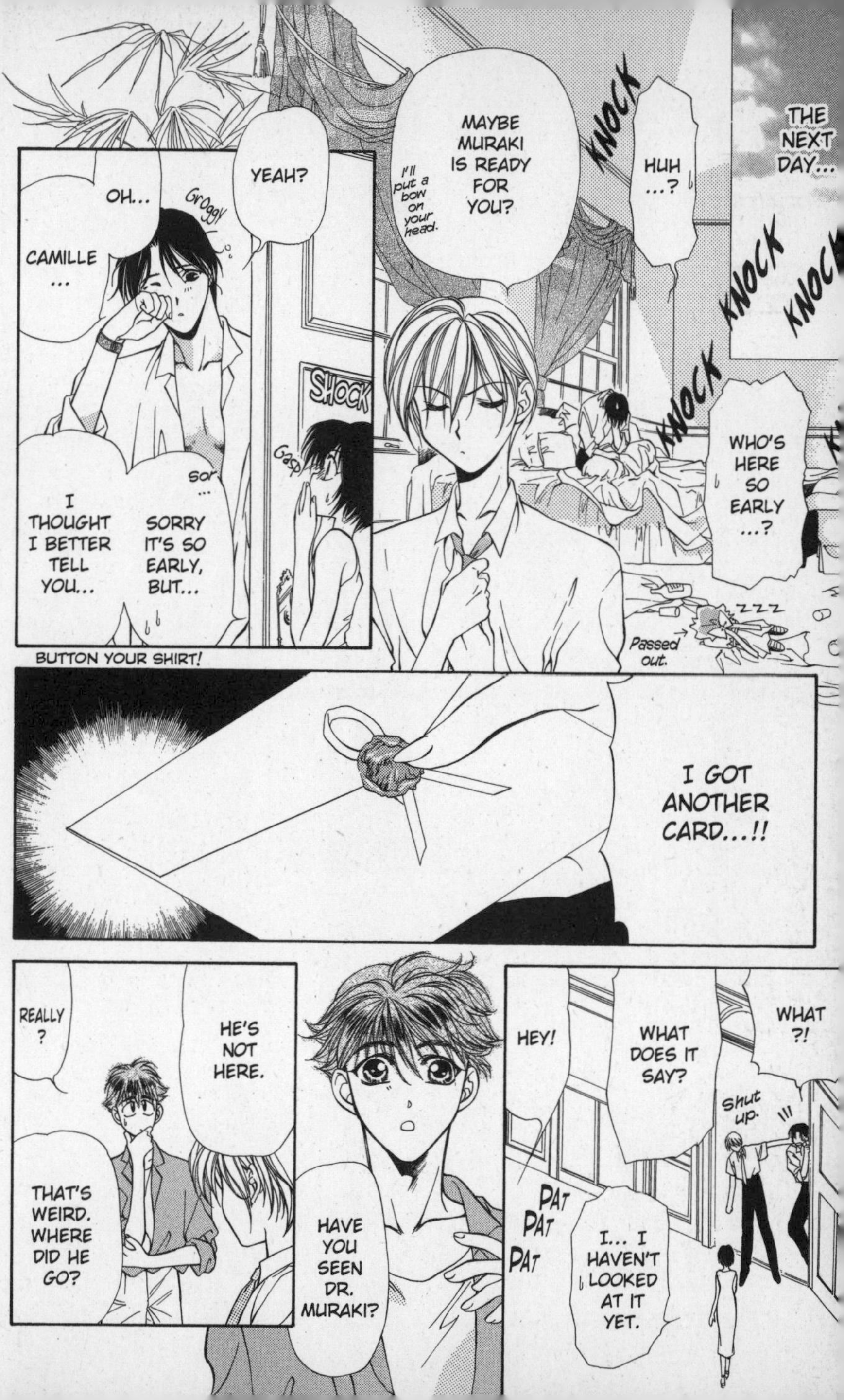
THE NEXT DAY...
KNOCK KNOCK KNOCK KNOCK
HUH ...?
WHO'S HERE SO EARLY ...?
Passed out.
ZZZ
MAYBE MURAKI IS READY FOR YOU?
I'll put a bow on your head.
YEAH?
OH... CAMILLE ...
Groggy
SHOCK
Gasp
Sor ...
SORRY IT'S SO EARLY, BUT...
I THOUGHT I BETTER TELL YOU...
BUTTON YOUR SHIRT!
I GOT ANOTHER CARD...!!
WHAT ?!
Shut up.
WHAT DOES IT SAY?
HEY!
PAT PAT PAT
I... I HAVEN'T LOOKED AT IT YET.
HAVE YOU SEEN DR. MURAKI?
HE'S NOT HERE.
REALLY ?
THAT'S WEIRD. WHERE DID HE GO?

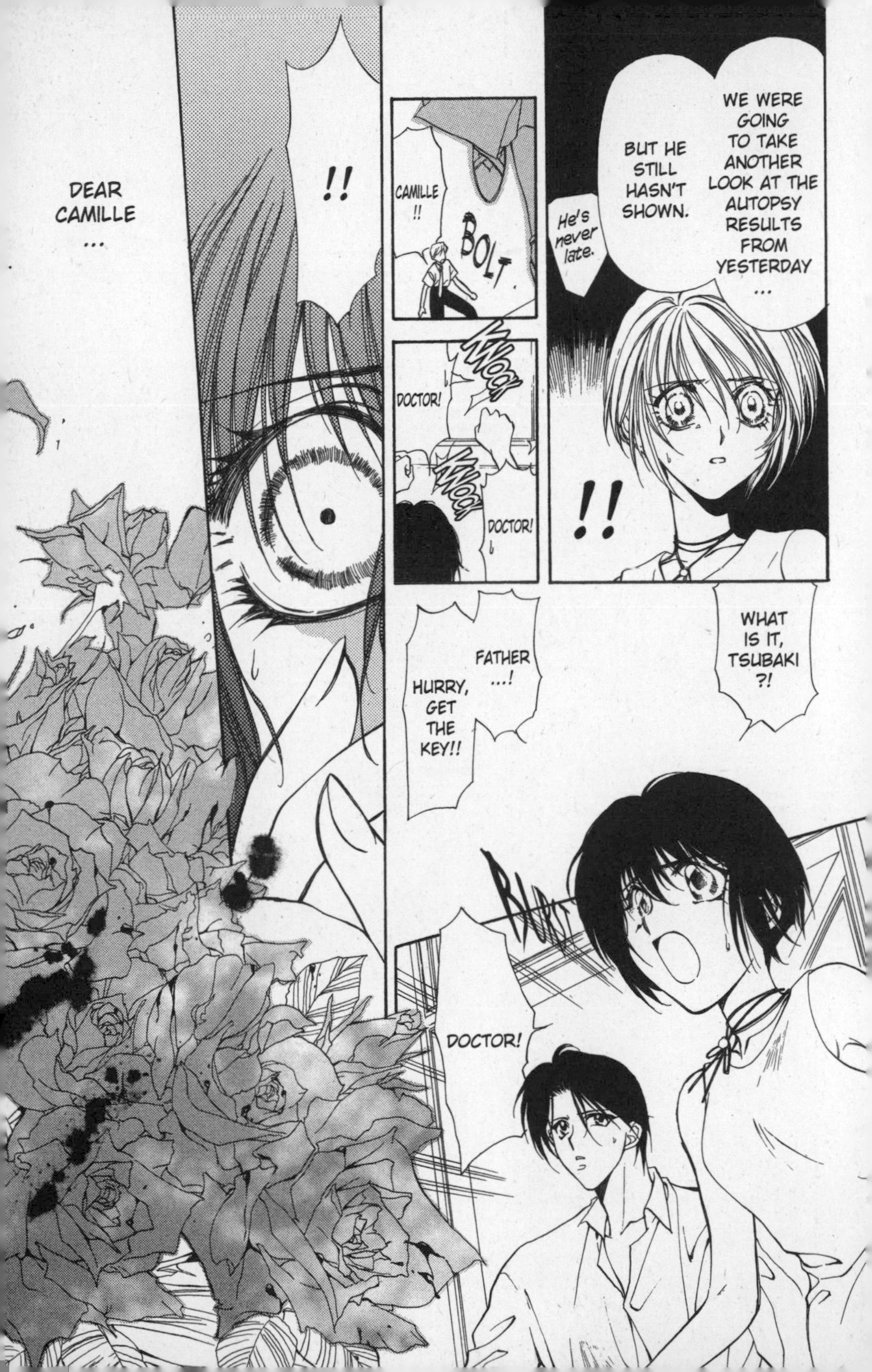
WE WERE GOING TO TAKE ANOTHER LOOK AT THE AUTOPSY RESULTS FROM YESTERDAY ...
BUT HE STILL HASN'T SHOWN.
He's never late.
!!
CAMILLE !!
BOLT
KNOCK
DOCTOR!
KNOCK
DOCTOR!
WHAT IS IT, TSUBAKI ?!
FATHER ...!
HURRY, GET THE KEY!!
BURST
DOCTOR!
!!
DEAR CAMILLE ...

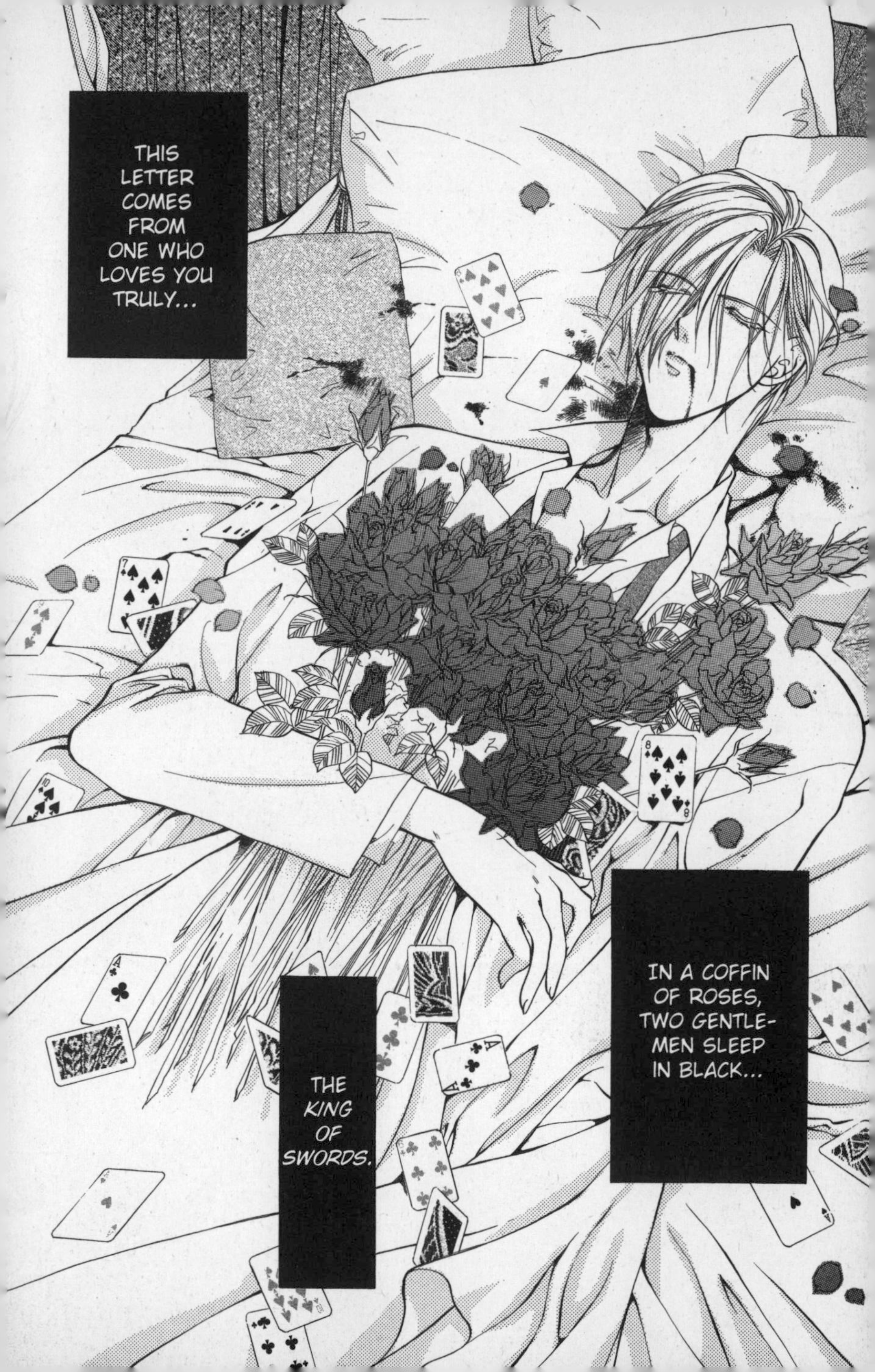
THIS LETTER COMES FROM ONE WHO LOVES YOU TRULY...
IN A COFFIN OF ROSES, TWO GENTLEMEN SLEEP IN BLACK...
THE KING OF SWORDS.

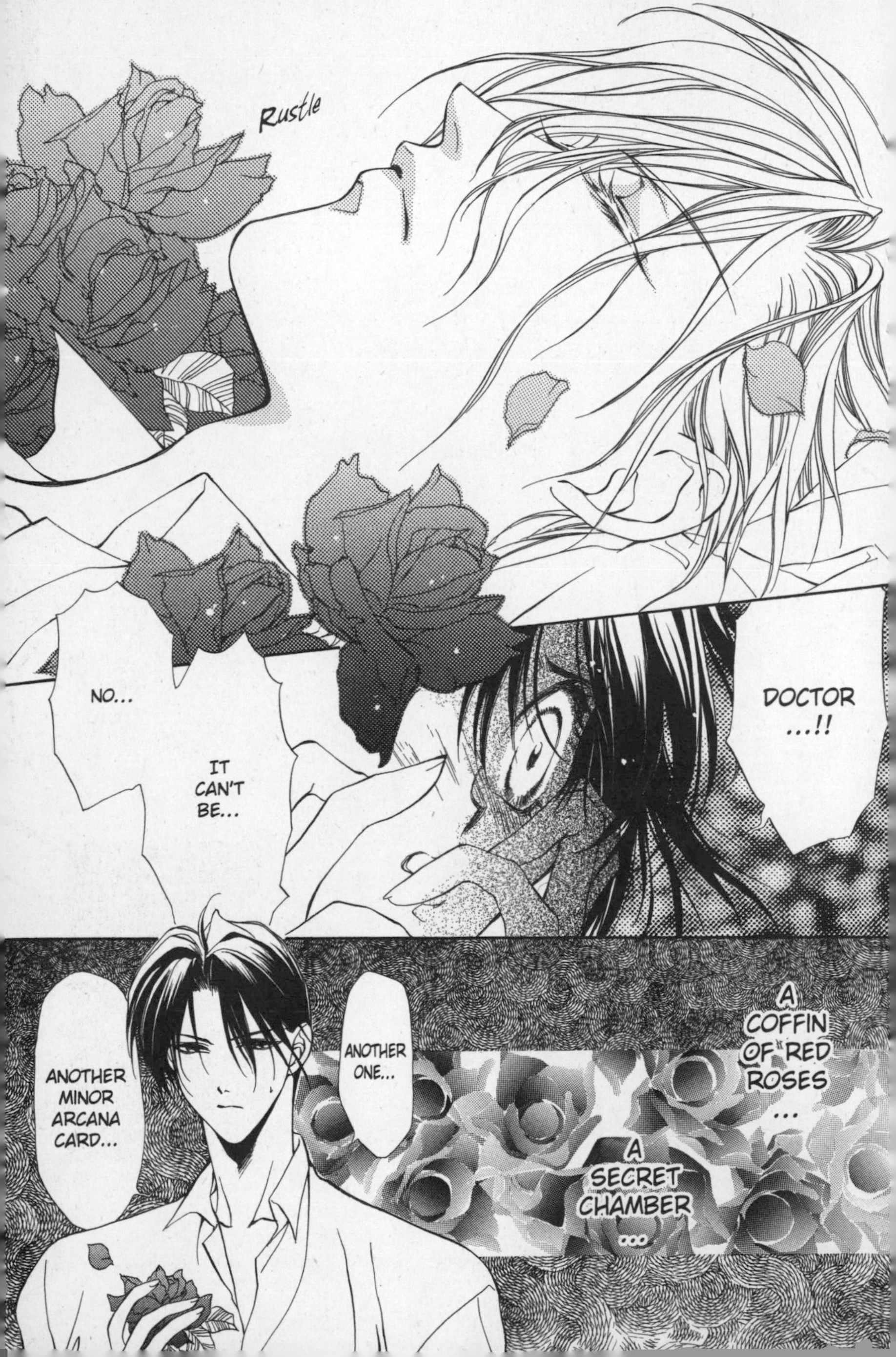
Rustle
DOCTOR ...!!
NO...
IT CAN'T BE...
A COFFIN OF RED ROSES ...
A SECRET CHAMBER ...
ANOTHER ONE...
ANOTHER MINOR ARCANA CARD...

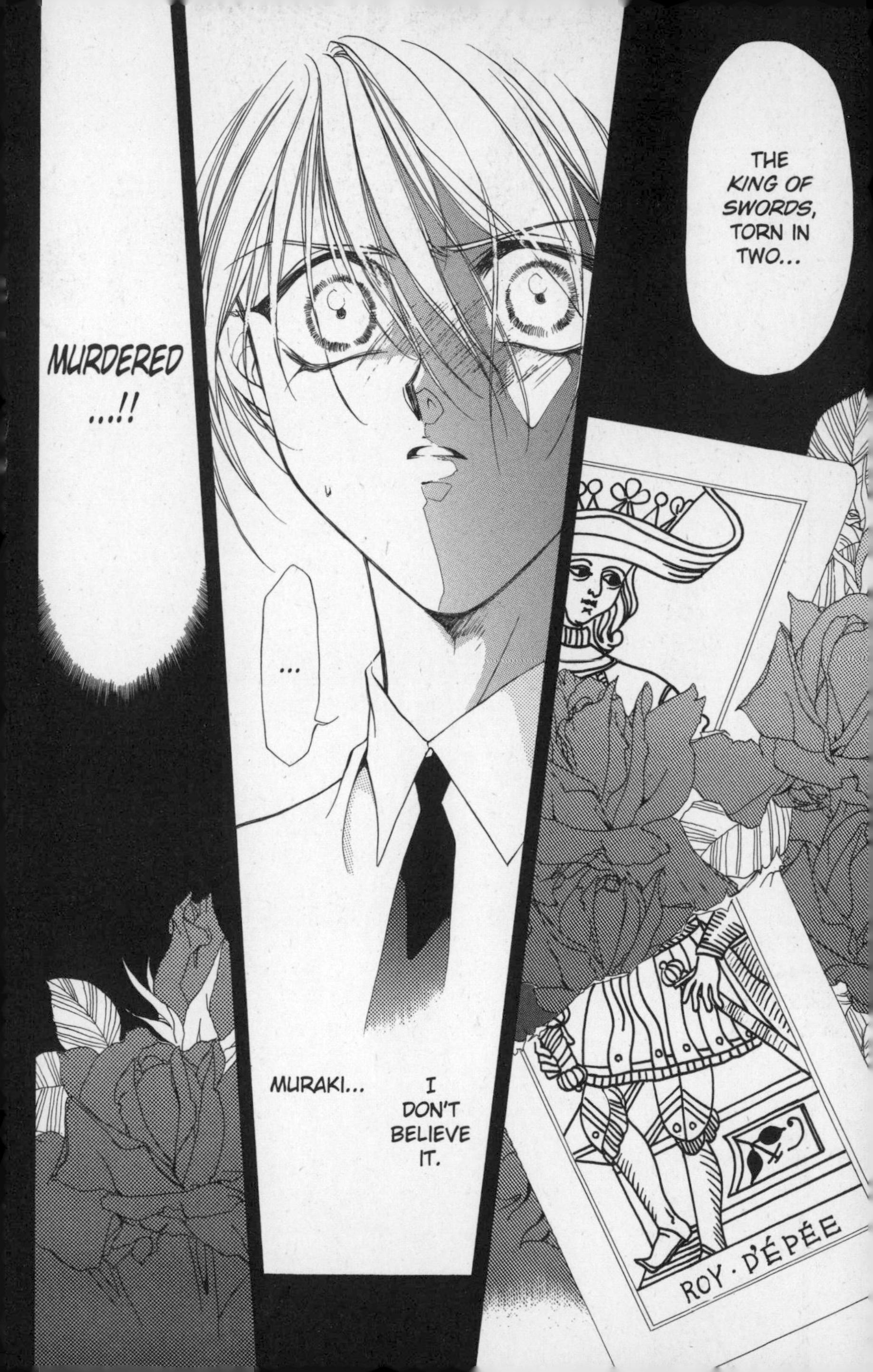
THE KING OF SWORDS, TORN IN TWO...
ROY · D'ÉPÉE
...
I DON'T BELIEVE IT.
MURAKI...
MURDERED ...!!

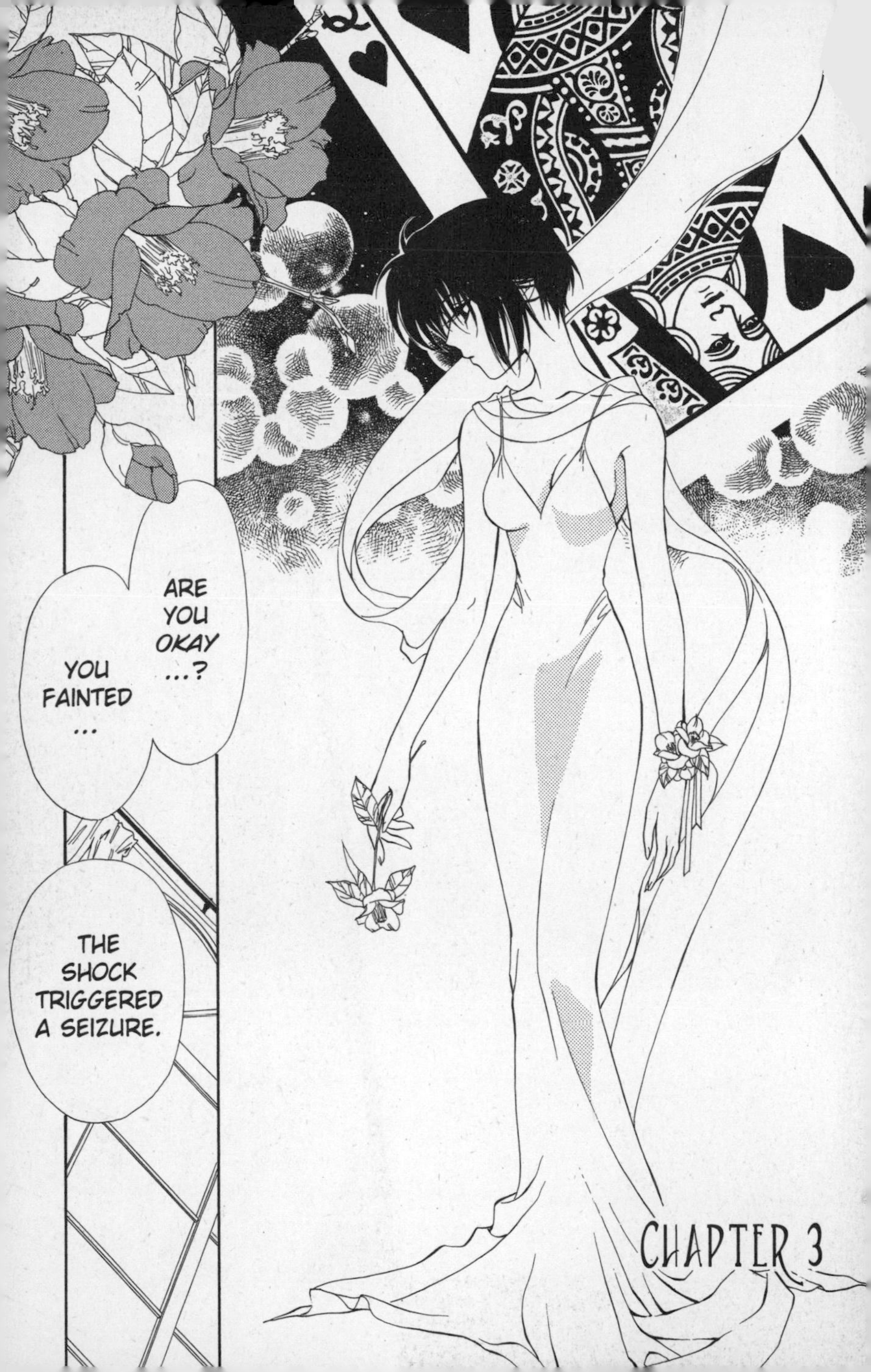
ARE YOU OKAY ...?
YOU FAINTED ...
THE SHOCK TRIGGERED A SEIZURE.
CHAPTER 3

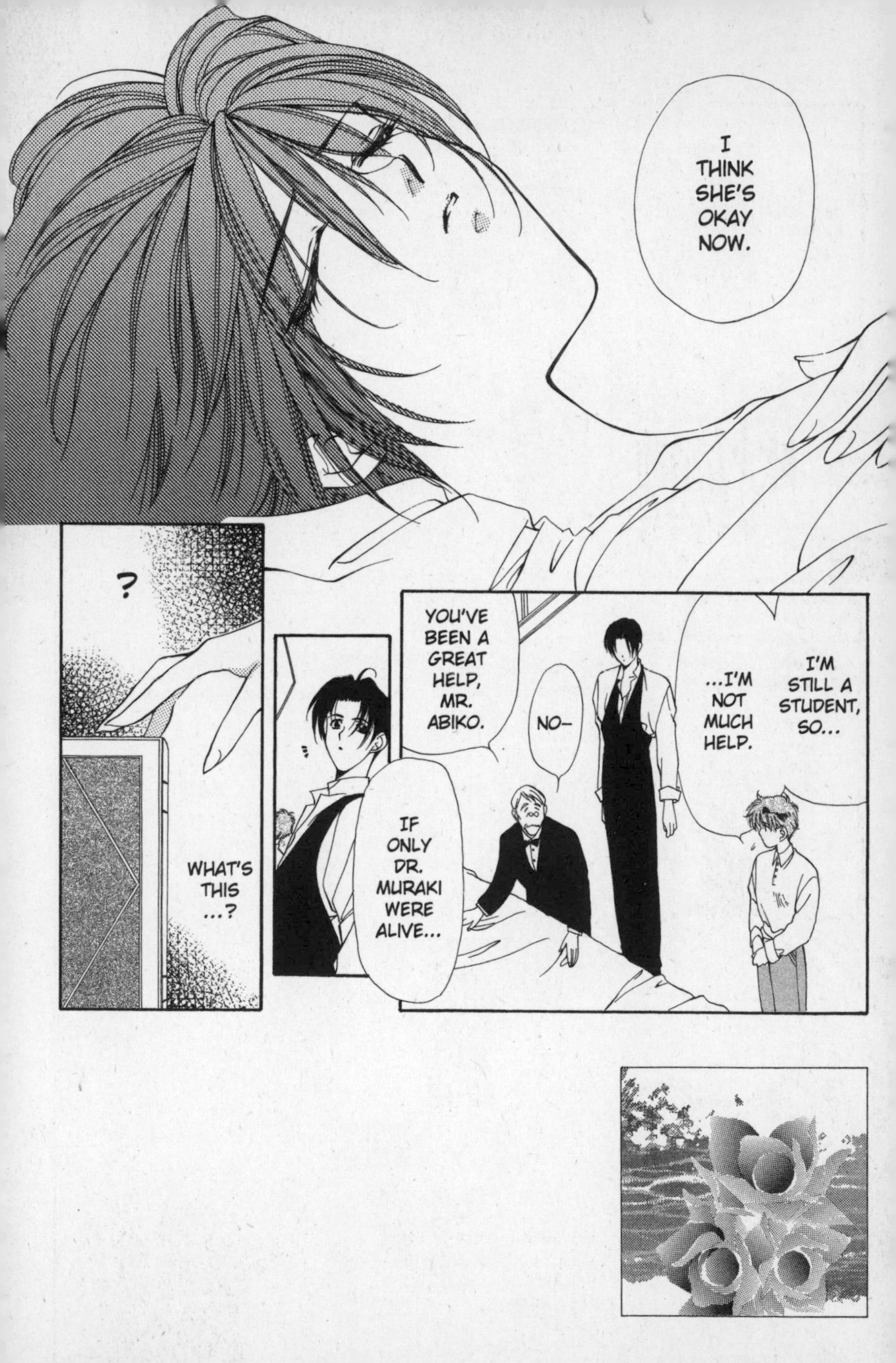
I THINK SHE'S OKAY NOW.
I'M STILL A STUDENT, SO...
...I'M NOT MUCH HELP.
NO-
YOU'VE BEEN A GREAT HELP, MR. ABIKO.
IF ONLY DR. MURAKI WERE ALIVE...
?
WHAT'S THIS ...?

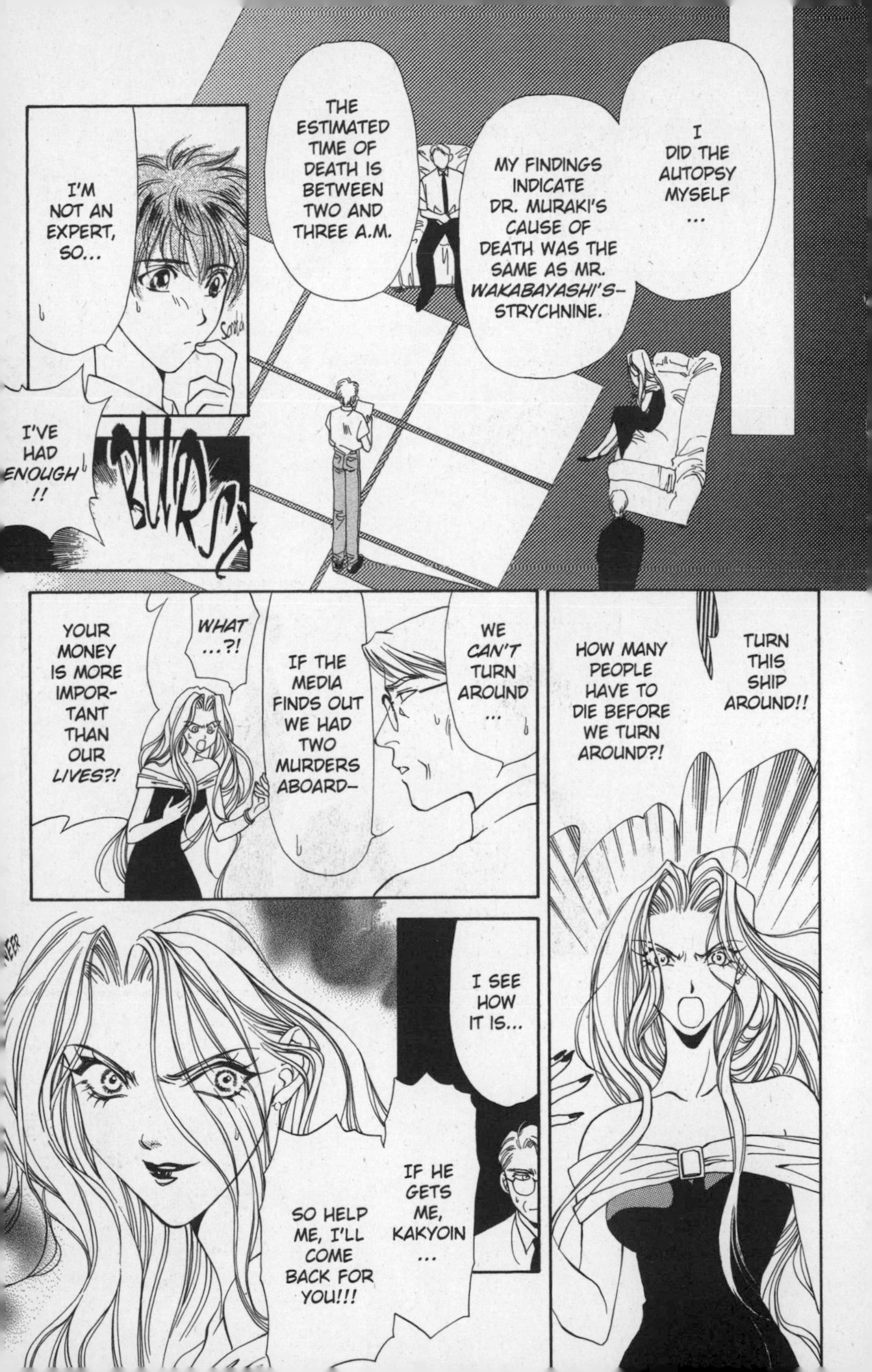
I DID THE AUTOPSY MYSELF ...
MY FINDINGS INDICATE DR. MURAKI'S CAUSE OF DEATH WAS THE SAME AS MR. *WAKABAYASHI'S*—STRYCHNINE.
THE ESTIMATED TIME OF DEATH IS BETWEEN TWO AND THREE A.M.
I'M NOT AN EXPERT, SO...
I'VE HAD *ENOUGH* !!
TURN THIS SHIP AROUND!!
HOW MANY PEOPLE HAVE TO DIE BEFORE WE TURN AROUND?!
WE *CAN'T* TURN AROUND ...
IF THE MEDIA FINDS OUT WE HAD TWO MURDERS ABOARD—
WHAT ...?!
YOUR MONEY IS MORE IMPOR-TANT THAN OUR *LIVES?!*
I SEE HOW IT IS...
IF HE GETS ME, KAKYOIN ...
SO HELP ME, I'LL COME BACK FOR YOU!!!

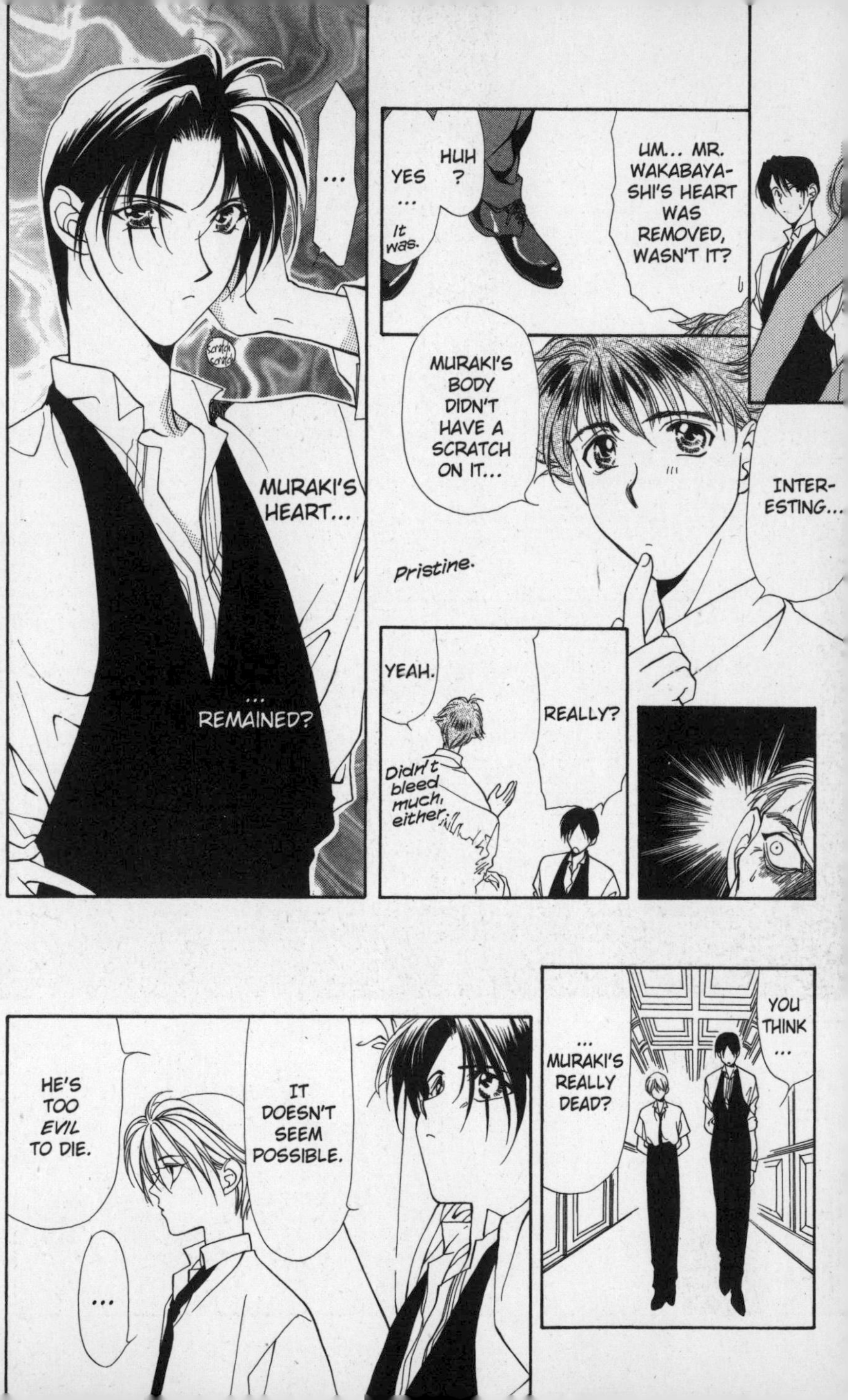
UM... MR. WAKABAYASHI'S HEART WAS REMOVED, WASN'T IT?
HUH?
YES...
It was.
INTERESTING...
MURAKI'S BODY DIDN'T HAVE A SCRATCH ON IT...
Pristine.
REALLY?
YEAH.
Didn't bleed much, either.
...
scratch scratch
MURAKI'S HEART...
... REMAINED?
YOU THINK...
... MURAKI'S REALLY DEAD?
IT DOESN'T SEEM POSSIBLE.
HE'S TOO *EVIL* TO DIE.
...

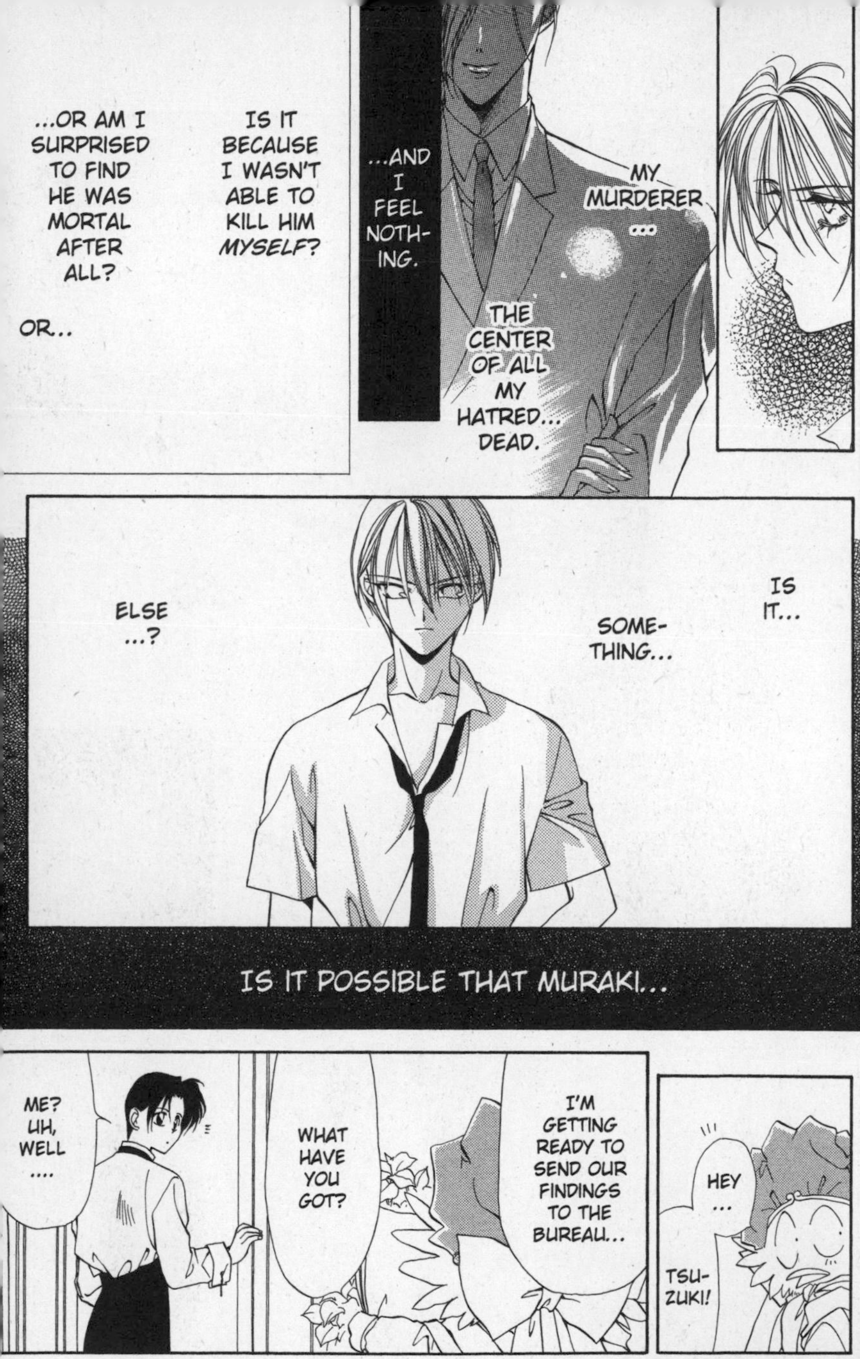
MY MURDERER ...
THE CENTER OF ALL MY HATRED... DEAD.
...AND I FEEL NOTH-ING.
IS IT BECAUSE I WASN'T ABLE TO KILL HIM *MYSELF*?
...OR AM I SURPRISED TO FIND HE WAS MORTAL AFTER ALL?
OR...
IS IT...
SOME-THING...
ELSE ...?
IS IT POSSIBLE THAT MURAKI...
HEY ...
TSU-ZUKI!
I'M GETTING READY TO SEND OUR FINDINGS TO THE BUREAU...
WHAT HAVE YOU GOT?
ME? UH, WELL ....

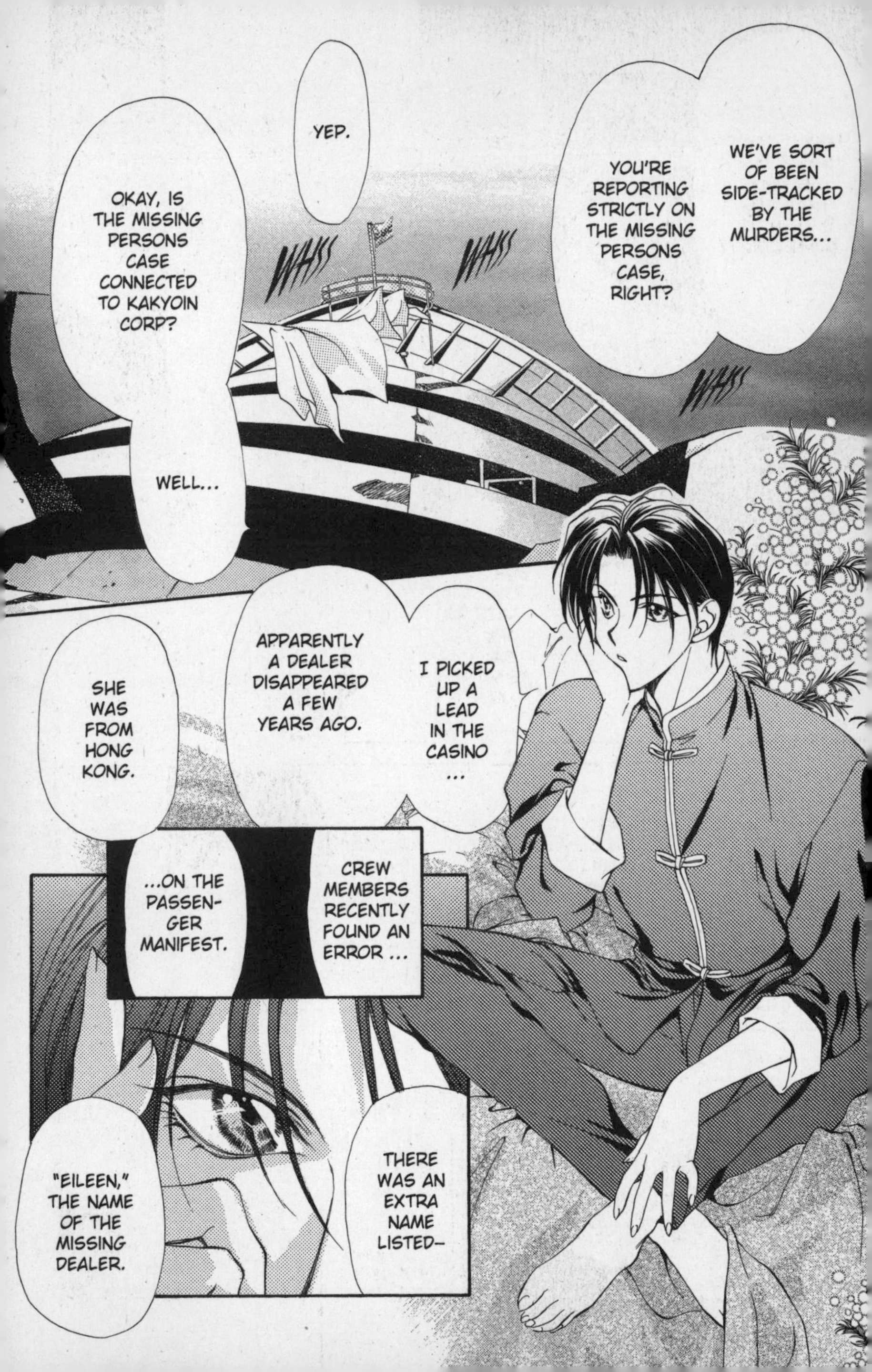
WE'VE SORT OF BEEN SIDE-TRACKED BY THE MURDERS...
YOU'RE REPORTING STRICTLY ON THE MISSING PERSONS CASE, RIGHT?
WHSS
YEP.
WHSS
WHSS
OKAY, IS THE MISSING PERSONS CASE CONNECTED TO KAKYOIN CORP?
WELL...
I PICKED UP A LEAD IN THE CASINO ...
APPARENTLY A DEALER DISAPPEARED A FEW YEARS AGO.
SHE WAS FROM HONG KONG.
CREW MEMBERS RECENTLY FOUND AN ERROR ...
...ON THE PASSENGER MANIFEST.
THERE WAS AN EXTRA NAME LISTED–
"EILEEN," THE NAME OF THE MISSING DEALER.

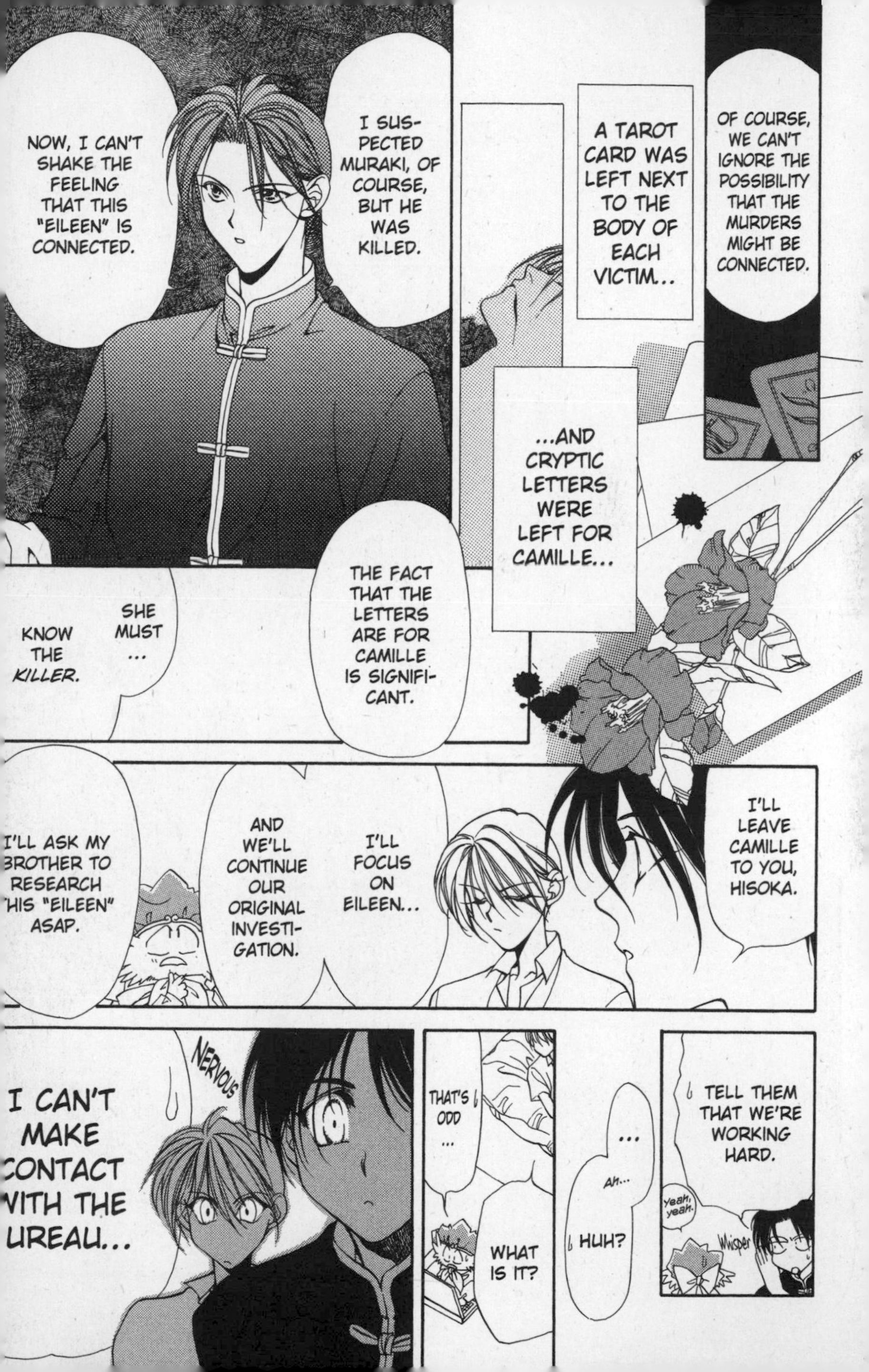
OF COURSE, WE CAN'T IGNORE THE POSSIBILITY THAT THE MURDERS MIGHT BE CONNECTED.
A TAROT CARD WAS LEFT NEXT TO THE BODY OF EACH VICTIM...
...AND CRYPTIC LETTERS WERE LEFT FOR CAMILLE...
I SUS-PECTED MURAKI, OF COURSE, BUT HE WAS KILLED.
NOW, I CAN'T SHAKE THE FEELING THAT THIS "EILEEN" IS CONNECTED.
THE FACT THAT THE LETTERS ARE FOR CAMILLE IS SIGNIFI-CANT.
SHE MUST ...
KNOW THE *KILLER.*
I'LL LEAVE CAMILLE TO YOU, HISOKA.
I'LL FOCUS ON EILEEN...
AND WE'LL CONTINUE OUR ORIGINAL INVESTI-GATION.
I'LL ASK MY BROTHER TO RESEARCH THIS "EILEEN" ASAP.
TELL THEM THAT WE'RE WORKING HARD.
Yeah, yeah.
Whisper
...
Ah...
HUH?
THAT'S ODD ...
WHAT IS IT?
NERVOUS
I CAN'T MAKE CONTACT WITH THE UREAU...

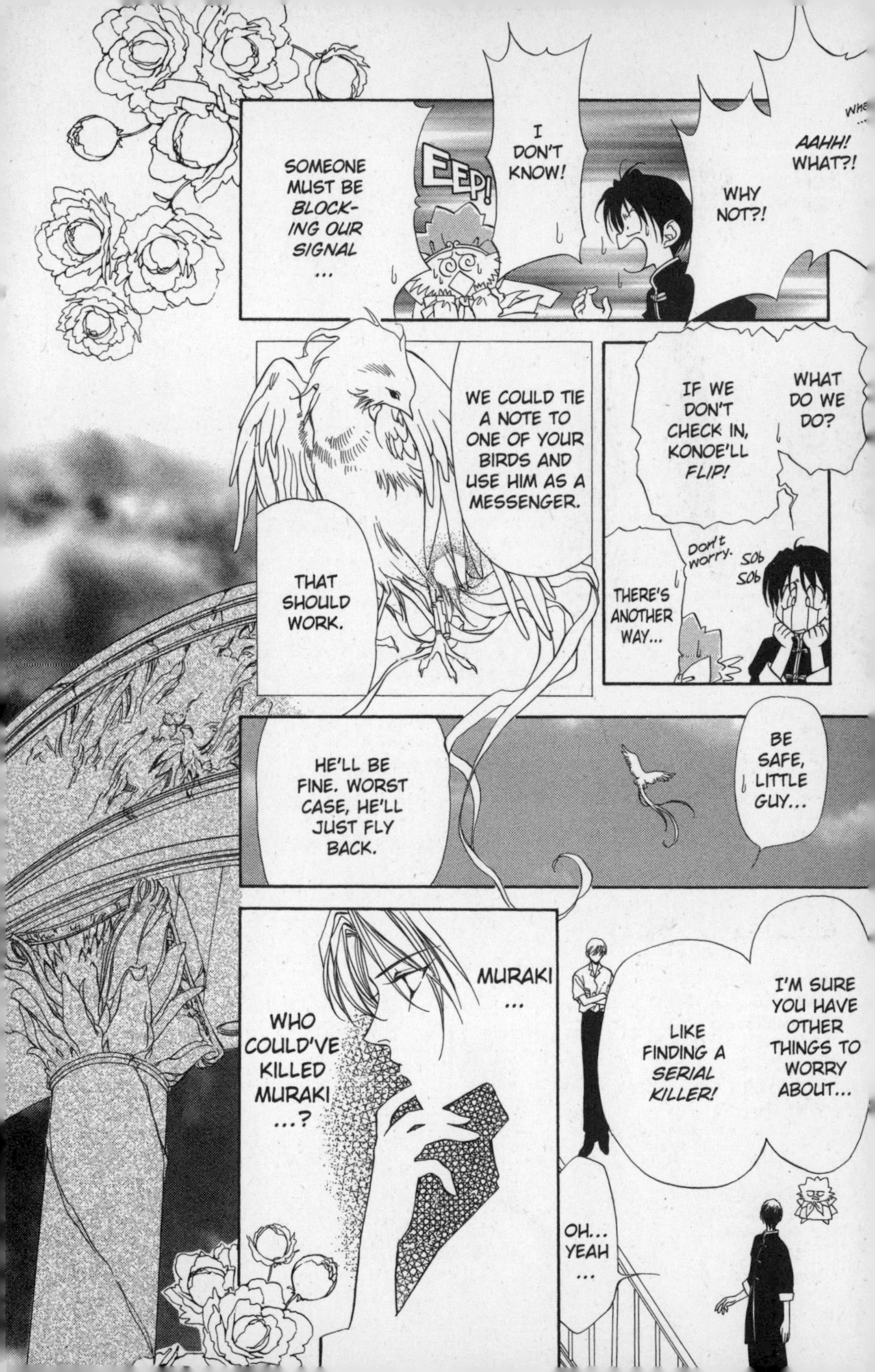
Wha...
AAHH! WHAT?!
WHY NOT?!
I DON'T KNOW!
EEP!
SOMEONE MUST BE BLOCKING OUR SIGNAL ...
WHAT DO WE DO?
IF WE DON'T CHECK IN, KONOE'LL FLIP!
Don't worry.
Sob Sob
THERE'S ANOTHER WAY...
WE COULD TIE A NOTE TO ONE OF YOUR BIRDS AND USE HIM AS A MESSENGER.
THAT SHOULD WORK.
BE SAFE, LITTLE GUY...
HE'LL BE FINE. WORST CASE, HE'LL JUST FLY BACK.
I'M SURE YOU HAVE OTHER THINGS TO WORRY ABOUT...
LIKE FINDING A SERIAL KILLER!
OH... YEAH ...
MURAKI ...
WHO COULD'VE KILLED MURAKI ...?

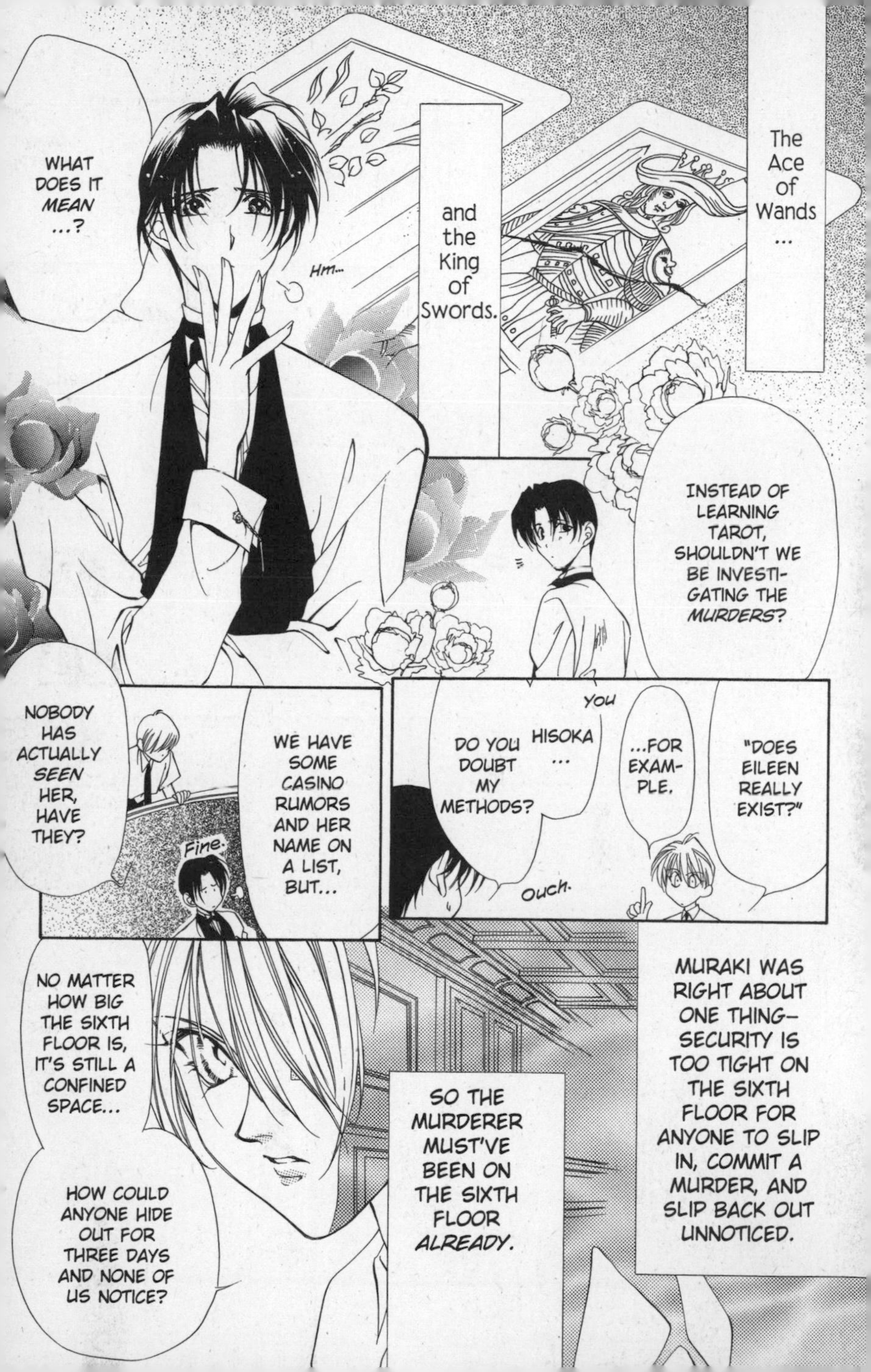
The Ace of Wands ...
and the King of Swords.
Hm...
WHAT DOES IT MEAN ...?
INSTEAD OF LEARNING TAROT, SHOULDN'T WE BE INVESTIGATING THE MURDERS?
"DOES EILEEN REALLY EXIST?"
...FOR EXAMPLE.
HISOKA ...
YOU
DO YOU DOUBT MY METHODS?
Ouch.
WE HAVE SOME CASINO RUMORS AND HER NAME ON A LIST, BUT...
Fine.
NOBODY HAS ACTUALLY SEEN HER, HAVE THEY?
MURAKI WAS RIGHT ABOUT ONE THING–SECURITY IS TOO TIGHT ON THE SIXTH FLOOR FOR ANYONE TO SLIP IN, COMMIT A MURDER, AND SLIP BACK OUT UNNOTICED.
SO THE MURDERER MUST'VE BEEN ON THE SIXTH FLOOR ALREADY.
NO MATTER HOW BIG THE SIXTH FLOOR IS, IT'S STILL A CONFINED SPACE...
HOW COULD ANYONE HIDE OUT FOR THREE DAYS AND NONE OF US NOTICE?

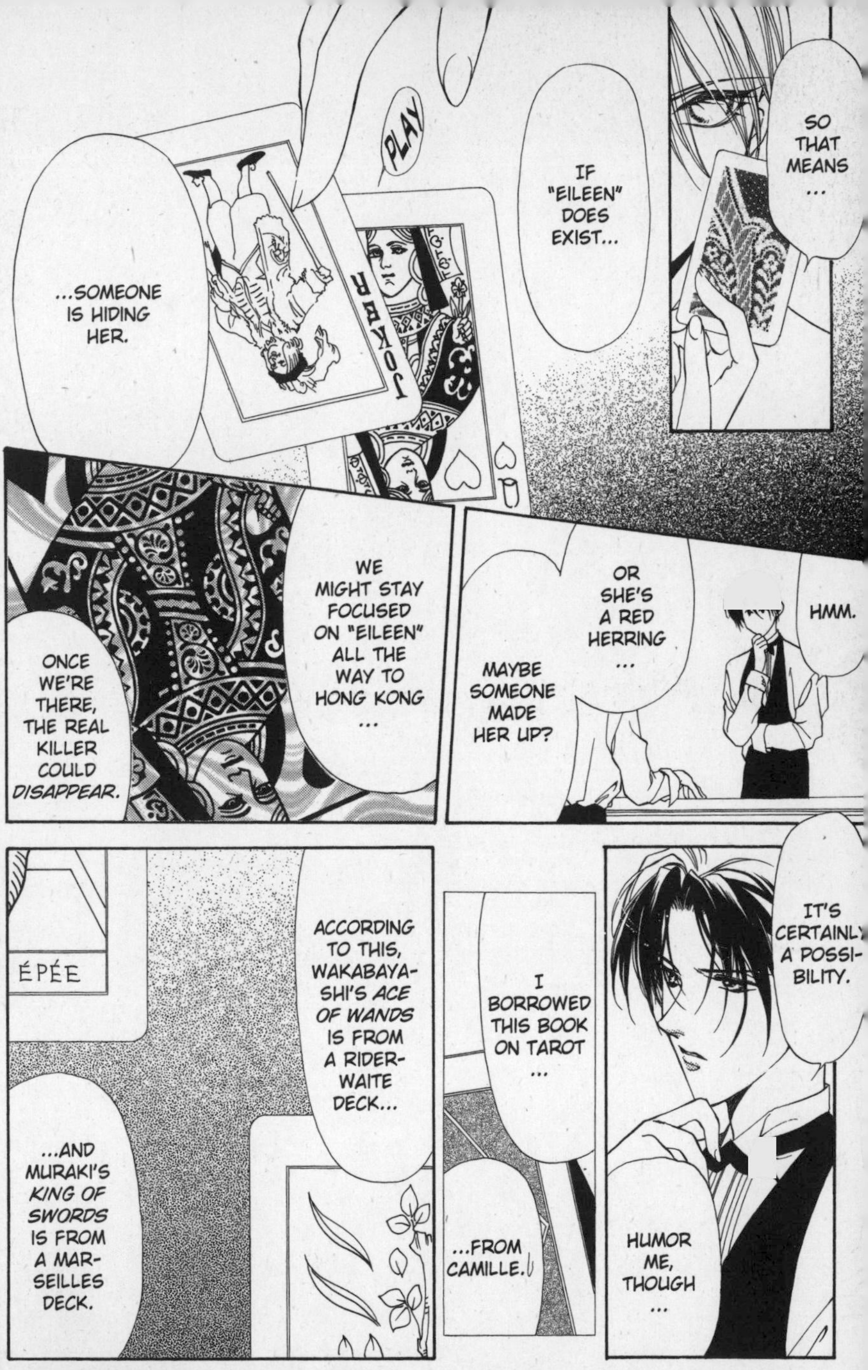
SO THAT MEANS ...
IF "EILEEN" DOES EXIST...
PLAY
JOKER
...SOMEONE IS HIDING HER.
HMM.
OR SHE'S A RED HERRING ...
MAYBE SOMEONE MADE HER UP?
WE MIGHT STAY FOCUSED ON "EILEEN" ALL THE WAY TO HONG KONG ...
ONCE WE'RE THERE, THE REAL KILLER COULD *DISAPPEAR.*
IT'S CERTAINLY A POSSIBILITY.
HUMOR ME, THOUGH ...
I BORROWED THIS BOOK ON TAROT ...
...FROM CAMILLE.
ÉPÉE
ACCORDING TO THIS, WAKABAYASHI'S *ACE OF WANDS* IS FROM A RIDER-WAITE DECK...
...AND MURAKI'S *KING OF SWORDS* IS FROM A MARSEILLES DECK.

THE RIDER-WAITE DECK IS FROM ENGLAND, THE MARSEILLES IS FRENCH.

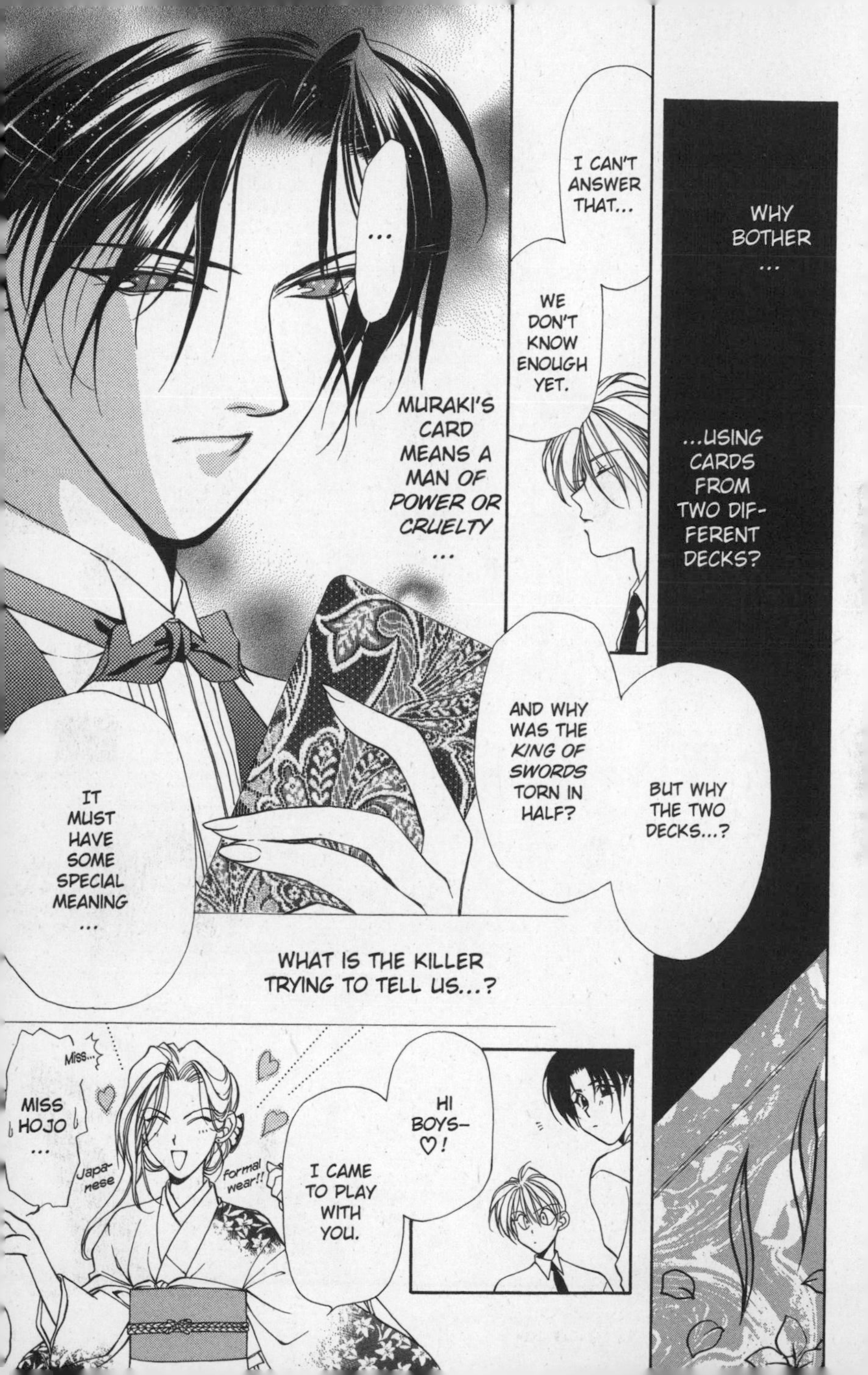
WHY BOTHER ...
...USING CARDS FROM TWO DIF-FERENT DECKS?
I CAN'T ANSWER THAT...
WE DON'T KNOW ENOUGH YET.
...
MURAKI'S CARD MEANS A MAN OF POWER OR CRUELTY ...
BUT WHY THE TWO DECKS...?
AND WHY WAS THE KING OF SWORDS TORN IN HALF?
IT MUST HAVE SOME SPECIAL MEANING ...
WHAT IS THE KILLER TRYING TO TELL US...?
HI BOYS-♡!
I CAME TO PLAY WITH YOU.
Miss...
MISS HOJO ...
Japa-nese formal wear!!

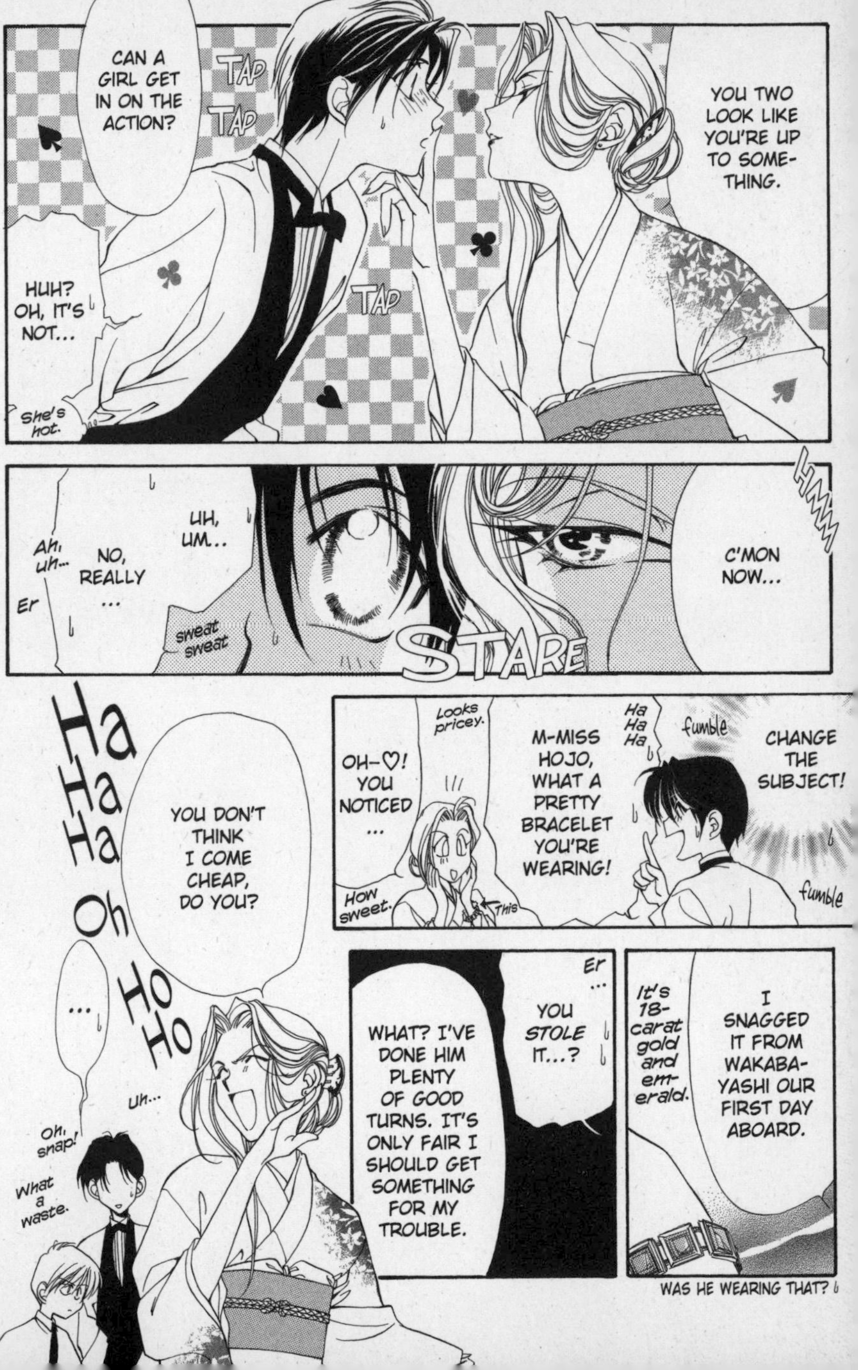

YOU TWO LOOK LIKE YOU'RE UP TO SOME-THING.
TAP
TAP
CAN A GIRL GET IN ON THE ACTION?
TAP
HUH? OH, IT'S NOT...
She's hot.
HMM
C'MON NOW...
STARE
UH, UM...
NO, REALLY ...
Ah, uh...
Er
sweat sweat
CHANGE THE SUBJECT!
fumble
fumble
Ha Ha Ha
M-MISS HOJO, WHAT A PRETTY BRACELET YOU'RE WEARING!
Looks pricey.
OH–♡! YOU NOTICED ...
How sweet.
This
I SNAGGED IT FROM WAKABA-YASHI OUR FIRST DAY ABOARD.
It's 18-carat gold and em-erald.
WAS HE WEARING THAT?
Er ...
YOU STOLE IT...?
WHAT? I'VE DONE HIM PLENTY OF GOOD TURNS. IT'S ONLY FAIR I SHOULD GET SOMETHING FOR MY TROUBLE.
YOU DON'T THINK I COME CHEAP, DO YOU?
Ha Ha Ha Oh Ho Ho
...
uh...
Oh, snap!
What a waste.

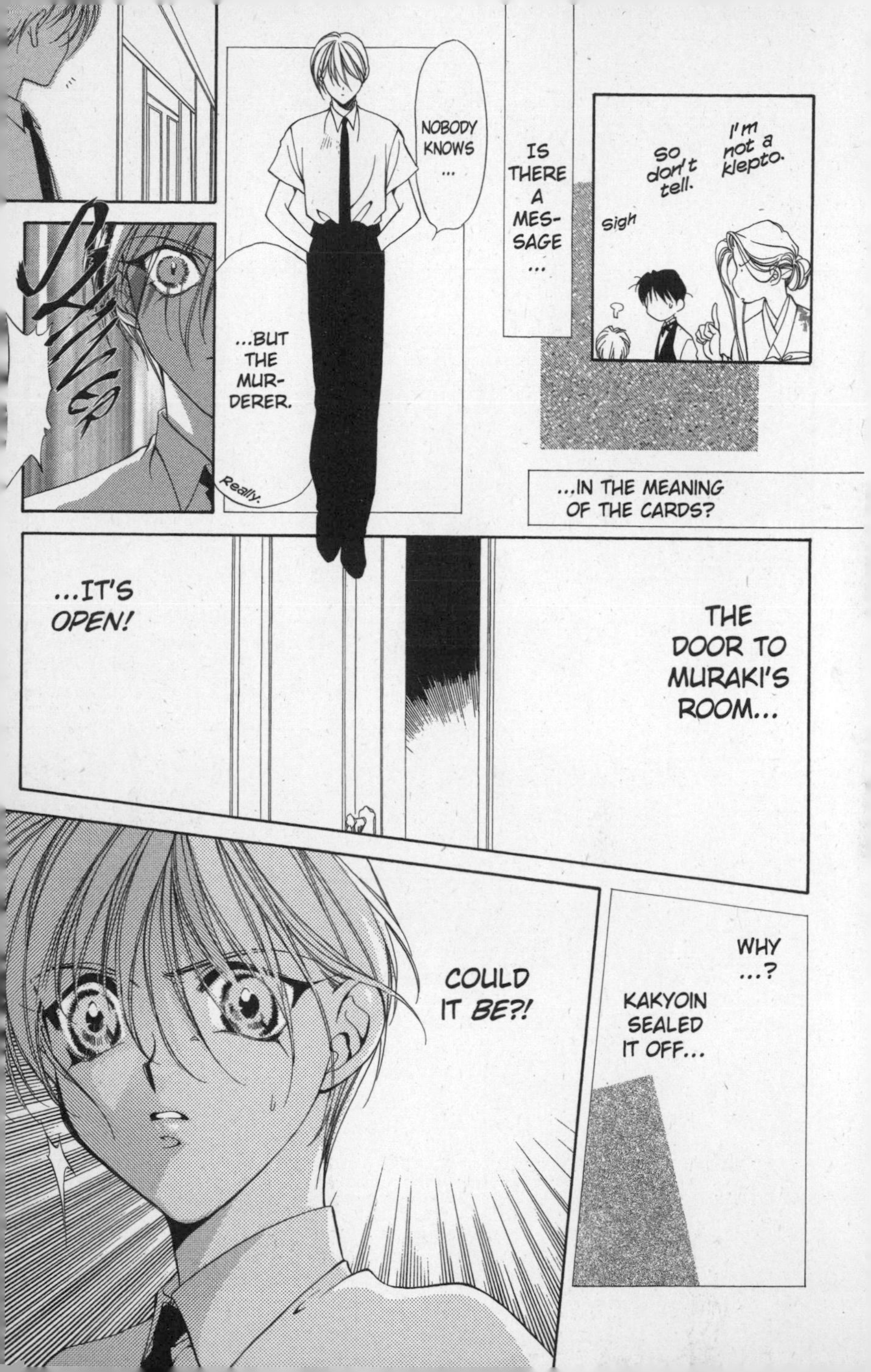

I'm not a klepto.
So don't tell.
Sigh
IS THERE A MES-SAGE...
...IN THE MEANING OF THE CARDS?
NOBODY KNOWS...
...BUT THE MUR-DERER.
Really.
THE DOOR TO MURAKI'S ROOM...
...IT'S OPEN!
WHY...?
KAKYOIN SEALED IT OFF...
COULD IT BE?!

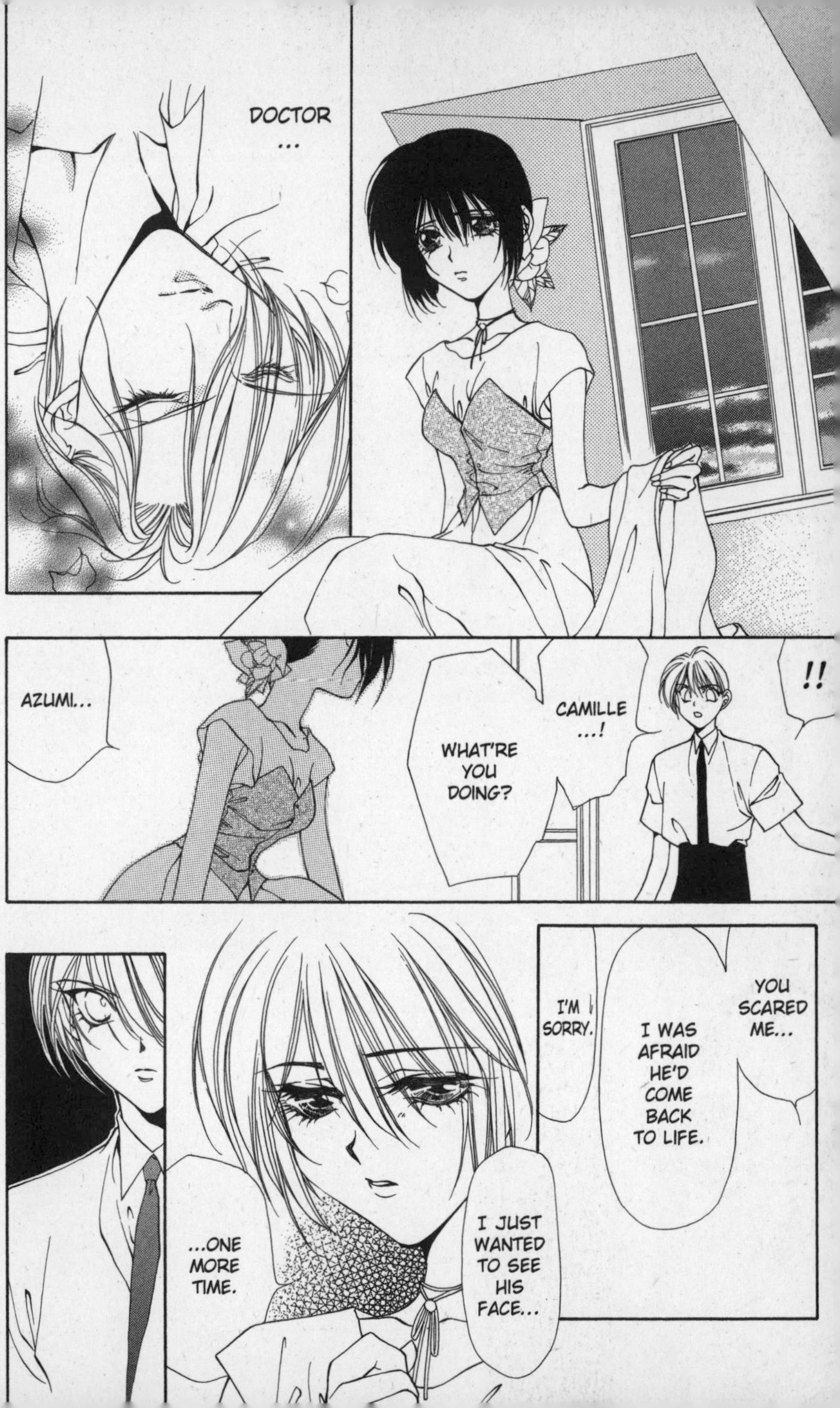
DOCTOR ...
!!
CAMILLE ...!
WHAT'RE YOU DOING?
AZUMI...
YOU SCARED ME...
I WAS AFRAID HE'D COME BACK TO LIFE.
I'M SORRY.
I JUST WANTED TO SEE HIS FACE...
...ONE MORE TIME.

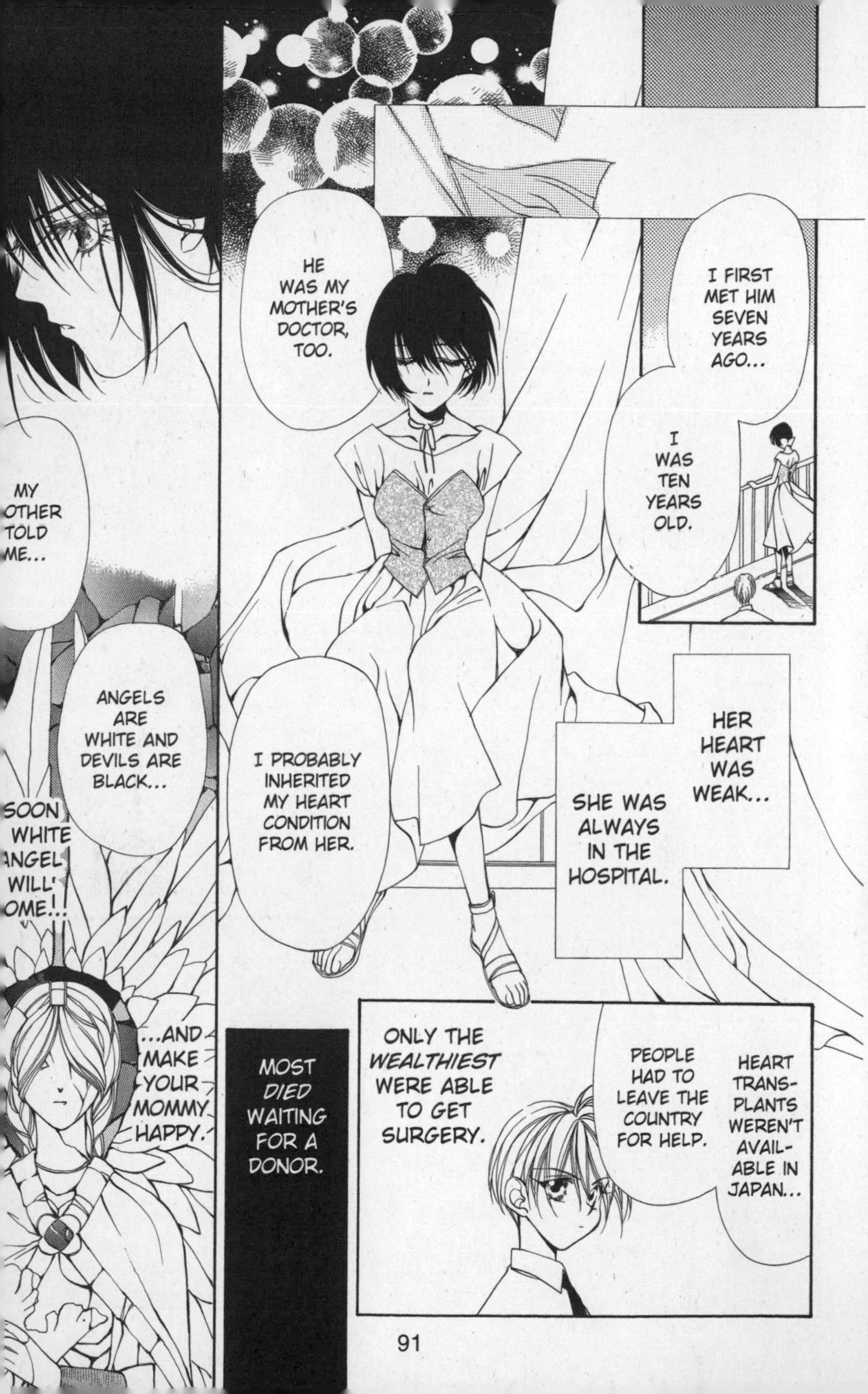
I FIRST MET HIM SEVEN YEARS AGO...
I WAS TEN YEARS OLD.
HE WAS MY MOTHER'S DOCTOR, TOO.
HER HEART WAS WEAK...
SHE WAS ALWAYS IN THE HOSPITAL.
I PROBABLY INHERITED MY HEART CONDITION FROM HER.
HEART TRANSPLANTS WEREN'T AVAILABLE IN JAPAN...
PEOPLE HAD TO LEAVE THE COUNTRY FOR HELP.
ONLY THE *WEALTHIEST* WERE ABLE TO GET SURGERY.
MOST *DIED* WAITING FOR A DONOR.
MY OTHER TOLD ME...
ANGELS ARE WHITE AND DEVILS ARE BLACK...
SOON WHITE NGEL WILL OME!...
...AND MAKE YOUR MOMMY HAPPY.

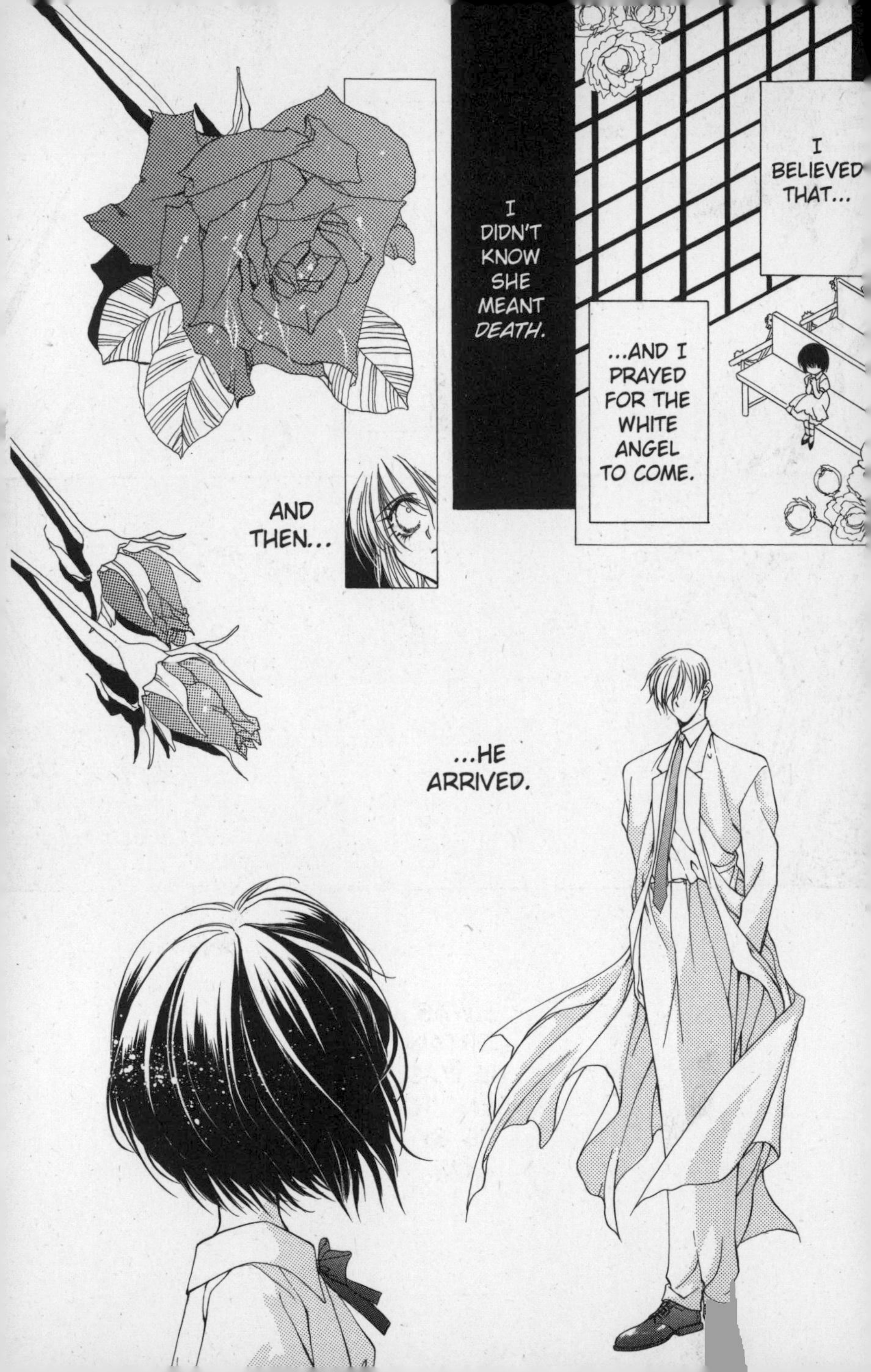
I BELIEVED THAT...
...AND I PRAYED FOR THE WHITE ANGEL TO COME.
I DIDN'T KNOW SHE MEANT *DEATH*.
AND THEN...
...HE ARRIVED.

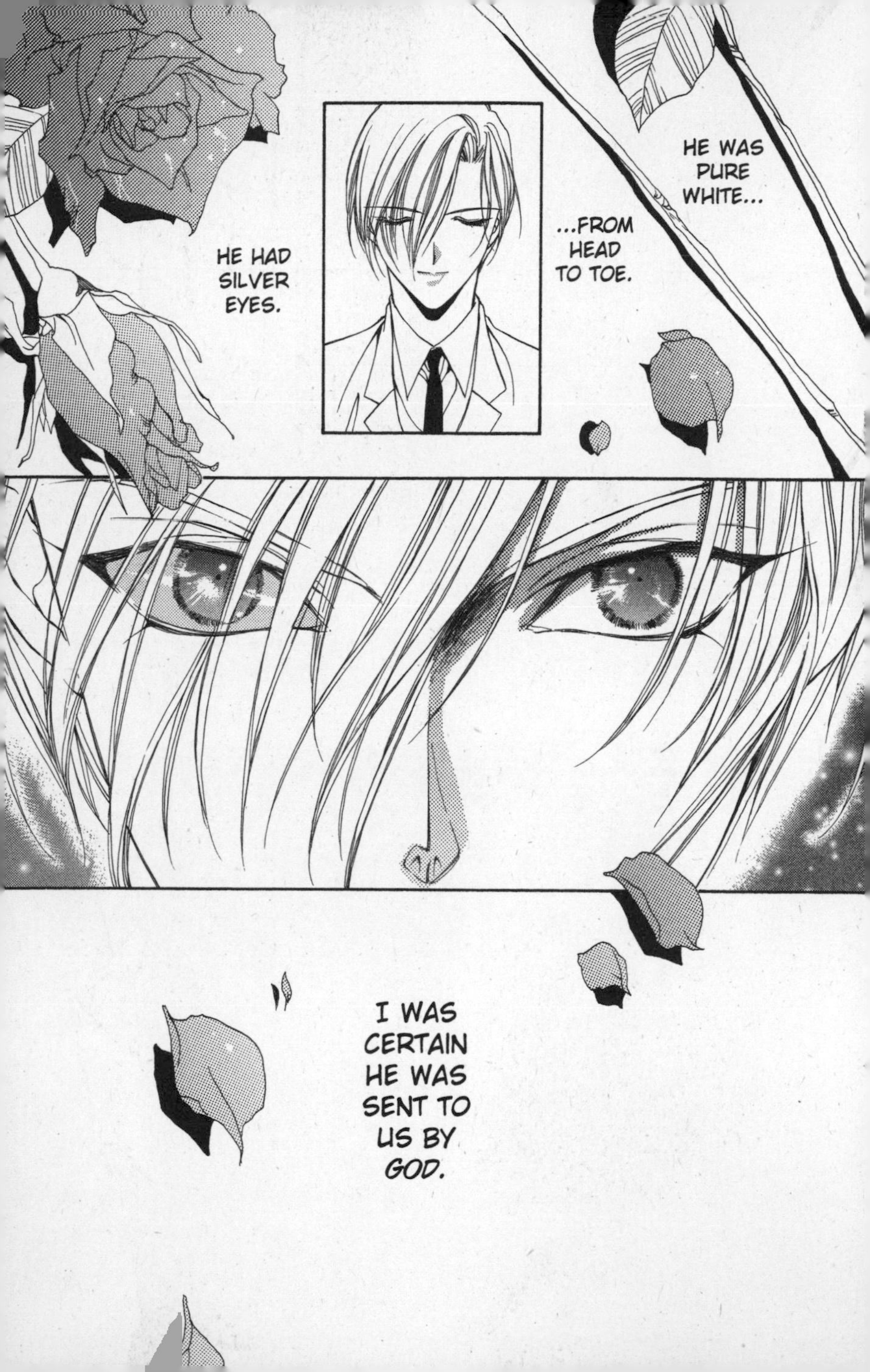
HE WAS PURE WHITE...
...FROM HEAD TO TOE.
HE HAD SILVER EYES.
I WAS CERTAIN HE WAS SENT TO US BY GOD.

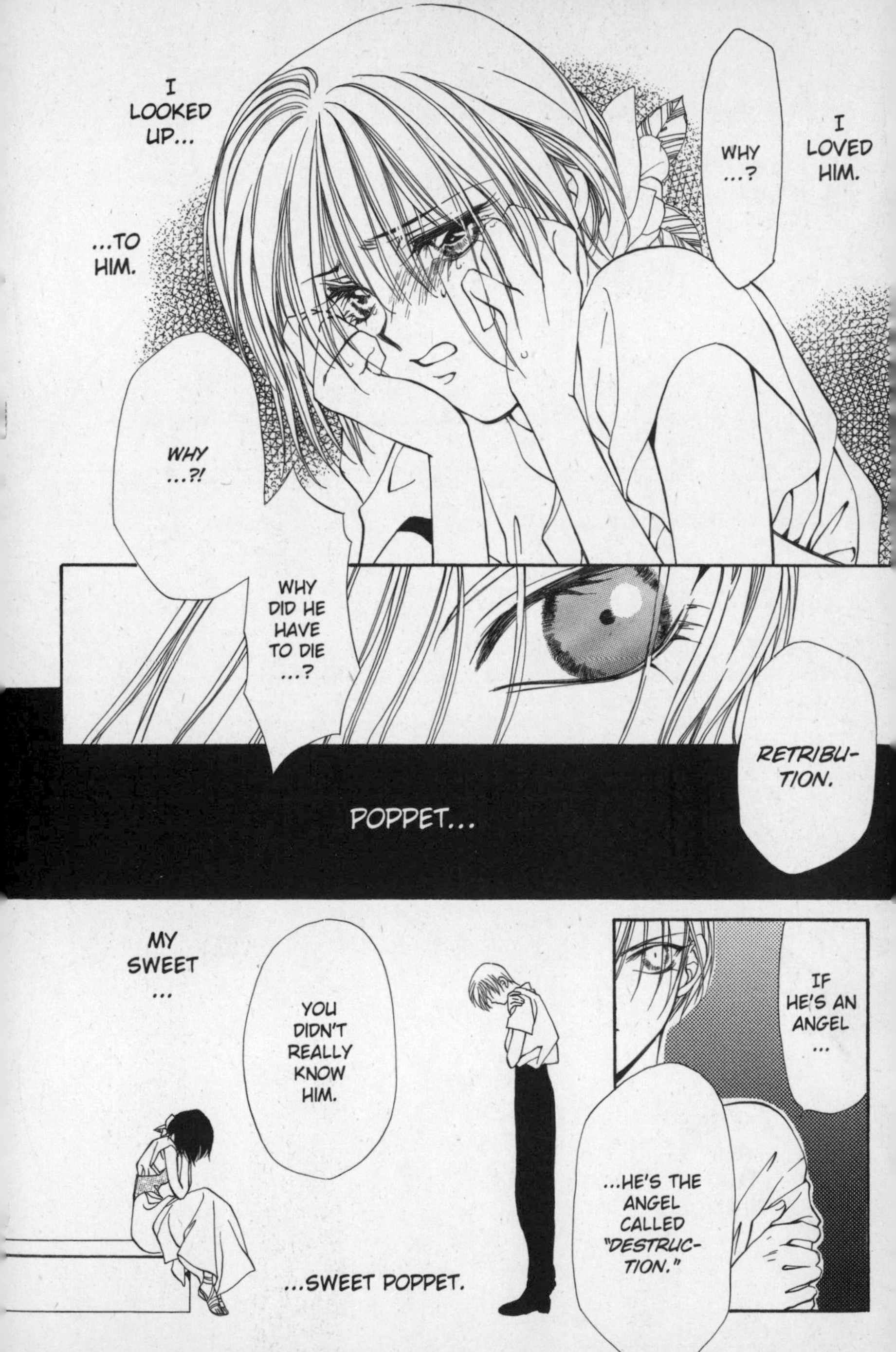
I LOVED HIM.
WHY ...?
I LOOKED UP...
...TO HIM.
WHY ...?!
WHY DID HE HAVE TO DIE ...?
RETRIBU-TION.
POPPET...
IF HE'S AN ANGEL ...
...HE'S THE ANGEL CALLED "DESTRUC-TION."
MY SWEET ...
YOU DIDN'T REALLY KNOW HIM.
...SWEET POPPET.

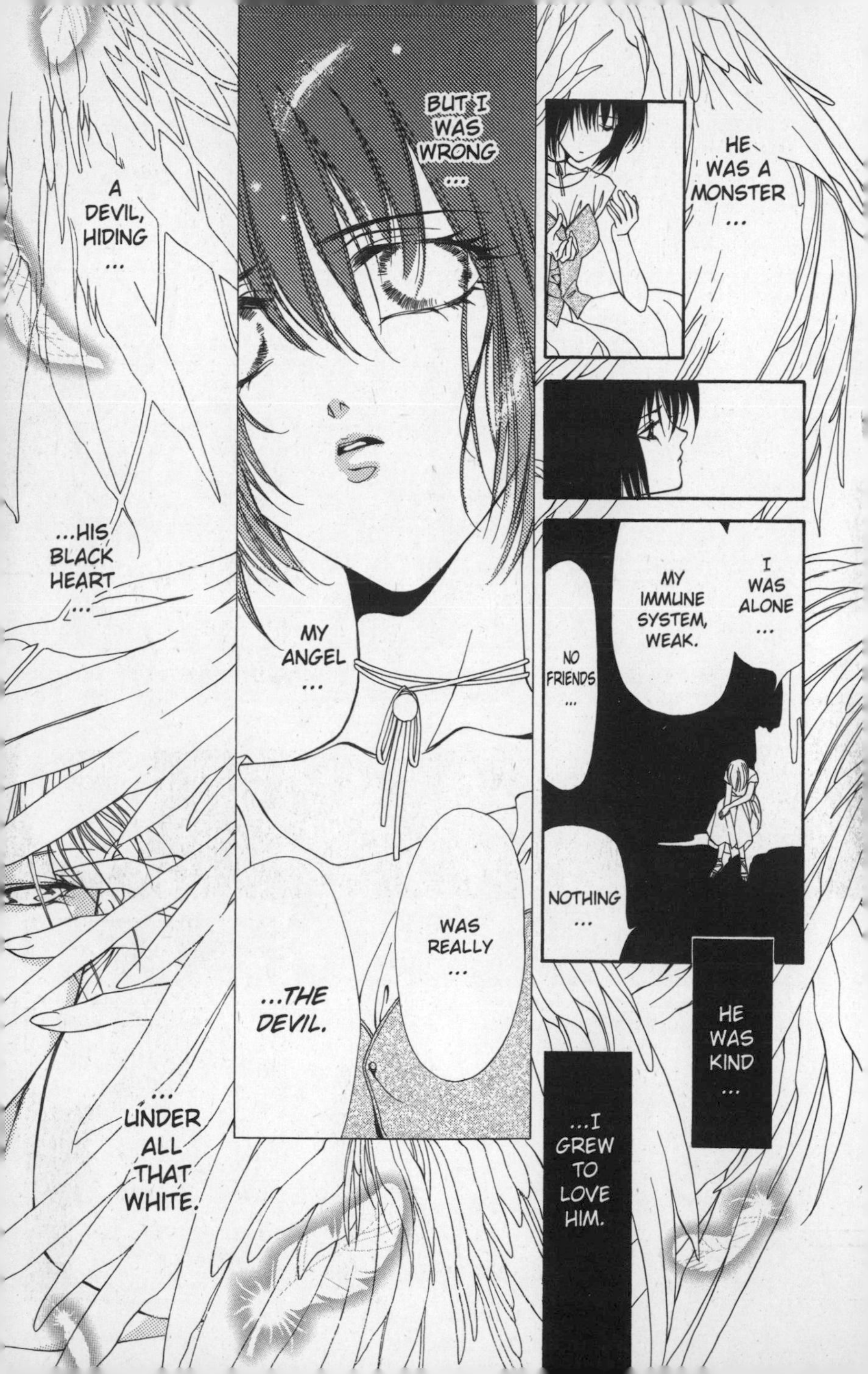
HE WAS A MONSTER ...
I WAS ALONE ...
MY IMMUNE SYSTEM, WEAK.
NO FRIENDS ...
NOTHING ...
HE WAS KIND ...
...I GREW TO LOVE HIM.
BUT I WAS WRONG ...
MY ANGEL ...
WAS REALLY ...
...THE DEVIL.
A DEVIL, HIDING ...
...HIS BLACK HEART ...
... UNDER ALL THAT WHITE.

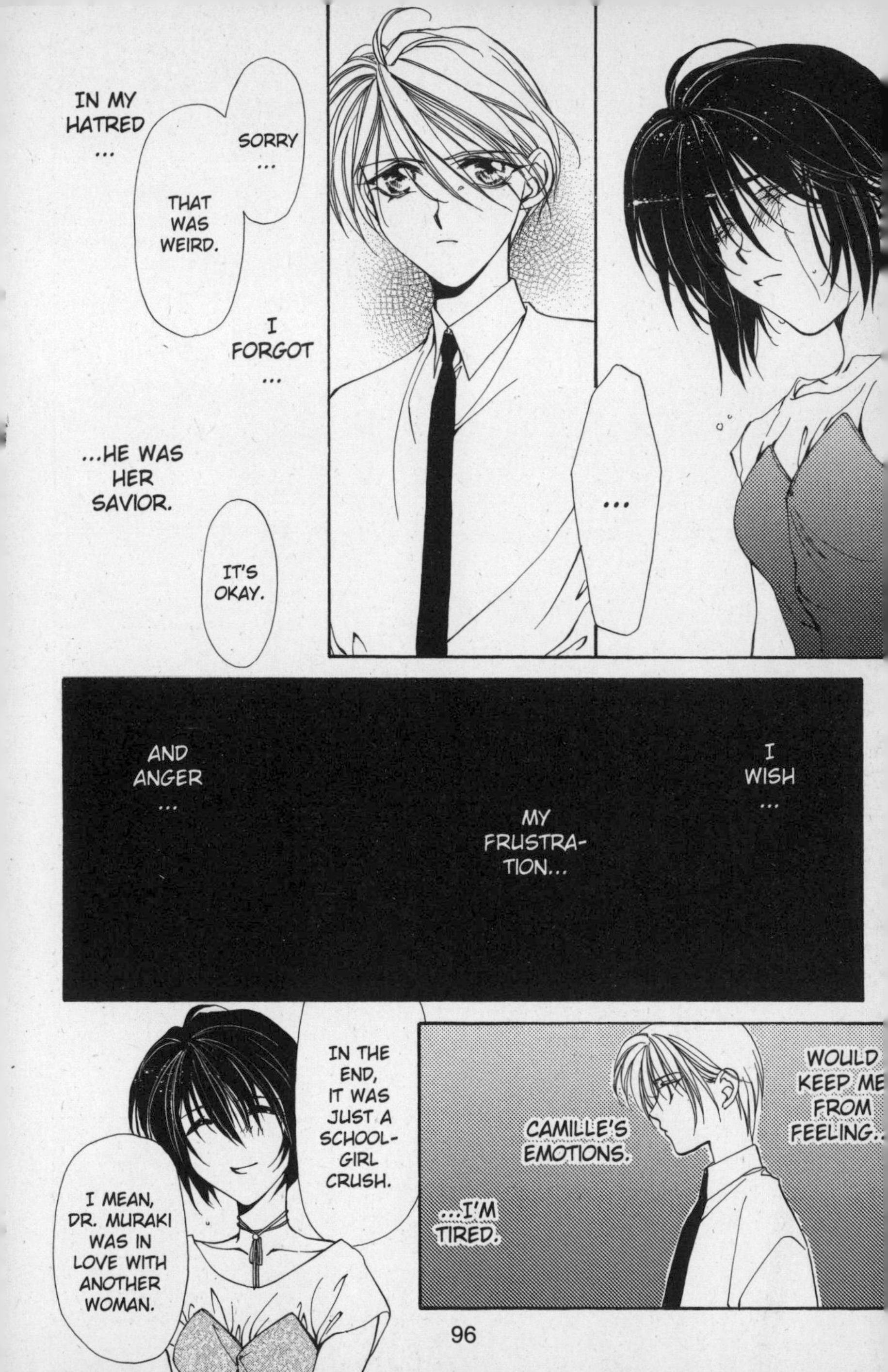
...
SORRY... THAT WAS WEIRD.
IN MY HATRED...
I FORGOT...
...HE WAS HER SAVIOR.
IT'S OKAY.
I WISH...
MY FRUSTRATION...
AND ANGER...
WOULD KEEP ME FROM FEELING...
CAMILLE'S EMOTIONS.
...I'M TIRED.
IN THE END, IT WAS JUST A SCHOOL-GIRL CRUSH.
I MEAN, DR. MURAKI WAS IN LOVE WITH ANOTHER WOMAN.

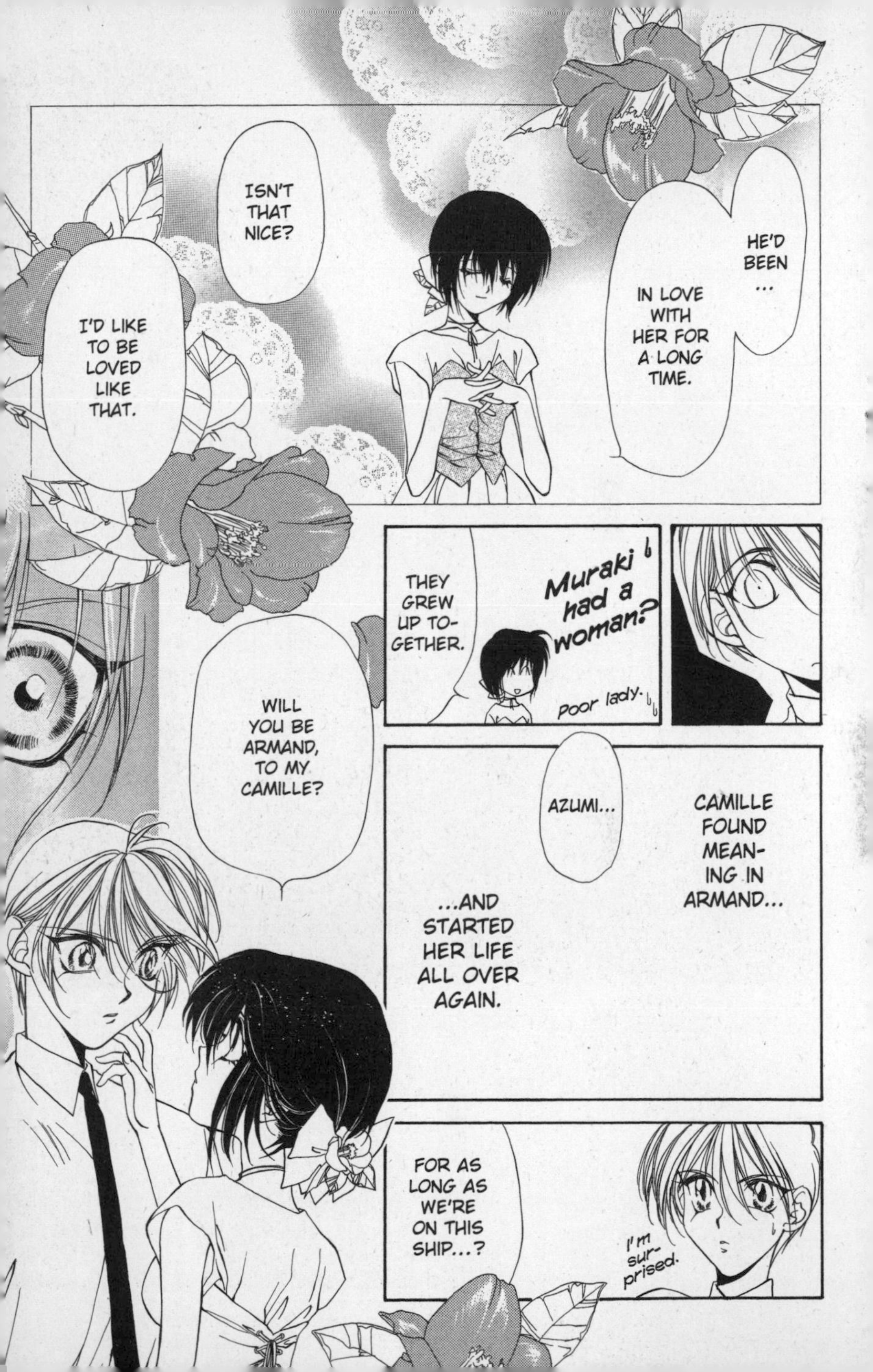

HE'D BEEN ...
IN LOVE WITH HER FOR A LONG TIME.
ISN'T THAT NICE?
I'D LIKE TO BE LOVED LIKE THAT.
THEY GREW UP TO-GETHER.
Muraki had a woman?
Poor lady.
CAMILLE FOUND MEAN-ING IN ARMAND...
...AND STARTED HER LIFE ALL OVER AGAIN.
AZUMI...
WILL YOU BE ARMAND, TO MY CAMILLE?
FOR AS LONG AS WE'RE ON THIS SHIP...?
I'm sur-prised.

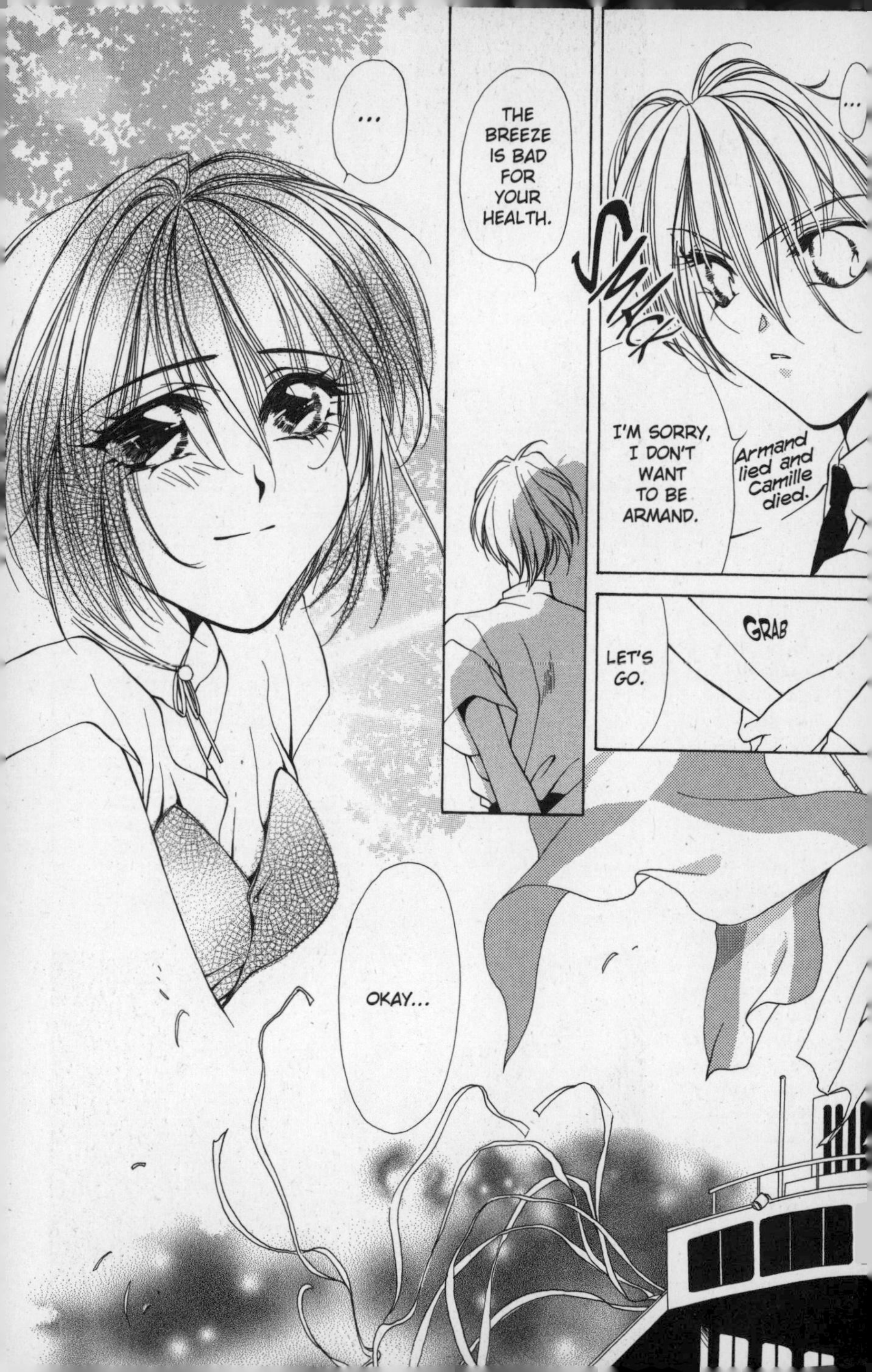
...
SMACK
Armand lied and Camille died.
I'M SORRY, I DON'T WANT TO BE ARMAND.
GRAB
LET'S GO.
THE BREEZE IS BAD FOR YOUR HEALTH.
...
OKAY...

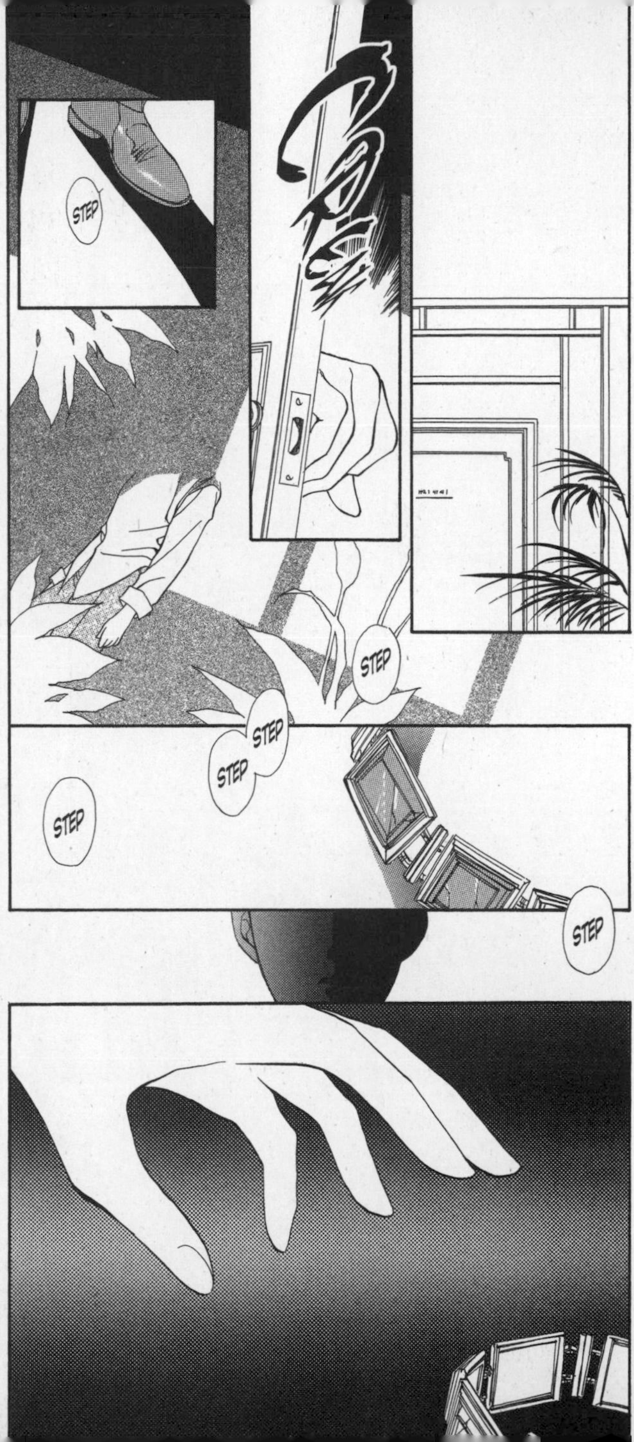
STEP
STEP
STEP
STEP
STEP
STEP

Muraki's Story
Unfolds!!

Is everybody still with me? I drew Muraki in color for the first time ever for this books cover. I know you don't care, but it's really hard to color blonde hair. If you don't do it right, it comes out looking gray. I redid it twice. That guy is so high maintenance!

If you're wondering why a Japanese doctor has blonde hair, well... it's a secret. You'll find out when you learn about his family and his family tree. I hope you're looking forward to it!!

If you're interested in what tools and techniques I use to color, well, I'm still a novice, so I just use regular colored inks. Occasionally, I experiment with special architectural drafting paint that I get from my friend, but I find it intimidating.

COLORED INK IS SO EXPENSIVE!!

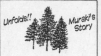

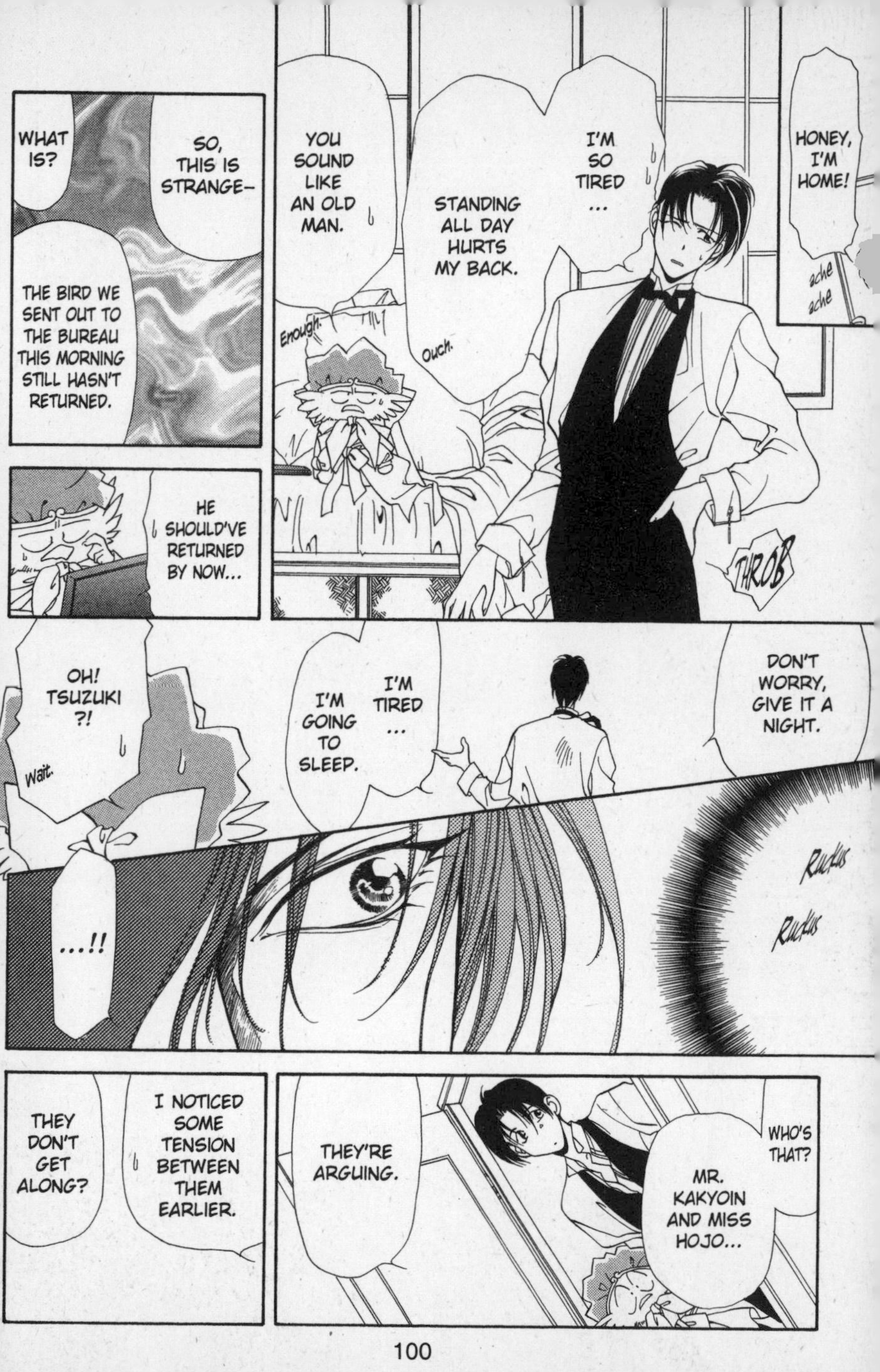
HONEY, I'M HOME!
ache
ache
I'M SO TIRED ...
STANDING ALL DAY HURTS MY BACK.
Ouch.
YOU SOUND LIKE AN OLD MAN.
Enough.
THROB
SO, THIS IS STRANGE-
WHAT IS?
THE BIRD WE SENT OUT TO THE BUREAU THIS MORNING STILL HASN'T RETURNED.
HE SHOULD'VE RETURNED BY NOW...
DON'T WORRY, GIVE IT A NIGHT.
I'M TIRED ...
I'M GOING TO SLEEP.
OH! TSUZUKI ?!
Wait.
Ruckus
Ruckus
...!!
WHO'S THAT?
MR. KAKYOIN AND MISS HOJO...
THEY'RE ARGUING.
I NOTICED SOME TENSION BETWEEN THEM EARLIER.
THEY DON'T GET ALONG?

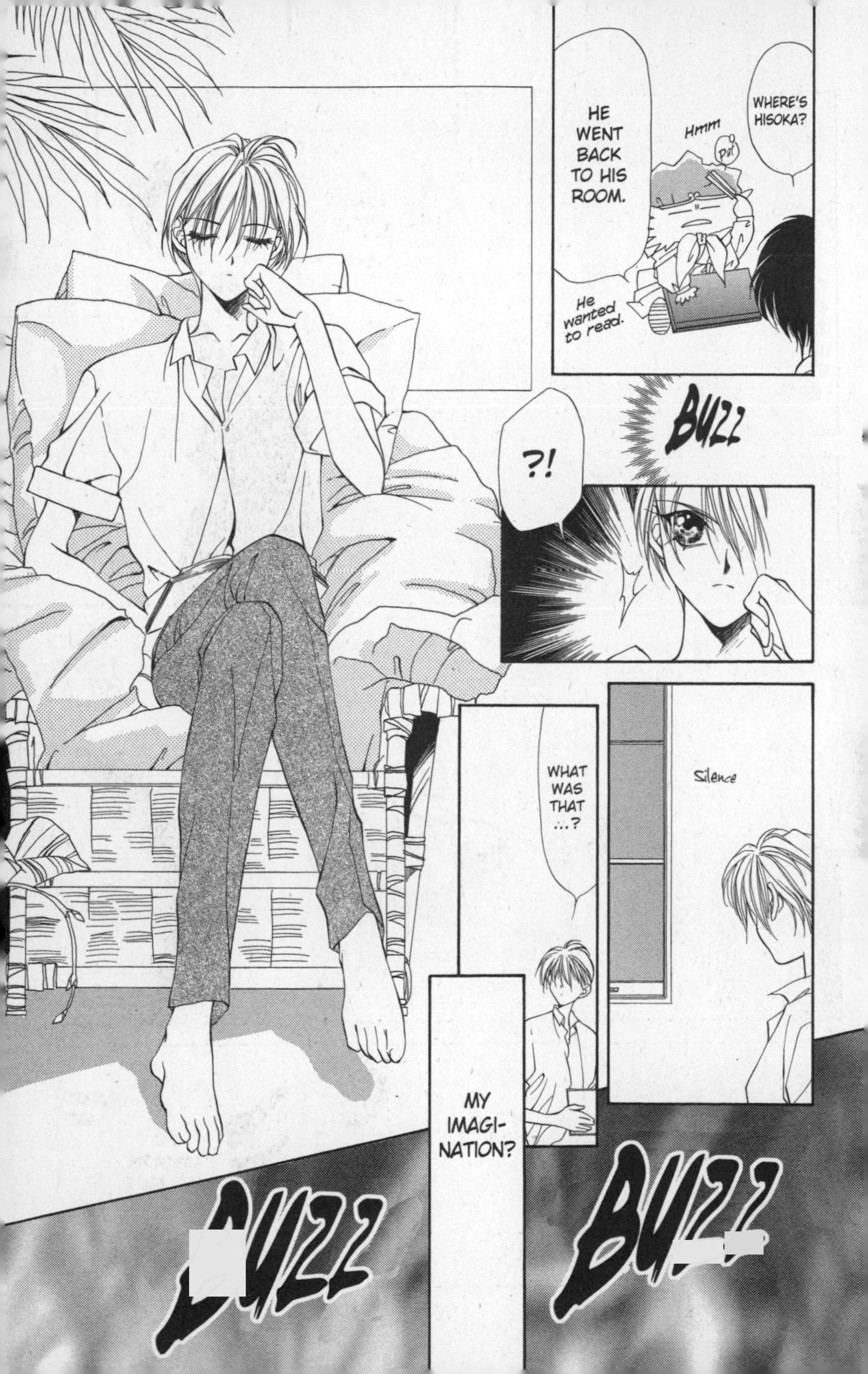

WHERE'S HISOKA?
HE WENT BACK TO HIS ROOM.
Hmm
Pat
He wanted to read.
BUZZ
?!
Silence
WHAT WAS THAT ...?
MY IMAGINATION?
UZZ
BU

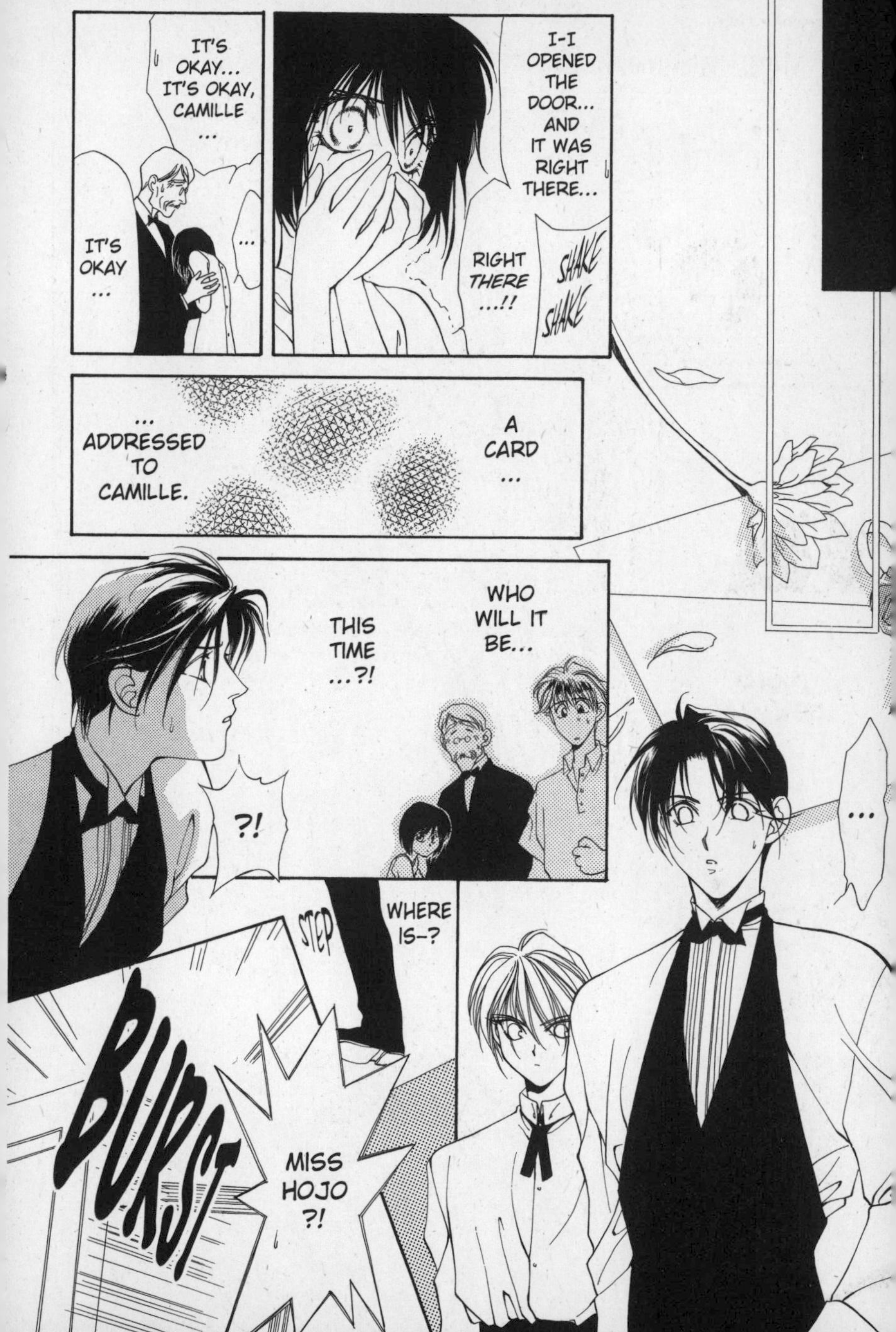
I-I OPENED THE DOOR... AND IT WAS RIGHT THERE...
RIGHT THERE ...!!
SHAKE SHAKE
IT'S OKAY... IT'S OKAY, CAMILLE ...
...
IT'S OKAY ...
A CARD ...
... ADDRESSED TO CAMILLE.
...
WHO WILL IT BE...
THIS TIME ...?!
?!
WHERE IS-?
STEP
BURST
MISS HOJO ?!

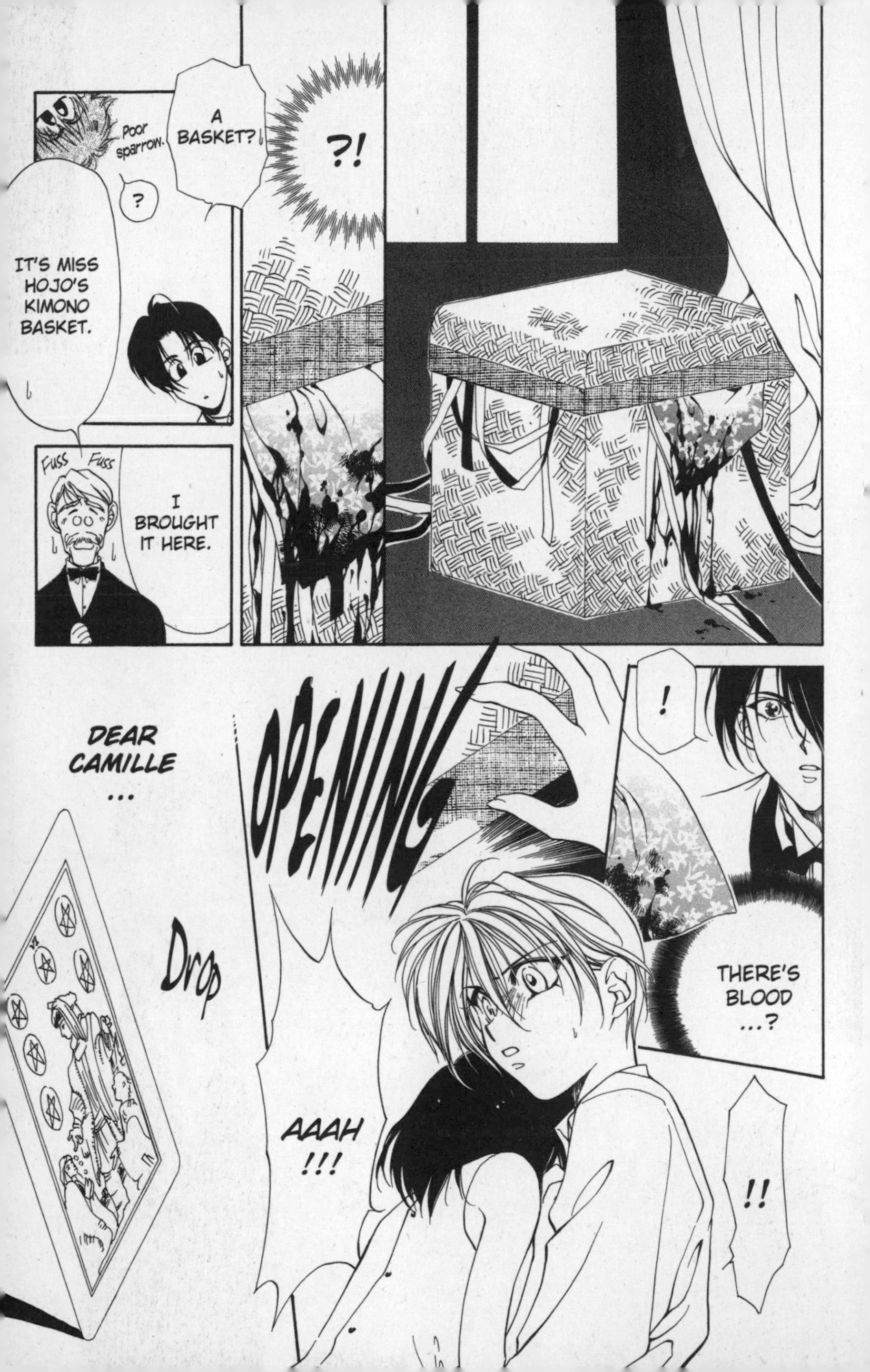
?!
A BASKET?
?
Poor sparrow.
IT'S MISS HOJO'S KIMONO BASKET.
Fuss Fuss
I BROUGHT IT HERE.
!
THERE'S BLOOD ...?
OPENING
Drop
DEAR CAMILLE ...
!!
AAAH !!!

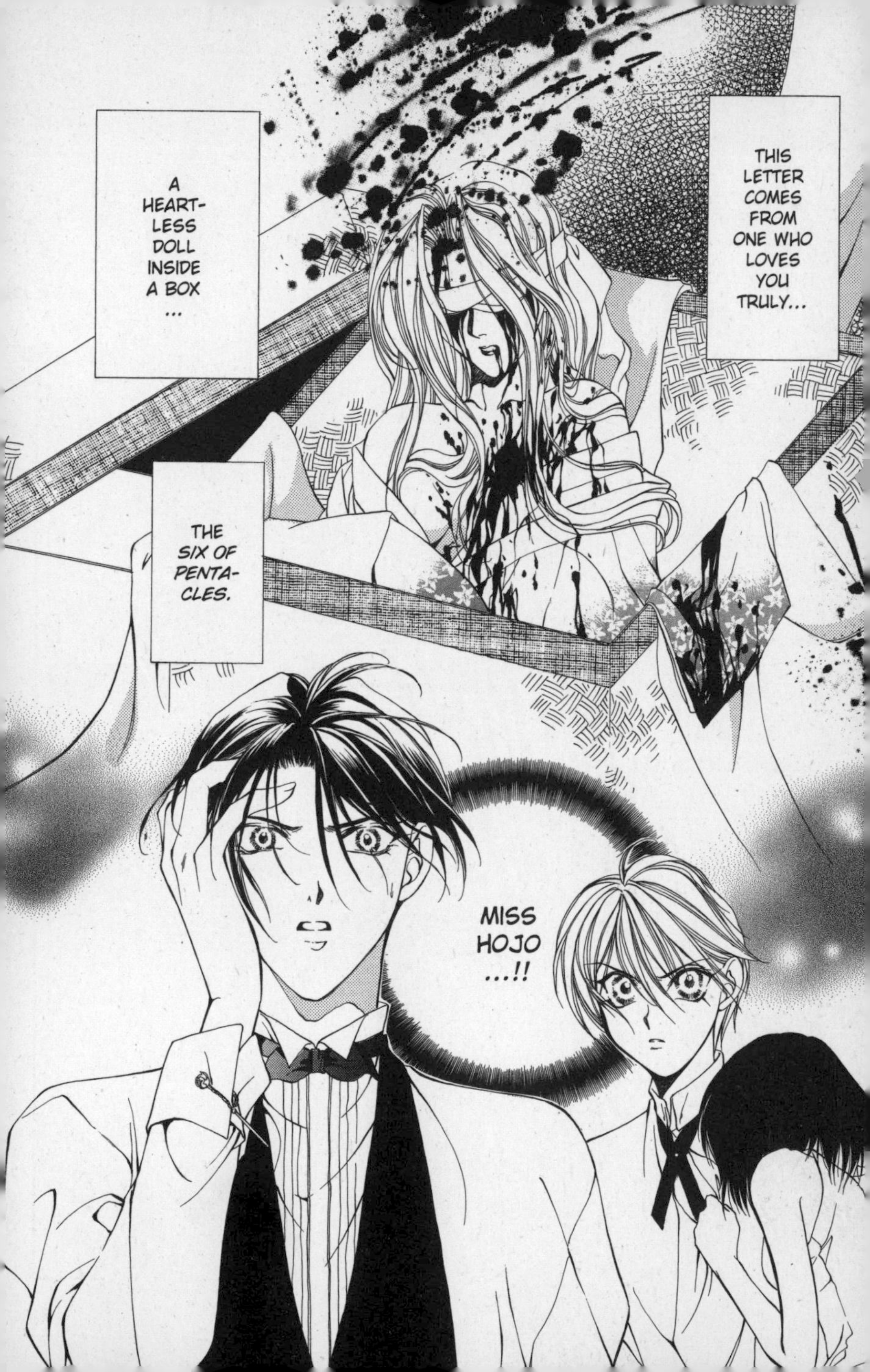
THIS LETTER COMES FROM ONE WHO LOVES YOU TRULY...
A HEART-LESS DOLL INSIDE A BOX ...
THE SIX OF PENTA-CLES.
MISS HOJO ...!!

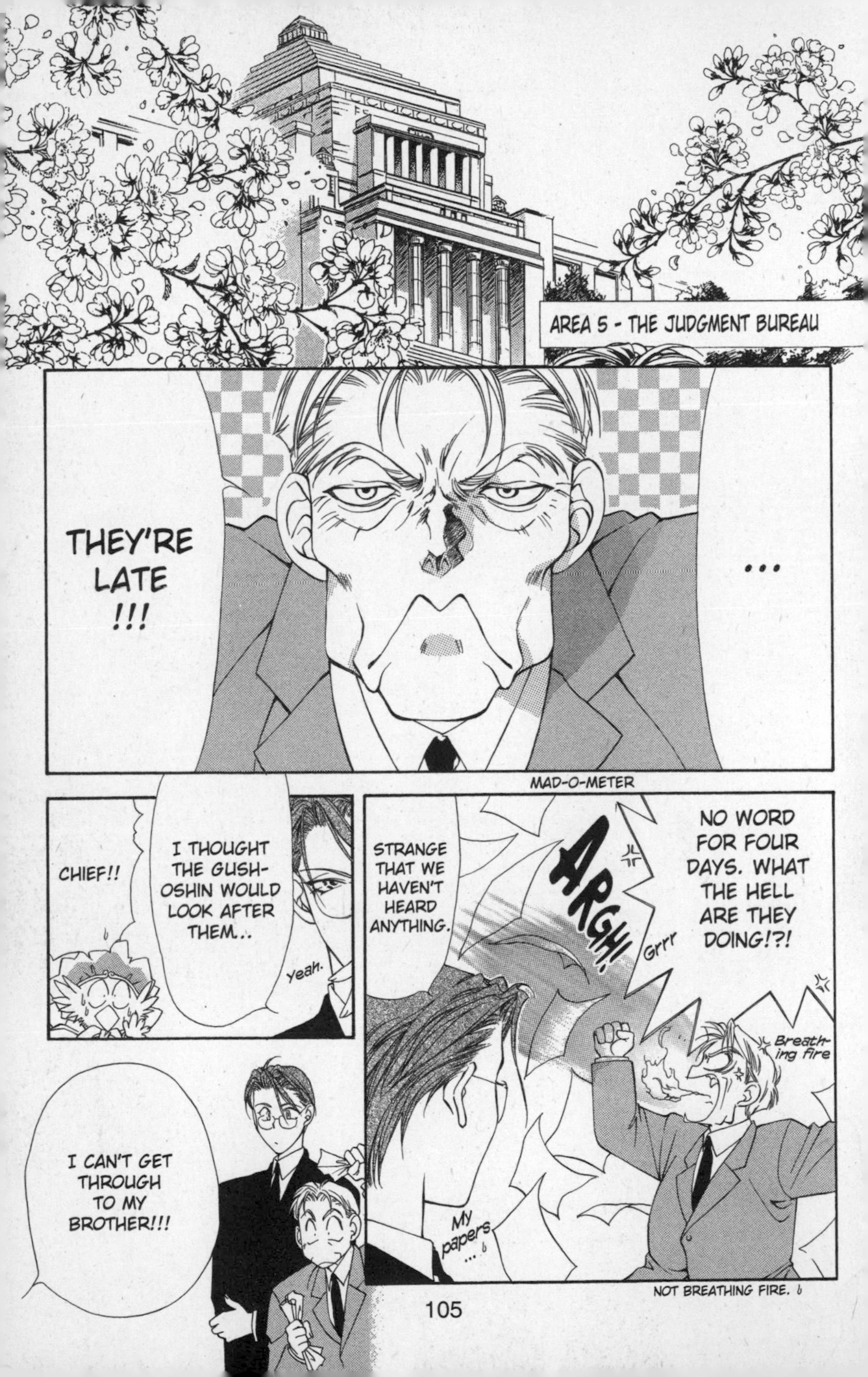
AREA 5 - THE JUDGMENT BUREAU
...
THEY'RE LATE !!!
MAD-O-METER
NO WORD FOR FOUR DAYS. WHAT THE HELL ARE THEY DOING!?!
ARGH!!
Grrr
Breathing fire
STRANGE THAT WE HAVEN'T HEARD ANYTHING.
My papers...
NOT BREATHING FIRE.
I THOUGHT THE GUSHOSHIN WOULD LOOK AFTER THEM..
Yeah.
CHIEF!!
I CAN'T GET THROUGH TO MY BROTHER!!!

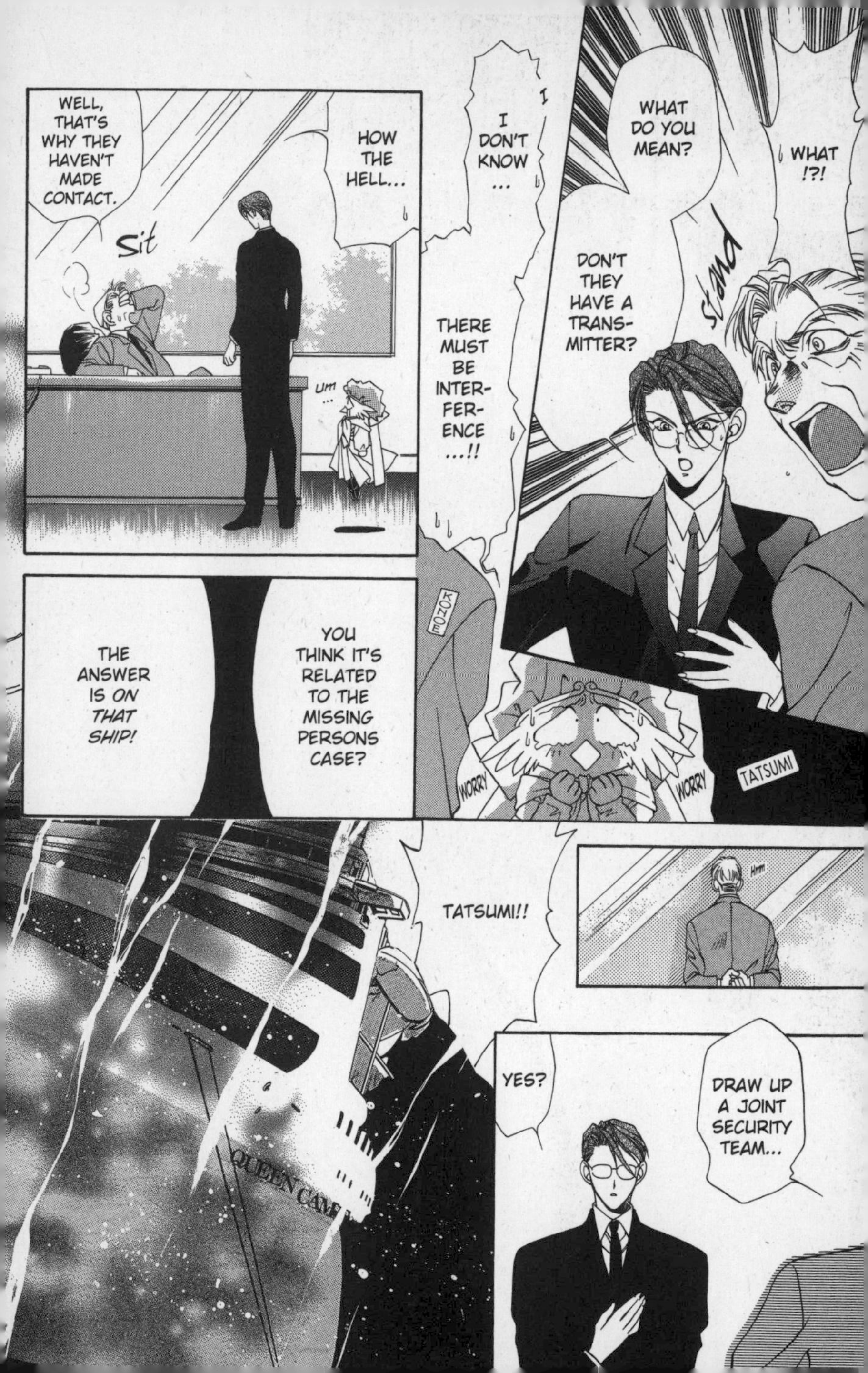

WHAT !?!
stand
WHAT DO YOU MEAN?
DON'T THEY HAVE A TRANSMITTER?
I
I DON'T KNOW ...
THERE MUST BE INTERFERENCE ...!!
KONOE
TATSUMI
WORRY
WORRY
HOW THE HELL...
WELL, THAT'S WHY THEY HAVEN'T MADE CONTACT.
Sit
um ...
YOU THINK IT'S RELATED TO THE MISSING PERSONS CASE?
THE ANSWER IS ON THAT SHIP!
Hmm
TATSUMI!!
DRAW UP A JOINT SECURITY TEAM...
YES?

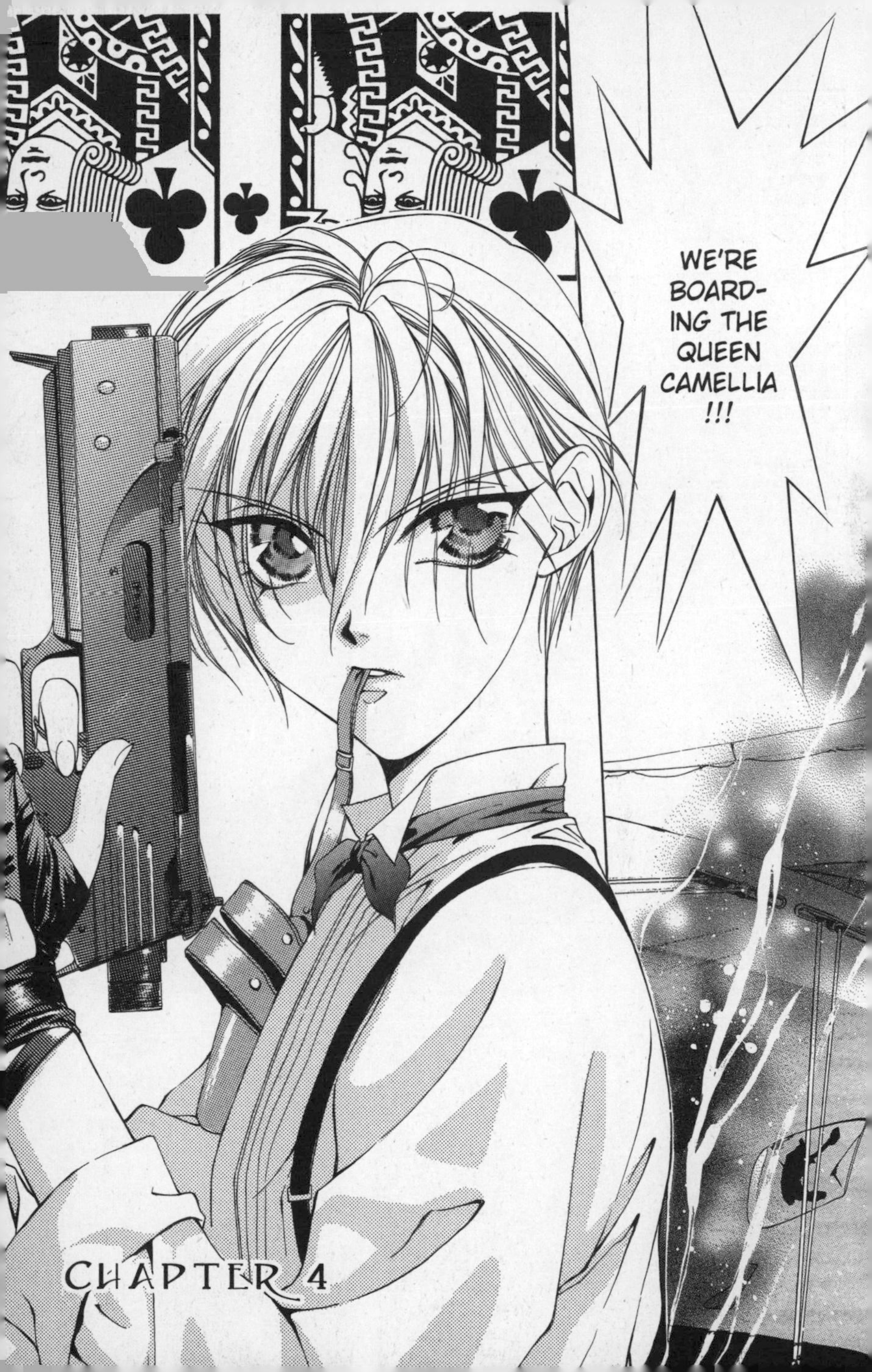
WE'RE BOARDING THE QUEEN CAMELLIA !!!
CHAPTER 4

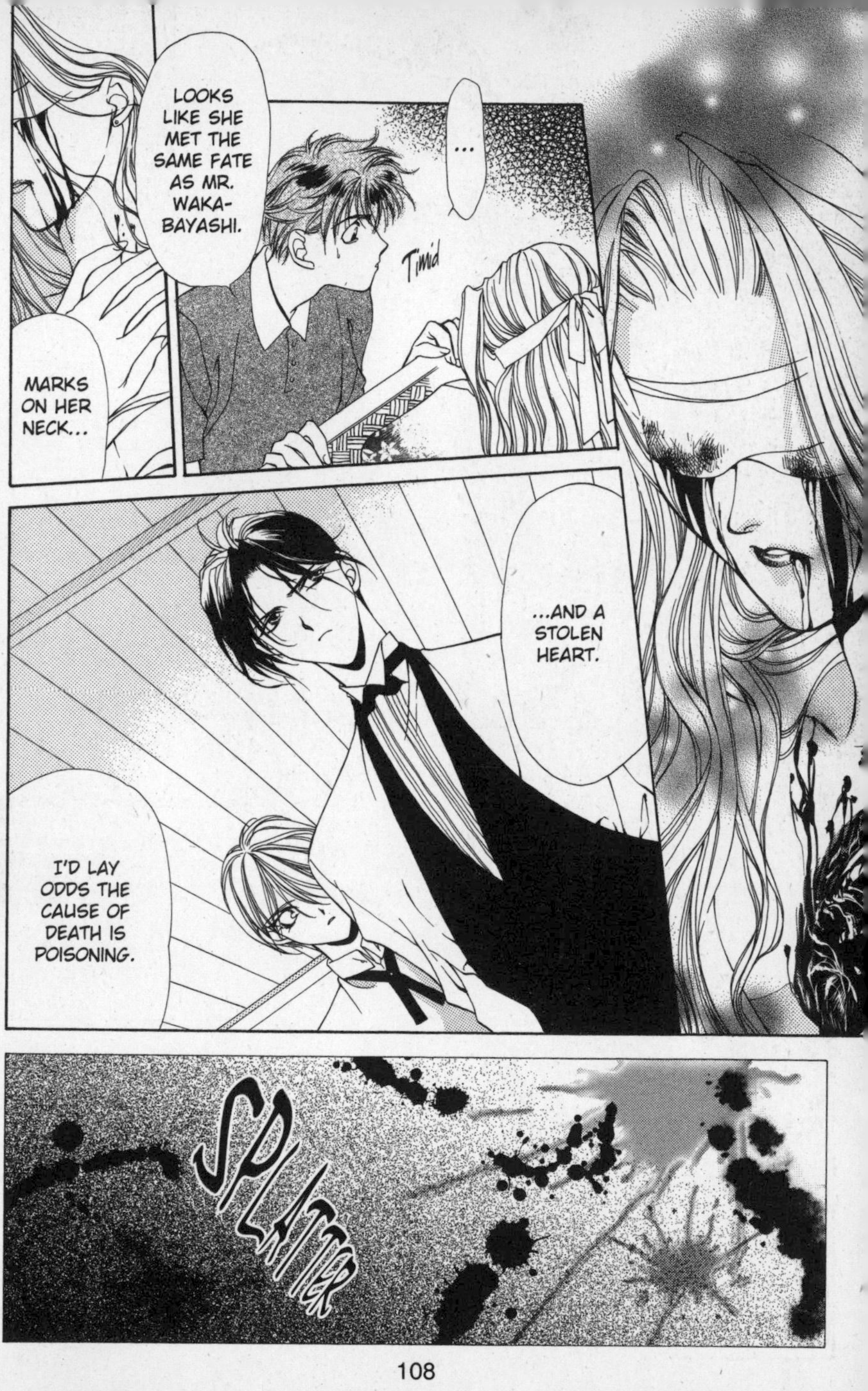
...
Timid
LOOKS LIKE SHE MET THE SAME FATE AS MR. WAKA-BAYASHI.
MARKS ON HER NECK...
...AND A STOLEN HEART.
I'D LAY ODDS THE CAUSE OF DEATH IS POISONING.
SPLATTER

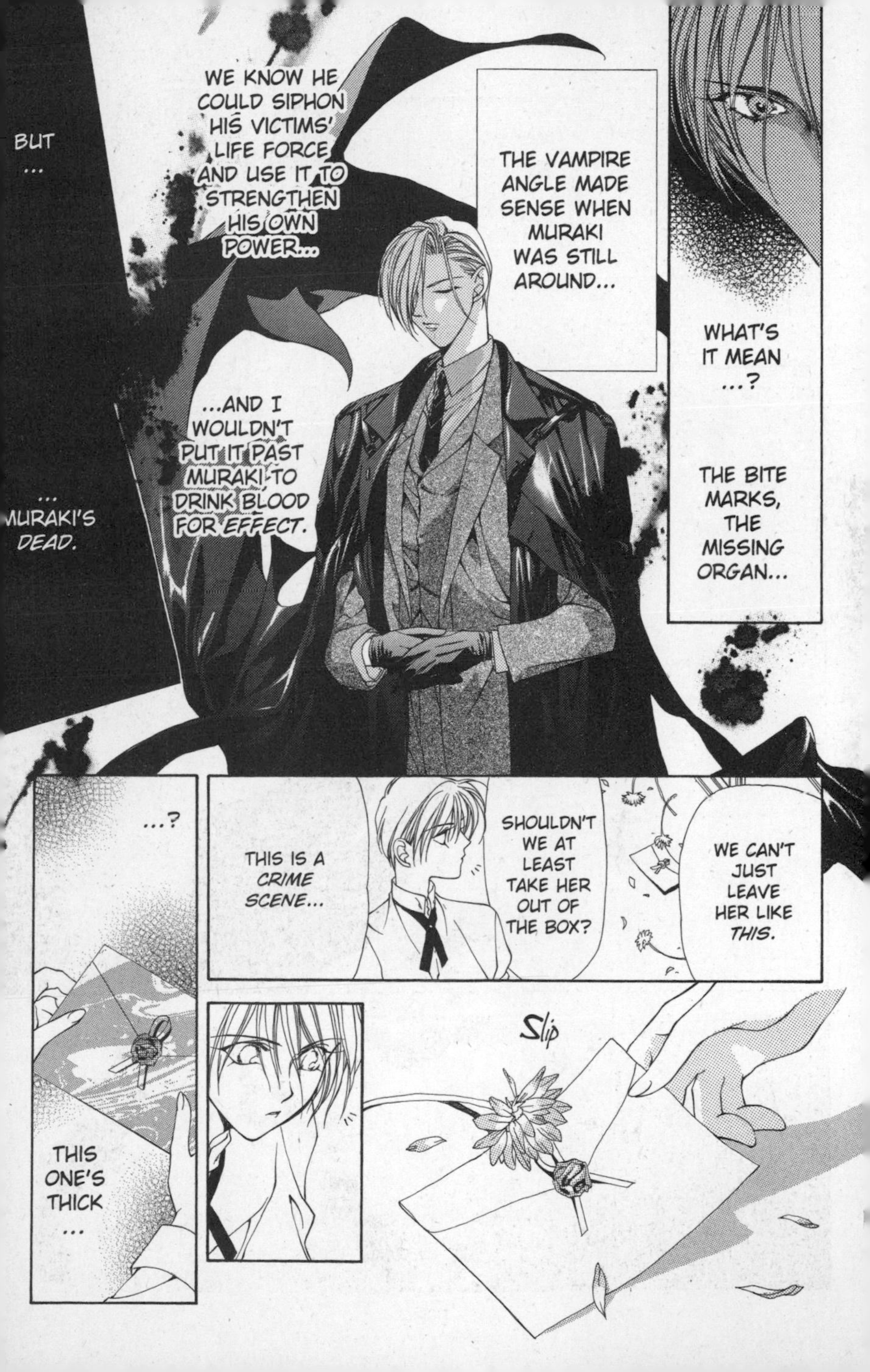
WHAT'S IT MEAN ...?
THE BITE MARKS, THE MISSING ORGAN...
THE VAMPIRE ANGLE MADE SENSE WHEN MURAKI WAS STILL AROUND...
WE KNOW HE COULD SIPHON HIS VICTIMS' LIFE FORCE AND USE IT TO STRENGTHEN HIS OWN POWER...
...AND I WOULDN'T PUT IT PAST MURAKI TO DRINK BLOOD FOR *EFFECT*.
BUT ...
...MURAKI'S *DEAD*.
WE CAN'T JUST LEAVE HER LIKE *THIS*.
SHOULDN'T WE AT LEAST TAKE HER OUT OF THE BOX?
THIS IS A *CRIME SCENE*...
Slip
...?
THIS ONE'S THICK ...

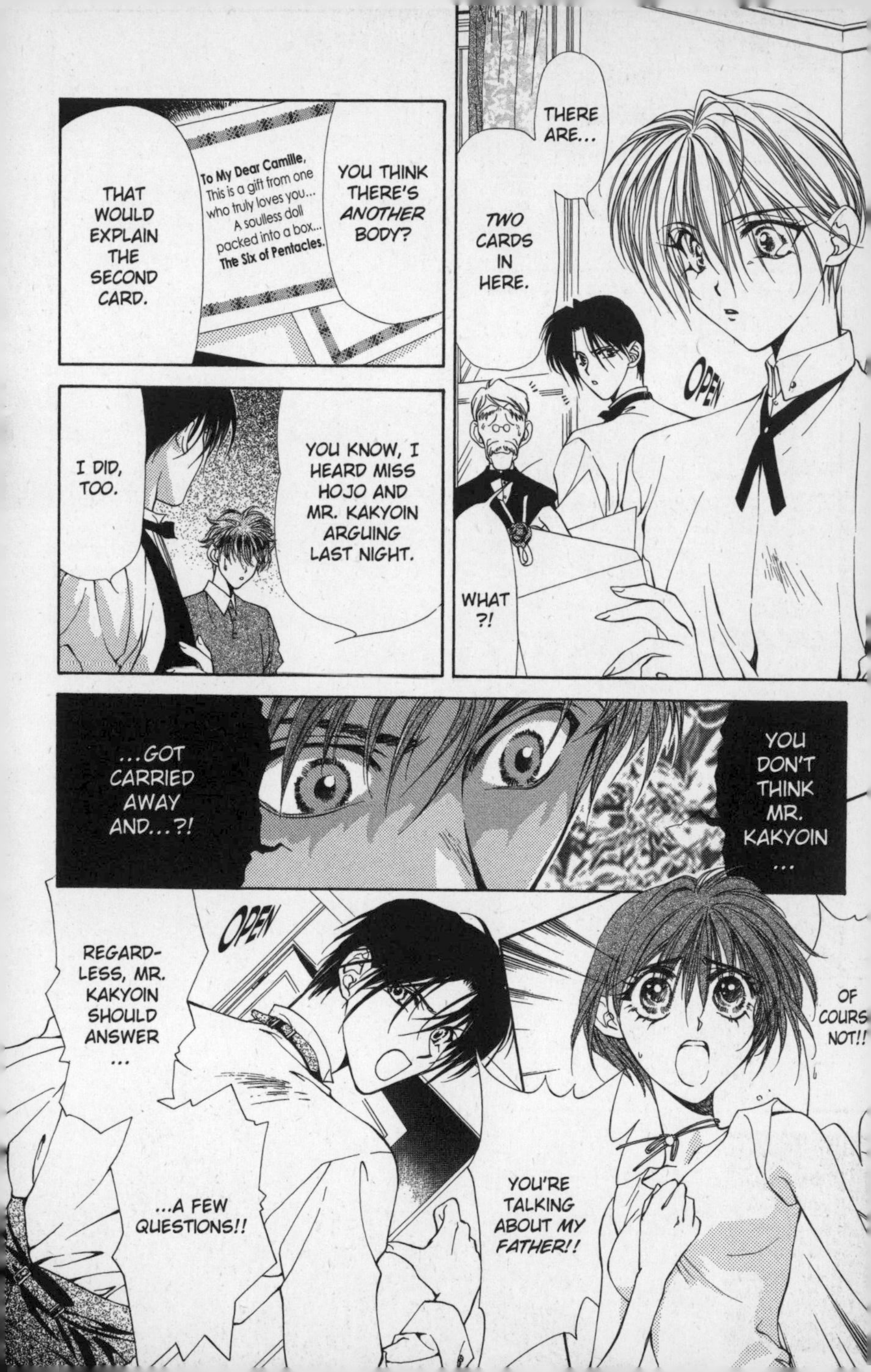
THERE ARE...
TWO CARDS IN HERE.
OPEN
WHAT?!
To My Dear Camille,
This is a gift from one who truly loves you...
A soulless doll packed into a box...
The Six of Pentacles.
YOU THINK THERE'S ANOTHER BODY?
THAT WOULD EXPLAIN THE SECOND CARD.
YOU KNOW, I HEARD MISS HOJO AND MR. KAKYOIN ARGUING LAST NIGHT.
I DID, TOO.
YOU DON'T THINK MR. KAKYOIN...
...GOT CARRIED AWAY AND...?!
OF COURS NOT!!
YOU'RE TALKING ABOUT MY FATHER!!
OPEN
REGARDLESS, MR. KAKYOIN SHOULD ANSWER...
...A FEW QUESTIONS!!

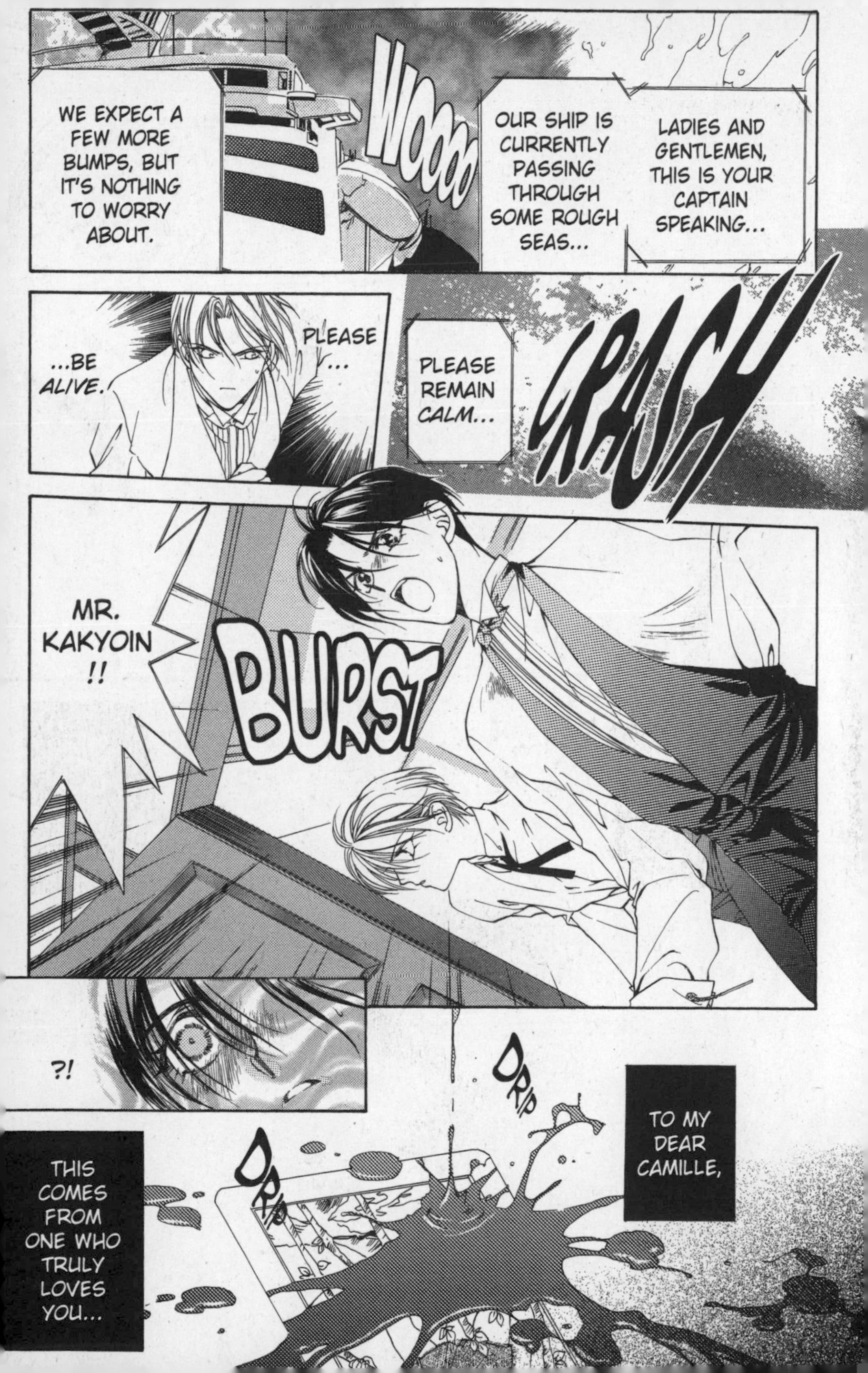
LADIES AND GENTLEMEN, THIS IS YOUR CAPTAIN SPEAKING...
OUR SHIP IS CURRENTLY PASSING THROUGH SOME ROUGH SEAS...
WOOOO
WE EXPECT A FEW MORE BUMPS, BUT IT'S NOTHING TO WORRY ABOUT.
CRASH
PLEASE REMAIN CALM...
PLEASE...
...BE ALIVE.
BURST
MR. KAKYOIN!!
?!
TO MY DEAR CAMILLE,
DRIP
DRIP
DRIP
THIS COMES FROM ONE WHO TRULY LOVES YOU...

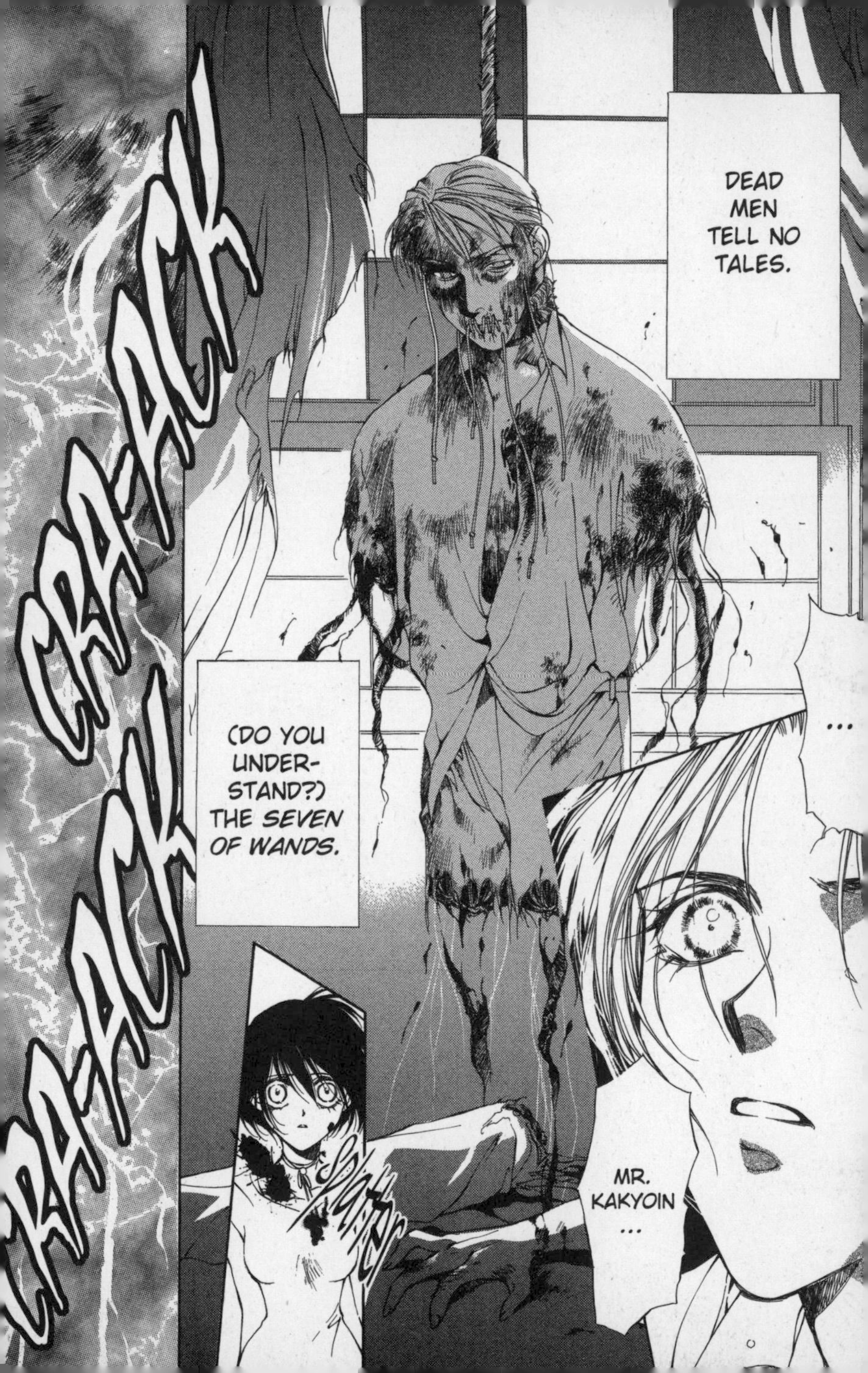
DEAD MEN TELL NO TALES.
CRA-ACK
CRACK
(DO YOU UNDER-STAND?) THE SEVEN OF WANDS.
...
MR. KAKYOIN ...

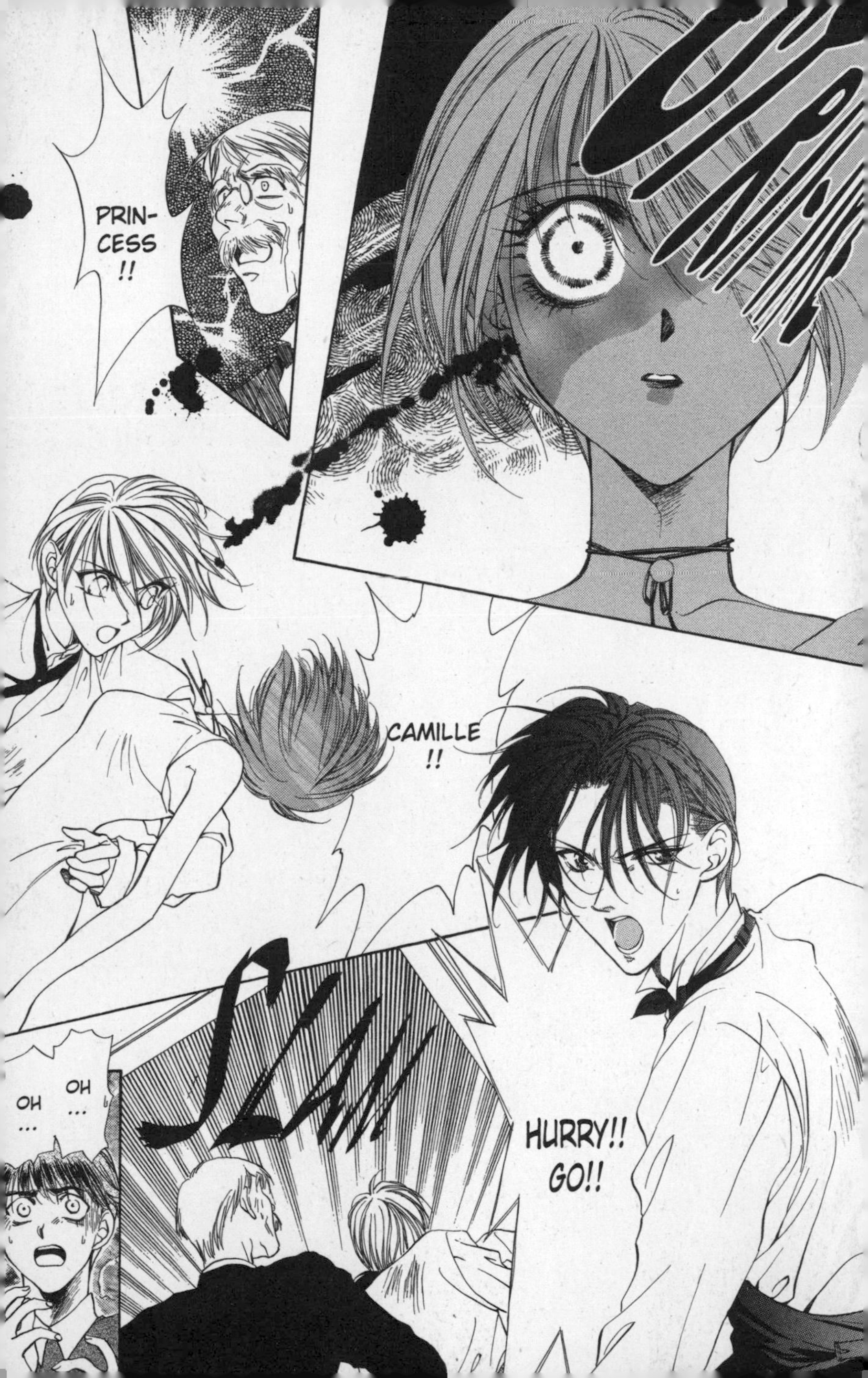
PRIN-
CESS
!!
CAMILLE
!!
HURRY!!
GO!!
SLAM
OH
...
OH
...

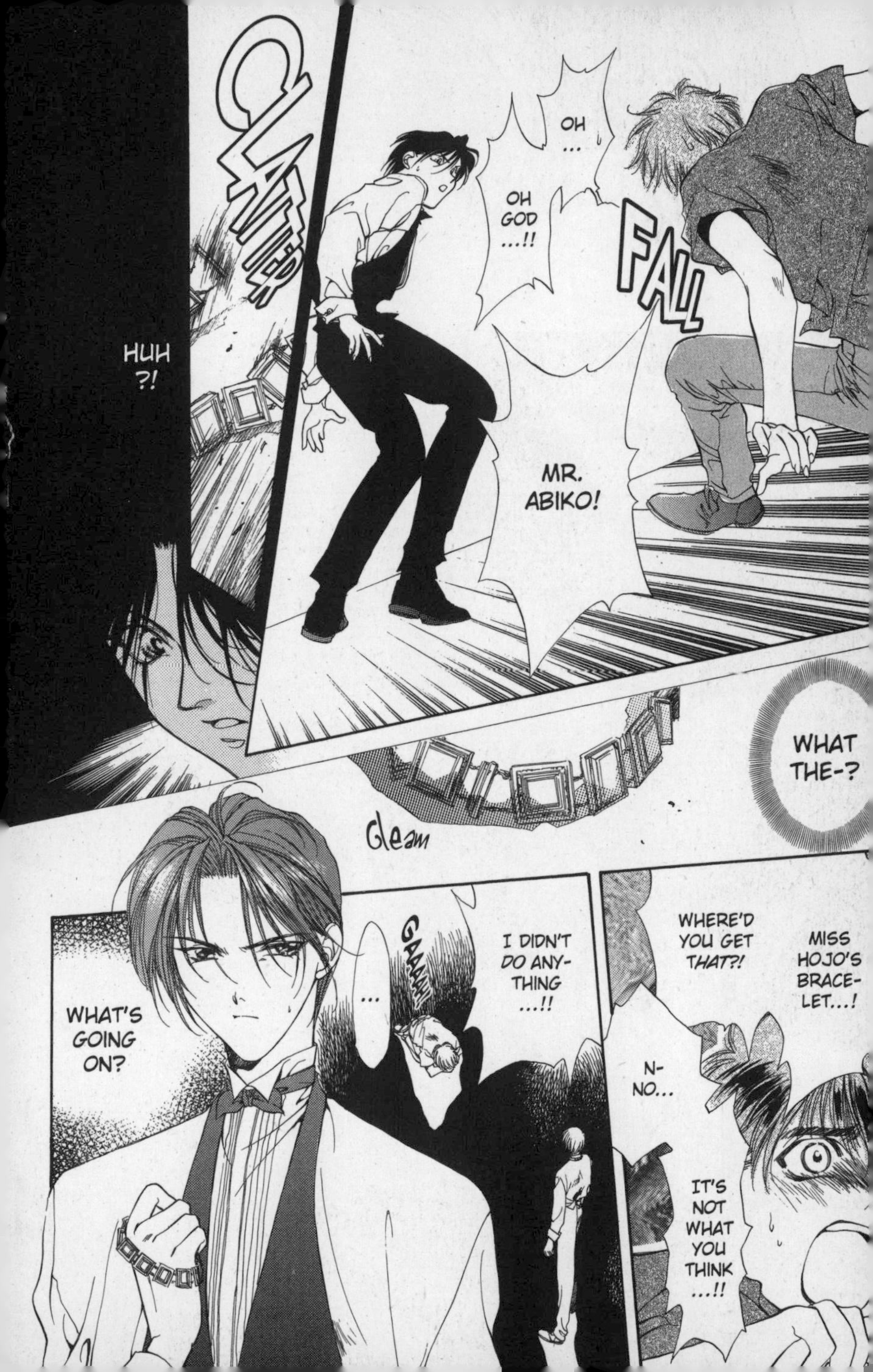
FALL
OH ...
OH GOD ...!!
MR. ABIKO!
CLATTER
HUH ?!
WHAT THE-?
Gleam
WHERE'D YOU GET THAT?!
MISS HOJO'S BRACE-LET...!
N-NO...
IT'S NOT WHAT YOU THINK ...!!
I DIDN'T DO ANY-THING ...!!
GAAAAH
...
WHAT'S GOING ON?

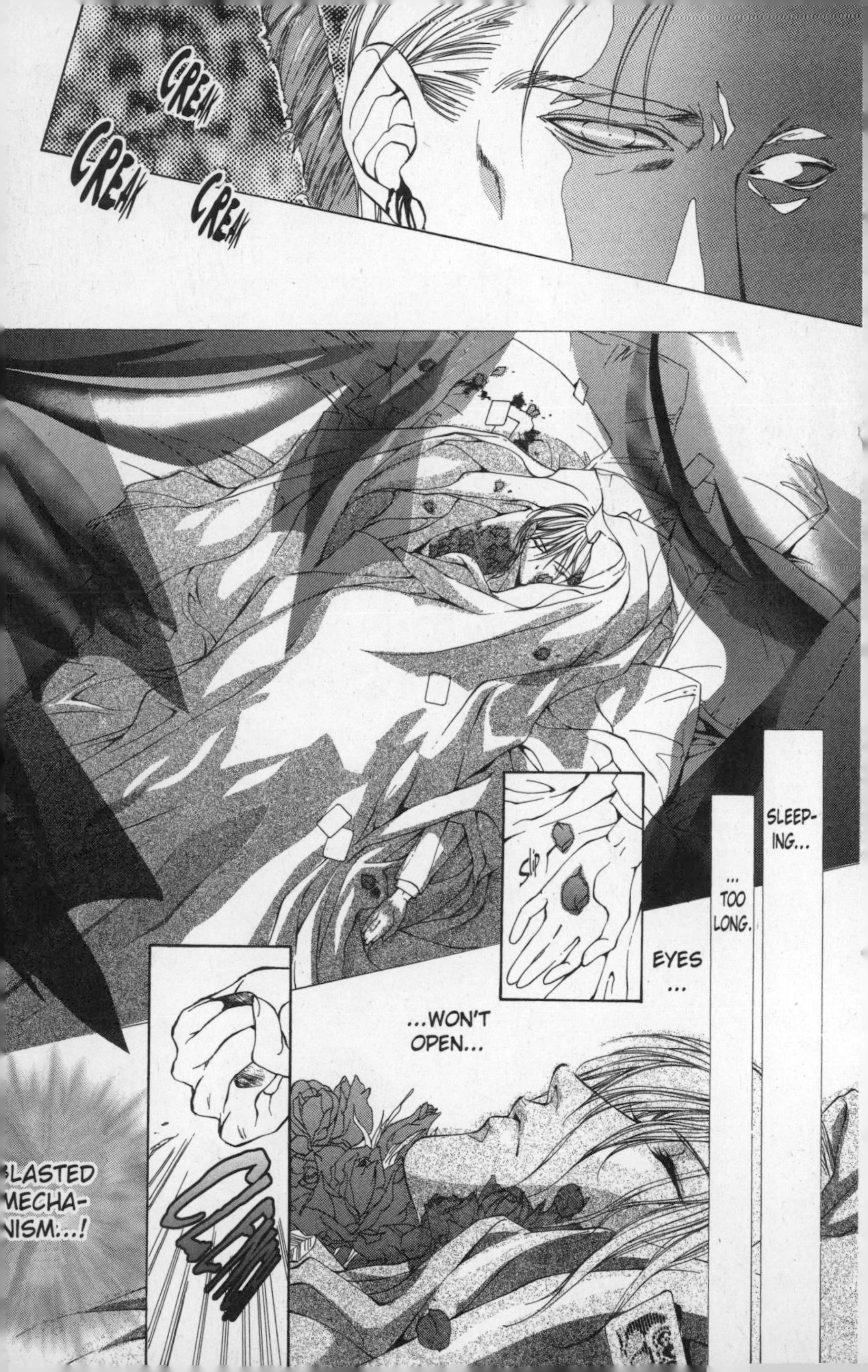
CREAK
CREAK
CREAK
SLEEPING...
...TOO LONG.
EYES...
SLIP
...WON'T OPEN...
BLASTED MECHANISM...!

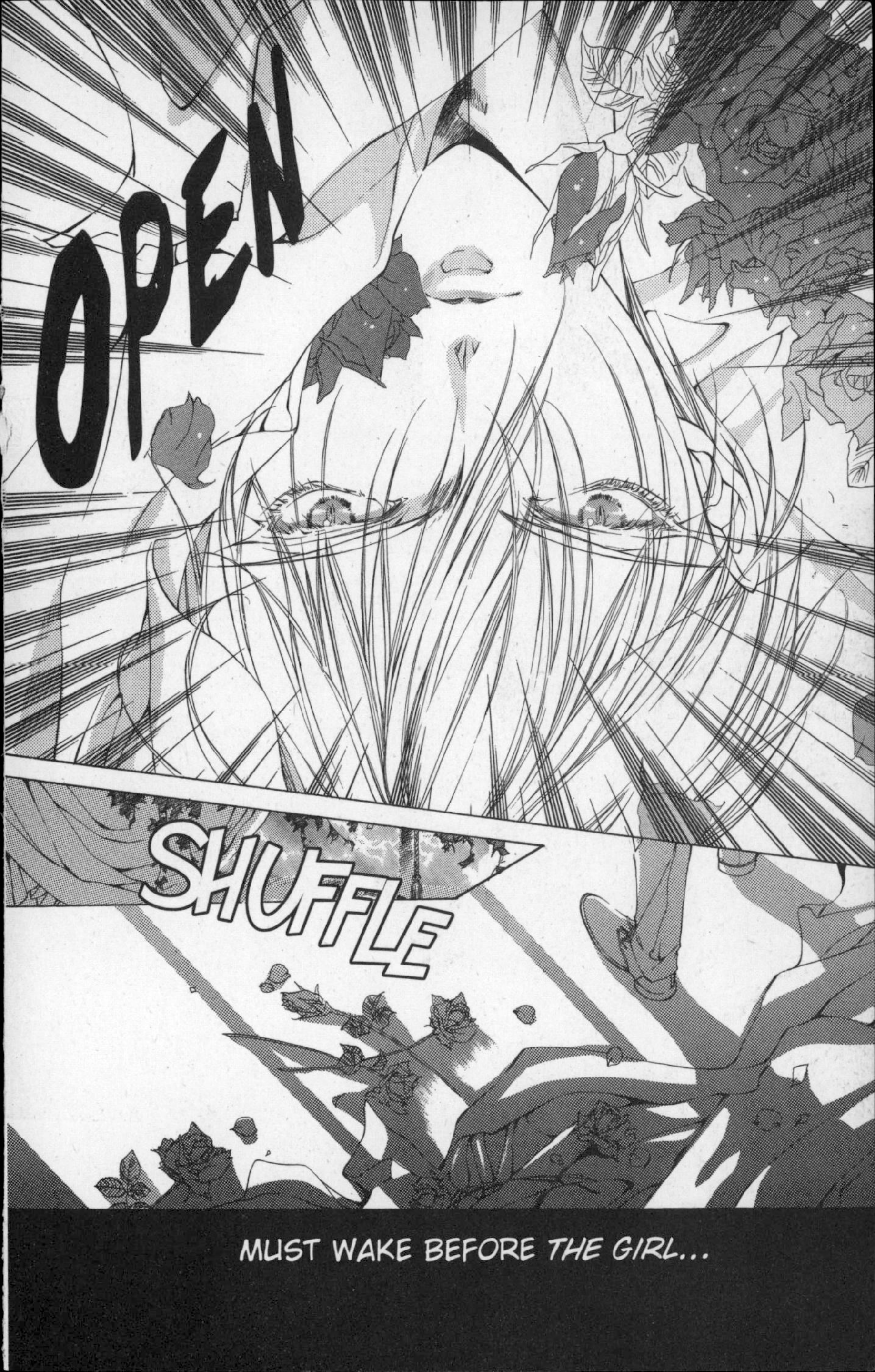
OPEN
SHUFFLE
MUST WAKE BEFORE THE GIRL...

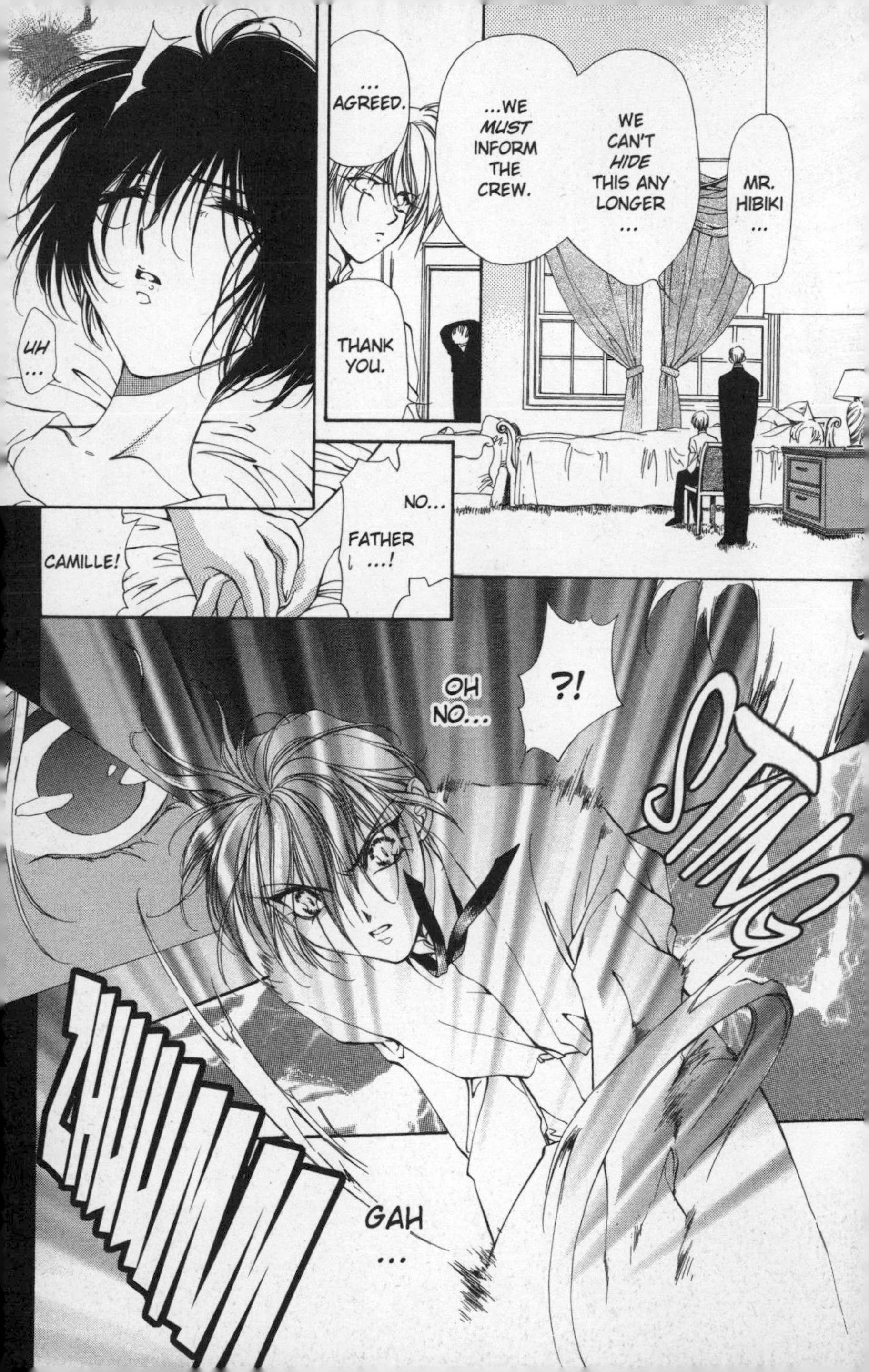
MR. HIBIKI ...
WE CAN'T *HIDE* THIS ANY LONGER ...
...WE *MUST* INFORM THE CREW.
... AGREED.
THANK YOU.
UH ...
NO... FATHER ...!
CAMILLE!
?!
OH NO...
STING
GAH ...

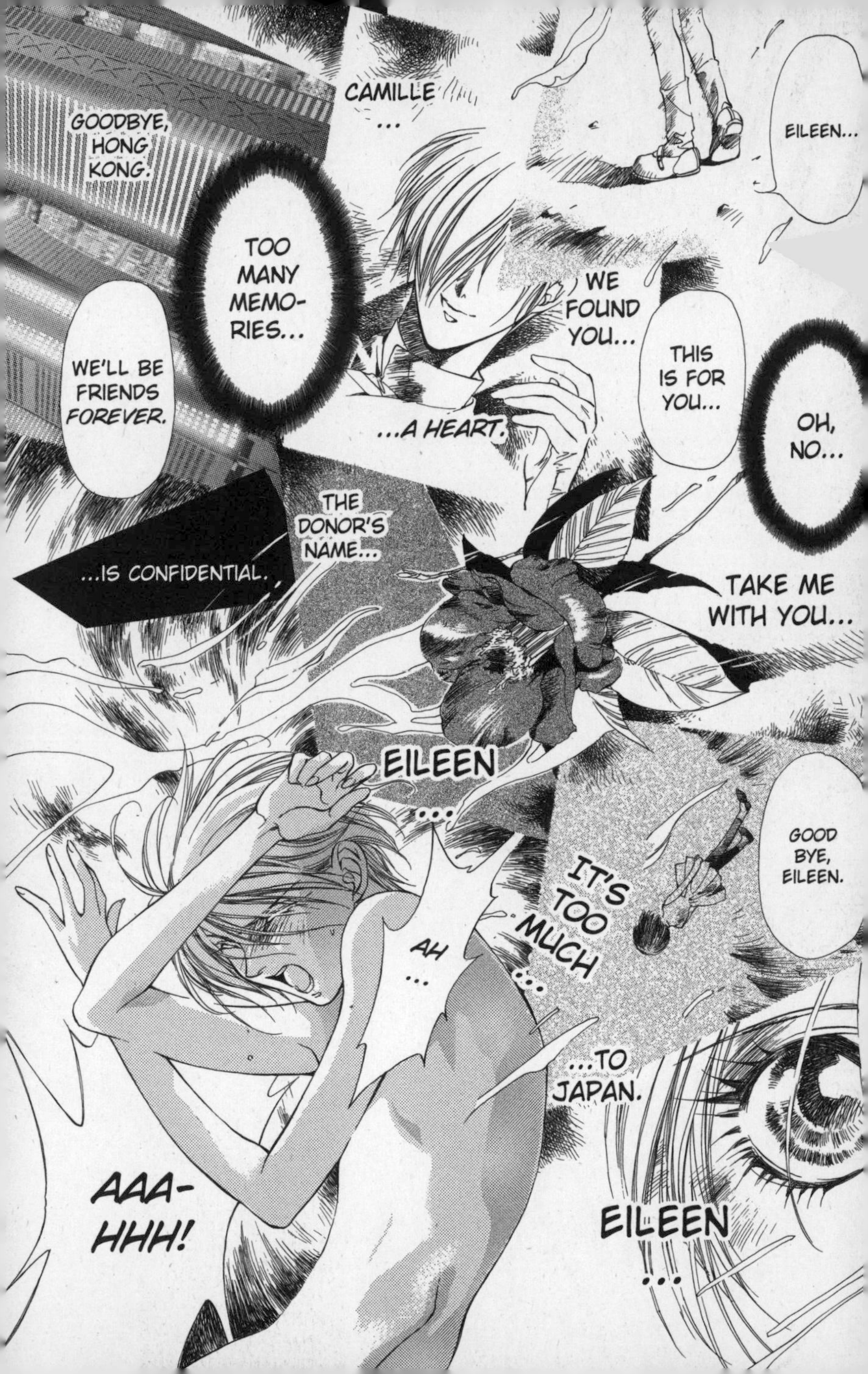
EILEEN...
CAMILLE...
GOODBYE, HONG KONG.
OH, NO...
THIS IS FOR YOU...
WE FOUND YOU...
TOO MANY MEMO-RIES...
...A HEART.
WE'LL BE FRIENDS FOREVER.
TAKE ME WITH YOU...
THE DONOR'S NAME...
...IS CONFIDENTIAL.
GOOD BYE, EILEEN.
IT'S TOO MUCH...
EILEEN...
AH...
...TO JAPAN.
EILEEN...
AAA-HHH!

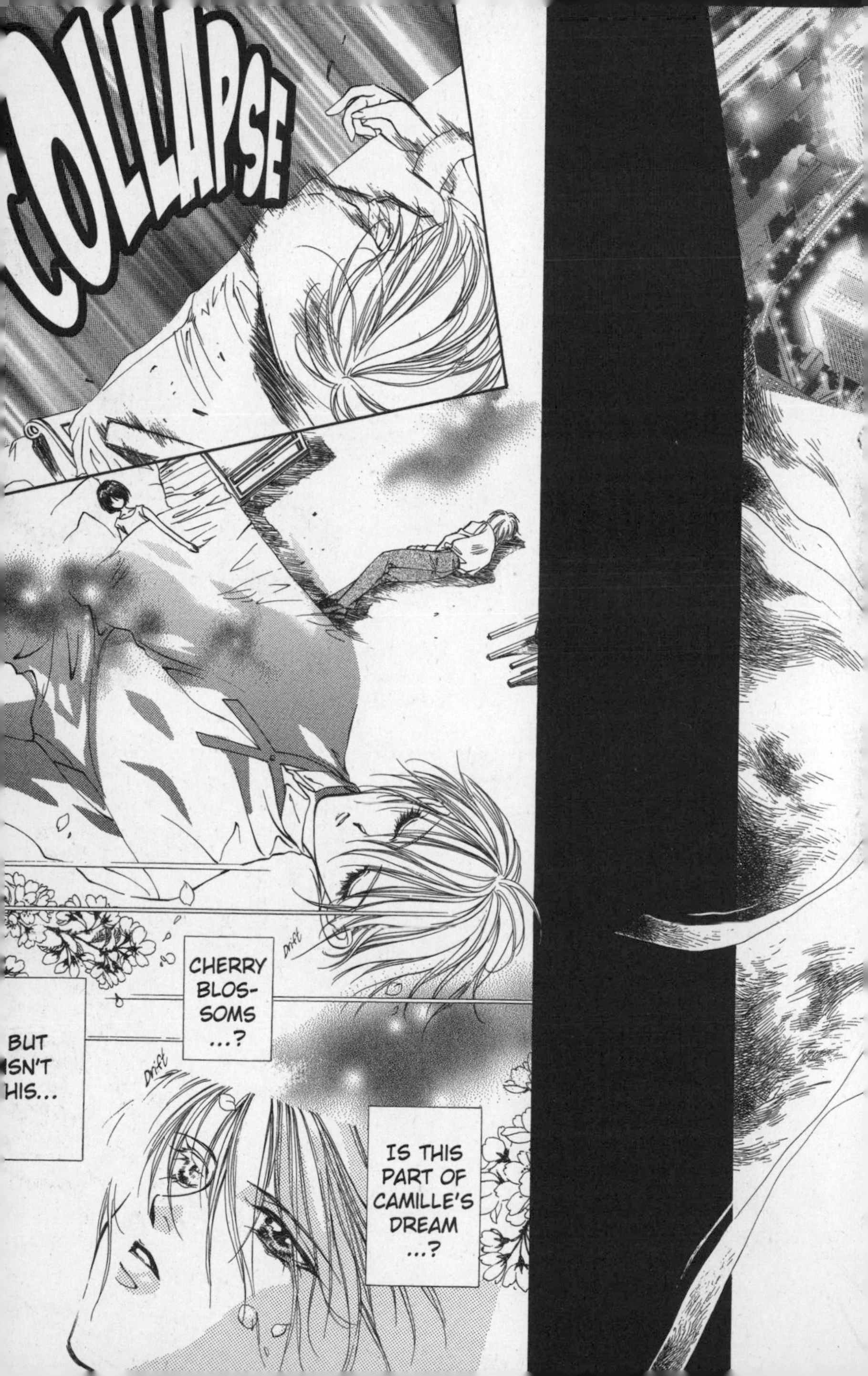
COLLAPSE
Drift
CHERRY BLOSSOMS ...?
IS THIS PART OF CAMILLE'S DREAM ...?
Drift
BUT ISN'T THIS...

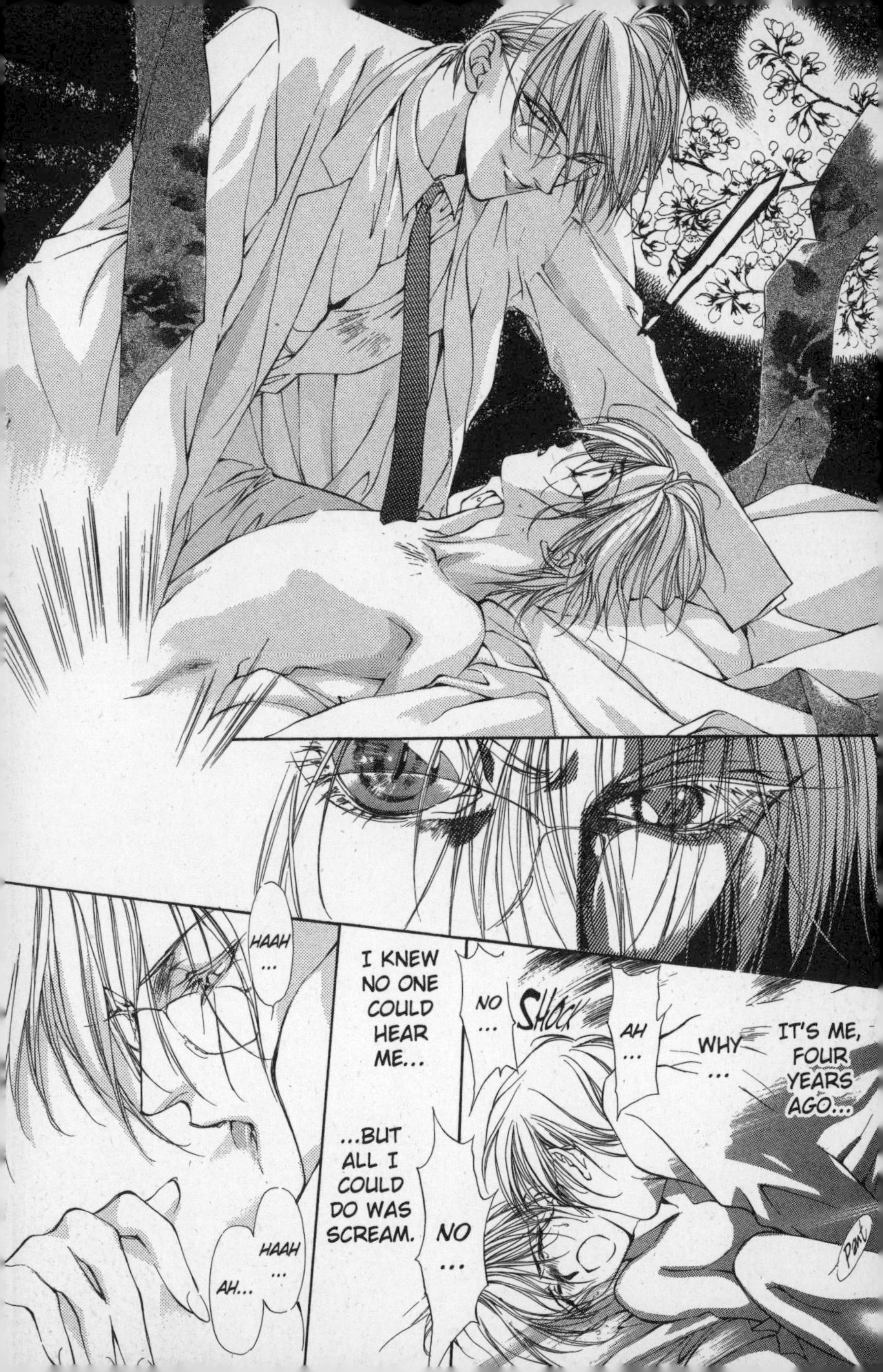
IT'S ME, FOUR YEARS AGO...
WHY...
AH...
SHOCK
NO...
Pant
I KNEW NO ONE COULD HEAR ME...
...BUT ALL I COULD DO WAS SCREAM.
NO...
HAAH...
HAAH...
AH...

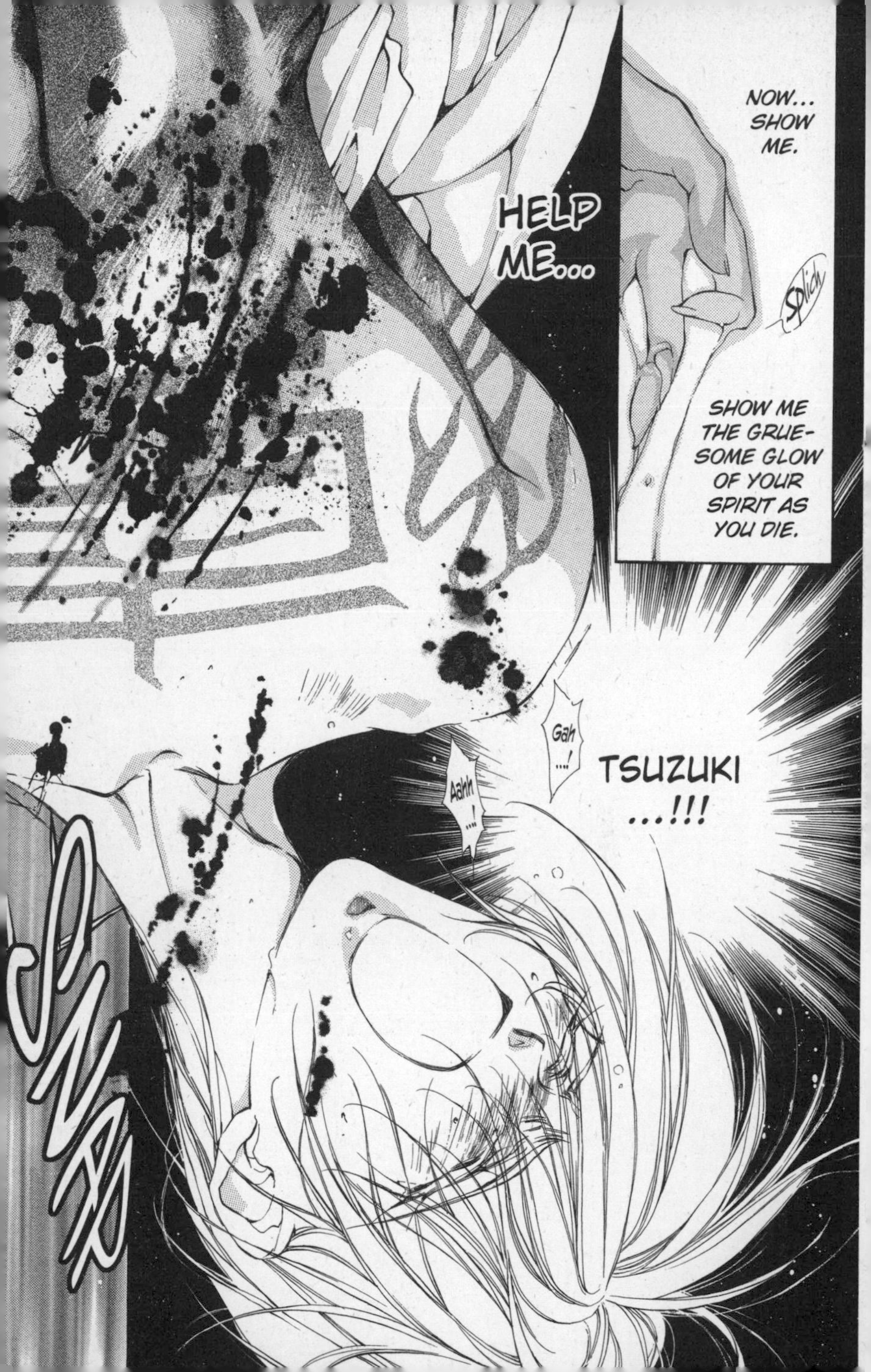
NOW... SHOW ME.
Splich
SHOW ME THE GRUE-SOME GLOW OF YOUR SPIRIT AS YOU DIE.
HELP ME...
TSUZUKI ...!!!
Gah ...!
Aahh ...!
SNAP

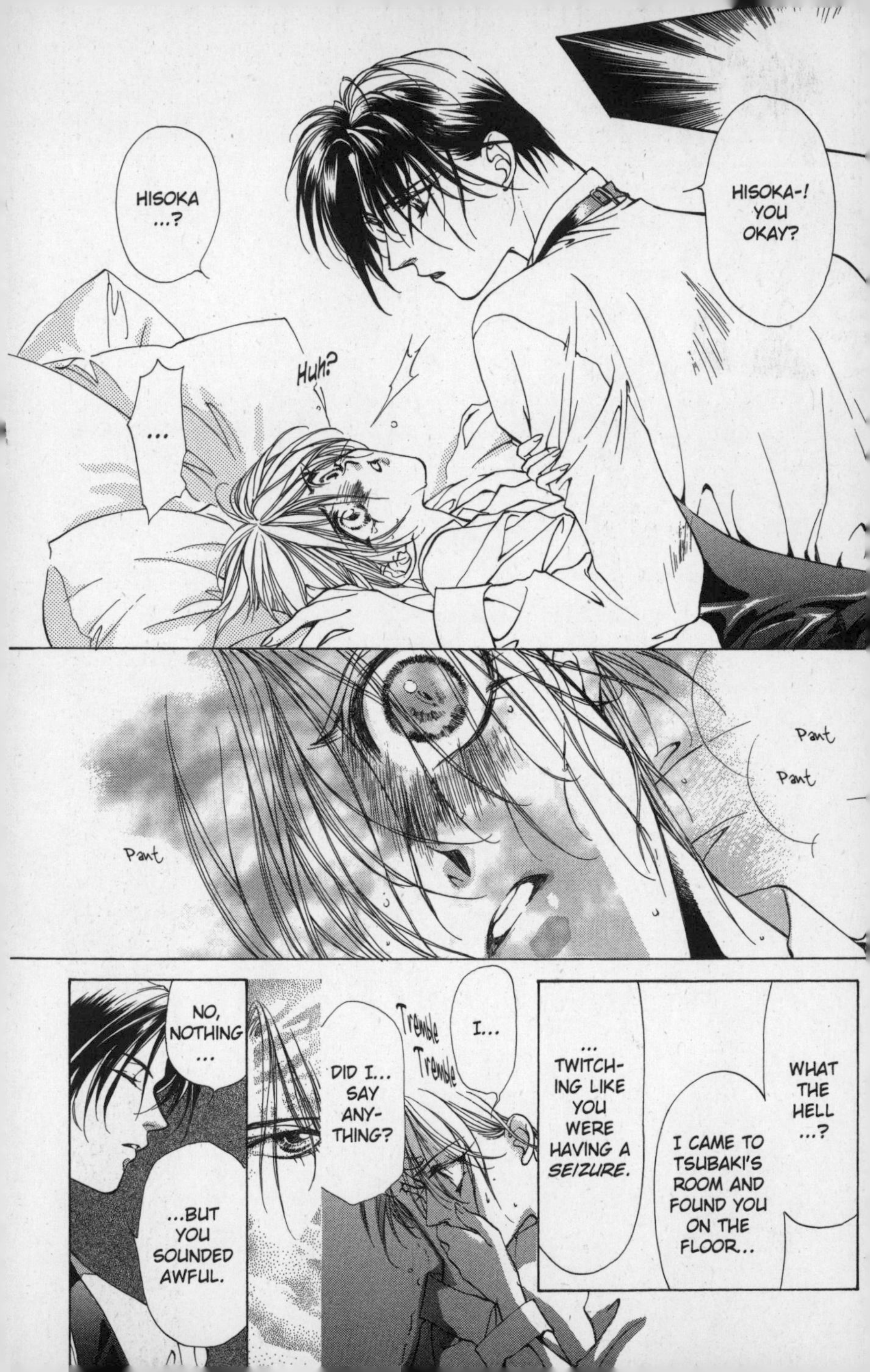
HISOKA-! YOU OKAY?
HISOKA ...?
Huh?
...
Pant
Pant
Pant
WHAT THE HELL ...?
I CAME TO TSUBAKI'S ROOM AND FOUND YOU ON THE FLOOR..
... TWITCHING LIKE YOU WERE HAVING A SEIZURE.
I...
Tremble Tremble
DID I... SAY ANY-THING?
NO, NOTHING ...
...BUT YOU SOUNDED AWFUL.

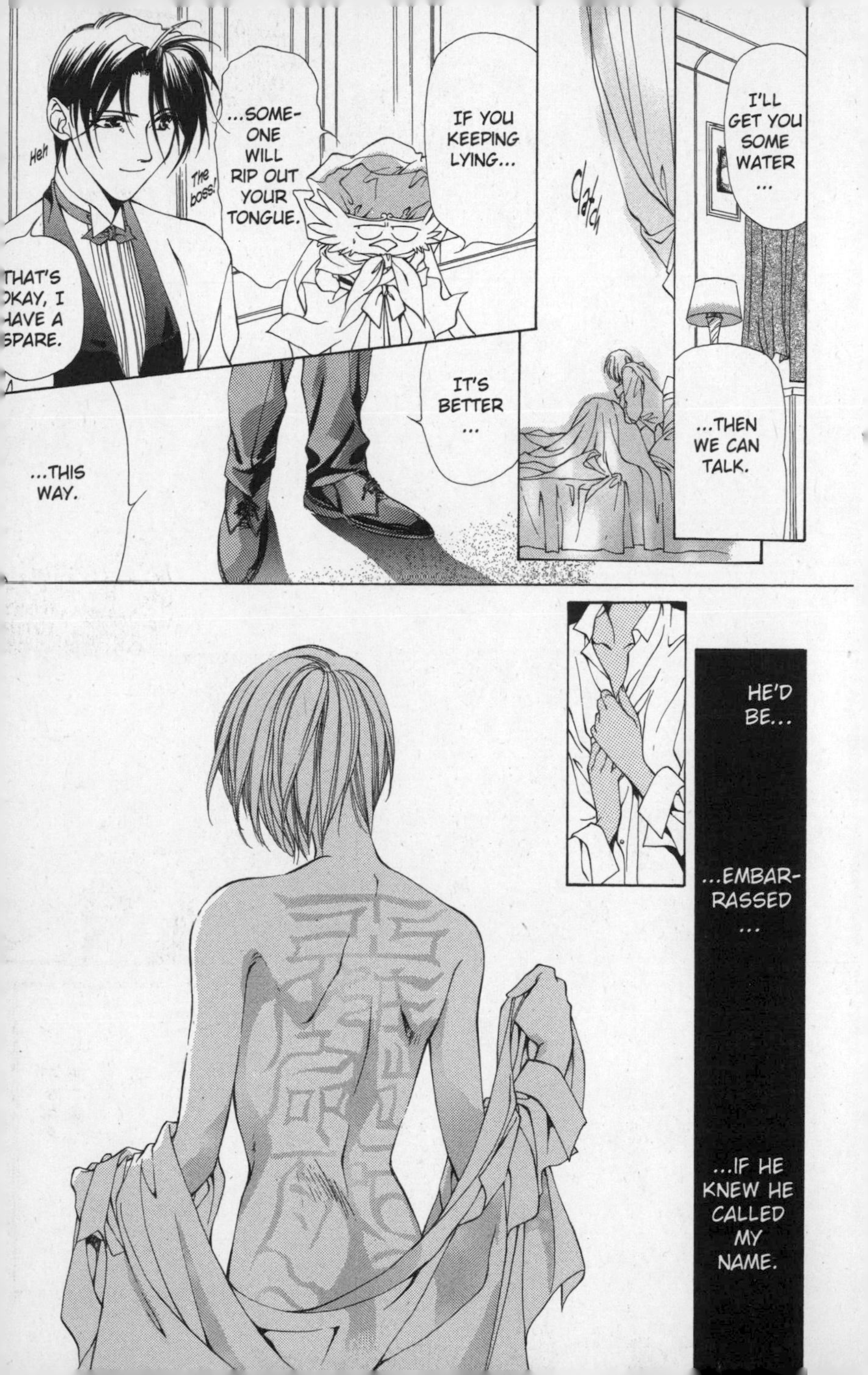
I'LL GET YOU SOME WATER ...
...THEN WE CAN TALK.
Clatch
IF YOU KEEPING LYING...
...SOME-ONE WILL RIP OUT YOUR TONGUE.
The boss!
Heh
THAT'S OKAY, I HAVE A SPARE.
IT'S BETTER ...
...THIS WAY.
HE'D BE...
...EMBAR-RASSED ...
...IF HE KNEW HE CALLED MY NAME.

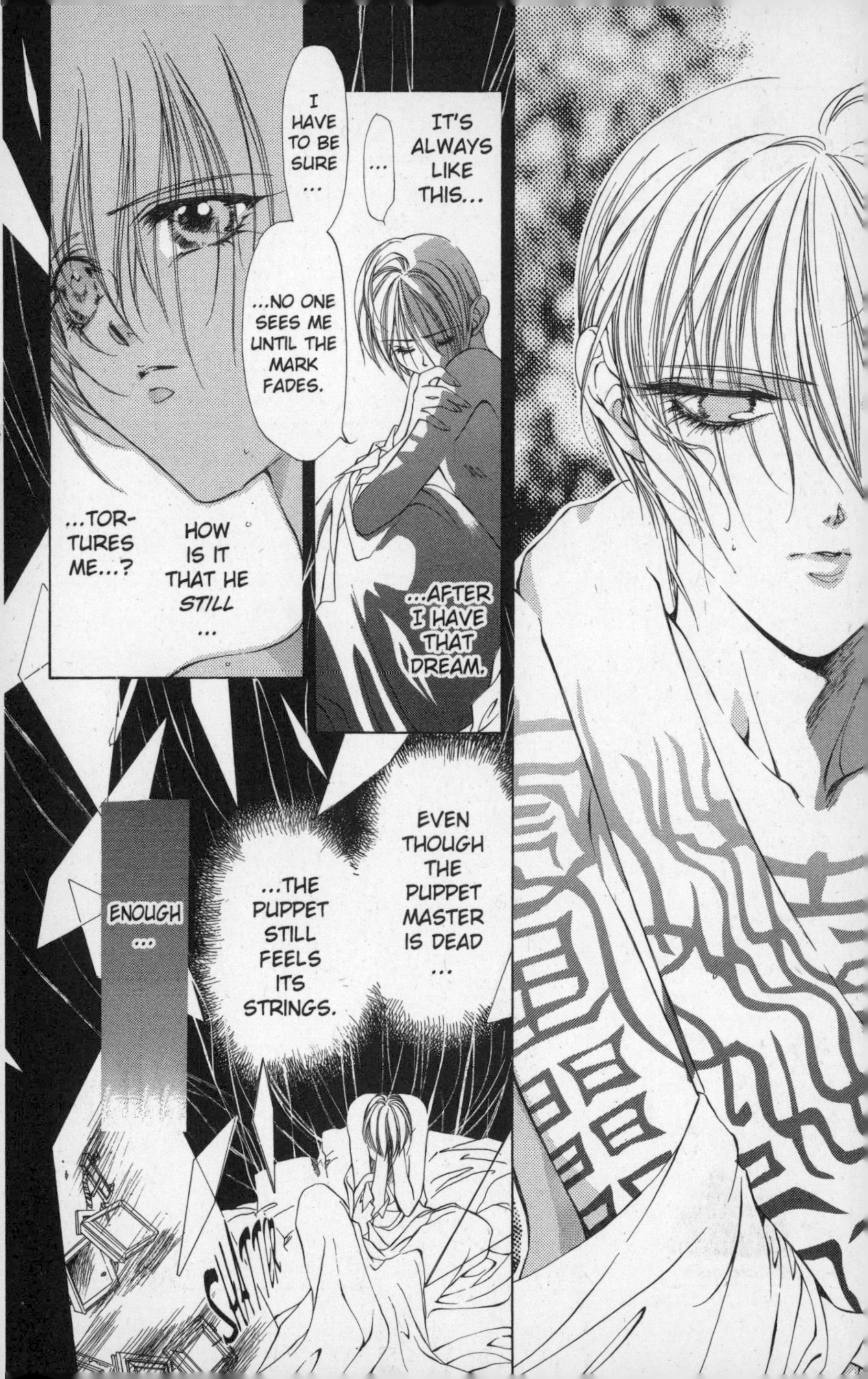

IT'S ALWAYS LIKE THIS...
...
I HAVE TO BE SURE ...
...NO ONE SEES ME UNTIL THE MARK FADES.
...AFTER I HAVE THAT DREAM.
HOW IS IT THAT HE STILL ...
...TOR-TURES ME...?
EVEN THOUGH THE PUPPET MASTER IS DEAD ...
...THE PUPPET STILL FEELS ITS STRINGS.
ENOUGH ...
SHATTER

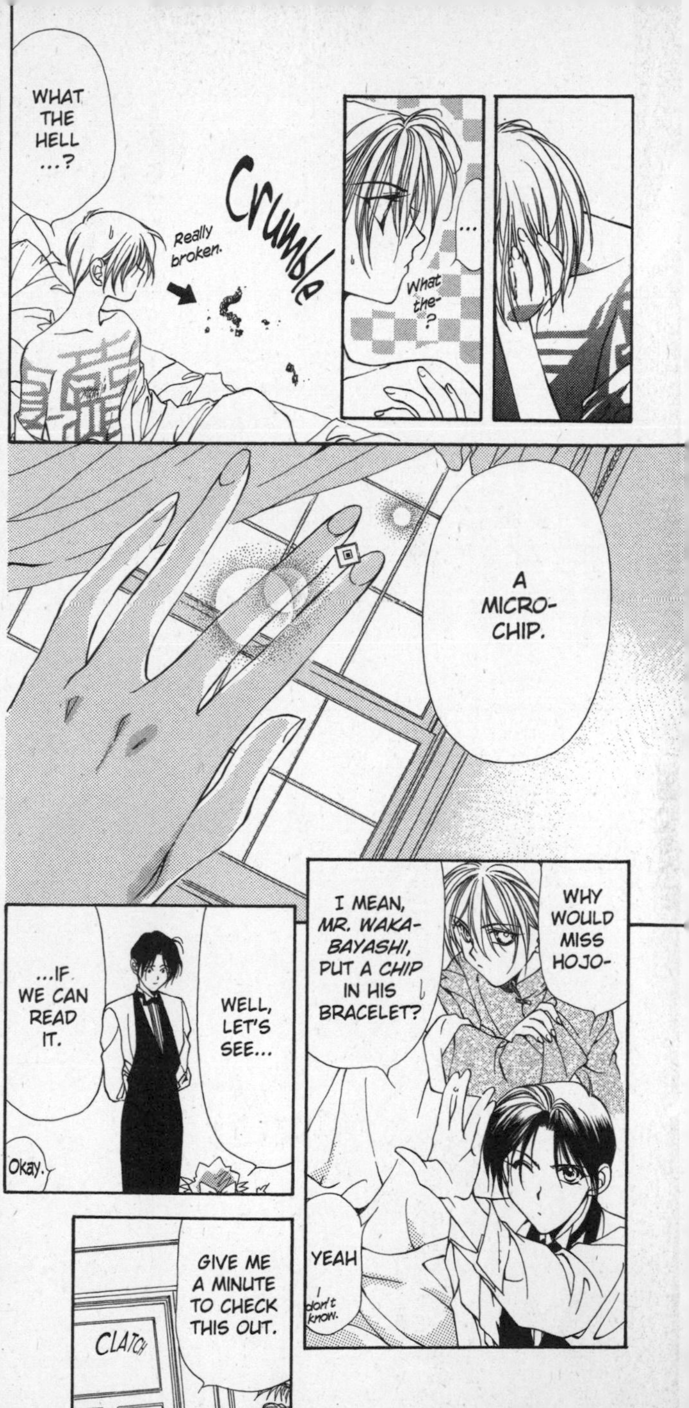
...
What the-?
WHAT THE HELL ...?
Crumble
Really broken.
A MICRO-CHIP.
WHY WOULD MISS HOJO-
I MEAN, MR. WAKA-BAYASHI, PUT A CHIP IN HIS BRACELET?
YEAH
I don't know.
WELL, LET'S SEE...
...IF WE CAN READ IT.
Okay.
GIVE ME A MINUTE TO CHECK THIS OUT.
CLATCH

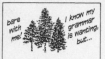

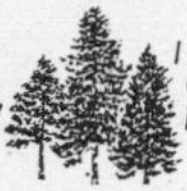
bare with me!
I know my grammar is wanting, but...

I'm sorry about the rape scene, Hisoka. I had to include it because it's part of the story. I know it was humiliating but hang in there, maybe you'll get Muraki in the end. (Not like that, you pervs!)

I've been getting a lot of fan letters lately – which is great – but I've got a couple of pet peeves I want to vent about, okay?

Pet Peeve #1) Writing in pencil. What's with the pencil?! It's hard to read. What are you afraid of? Commit to your ideas, scratch out if you have to, but write in black ink, please. Just humor me.

Pet Peeve #2) Writing to me about other writers. Are you trying to kill me here? I have an ego and you're bruising it! If you want to talk about someone else's works, write to them. Sheesh. Also, don't write to me on fancy paper.

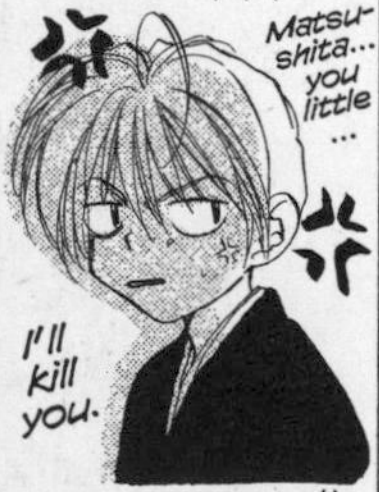
Matsu-shita... you little ...
I'll kill you.

Hisoka's pissed.

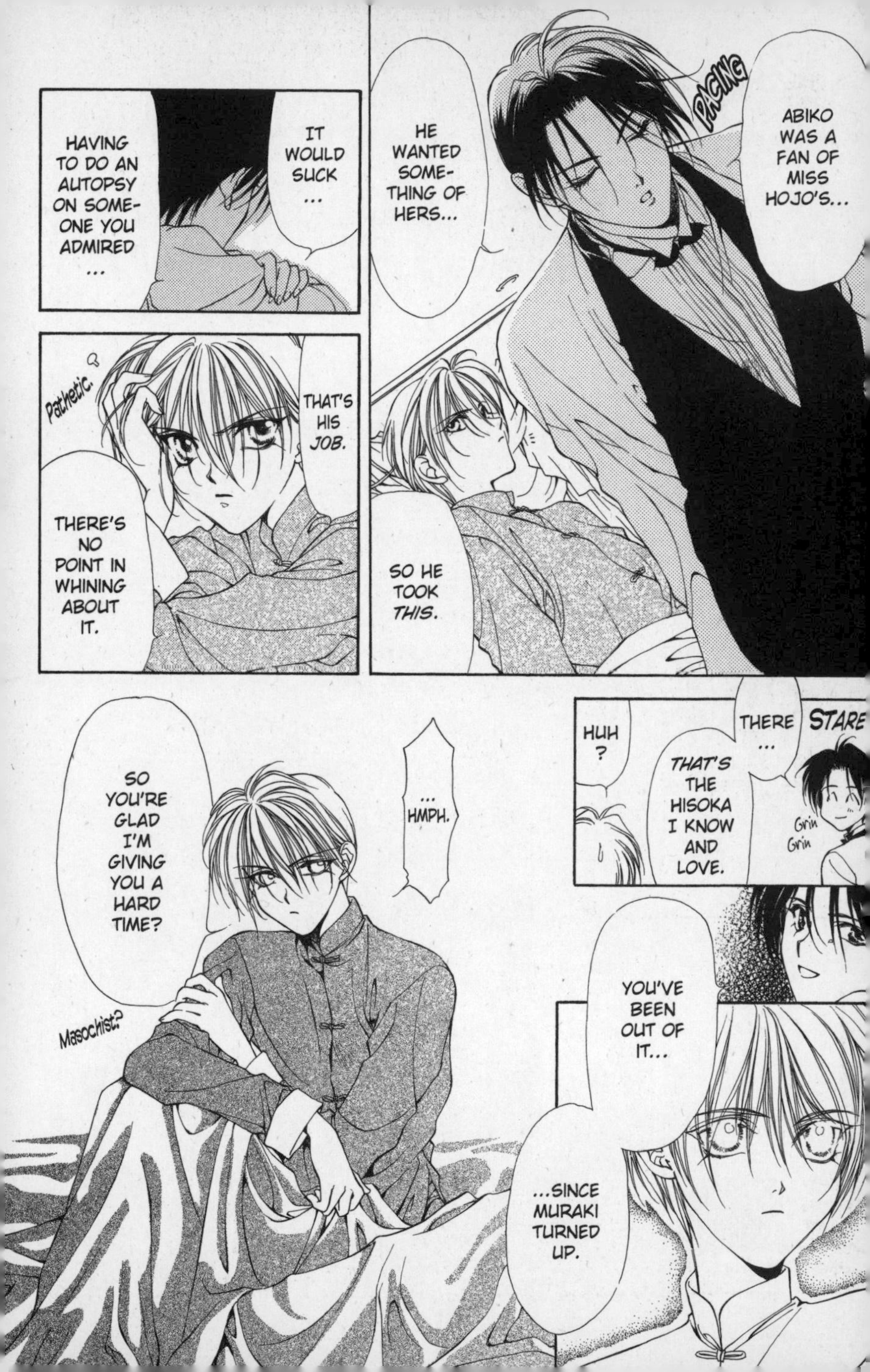
PACING
ABIKO WAS A FAN OF MISS HOJO'S...
HE WANTED SOME-THING OF HERS...
SO HE TOOK *THIS.*
IT WOULD SUCK ...
HAVING TO DO AN AUTOPSY ON SOME-ONE YOU ADMIRED ...
THAT'S HIS *JOB.*
Pathetic.
THERE'S NO POINT IN WHINING ABOUT IT.
STARE
THERE ...
THAT'S THE HISOKA I KNOW AND LOVE.
Grin Grin
HUH ?
YOU'VE BEEN OUT OF IT...
...SINCE MURAKI TURNED UP.
... HMPH.
SO YOU'RE GLAD I'M GIVING YOU A HARD TIME?
Masochist?

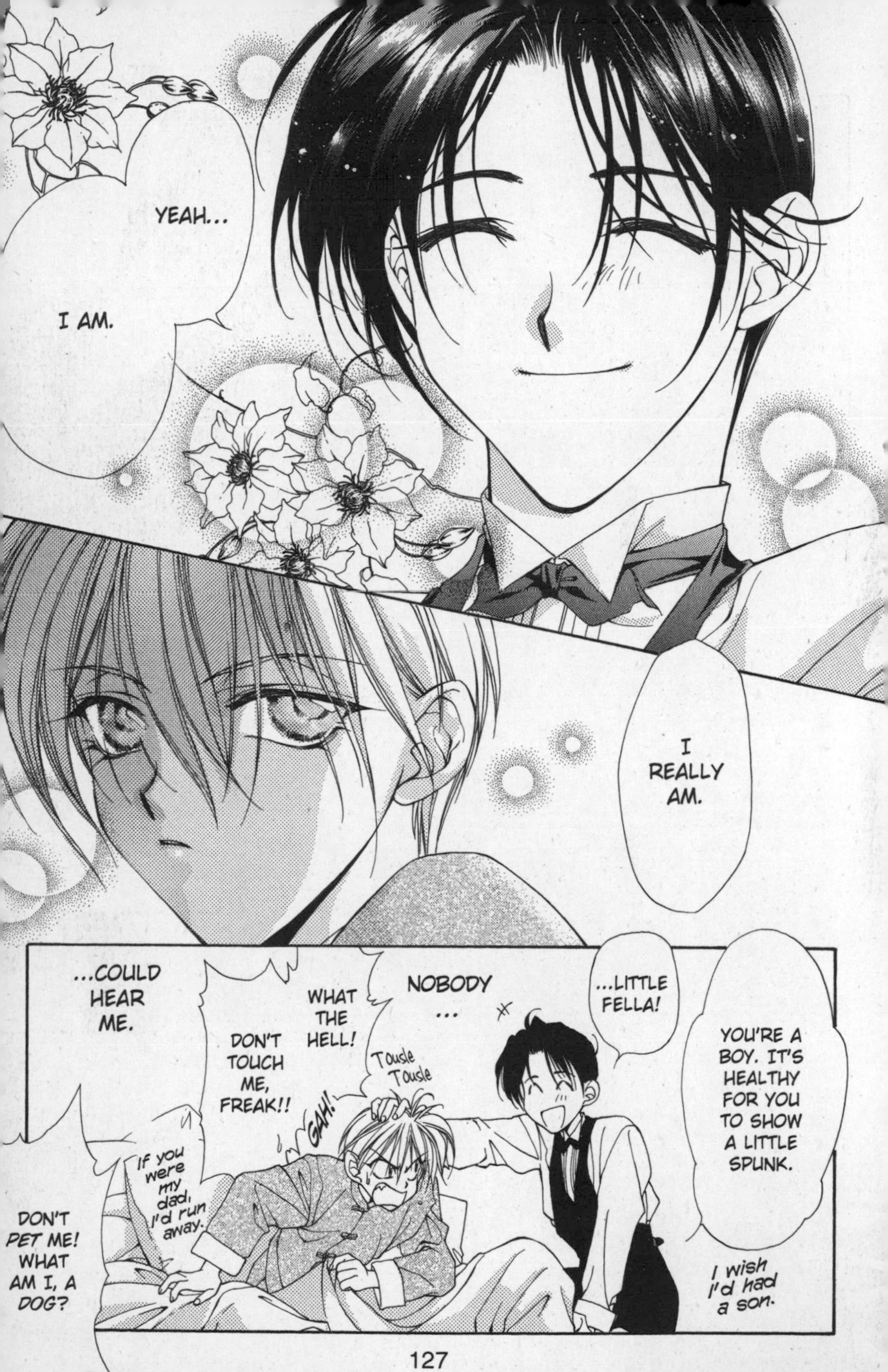
YEAH...
I AM.
I REALLY AM.
YOU'RE A BOY. IT'S HEALTHY FOR YOU TO SHOW A LITTLE SPUNK.
...LITTLE FELLA!
I wish I'd had a son.
NOBODY ...
...COULD HEAR ME.
WHAT THE HELL!
Tousle Tousle
DON'T TOUCH ME, FREAK!!
GAH!
If you were my dad, I'd run away.
DON'T PET ME! WHAT AM I, A DOG?

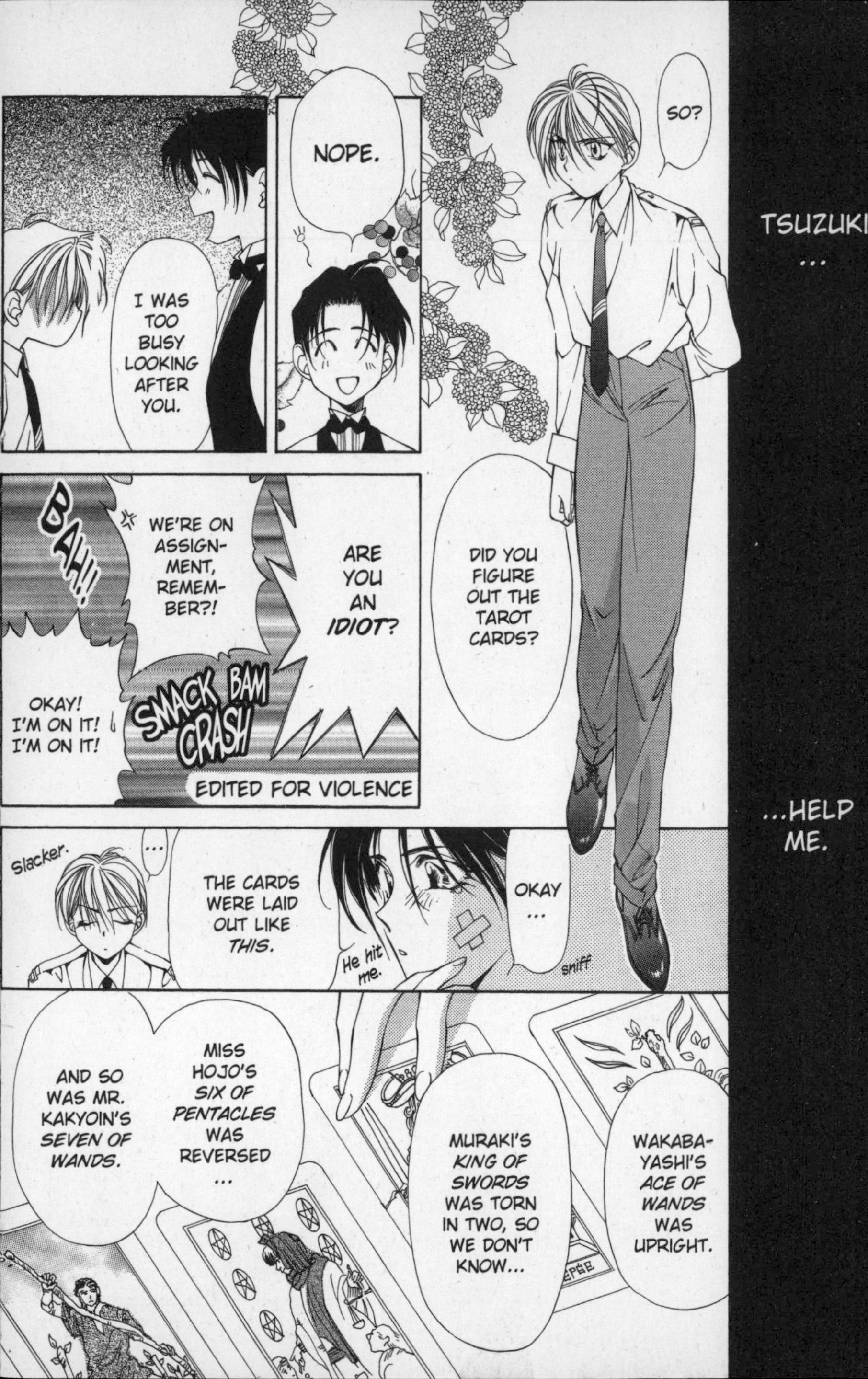
TSUZUKI ...
...HELP ME.
SO?
NOPE.
I WAS TOO BUSY LOOKING AFTER YOU.
DID YOU FIGURE OUT THE TAROT CARDS?
ARE YOU AN *IDIOT*?
WE'RE ON ASSIGN-MENT, REMEM-BER?!
BAH!!
SMACK BAM CRASH
OKAY! I'M ON IT! I'M ON IT!
EDITED FOR VIOLENCE
OKAY ...
sniff
He hit me.
THE CARDS WERE LAID OUT LIKE *THIS*.
...
Slacker.
WAKABA-YASHI'S *ACE OF WANDS* WAS UPRIGHT.
MURAKI'S *KING OF SWORDS* WAS TORN IN TWO, SO WE DON'T KNOW...
MISS HOJO'S *SIX OF PENTACLES* WAS REVERSED ...
AND SO WAS MR. KAKYOIN'S *SEVEN OF WANDS*.

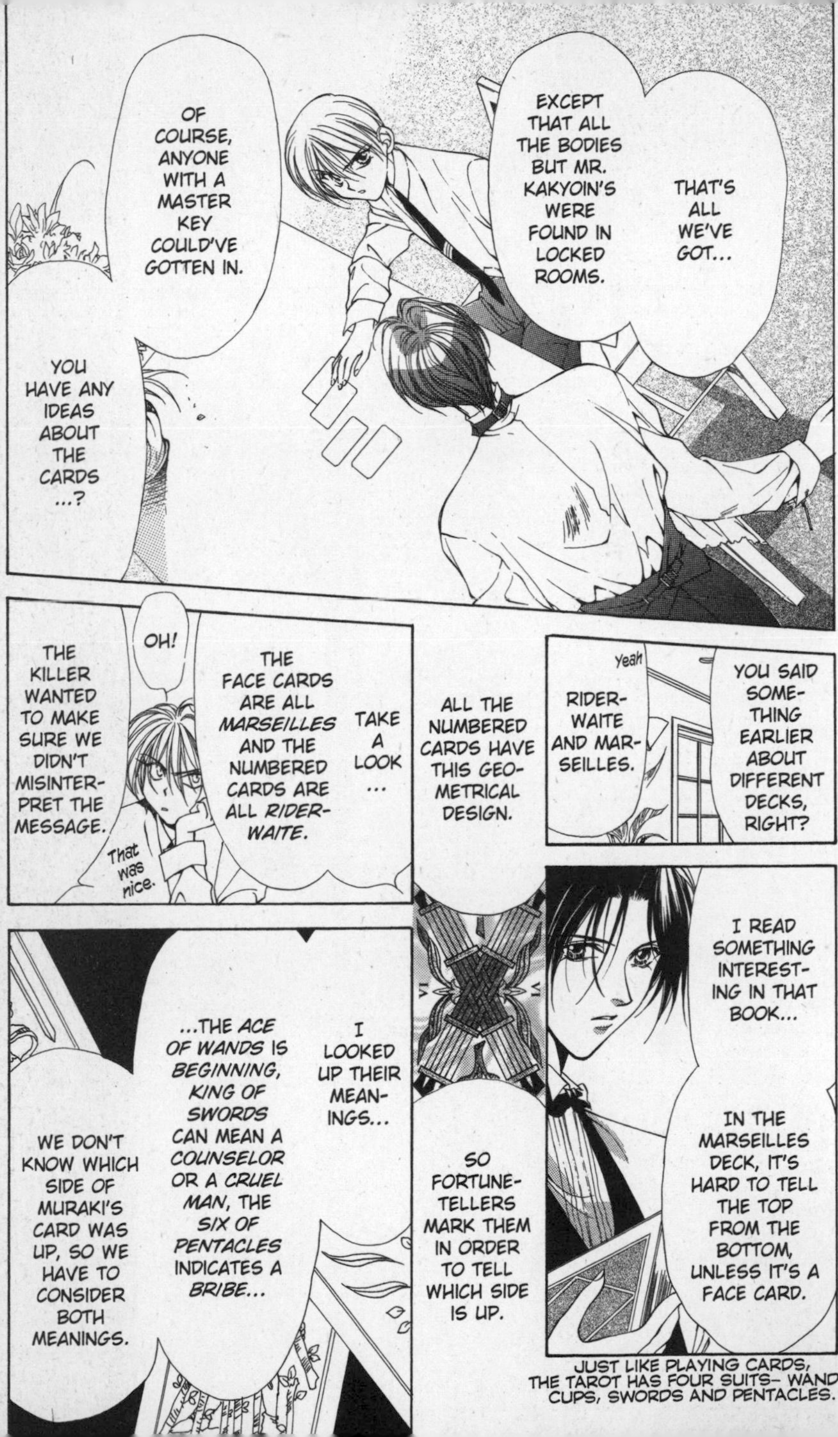
EXCEPT THAT ALL THE BODIES BUT MR. KAKYOIN'S WERE FOUND IN LOCKED ROOMS.
THAT'S ALL WE'VE GOT...
OF COURSE, ANYONE WITH A MASTER KEY COULD'VE GOTTEN IN.
YOU HAVE ANY IDEAS ABOUT THE CARDS ...?
YOU SAID SOMETHING EARLIER ABOUT DIFFERENT DECKS, RIGHT?
Yeah
RIDER-WAITE AND MARSEILLES.
ALL THE NUMBERED CARDS HAVE THIS GEOMETRICAL DESIGN.
TAKE A LOOK ...
THE FACE CARDS ARE ALL *MARSEILLES* AND THE NUMBERED CARDS ARE ALL *RIDER-WAITE*.
OH!
THE KILLER WANTED TO MAKE SURE WE DIDN'T MISINTERPRET THE MESSAGE.
That was nice.
I READ SOMETHING INTERESTING IN THAT BOOK...
IN THE MARSEILLES DECK, IT'S HARD TO TELL THE TOP FROM THE BOTTOM, UNLESS IT'S A FACE CARD.
SO FORTUNE-TELLERS MARK THEM IN ORDER TO TELL WHICH SIDE IS UP.
I LOOKED UP THEIR MEANINGS...
...THE *ACE OF WANDS* IS *BEGINNING*, *KING OF SWORDS* CAN MEAN A *COUNSELOR* OR A *CRUEL MAN*, THE *SIX OF PENTACLES* INDICATES A *BRIBE*...
WE DON'T KNOW WHICH SIDE OF MURAKI'S CARD WAS UP, SO WE HAVE TO CONSIDER BOTH MEANINGS.

JUST LIKE PLAYING CARDS, THE TAROT HAS FOUR SUITS– WANDS, CUPS, SWORDS AND PENTACLES.

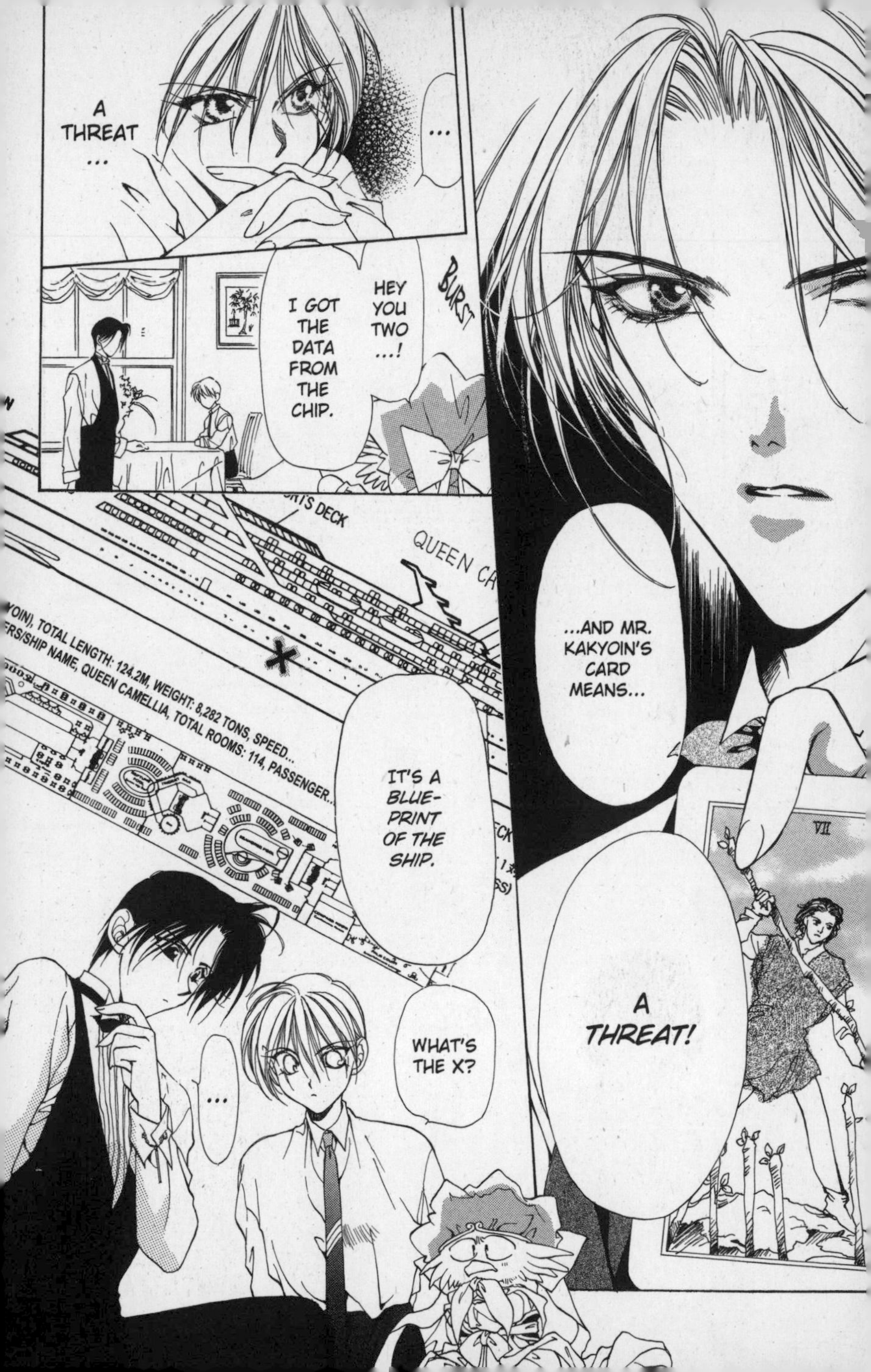
...AND MR. KAKYOIN'S CARD MEANS...
A THREAT!
VII
A THREAT ...
...
BURST
HEY YOU TWO ...!
I GOT THE DATA FROM THE CHIP.
QUEEN CA
YOIN), TOTAL LENGTH: 124.2M, WEIGHT: 8,282 TONS, SPEED...
ERS/SHIP NAME, QUEEN CAMELLIA, TOTAL ROOMS: 114, PASSENGER...
IT'S A BLUE-PRINT OF THE SHIP.
WHAT'S THE X?
...

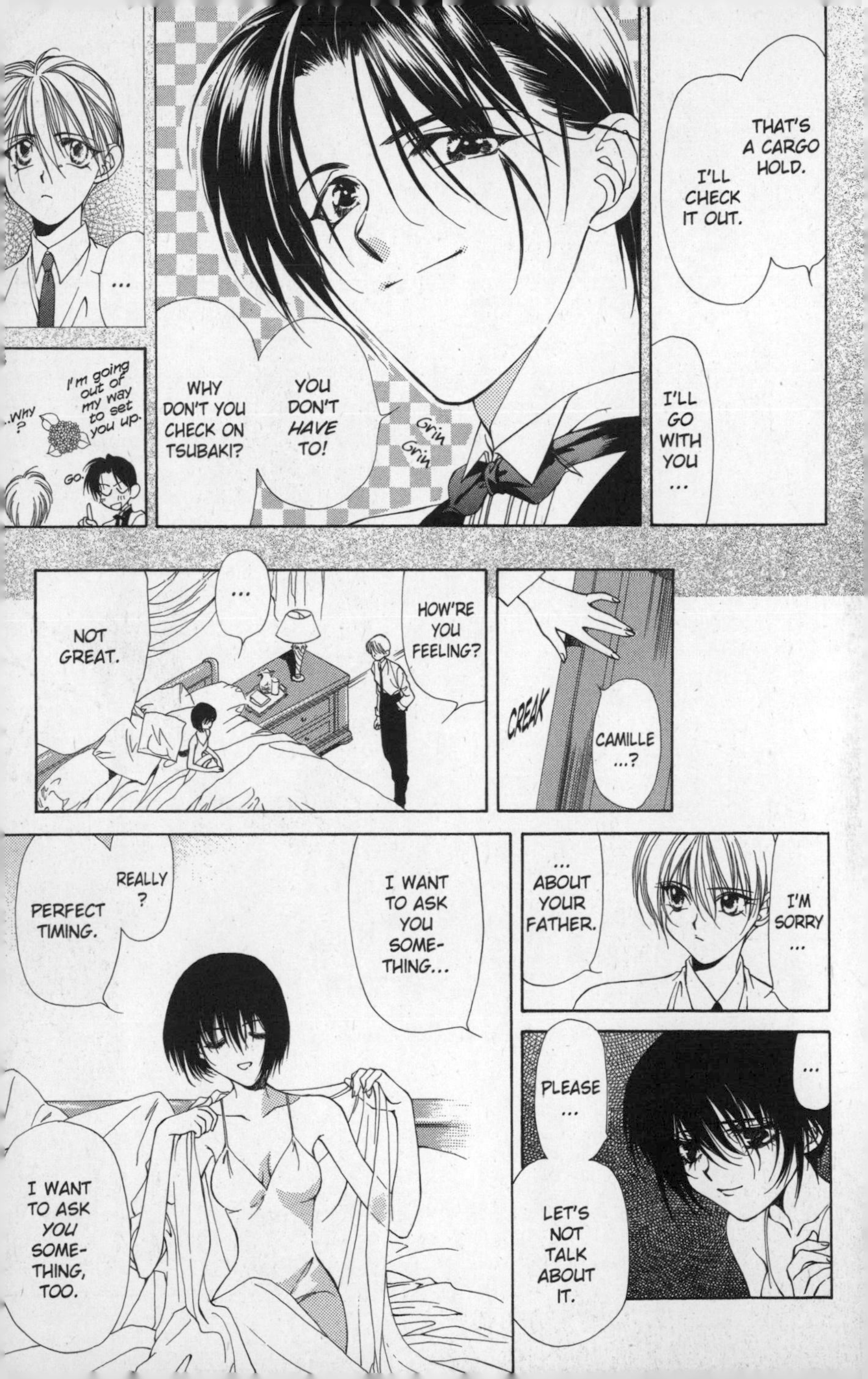
THAT'S A CARGO HOLD.
I'LL CHECK IT OUT.
I'LL GO WITH YOU ...
YOU DON'T *HAVE* TO!
WHY DON'T YOU CHECK ON TSUBAKI?
Grin Grin
...
I'm going out of my way to set you up.
...Why?
GO.
CREAK
CAMILLE ...?
HOW'RE YOU FEELING?
...
NOT GREAT.
I'M SORRY ...
... ABOUT YOUR FATHER.
...
PLEASE ...
LET'S NOT TALK ABOUT IT.
I WANT TO ASK YOU SOMETHING...
REALLY?
PERFECT TIMING.
I WANT TO ASK *YOU* SOMETHING, TOO.

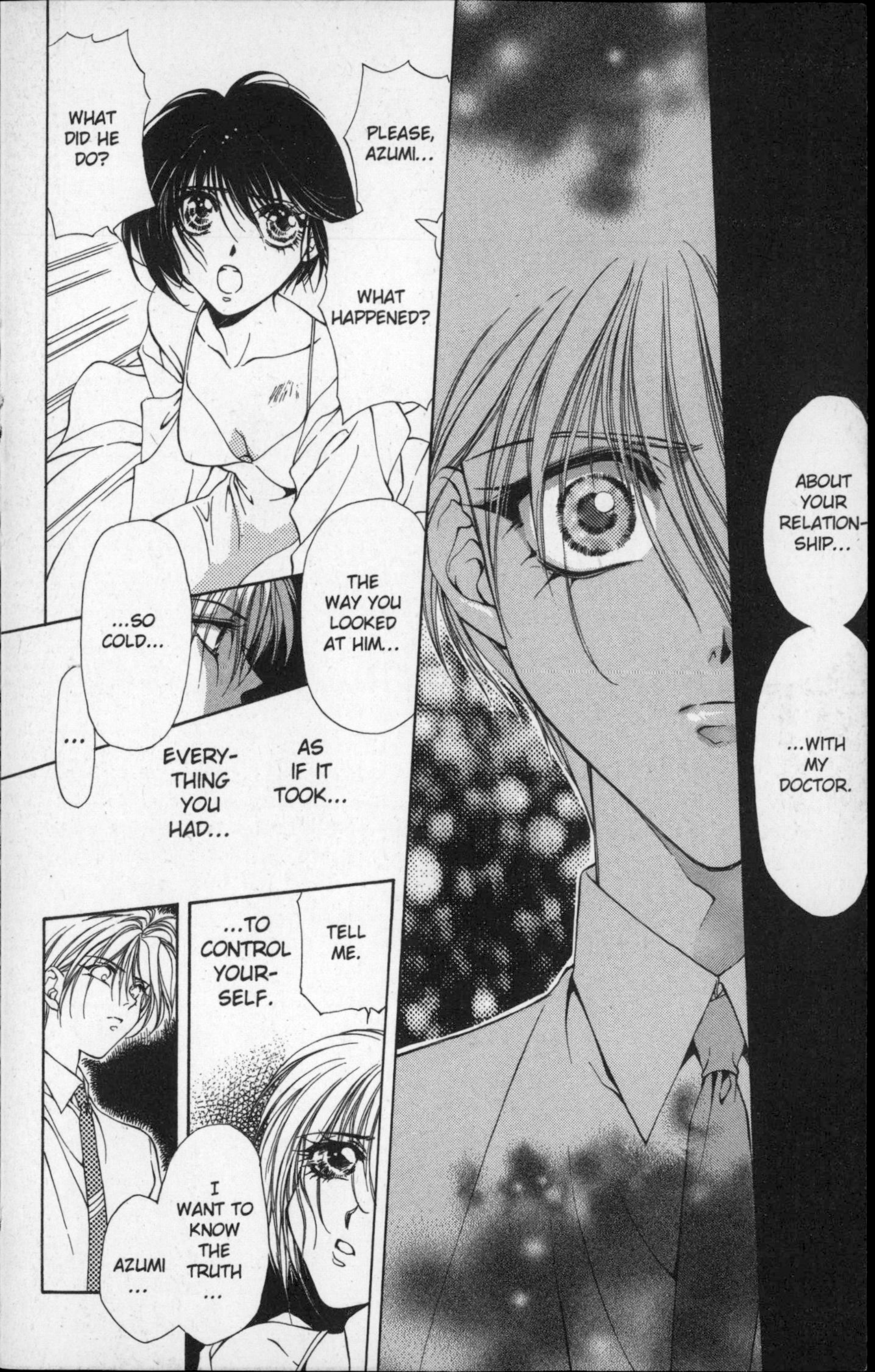

ABOUT YOUR RELATION-SHIP...
...WITH MY DOCTOR.
PLEASE, AZUMI...
WHAT DID HE DO?
WHAT HAPPENED?
THE WAY YOU LOOKED AT HIM...
...SO COLD...
...
AS IF IT TOOK...
EVERY-THING YOU HAD...
...TO CONTROL YOUR-SELF.
TELL ME.
I WANT TO KNOW THE TRUTH...
AZUMI...

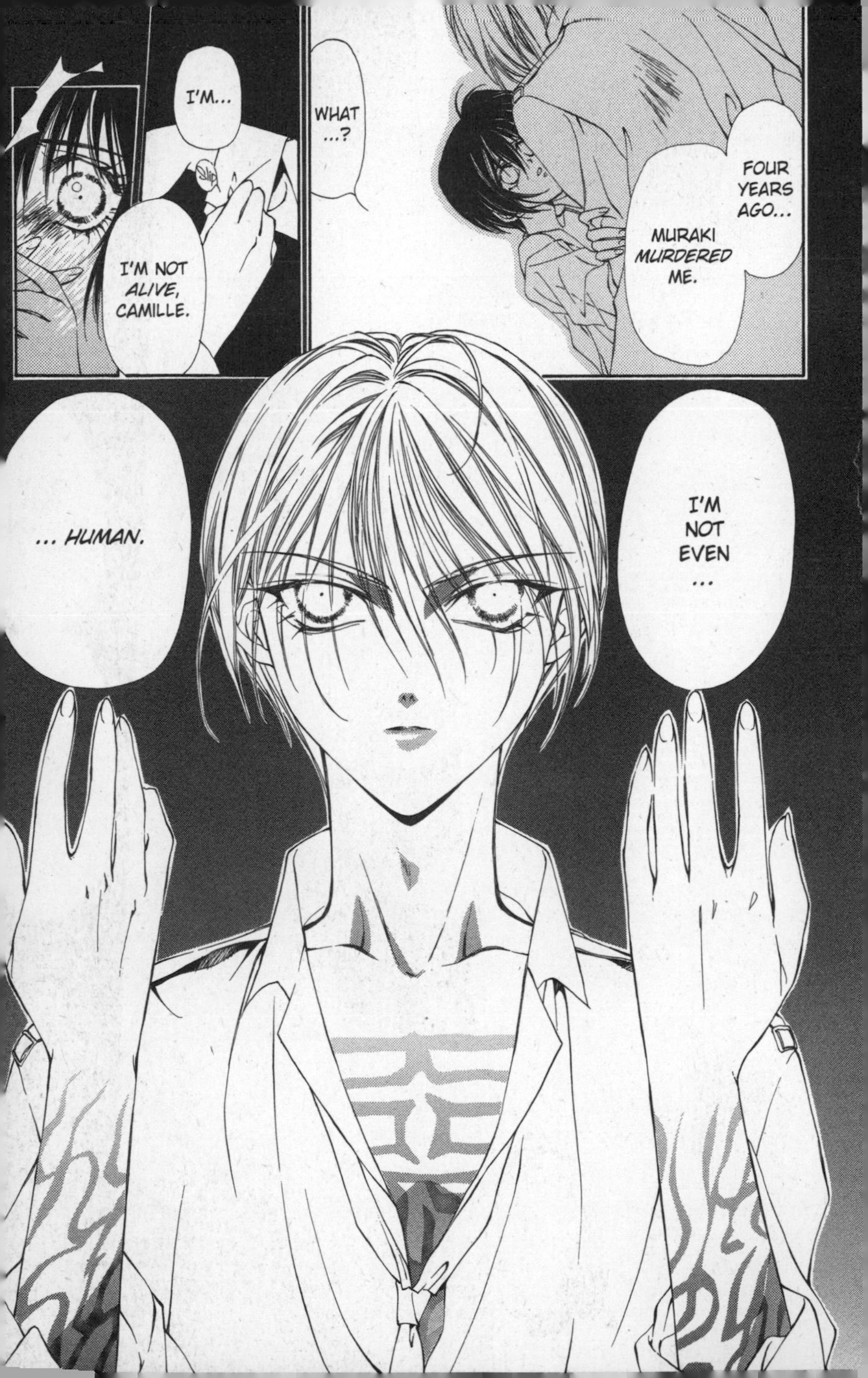
FOUR YEARS AGO...
MURAKI MURDERED ME.
WHAT ...?
I'M...
slip
I'M NOT ALIVE, CAMILLE.
I'M NOT EVEN ...
... HUMAN.

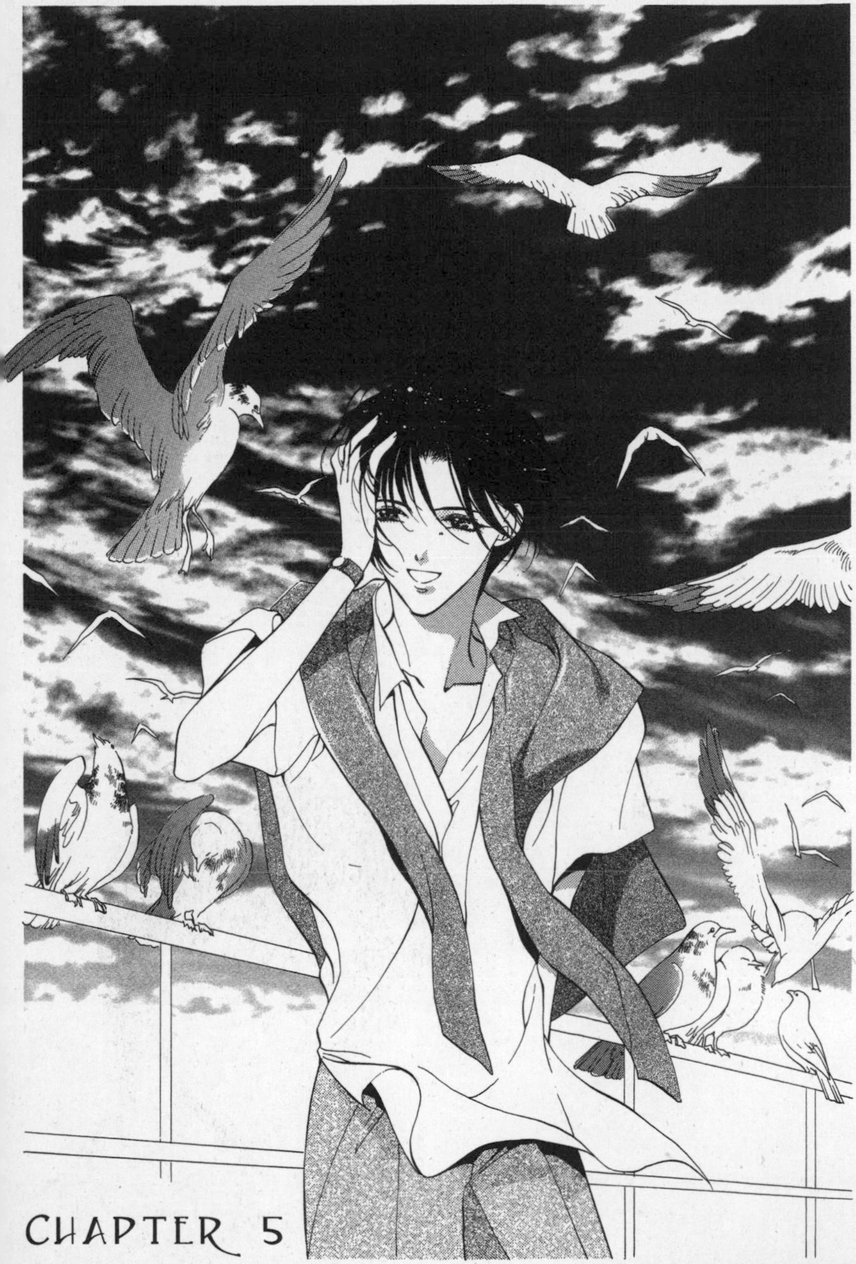
CHAPTER 5

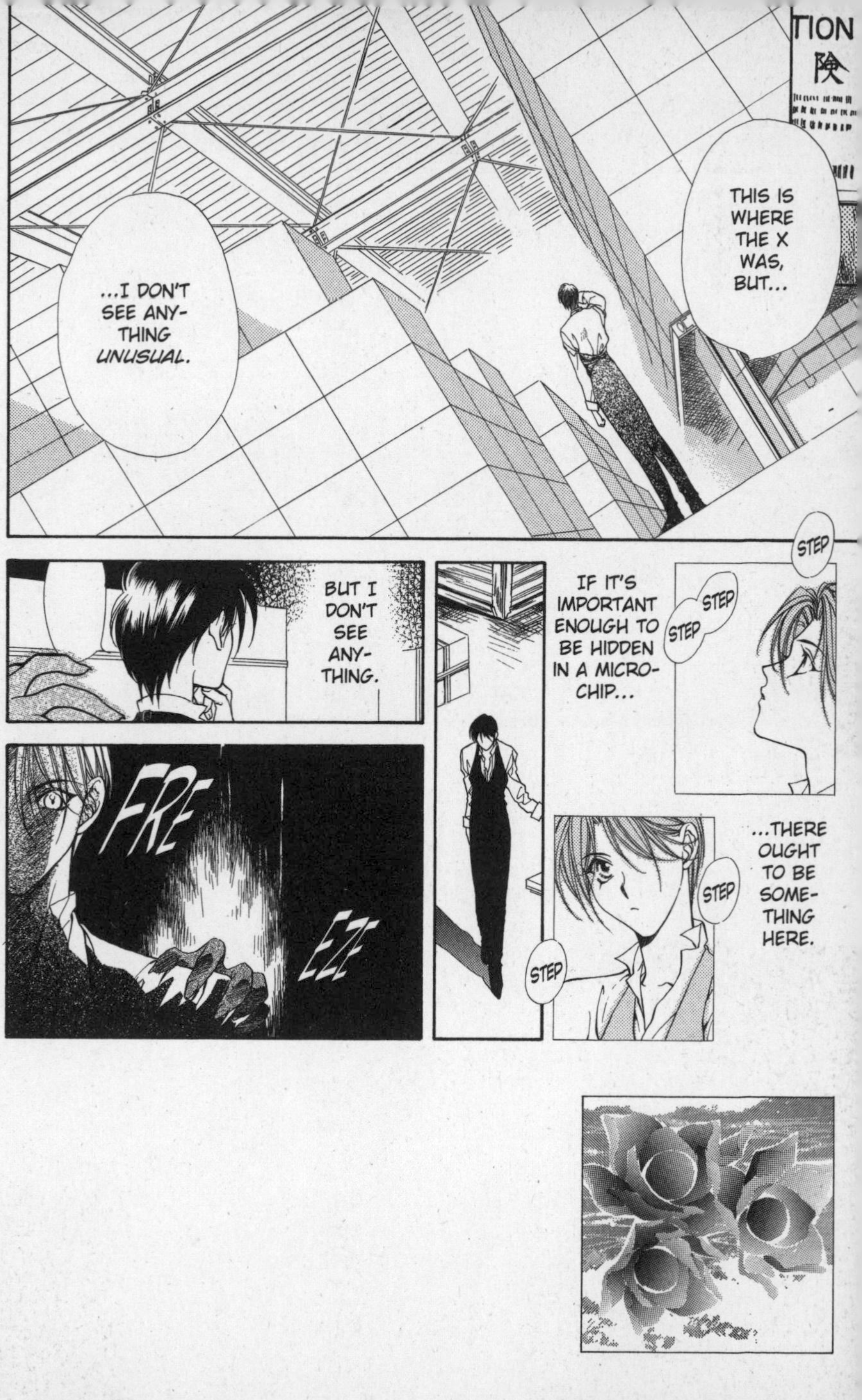
TION
THIS IS WHERE THE X WAS, BUT...
...I DON'T SEE ANYTHING UNUSUAL.
STEP
STEP
STEP
IF IT'S IMPORTANT ENOUGH TO BE HIDDEN IN A MICROCHIP...
STEP
...THERE OUGHT TO BE SOMETHING HERE.
STEP
BUT I DON'T SEE ANYTHING.
FREEZE

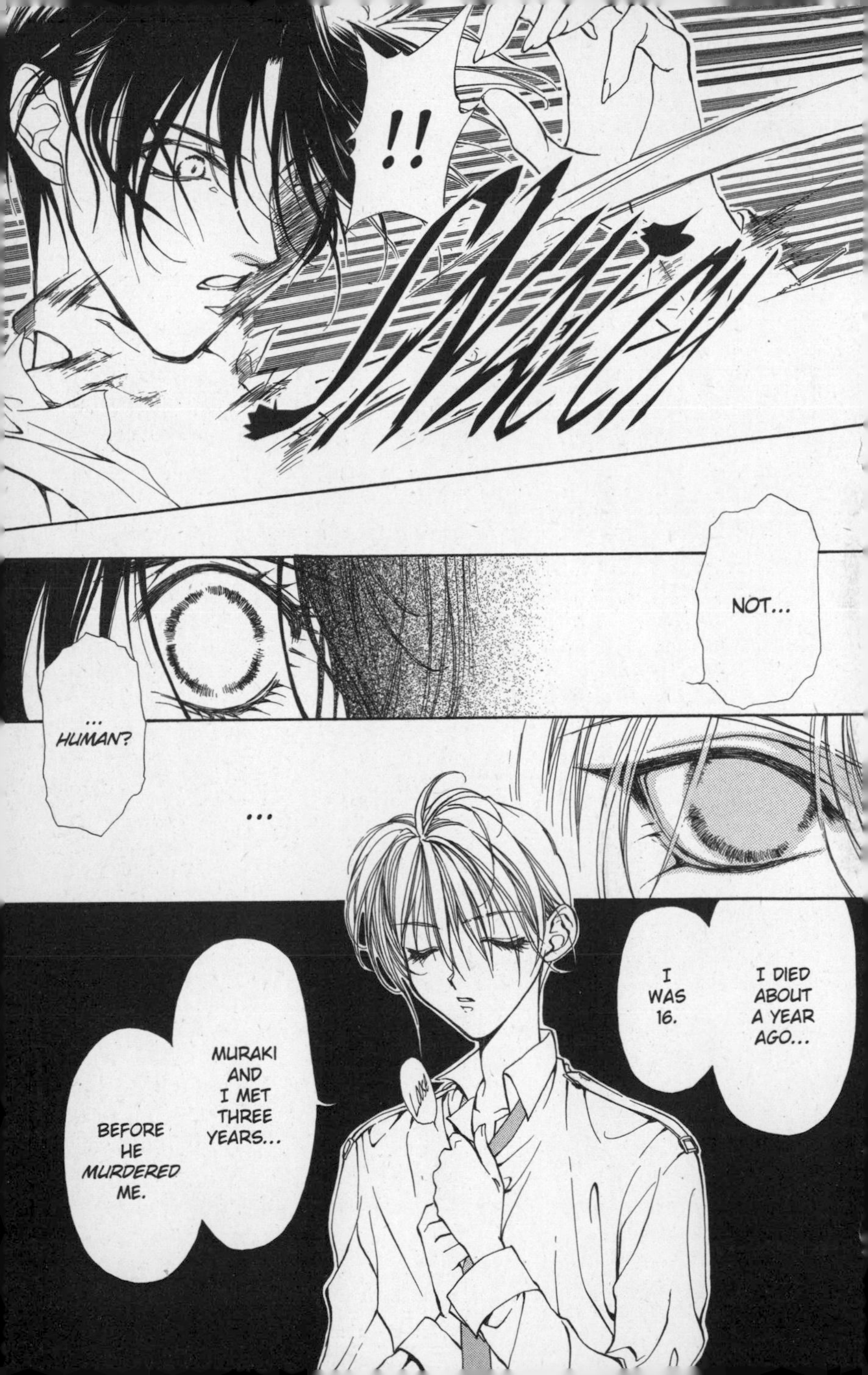
!!
NOT...
... HUMAN?
...
I DIED ABOUT A YEAR AGO...
I WAS 16.
MURAKI AND I MET THREE YEARS...
BEFORE HE MURDERED ME.

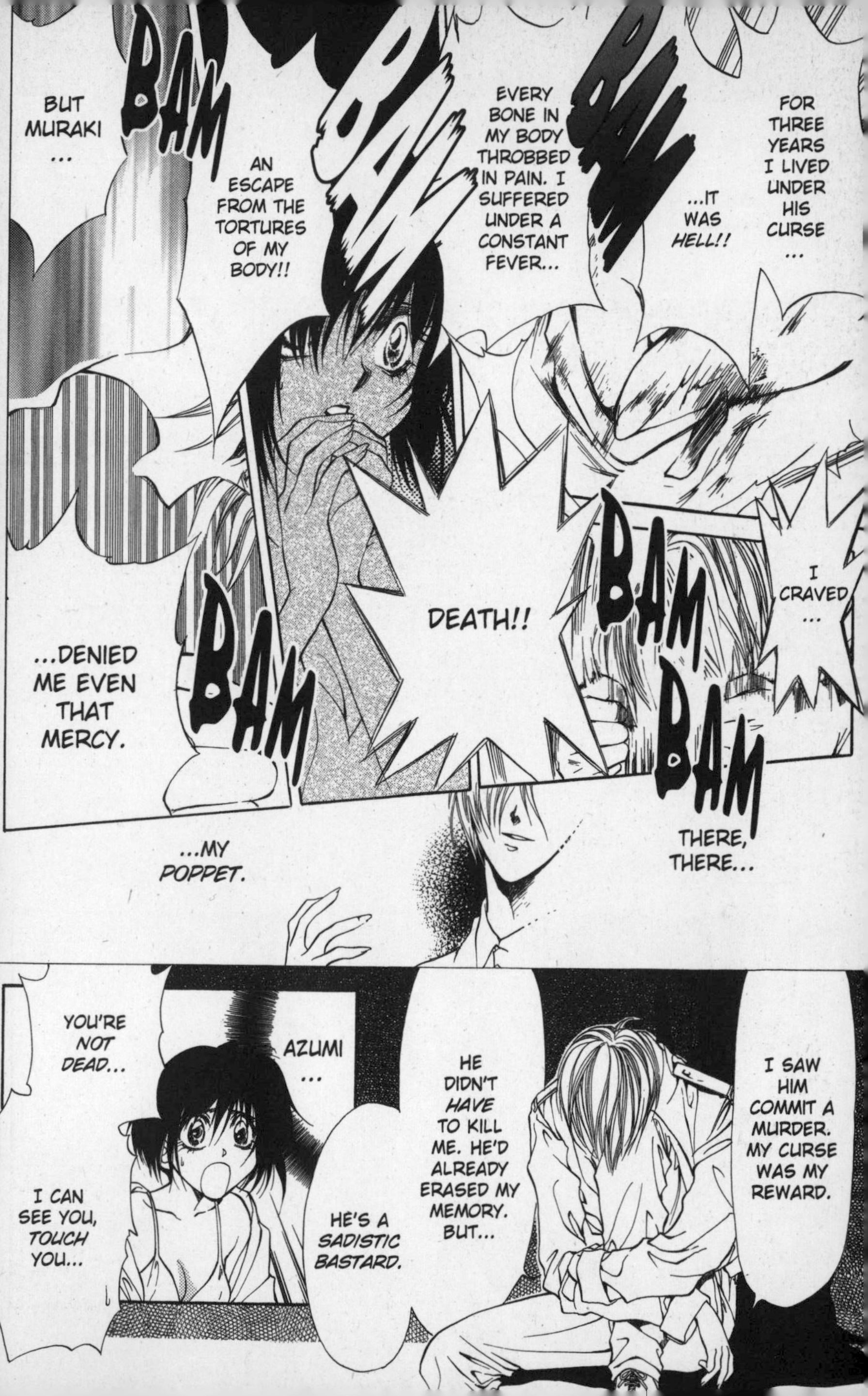
FOR THREE YEARS I LIVED UNDER HIS CURSE...
...IT WAS *HELL!!*
BAM
EVERY BONE IN MY BODY THROBBED IN PAIN. I SUFFERED UNDER A CONSTANT FEVER...
BAM
I CRAVED...
DEATH!!
BAM BAM
BAM BAM
AN ESCAPE FROM THE TORTURES OF MY BODY!!
BUT MURAKI...
BAM
...DENIED ME EVEN THAT MERCY.
THERE, THERE...
...MY *POPPET.*
I SAW HIM COMMIT A MURDER. MY CURSE WAS MY REWARD.
HE DIDN'T *HAVE* TO KILL ME. HE'D ALREADY ERASED MY MEMORY. BUT...
HE'S A *SADISTIC BASTARD.*
AZUMI...
YOU'RE *NOT DEAD...*
I CAN SEE YOU, *TOUCH* YOU...

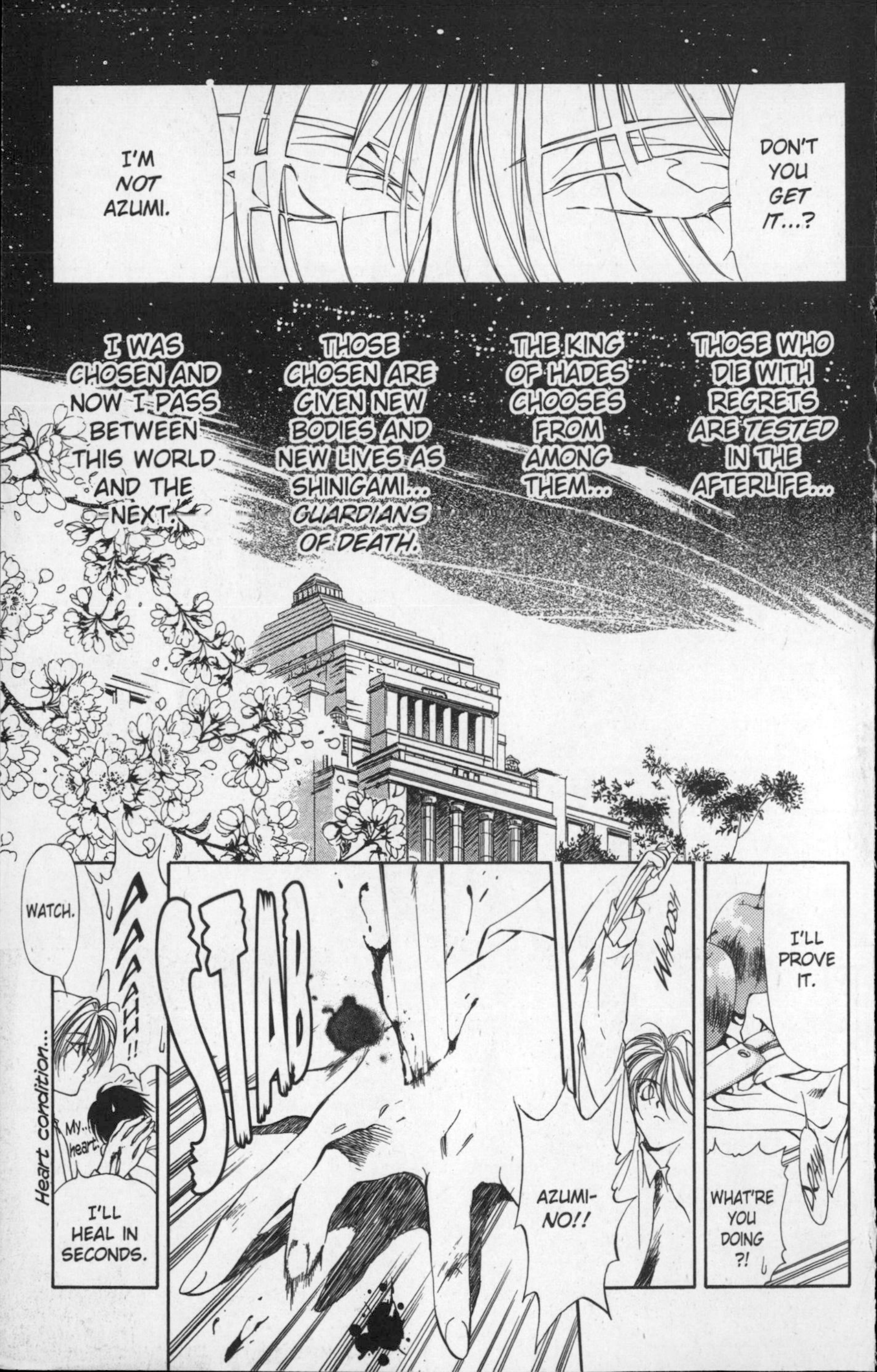
DON'T YOU GET IT...?
I'M NOT AZUMI.
THOSE WHO DIE WITH REGRETS ARE TESTED IN THE AFTERLIFE...
THE KING OF HADES CHOOSES FROM AMONG THEM...
THOSE CHOSEN ARE GIVEN NEW BODIES AND NEW LIVES AS SHINIGAMI... GUARDIANS OF DEATH.
I WAS CHOSEN AND NOW I PASS BETWEEN THIS WORLD AND THE NEXT.
I'LL PROVE IT.
WHAT'RE YOU DOING?!
WHOOSH
AZUMI-NO!!
STAB
WATCH.
My... heart.
Heart condition...
I'LL HEAL IN SECONDS.

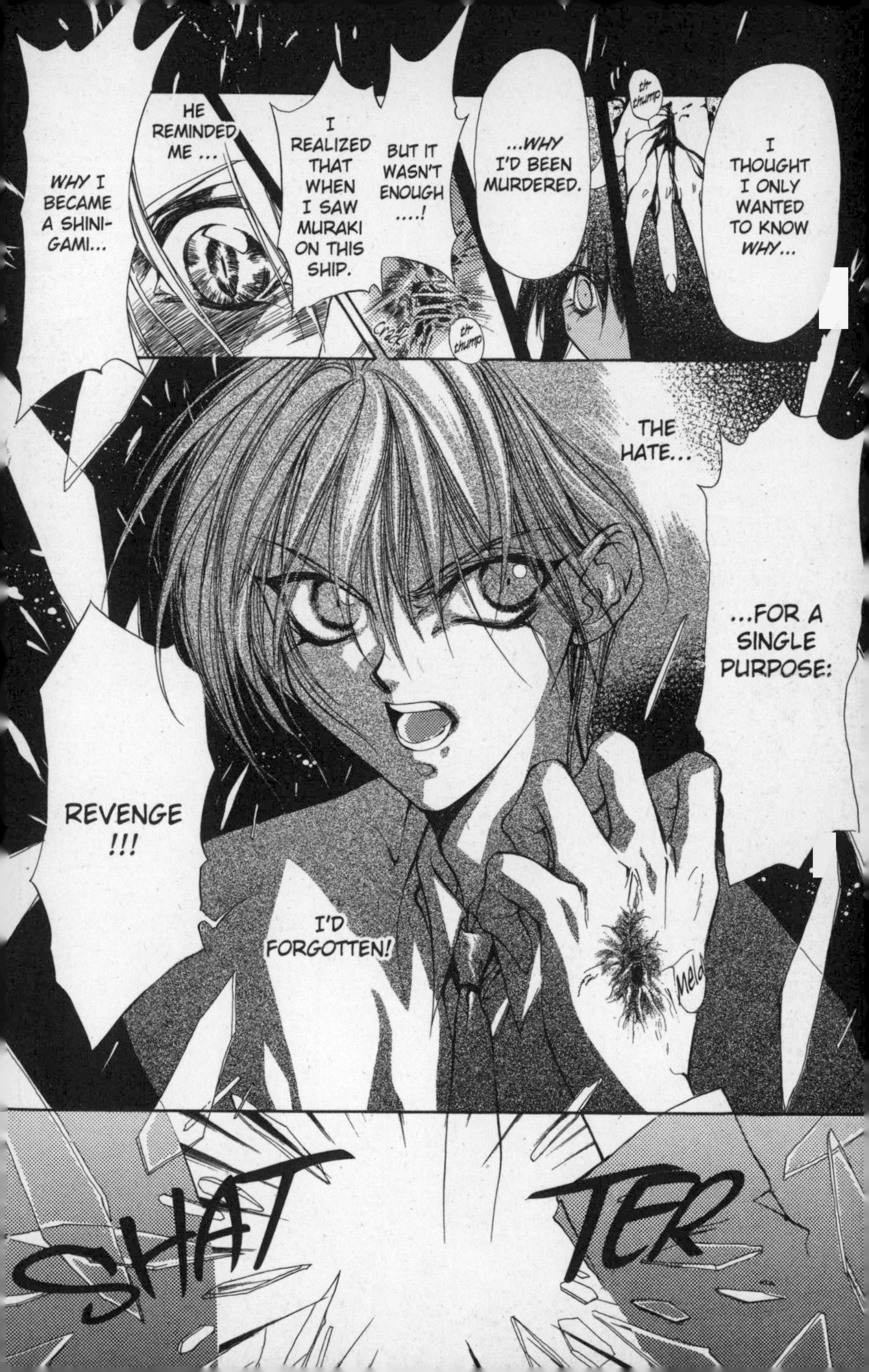
I THOUGHT I ONLY WANTED TO KNOW *WHY*...
th thump
...*WHY* I'D BEEN MURDERED.
BUT IT WASN'T ENOUGH ....!
I REALIZED THAT WHEN I SAW MURAKI ON THIS SHIP.
th thump
crack
HE REMINDED ME ...
WHY I BECAME A SHINI-GAMI...
THE HATE...
...FOR A SINGLE PURPOSE:
REVENGE !!!
meld
I'D FORGOTTEN!
SHAT TER

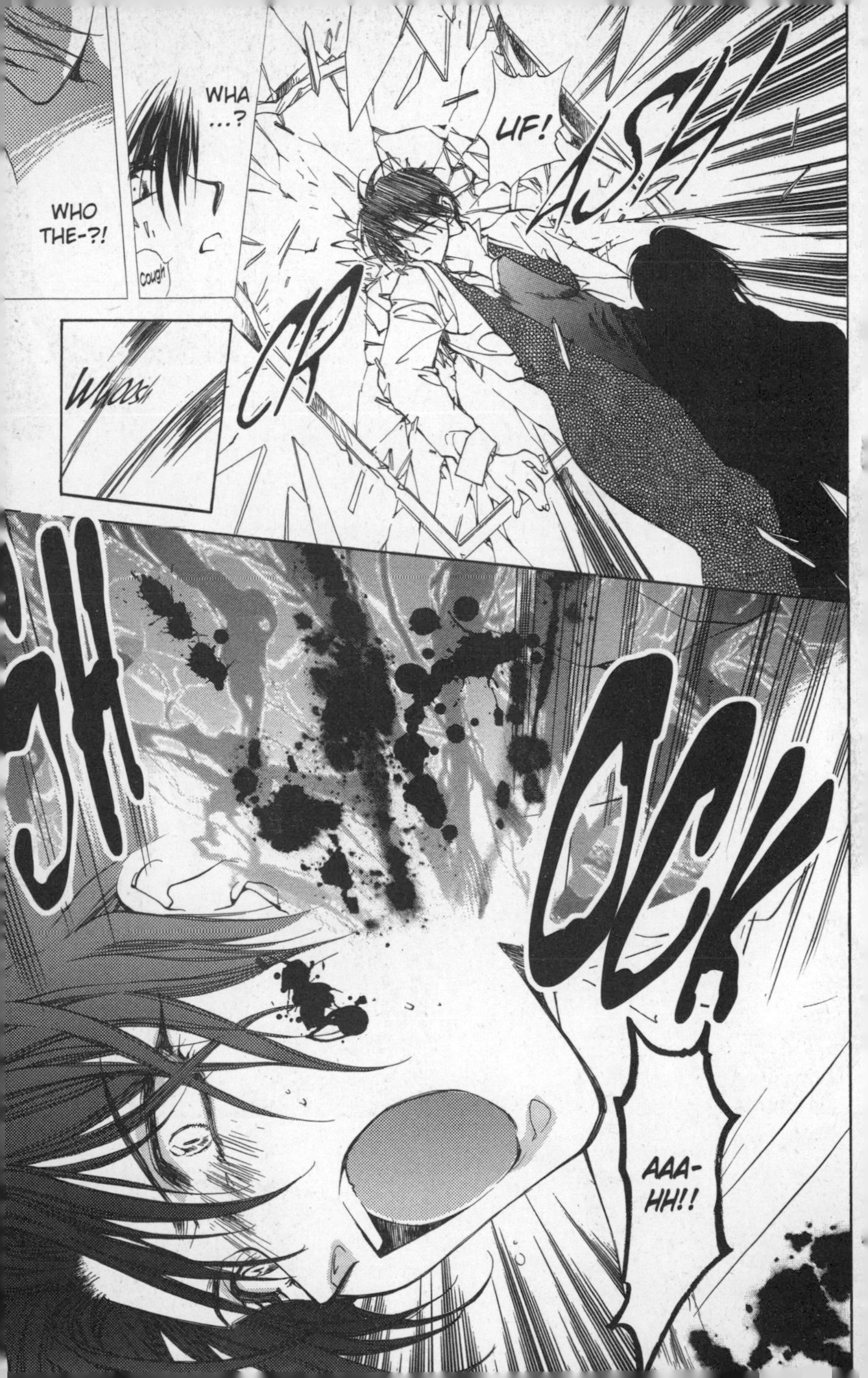
ASH
UF!
CR
WHA ...?
WHO THE-?!
cough
whoosh
OCK
AAA-HH!!
SH

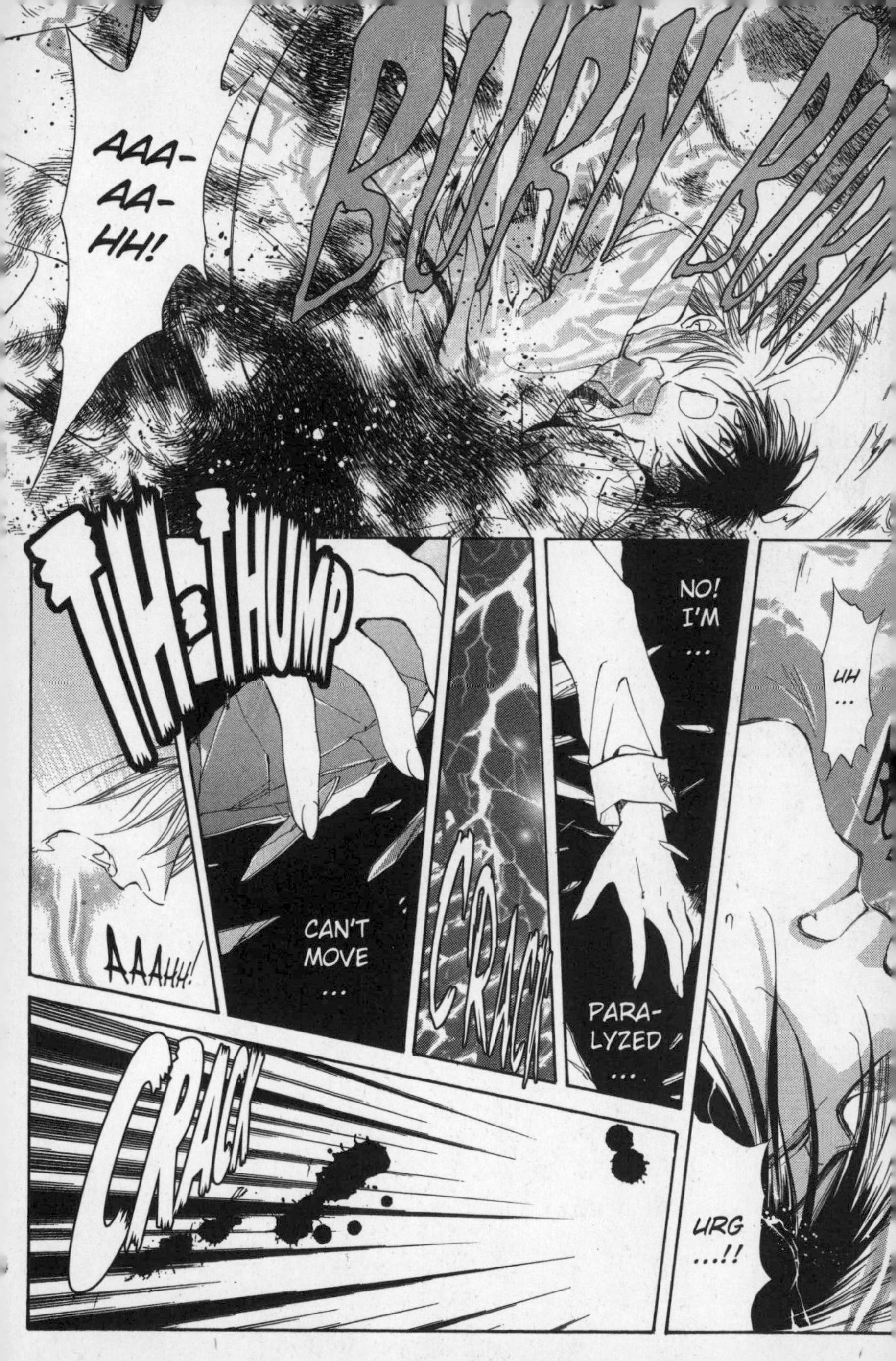
BURN
AAA-AA-HH!
UH ...
NO! I'M ...
PARA-LYZED ...
CRACK
CAN'T MOVE ...
TH-THUMP
AAAHH!
URG ...!!
CRACK

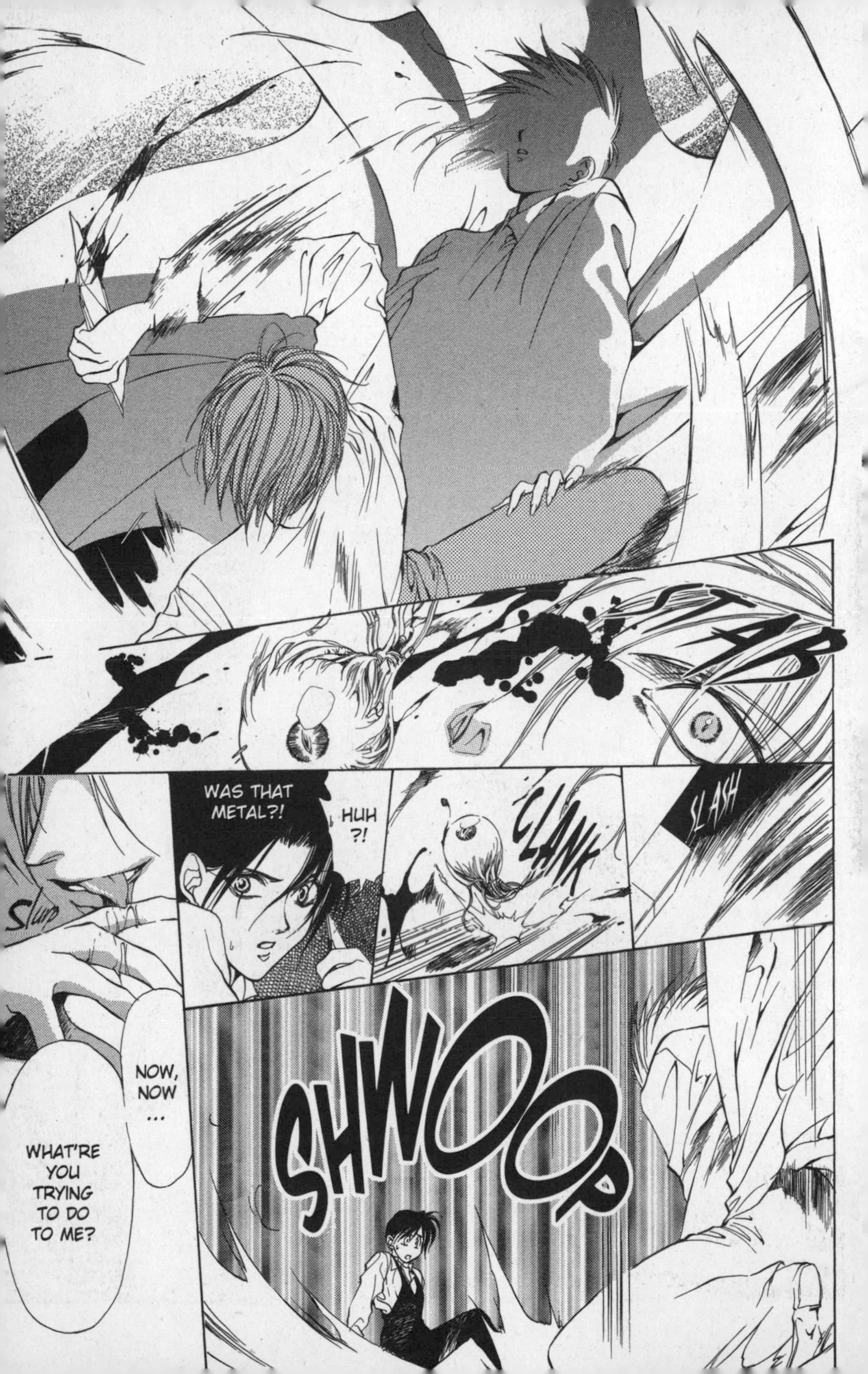
STAB
SLASH
CLANK
HUH ?!
WAS THAT METAL?!
SHWOOP
NOW, NOW ...
WHAT'RE YOU TRYING TO DO TO ME?

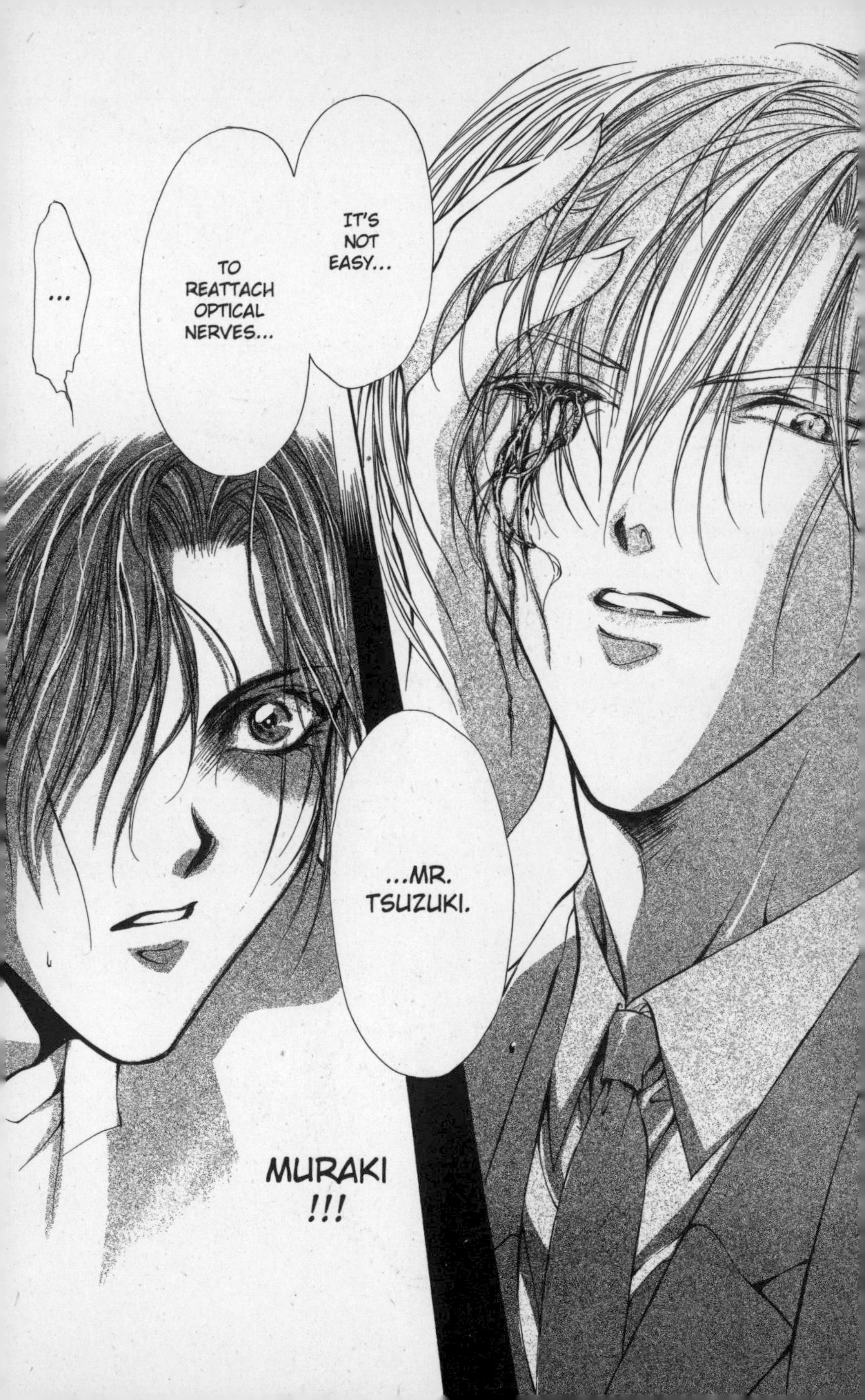
IT'S NOT EASY...
TO REATTACH OPTICAL NERVES...
...
...MR. TSUZUKI.
MURAKI !!!

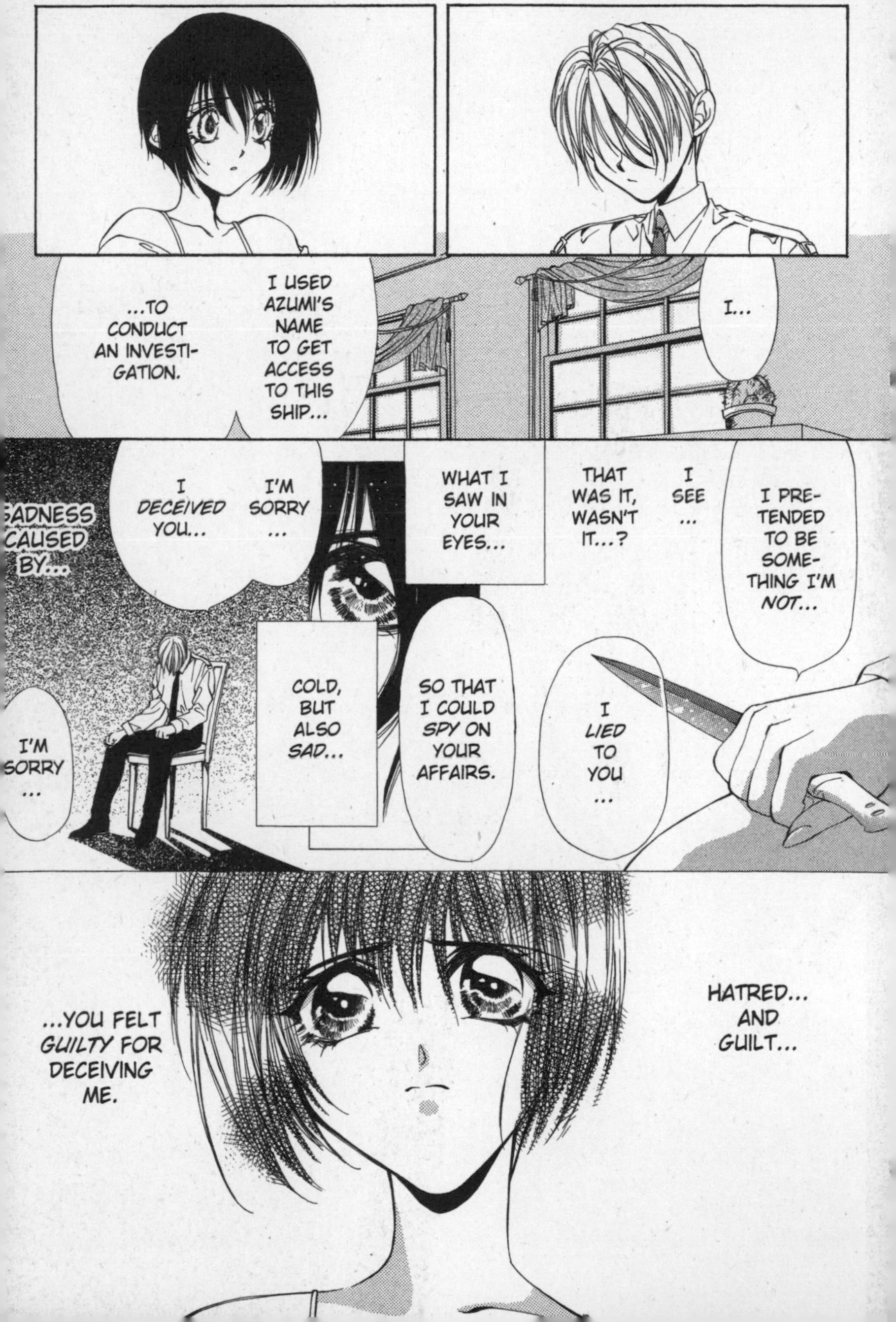
I...
I USED AZUMI'S NAME TO GET ACCESS TO THIS SHIP...
...TO CONDUCT AN INVESTIGATION.
I PRETENDED TO BE SOMETHING I'M *NOT*...
I SEE...
THAT WAS IT, WASN'T IT...?
WHAT I SAW IN YOUR EYES...
I *LIED* TO YOU...
SO THAT I COULD *SPY* ON YOUR AFFAIRS.
COLD, BUT ALSO SAD...
I'M SORRY...
I *DECEIVED* YOU...
SADNESS CAUSED BY...
I'M SORRY...
HATRED... AND GUILT...
...YOU FELT *GUILTY* FOR DECEIVING ME.

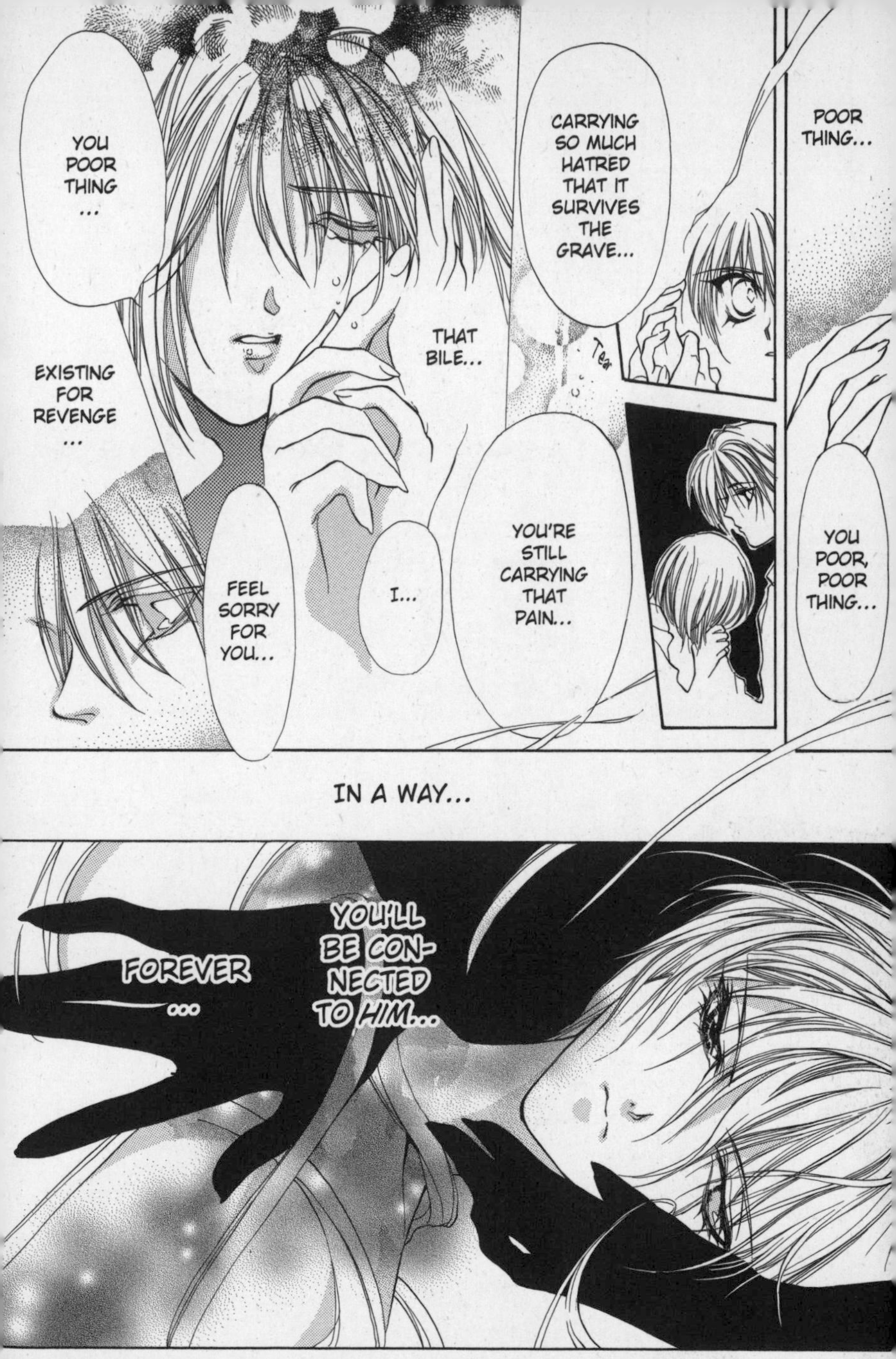
POOR THING...
YOU POOR, POOR THING...
Tear
CARRYING SO MUCH HATRED THAT IT SURVIVES THE GRAVE...
YOU POOR THING ...
THAT BILE...
EXISTING FOR REVENGE ...
YOU'RE STILL CARRYING THAT PAIN...
I...
FEEL SORRY FOR YOU...
IN A WAY...
YOU'LL BE CON-NECTED TO HIM...
FOREVER ...

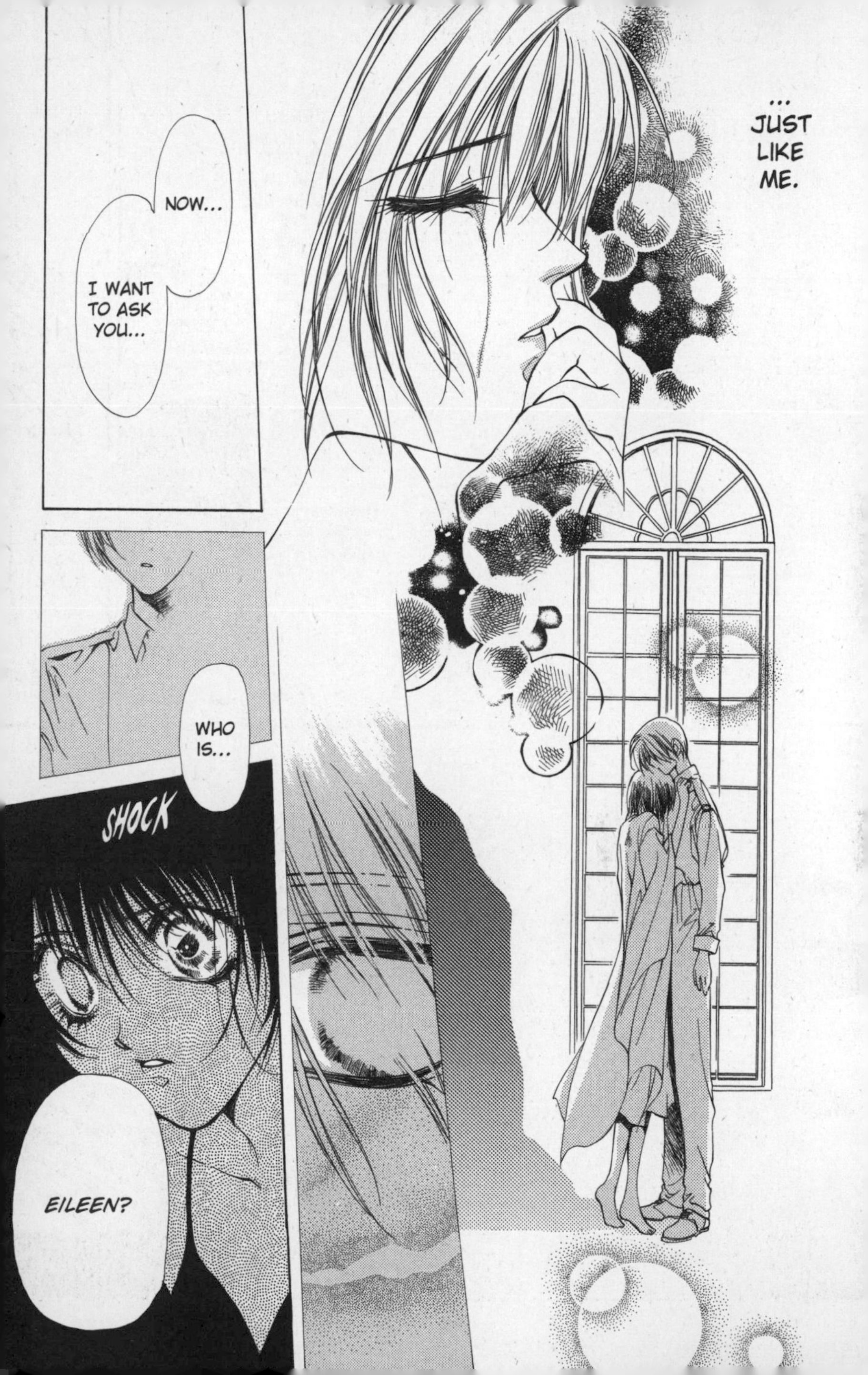
... JUST LIKE ME.
NOW...
I WANT TO ASK YOU...
WHO IS...
SHOCK
EILEEN?

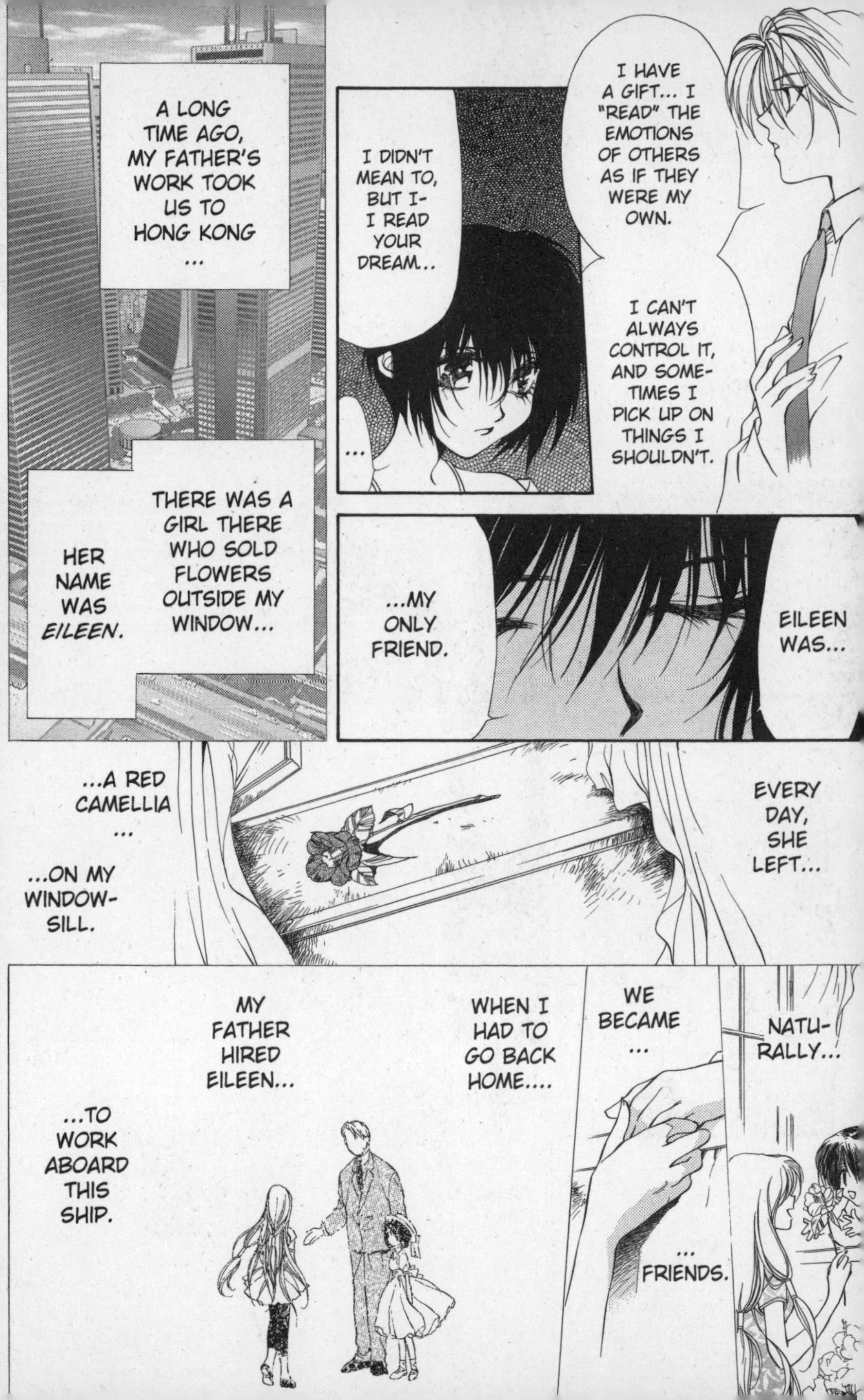
I HAVE A GIFT... I "READ" THE EMOTIONS OF OTHERS AS IF THEY WERE MY OWN.
I CAN'T ALWAYS CONTROL IT, AND SOME-TIMES I PICK UP ON THINGS I SHOULDN'T.
I DIDN'T MEAN TO, BUT I- I READ YOUR DREAM...
...
EILEEN WAS...
...MY ONLY FRIEND.
A LONG TIME AGO, MY FATHER'S WORK TOOK US TO HONG KONG ...
THERE WAS A GIRL THERE WHO SOLD FLOWERS OUTSIDE MY WINDOW...
HER NAME WAS *EILEEN*.
EVERY DAY, SHE LEFT...
...A RED CAMELLIA ...
...ON MY WINDOW-SILL.
NATU-RALLY...
WE BECAME ...
... FRIENDS.
WHEN I HAD TO GO BACK HOME....
MY FATHER HIRED EILEEN...
...TO WORK ABOARD THIS SHIP.

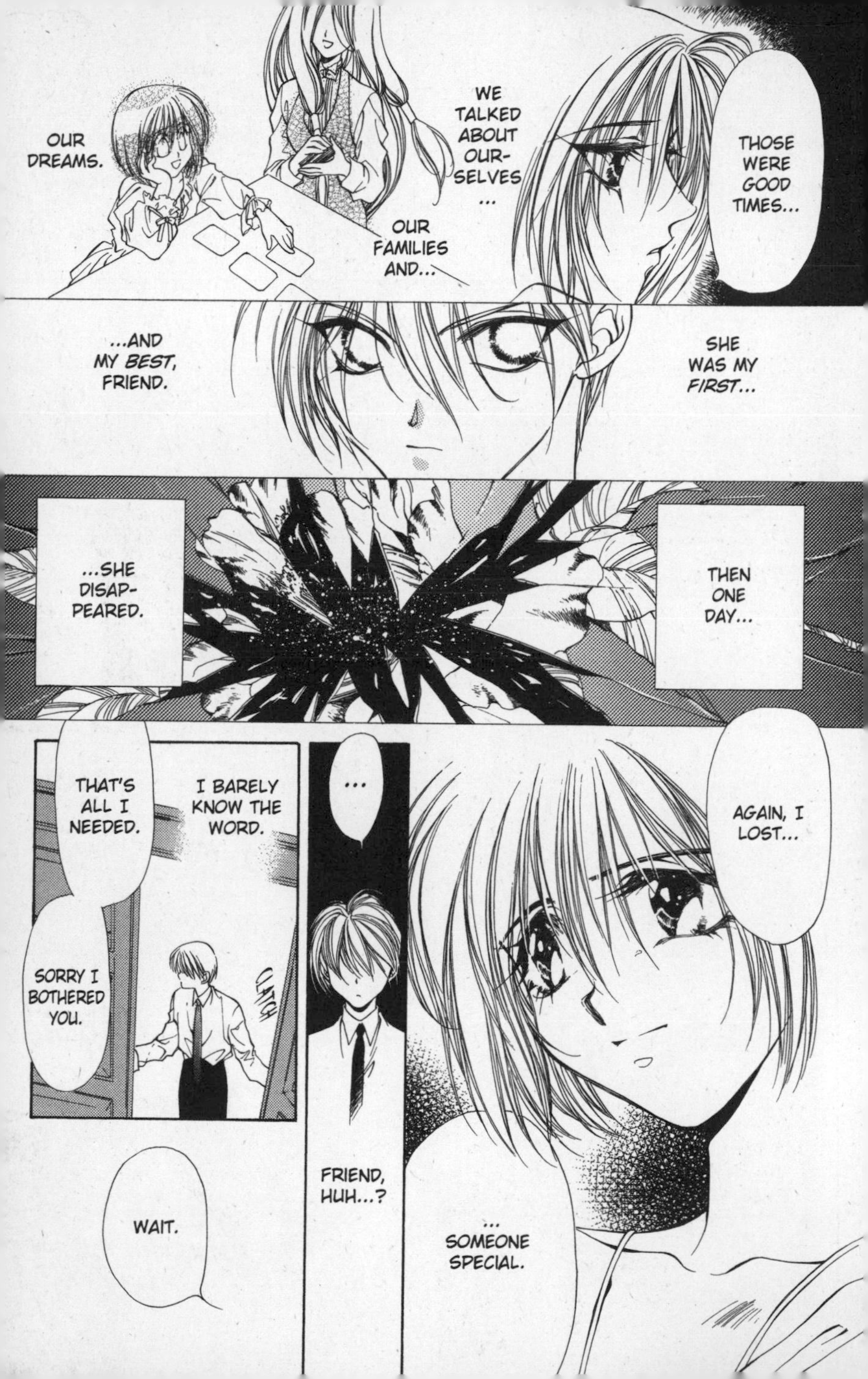
THOSE WERE GOOD TIMES...
WE TALKED ABOUT OUR-SELVES...
OUR FAMILIES AND...
OUR DREAMS.
SHE WAS MY *FIRST*...
...AND MY *BEST*, FRIEND.
THEN ONE DAY...
...SHE DISAP-PEARED.
AGAIN, I LOST...
...SOMEONE SPECIAL.
...
FRIEND, HUH...?
I BARELY KNOW THE WORD.
THAT'S ALL I NEEDED.
SORRY I BOTHERED YOU.
CLATCH
WAIT.

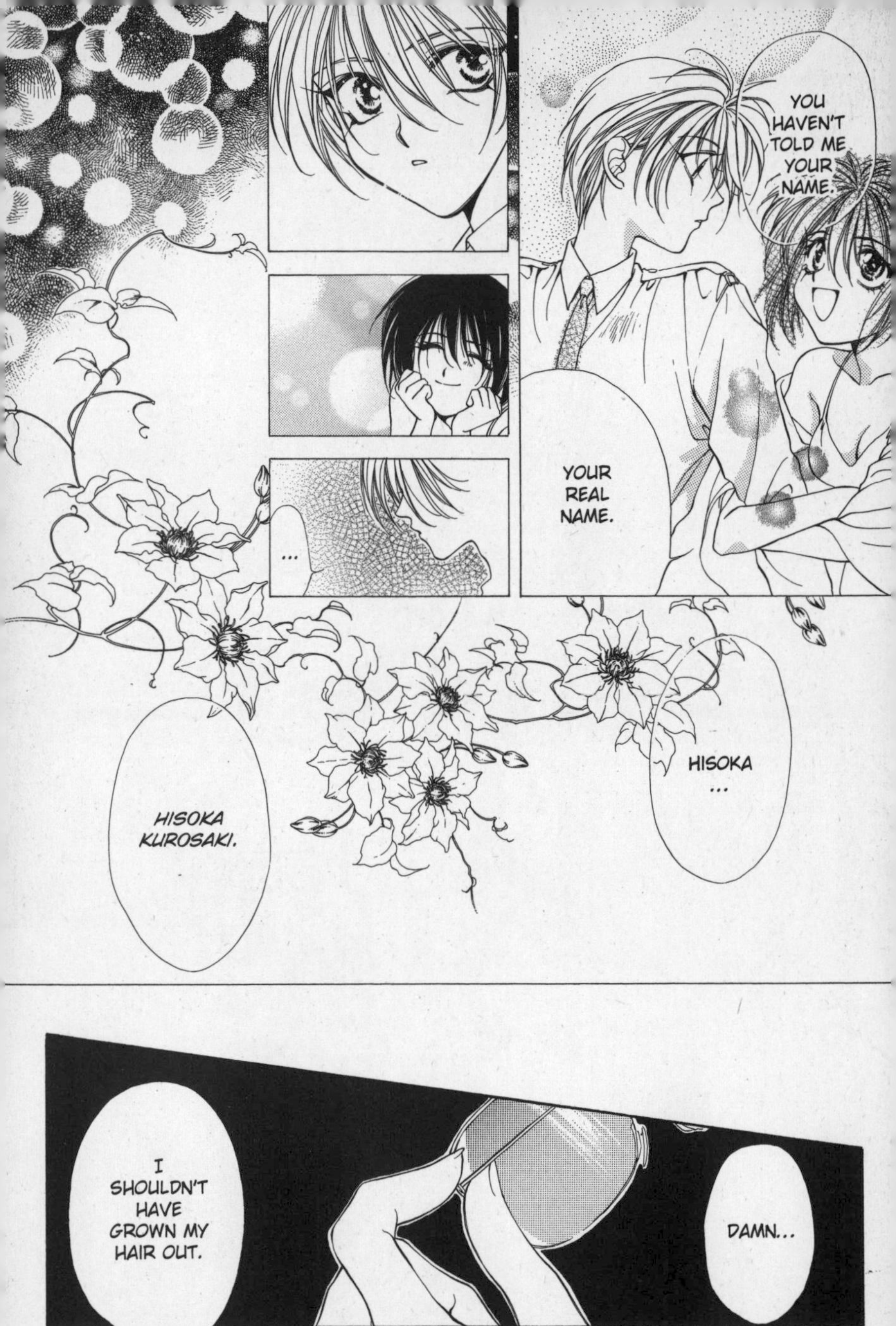
YOU HAVEN'T TOLD ME YOUR NAME.
YOUR REAL NAME.
...
HISOKA ...
HISOKA KUROSAKI.
DAMN...
I SHOULDN'T HAVE GROWN MY HAIR OUT.

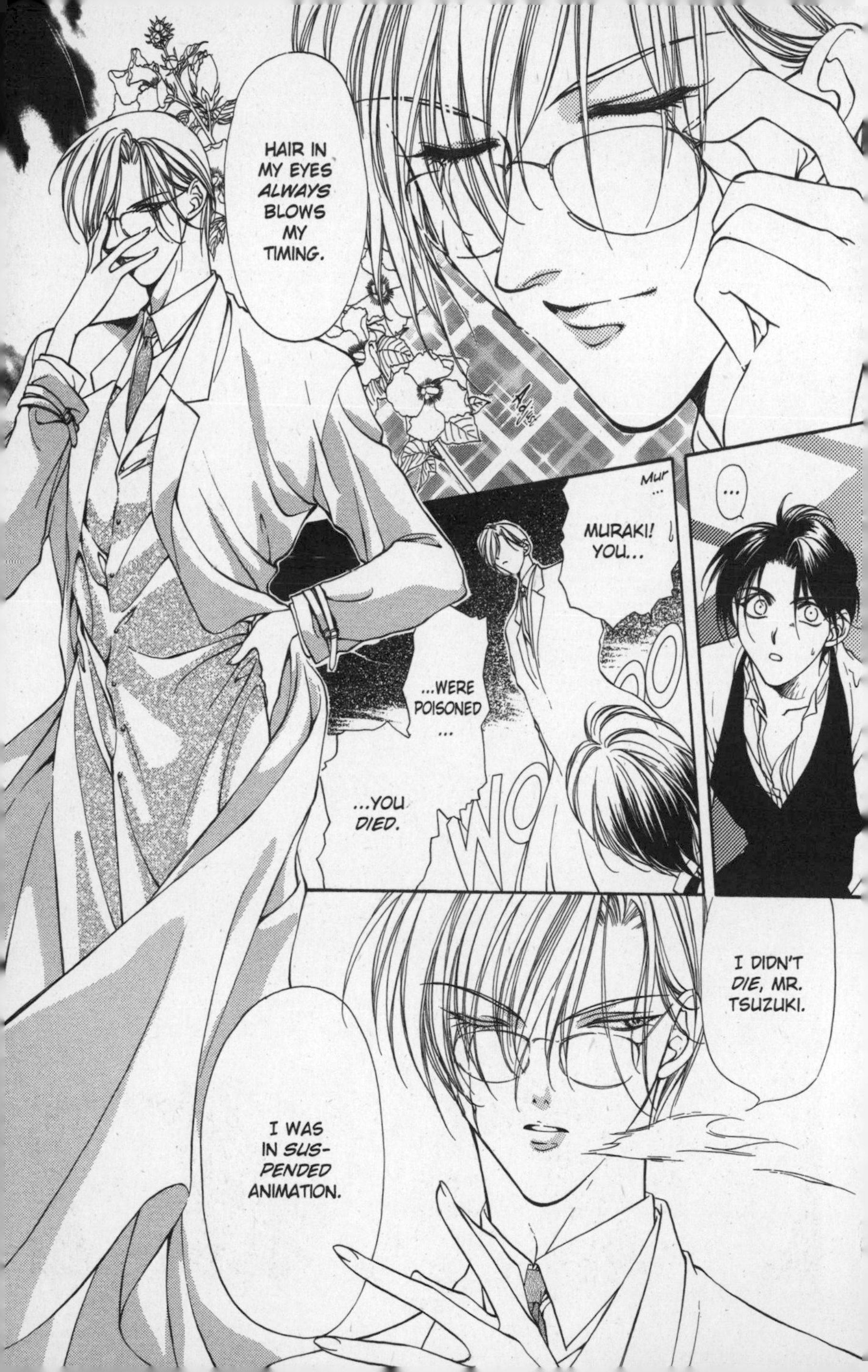
HAIR IN MY EYES ALWAYS BLOWS MY TIMING.
Adjust
...
Mur...
MURAKI! YOU...
...WERE POISONED...
...YOU DIED.
I DIDN'T DIE, MR. TSUZUKI.
I WAS IN SUS-PENDED ANIMATION.

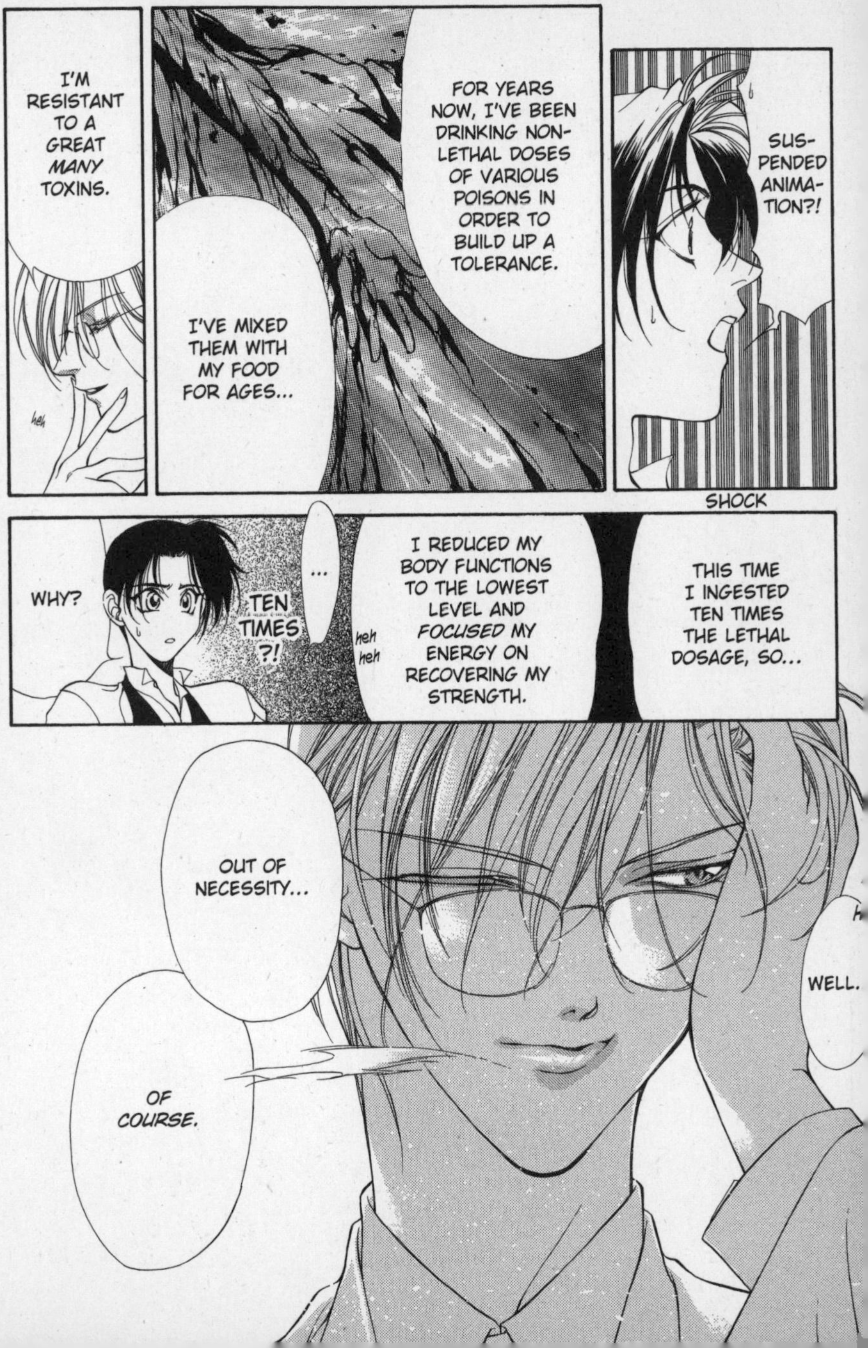
SUS-PENDED ANIMATION?!
SHOCK
FOR YEARS NOW, I'VE BEEN DRINKING NON-LETHAL DOSES OF VARIOUS POISONS IN ORDER TO BUILD UP A TOLERANCE.
I'VE MIXED THEM WITH MY FOOD FOR AGES...
I'M RESISTANT TO A GREAT *MANY* TOXINS.
heh
THIS TIME I INGESTED TEN TIMES THE LETHAL DOSAGE, SO...
I REDUCED MY BODY FUNCTIONS TO THE LOWEST LEVEL AND *FOCUSED* MY ENERGY ON RECOVERING MY STRENGTH.
heh heh
...
TEN TIMES ?!
WHY?
WELL.
OUT OF NECESSITY...
OF COURSE.

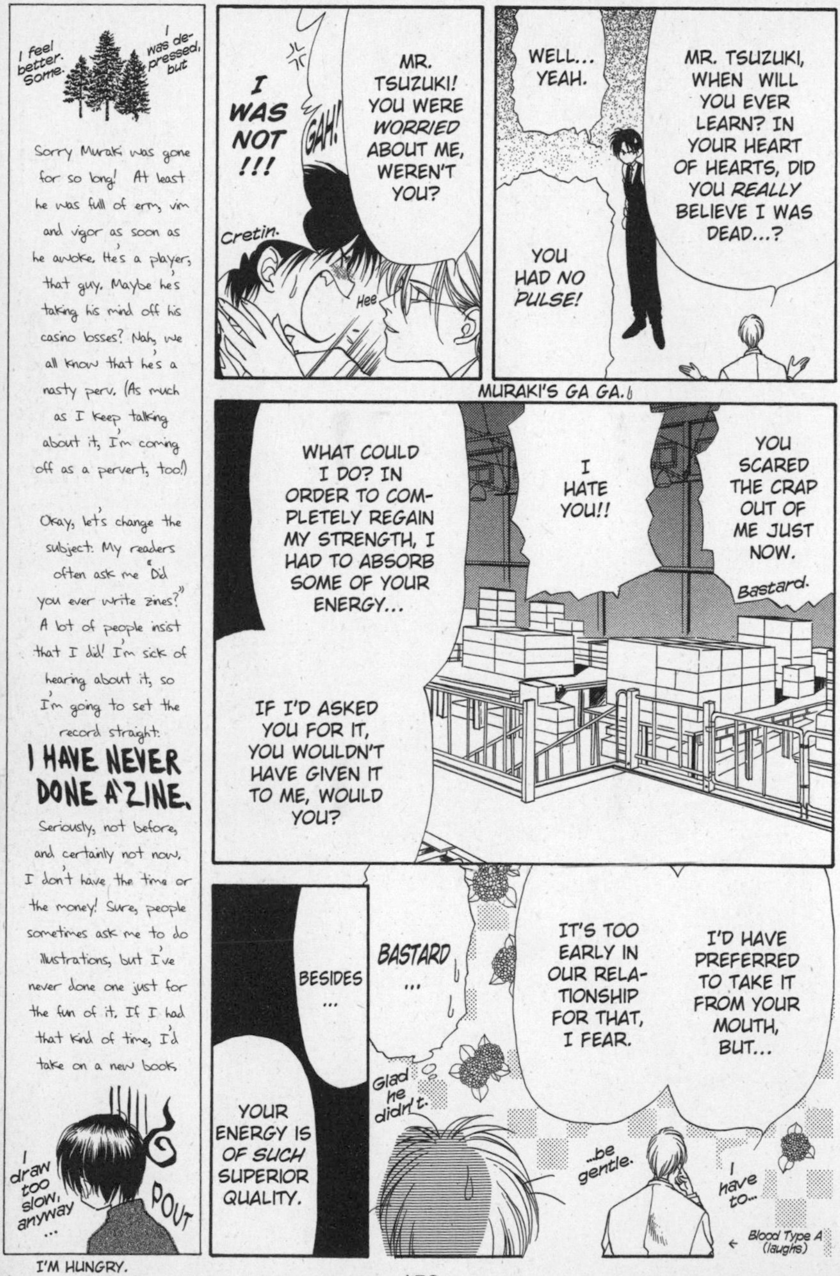
MR. TSUZUKI, WHEN WILL YOU EVER LEARN? IN YOUR HEART OF HEARTS, DID YOU *REALLY* BELIEVE I WAS DEAD...?
WELL... YEAH.
YOU HAD NO *PULSE!*
MR. TSUZUKI! YOU WERE *WORRIED* ABOUT ME, WEREN'T YOU?
I WAS NOT !!!
GAH!
Cretin.
Hee
MURAKI'S GA GA.
YOU SCARED THE CRAP OUT OF ME JUST NOW.
Bastard.
I HATE YOU!!
WHAT COULD I DO? IN ORDER TO COMPLETELY REGAIN MY STRENGTH, I HAD TO ABSORB SOME OF YOUR ENERGY...
IF I'D ASKED YOU FOR IT, YOU WOULDN'T HAVE GIVEN IT TO ME, WOULD YOU?
I'D HAVE PREFERRED TO TAKE IT FROM YOUR MOUTH, BUT...
IT'S TOO EARLY IN OUR RELATIONSHIP FOR THAT, I FEAR.
I have to...
...be gentle.
← Blood Type A (laughs)
Glad he didn't.
BASTARD...
BESIDES...
YOUR ENERGY IS OF *SUCH* SUPERIOR QUALITY.
I feel better. Some.
I was depressed, but
Sorry Muraki was gone for so long! At least he was full of erm, vim and vigor as soon as he awoke. He's a player, that guy. Maybe he's taking his mind off his casino losses? Nah, we all know that he's a nasty perv. (As much as I keep talking about it, I'm coming off as a pervert, too!)
Okay, let's change the subject: My readers often ask me "Did you ever write zines?" A lot of people insist that I did! I'm sick of hearing about it, so I'm going to set the record straight:
I HAVE NEVER DONE A 'ZINE.
Seriously, not before, and certainly not now. I don't have the time or the money! Sure, people sometimes ask me to do illustrations, but I've never done one just for the fun of it. If I had that kind of time, I'd take on a new books
I draw too slow, anyway ...
POUT
I'M HUNGRY.

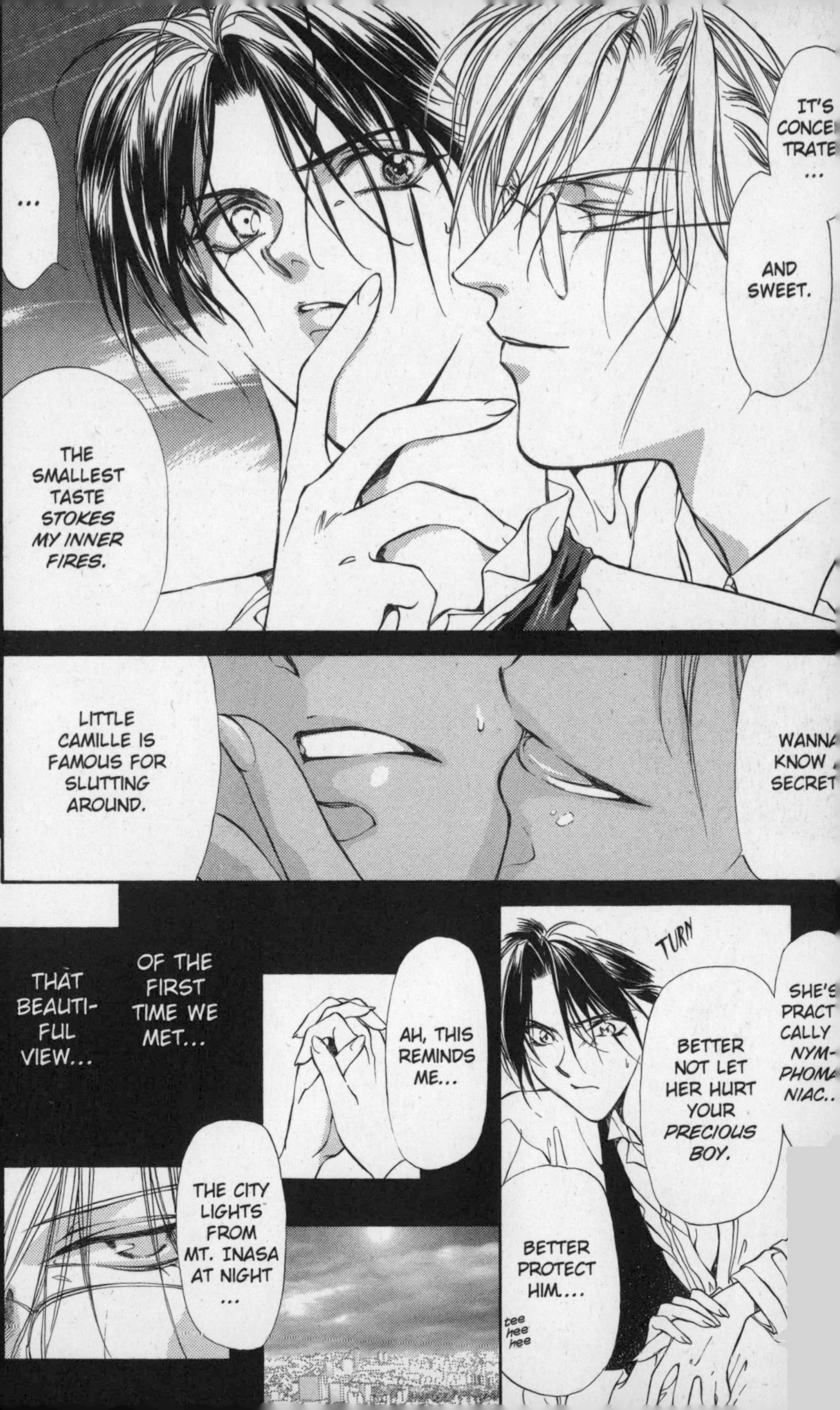
IT'S CONCE TRATE ...
AND SWEET.
...
THE SMALLEST TASTE STOKES *MY INNER FIRES.*
WANNA KNOW SECRET
LITTLE CAMILLE IS FAMOUS FOR SLUTTING AROUND.
SHE'S PRACT CALLY *NYM-PHOMA NIAC..*
TURN
BETTER NOT LET HER HURT YOUR *PRECIOUS* BOY.
BETTER PROTECT HIM...
tee hee hee
AH, THIS REMINDS ME...
OF THE FIRST TIME WE MET...
THAT BEAUTI-FUL VIEW...
THE CITY LIGHTS FROM MT. INASA AT NIGHT ...

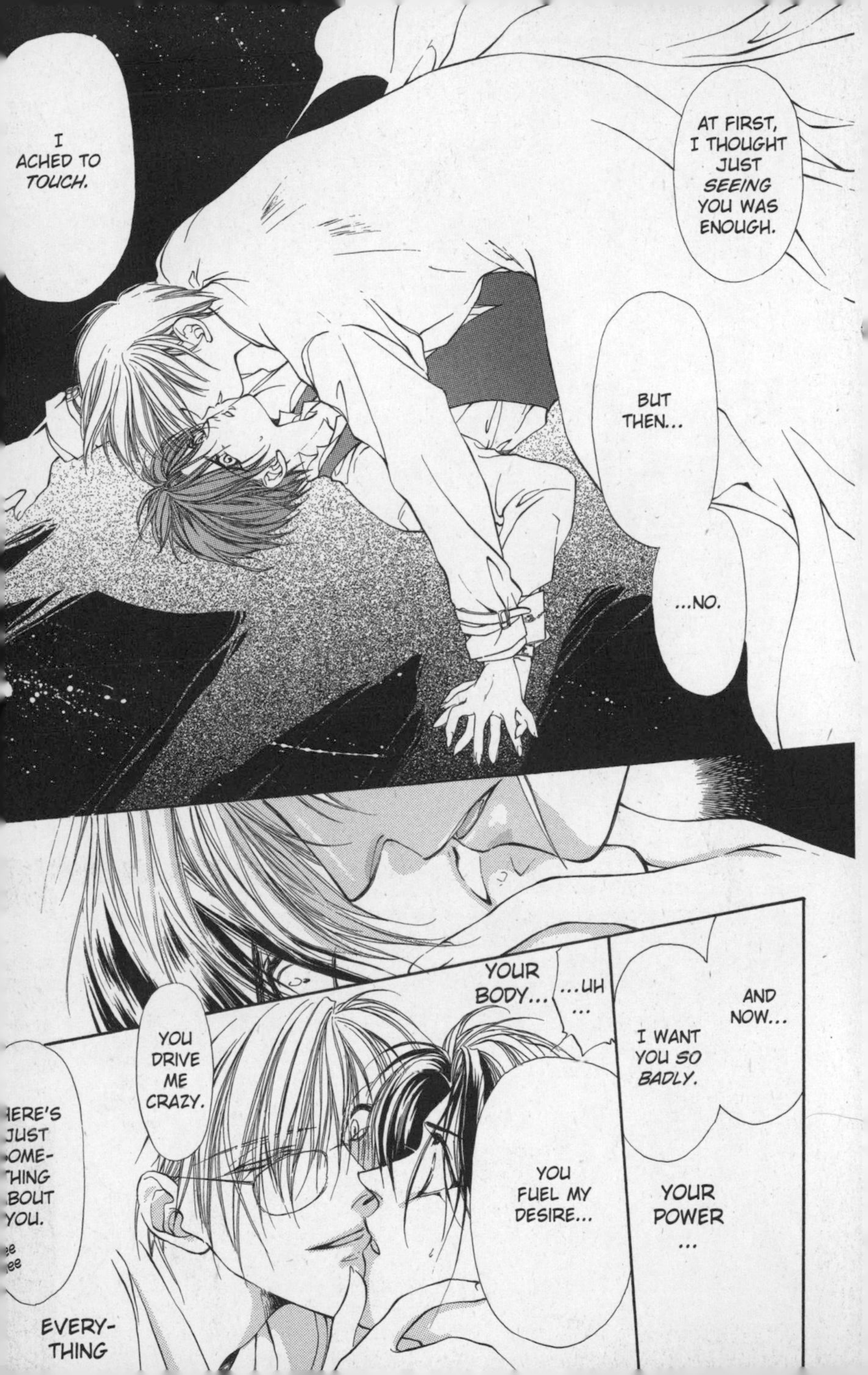
AT FIRST, I THOUGHT JUST *SEEING* YOU WAS ENOUGH.
BUT THEN...
...NO.
I ACHED TO *TOUCH*.
AND NOW...
I WANT YOU SO *BADLY*.
YOUR POWER ...
...UH ...
YOUR BODY...
YOU FUEL MY DESIRE...
YOU DRIVE ME CRAZY.
HERE'S JUST OME- THING BOUT YOU.
EVERY- THING

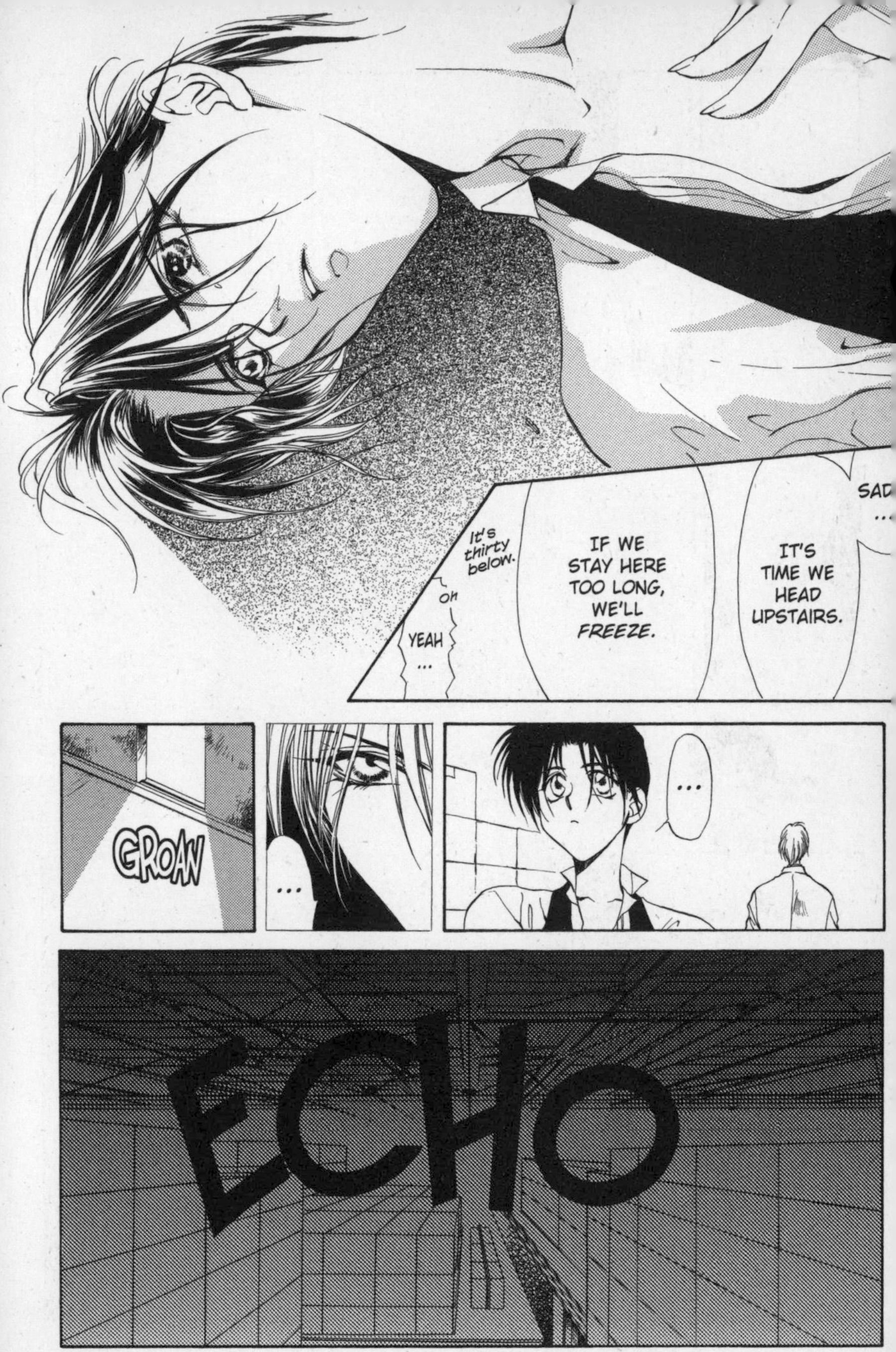
SAD ...
IT'S TIME WE HEAD UPSTAIRS.
IF WE STAY HERE TOO LONG, WE'LL FREEZE.
It's thirty below.
oh YEAH ...
...
...
GROAN
ECHO

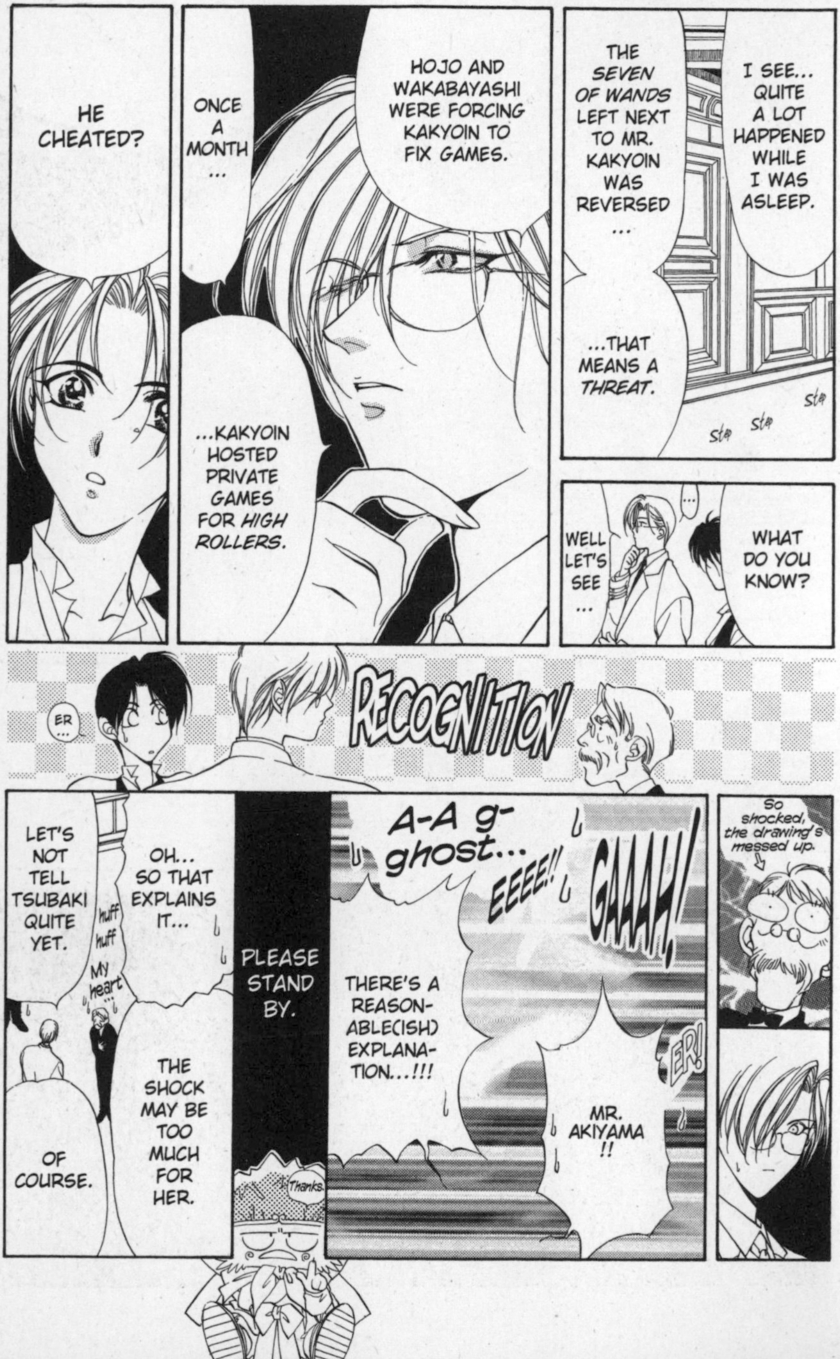
I SEE... QUITE A LOT HAPPENED WHILE I WAS ASLEEP.
THE SEVEN OF WANDS LEFT NEXT TO MR. KAKYOIN WAS REVERSED...
...THAT MEANS A THREAT.
step step step
WHAT DO YOU KNOW?
...
WELL LET'S SEE...
HOJO AND WAKABAYASHI WERE FORCING KAKYOIN TO FIX GAMES.
ONCE A MONTH...
...KAKYOIN HOSTED PRIVATE GAMES FOR HIGH ROLLERS.
HE CHEATED?
RECOGNITION
ER...
So shocked, the drawing's messed up.
A-A g-ghost...
EEEE!!
GAAAH!
ER!
MR. AKIYAMA!!
THERE'S A REASONABLE(ISH) EXPLANATION...!!!
Thanks.
PLEASE STAND BY.
OH... SO THAT EXPLAINS IT...
LET'S NOT TELL TSUBAKI QUITE YET.
huff huff My heart...
THE SHOCK MAY BE TOO MUCH FOR HER.
OF COURSE.

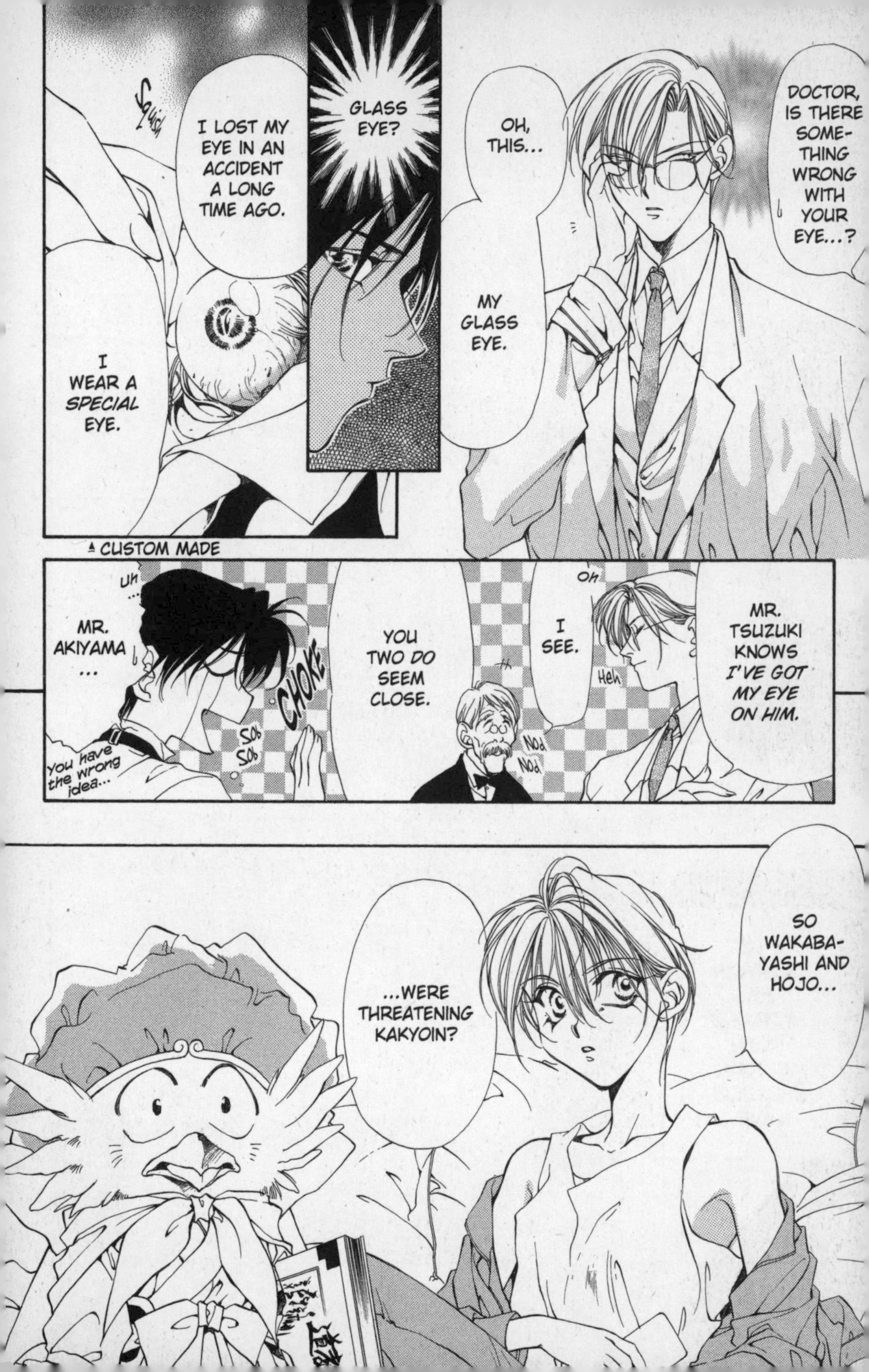
DOCTOR, IS THERE SOME-THING WRONG WITH YOUR EYE...?
OH, THIS...
MY GLASS EYE.
GLASS EYE?
Squish
I LOST MY EYE IN AN ACCIDENT A LONG TIME AGO.
I WEAR A SPECIAL EYE.
▲CUSTOM MADE
Oh
MR. TSUZUKI KNOWS I'VE GOT MY EYE ON HIM.
Heh
I SEE.
Nod Nod
YOU TWO DO SEEM CLOSE.
CHOKE
Sob Sob
uh...
MR. AKIYAMA...
You have the wrong idea...
SO WAKABA-YASHI AND HOJO...
...WERE THREATENING KAKYOIN?

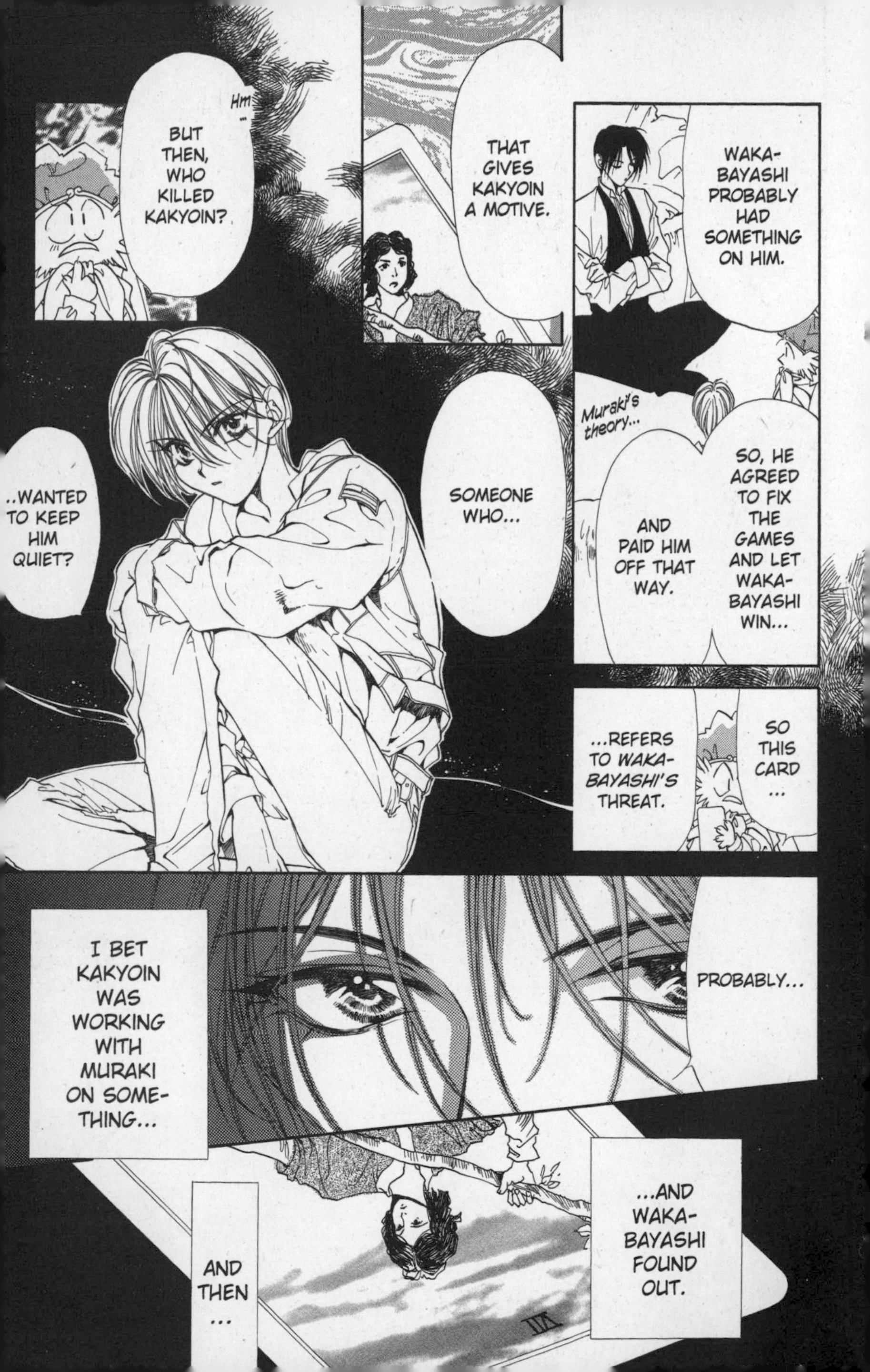
WAKA-BAYASHI PROBABLY HAD SOMETHING ON HIM.
Muraki's theory...
SO, HE AGREED TO FIX THE GAMES AND LET WAKA-BAYASHI WIN...
AND PAID HIM OFF THAT WAY.
THAT GIVES KAKYOIN A MOTIVE.
Hm ...
BUT THEN, WHO KILLED KAKYOIN?
SOMEONE WHO...
..WANTED TO KEEP HIM QUIET?
SO THIS CARD ...
...REFERS TO WAKA-BAYASHI'S THREAT.
PROBABLY...
I BET KAKYOIN WAS WORKING WITH MURAKI ON SOME-THING...
...AND WAKA-BAYASHI FOUND OUT.
AND THEN ...

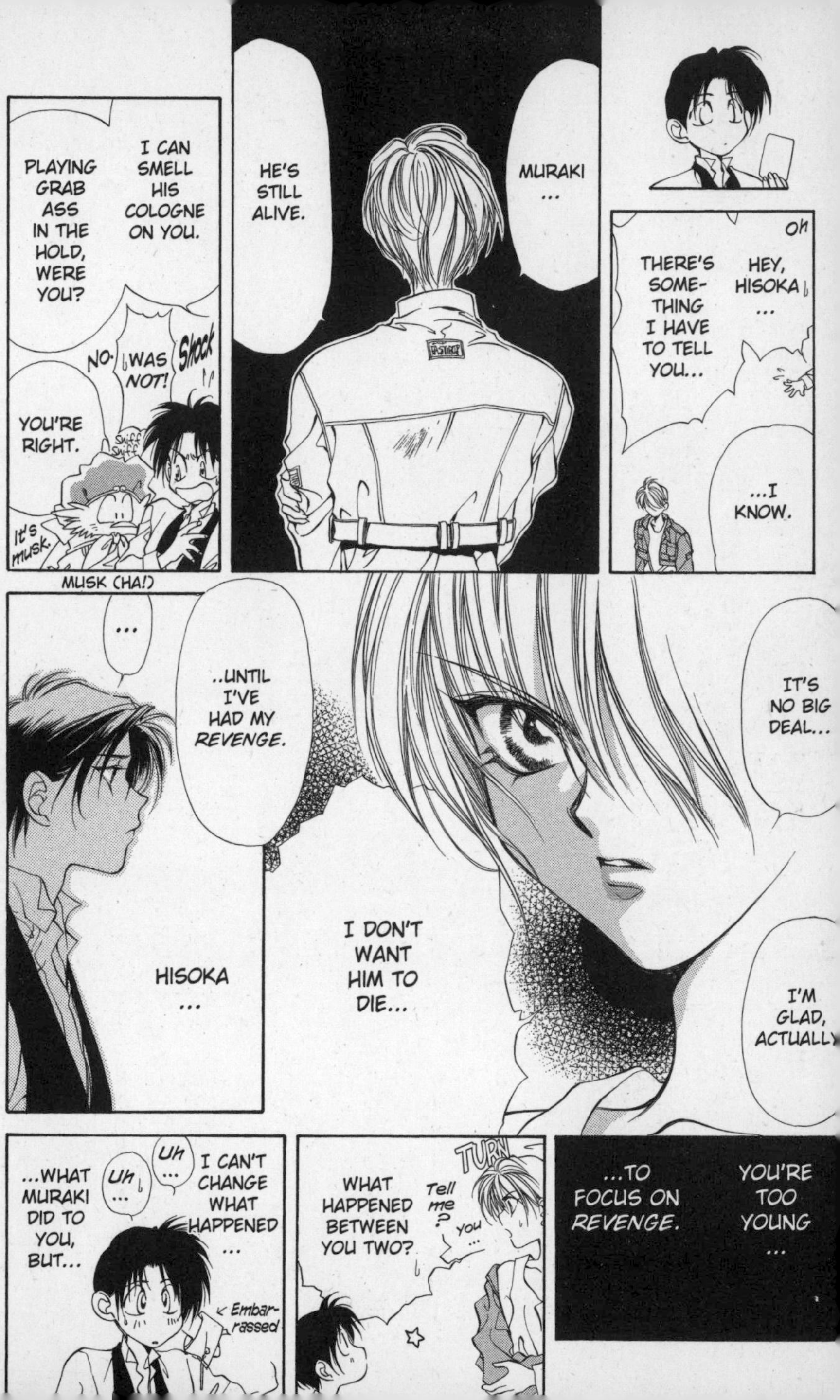
Oh
HEY, HISOKA...
THERE'S SOMETHING I HAVE TO TELL YOU...
...I KNOW.
MURAKI...
HE'S STILL ALIVE.
I CAN SMELL HIS COLOGNE ON YOU.
PLAYING GRAB ASS IN THE HOLD, WERE YOU?
Shock
NO- WAS NOT!
YOU'RE RIGHT.
Sniff Sniff
It's musk.
MUSK (HA!)
IT'S NO BIG DEAL...
I'M GLAD, ACTUALLY
I DON'T WANT HIM TO DIE...
..UNTIL I'VE HAD MY *REVENGE.*
...
HISOKA...
YOU'RE TOO YOUNG...
...TO FOCUS ON *REVENGE.*
TURN
You...
Tell me?
WHAT HAPPENED BETWEEN YOU TWO?
I CAN'T CHANGE WHAT HAPPENED...
Uh...
Uh...
...WHAT MURAKI DID TO YOU, BUT...
Embar-rassed

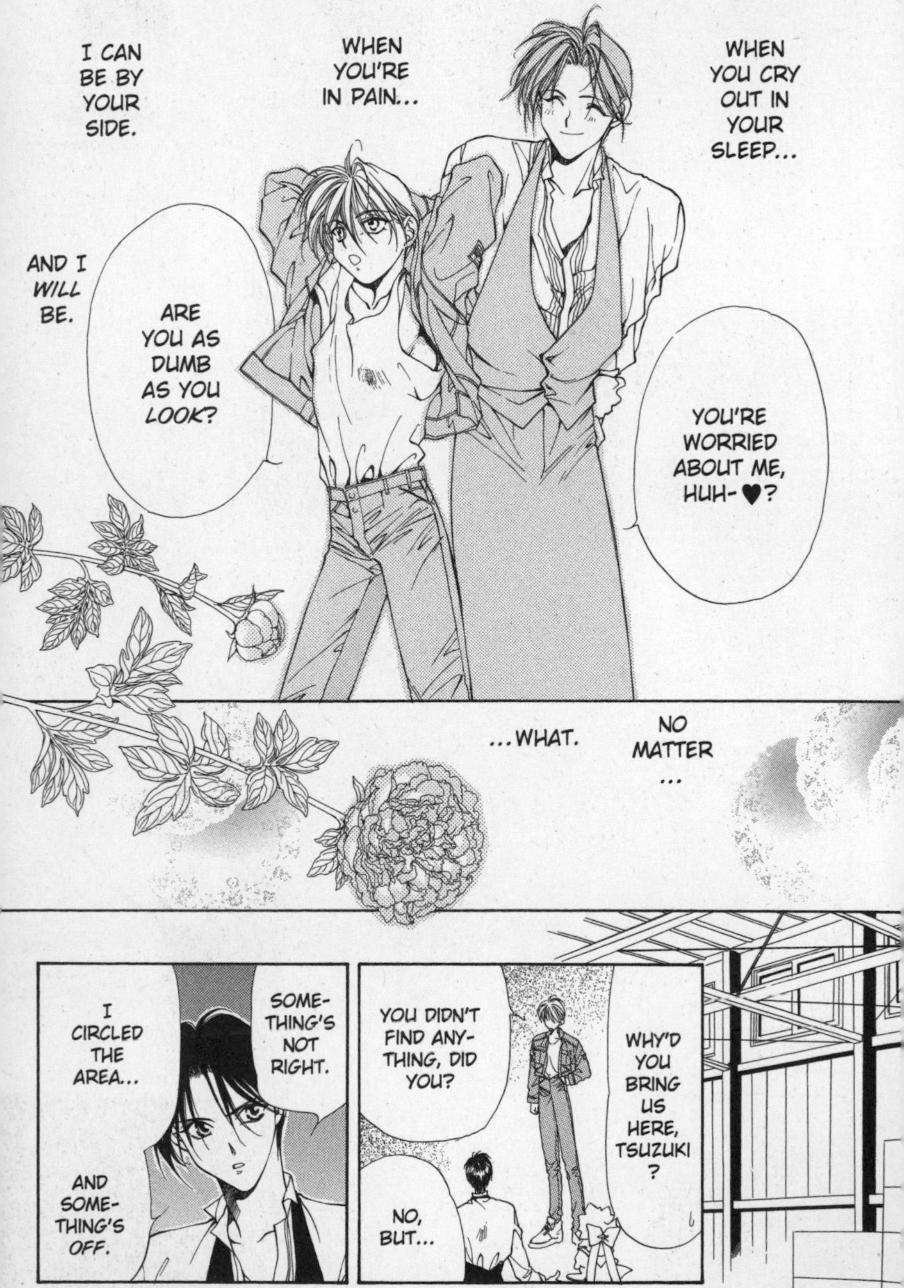
WHEN YOU CRY OUT IN YOUR SLEEP...
WHEN YOU'RE IN PAIN...
I CAN BE BY YOUR SIDE.
AND I *WILL* BE.
YOU'RE WORRIED ABOUT ME, HUH-♥?
ARE YOU AS DUMB AS YOU *LOOK*?
NO MATTER ...
...WHAT.
WHY'D YOU BRING US HERE, TSUZUKI?
YOU DIDN'T FIND ANY-THING, DID YOU?
NO, BUT...
SOME-THING'S NOT RIGHT.
I CIRCLED THE AREA...
AND SOME-THING'S *OFF*.

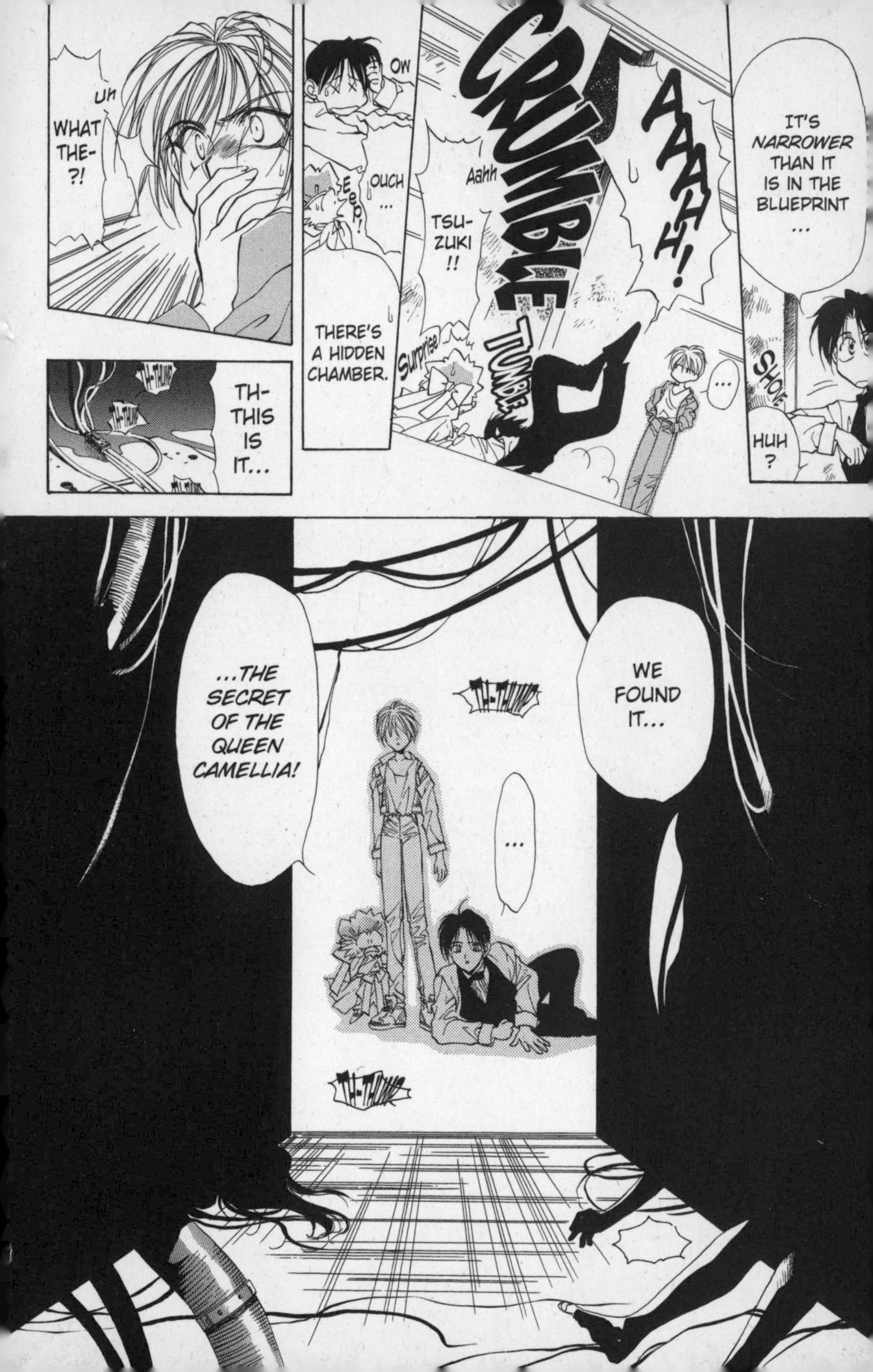
IT'S NARROWER THAN IT IS IN THE BLUEPRINT ...
SHOVE
HUH ?
...
AAAH!
CRUMBLE
TUMBLE
Aahh
TSU-ZUKI !!
Surprise
THERE'S A HIDDEN CHAMBER.
OW
OUCH ...
Eep!
Uh
WHAT THE- ?!
TH-THUMP
TH-THUMP
TH-THIS IS IT...
WE FOUND IT...
...THE SECRET OF THE QUEEN CAMELLIA!
TH-THUMP
...
TH-THUMP

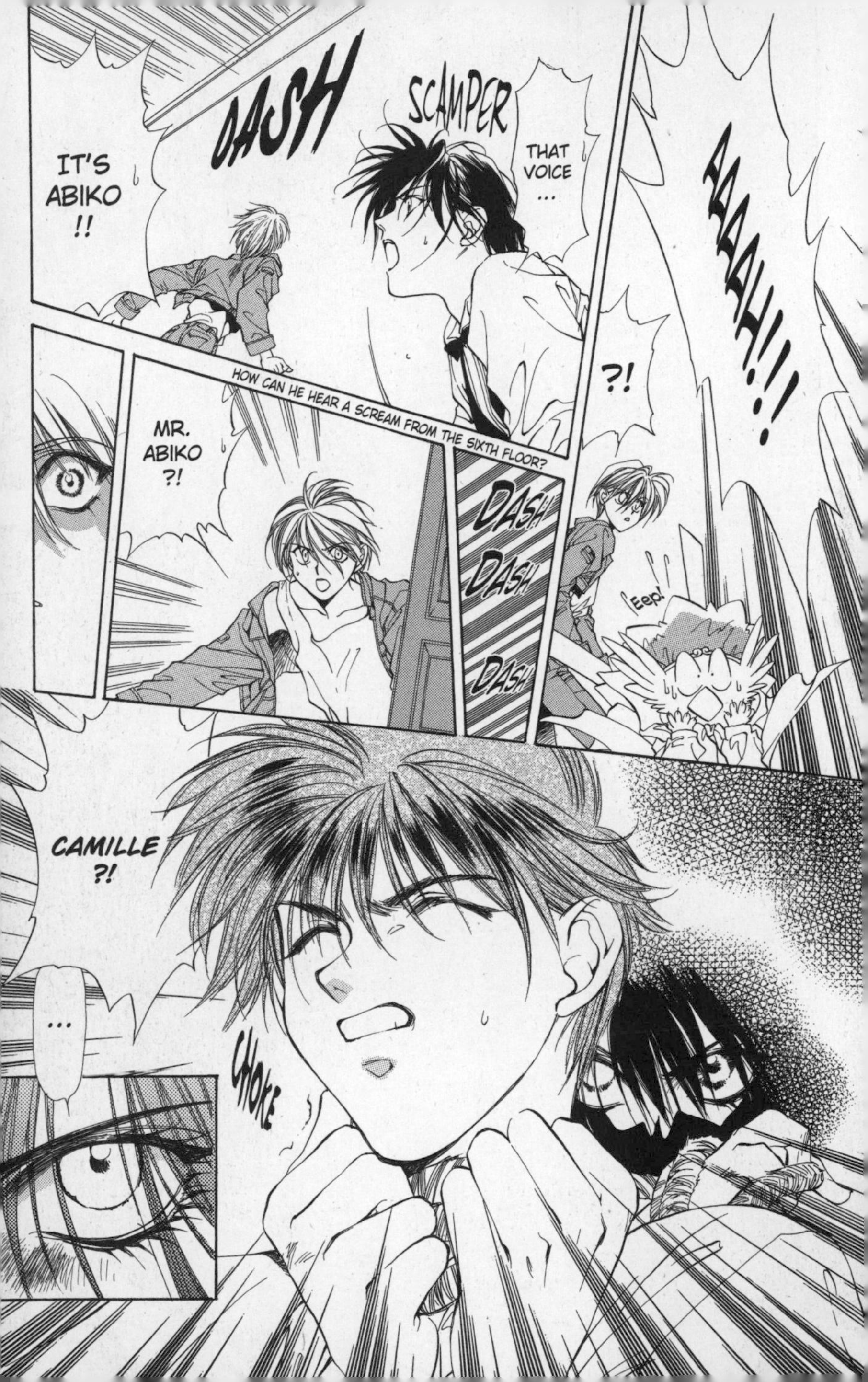
AAAAH!!!
?!
Eep!
THAT VOICE ...
SCAMPER
DASH
IT'S ABIKO !!
DASH DASH DASH
HOW CAN HE HEAR A SCREAM FROM THE SIXTH FLOOR?
MR. ABIKO ?!
CAMILLE ?!
CHOKE
...

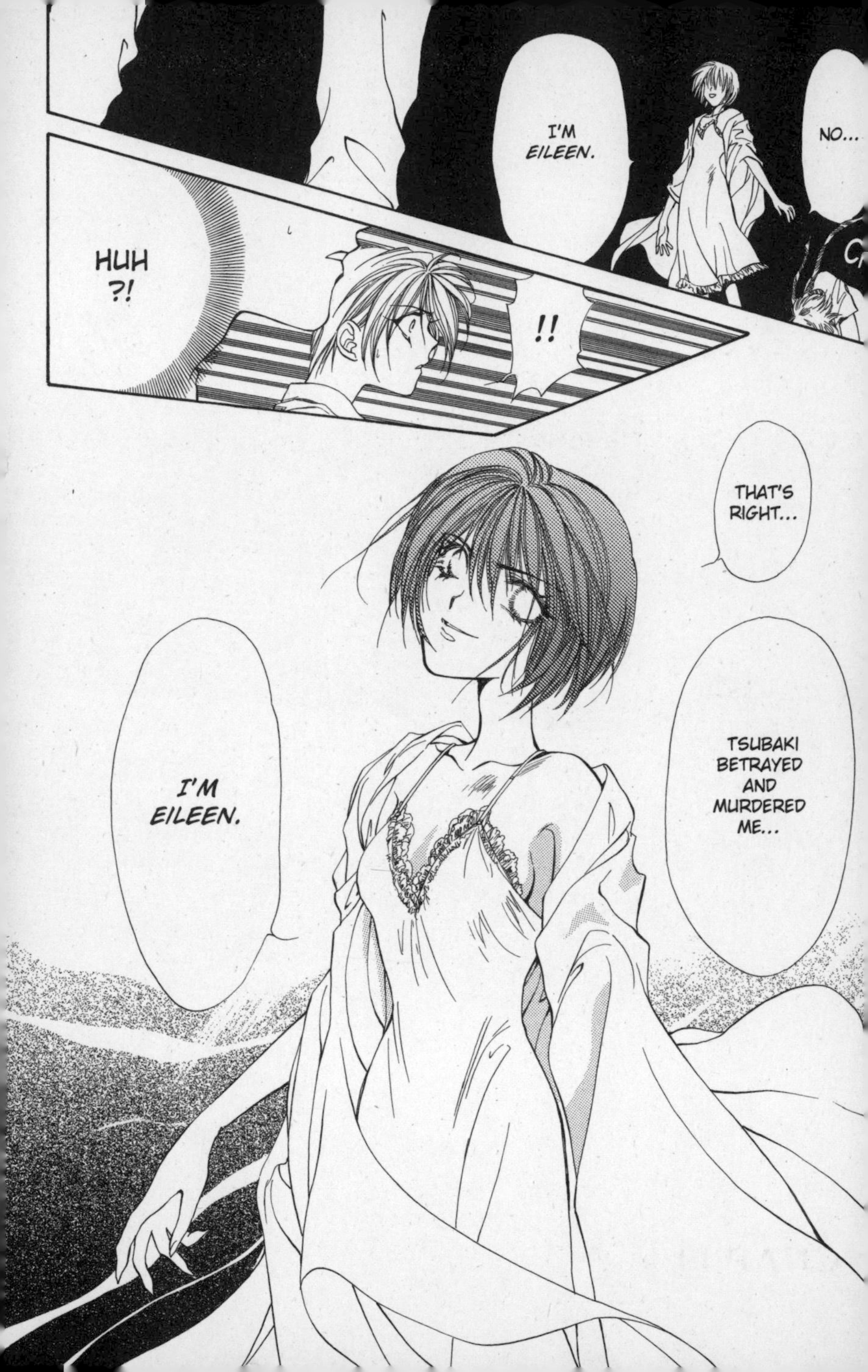
NO...
I'M EILEEN.
!!
HUH ?!
THAT'S RIGHT...
TSUBAKI BETRAYED AND MURDERED ME...
I'M EILEEN.

CHAPTER 6

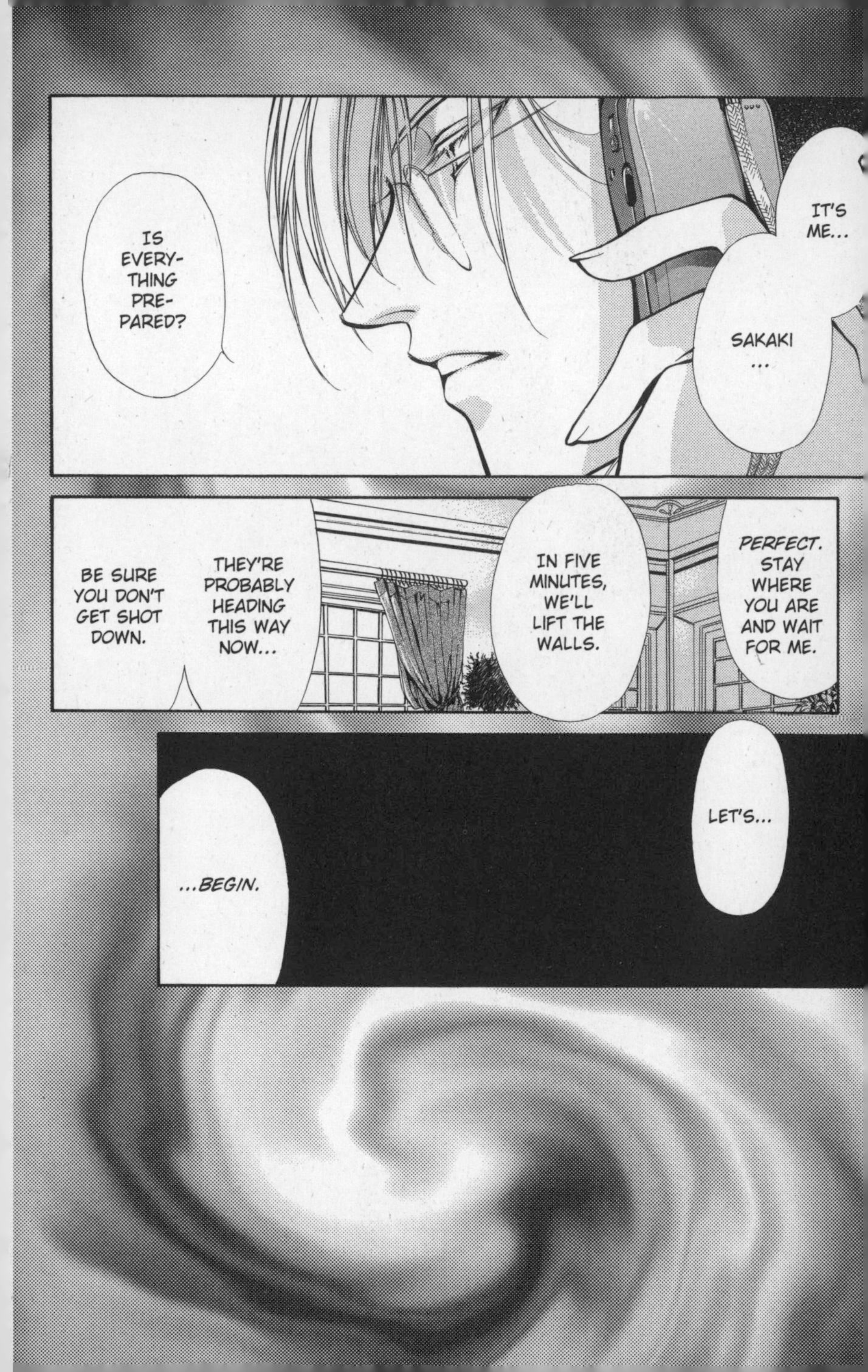
IT'S ME... SAKAKI ...
IS EVERY-THING PRE-PARED?
PERFECT. STAY WHERE YOU ARE AND WAIT FOR ME.
IN FIVE MINUTES, WE'LL LIFT THE WALLS.
THEY'RE PROBABLY HEADING THIS WAY NOW...
BE SURE YOU DON'T GET SHOT DOWN.
LET'S...
...BEGIN.

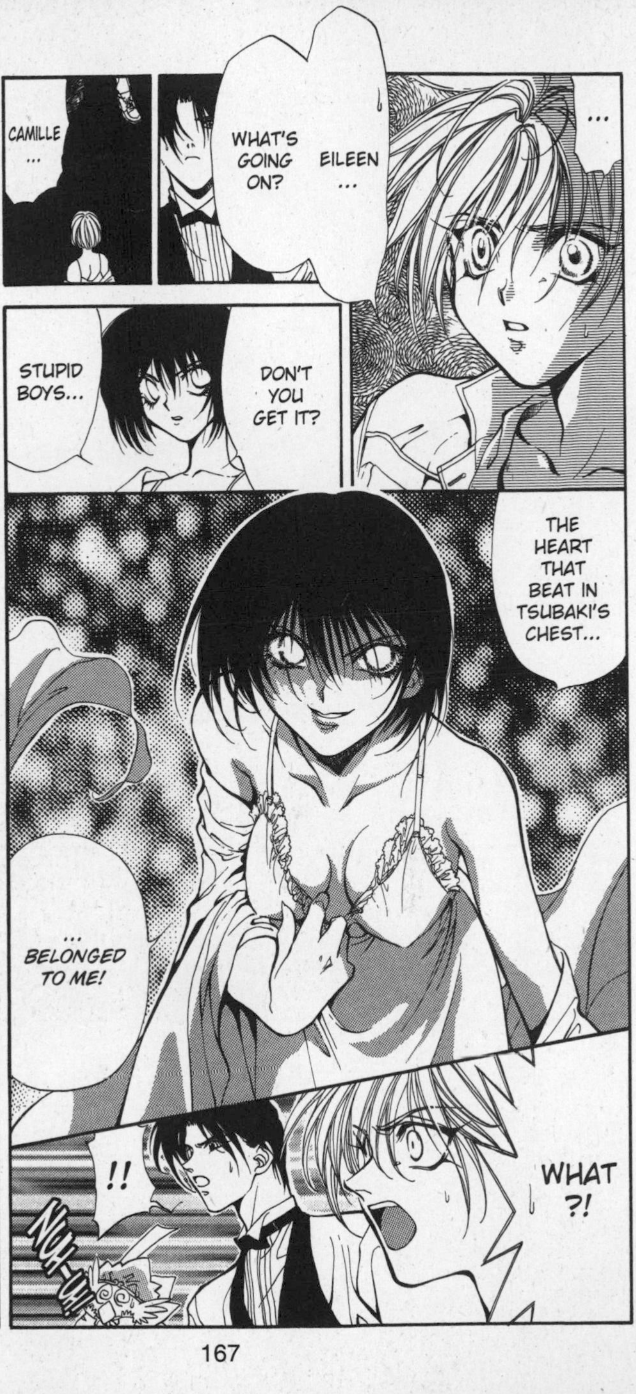
...
EILEEN ...
WHAT'S GOING ON?
CAMILLE ...
DON'T YOU GET IT?
STUPID BOYS...
THE HEART THAT BEAT IN TSUBAKI'S CHEST...
...BELONGED TO ME!
WHAT ?!
!!
NUH-UH

This is my last column in this volume. This story was really hard on me. I barely got the storyboards in on time. So much stress! I know it's seems weird considering that I'm the one writing the story, but I was really drawn in by Hisoka's pain. I cried. I empathized with Tsubaki and I cried. Even Muraki made me cry! These characters are my babies and I love them like they were flesh and blood. Hisoka's really matured, don't you think? I'm proud of him. I suspect the evil Doctor will make another appearance soon, so don't give up hope. One day, I'd like to write Muraki's history. What was he like as a child? Hmm, Sounds fun, doesn't it? (I'm still talking about the doctor... I'm obsessed.) Well, see you next time...!!

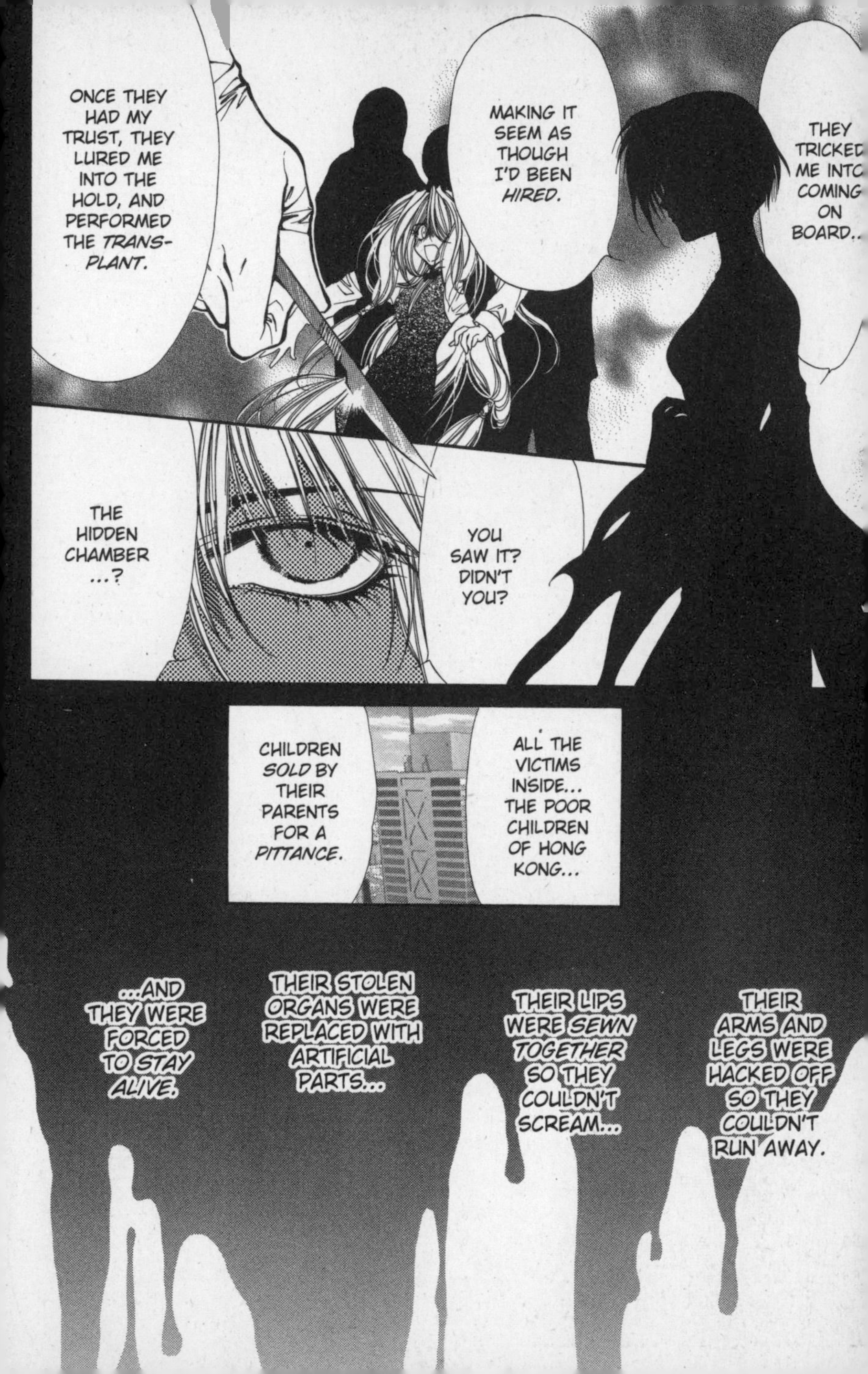
THEY TRICKED ME INTO COMING ON BOARD...
MAKING IT SEEM AS THOUGH I'D BEEN *HIRED*.
ONCE THEY HAD MY TRUST, THEY LURED ME INTO THE HOLD, AND PERFORMED THE *TRANS-PLANT*.
YOU SAW IT? DIDN'T YOU?
THE HIDDEN CHAMBER ...?
ALL THE VICTIMS INSIDE... THE POOR CHILDREN OF HONG KONG...
CHILDREN *SOLD* BY THEIR PARENTS FOR A *PITTANCE*.
THEIR ARMS AND LEGS WERE HACKED OFF SO THEY COULDN'T RUN AWAY.
THEIR LIPS WERE *SEWN TOGETHER* SO THEY COULDN'T SCREAM...
THEIR STOLEN ORGANS WERE REPLACED WITH ARTIFICIAL PARTS...
...AND THEY WERE FORCED TO *STAY ALIVE*.

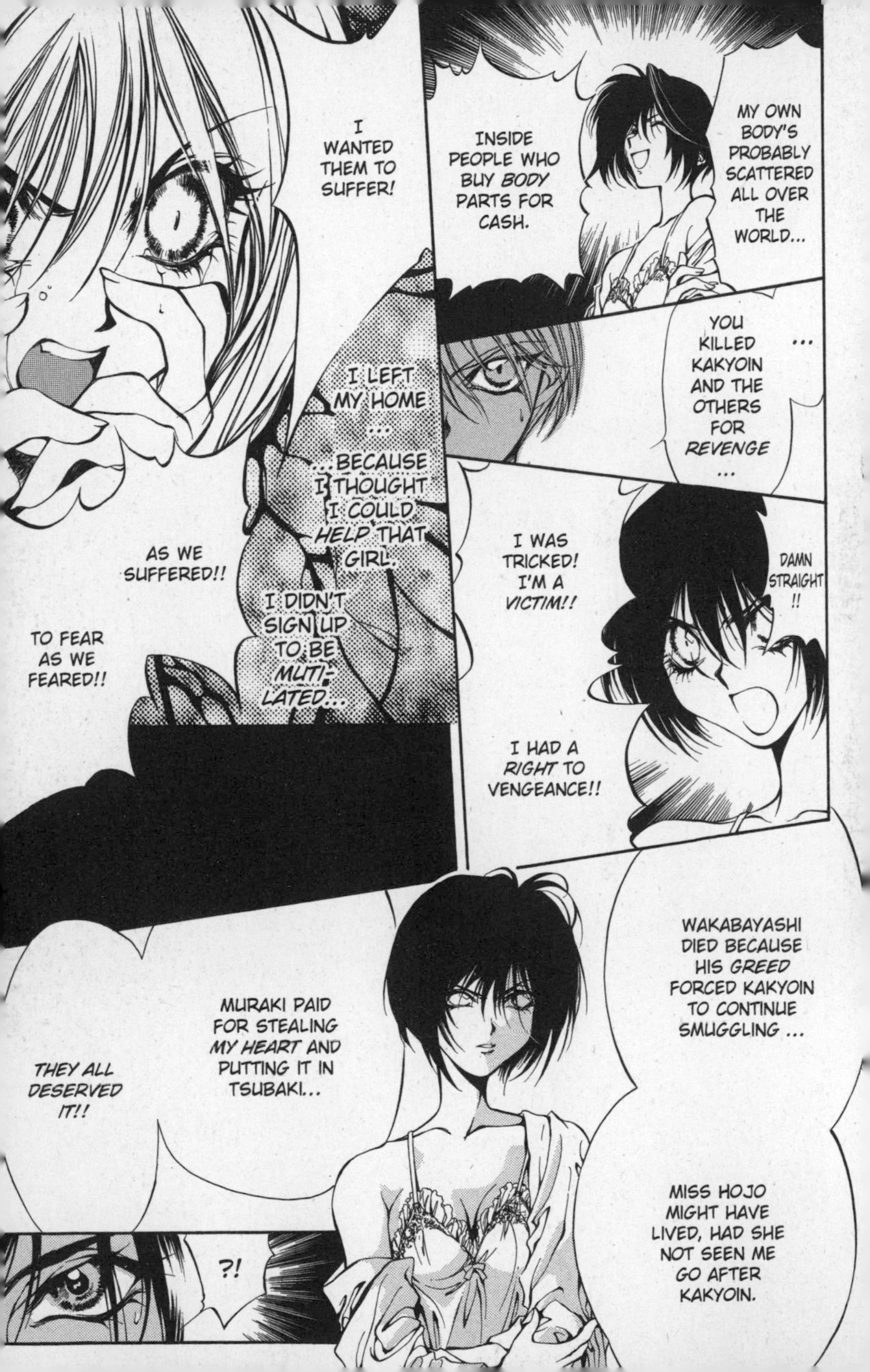

MY OWN BODY'S PROBABLY SCATTERED ALL OVER THE WORLD...
INSIDE PEOPLE WHO BUY *BODY* PARTS FOR CASH.
...
YOU KILLED KAKYOIN AND THE OTHERS FOR *REVENGE* ...
DAMN STRAIGHT !!
I WAS TRICKED! I'M A *VICTIM!!*
I HAD A *RIGHT* TO VENGEANCE!!
I WANTED THEM TO SUFFER!
I LEFT MY HOME ...
...BECAUSE I THOUGHT I COULD *HELP* THAT GIRL.
I DIDN'T SIGN UP TO BE *MUTI-LATED...*
AS WE SUFFERED!!
TO FEAR AS WE FEARED!!
WAKABAYASHI DIED BECAUSE HIS *GREED* FORCED KAKYOIN TO CONTINUE SMUGGLING ...
MISS HOJO MIGHT HAVE LIVED, HAD SHE NOT SEEN ME GO AFTER KAKYOIN.
MURAKI PAID FOR STEALING *MY HEART* AND PUTTING IT IN TSUBAKI...
THEY ALL DESERVED IT!!
?!

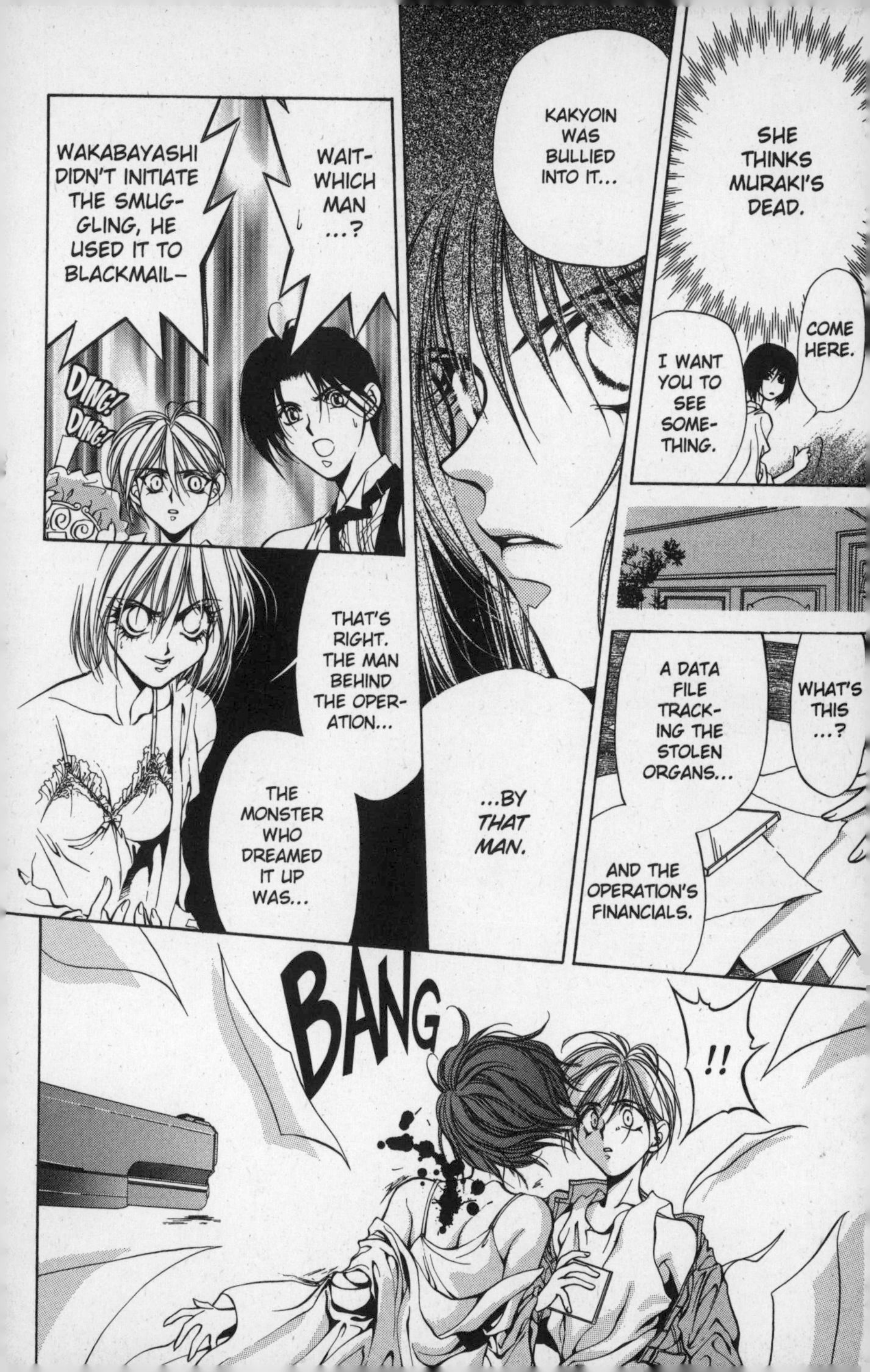
SHE THINKS MURAKI'S DEAD.
COME HERE.
I WANT YOU TO SEE SOME-THING.
WHAT'S THIS ...?
A DATA FILE TRACK-ING THE STOLEN ORGANS...
AND THE OPERATION'S FINANCIALS.
KAKYOIN WAS BULLIED INTO IT...
...BY THAT MAN.
WAKABAYASHI DIDN'T INITIATE THE SMUG-GLING, HE USED IT TO BLACKMAIL–
WAIT-WHICH MAN ...?
DING! DING!
THAT'S RIGHT. THE MAN BEHIND THE OPER-ATION...
THE MONSTER WHO DREAMED IT UP WAS...
BANG
!!

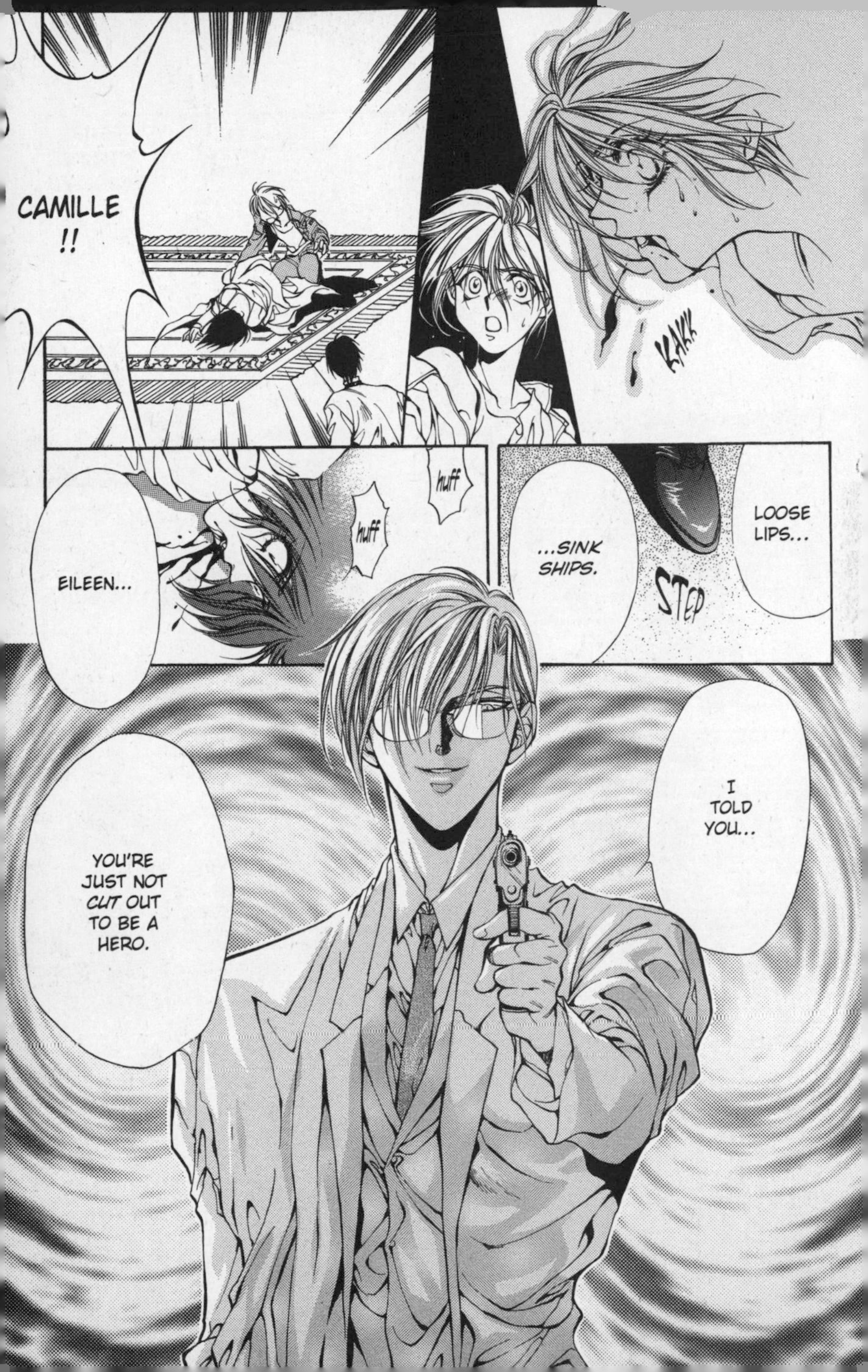
KAKK
CAMILLE !!
LOOSE LIPS...
STEP
...SINK SHIPS.
huff
huff
EILEEN...
I TOLD YOU...
YOU'RE JUST NOT CUT OUT TO BE A HERO.

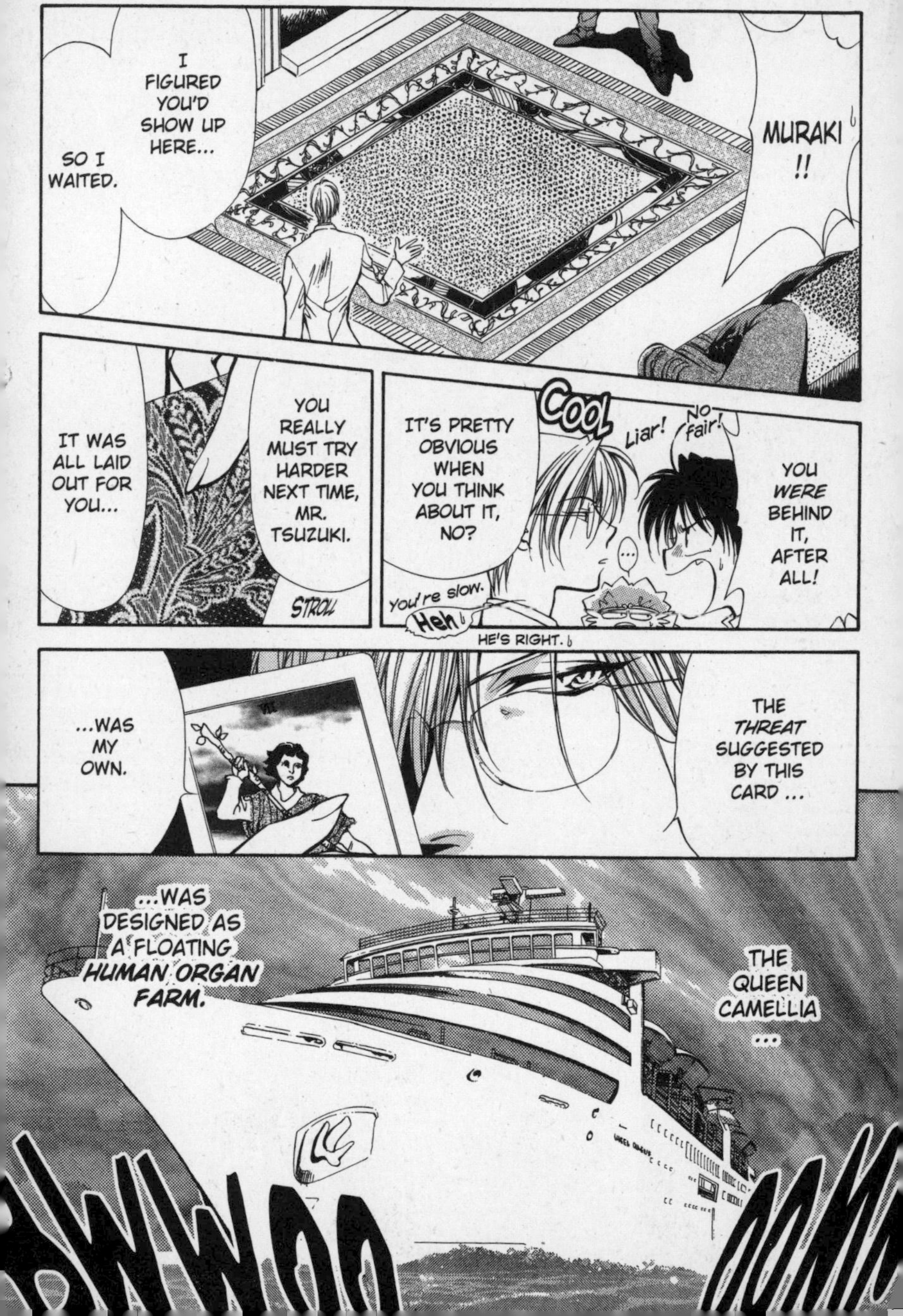
MURAKI !!
I FIGURED YOU'D SHOW UP HERE...
SO I WAITED.
YOU WERE BEHIND IT, AFTER ALL!
No fair!
Liar!
COOL
IT'S PRETTY OBVIOUS WHEN YOU THINK ABOUT IT, NO?
...
You're slow.
Heh
HE'S RIGHT.
YOU REALLY MUST TRY HARDER NEXT TIME, MR. TSUZUKI.
STROLL
IT WAS ALL LAID OUT FOR YOU...
THE THREAT SUGGESTED BY THIS CARD ...
...WAS MY OWN.
THE QUEEN CAMELLIA ...
...WAS DESIGNED AS A FLOATING HUMAN ORGAN FARM.

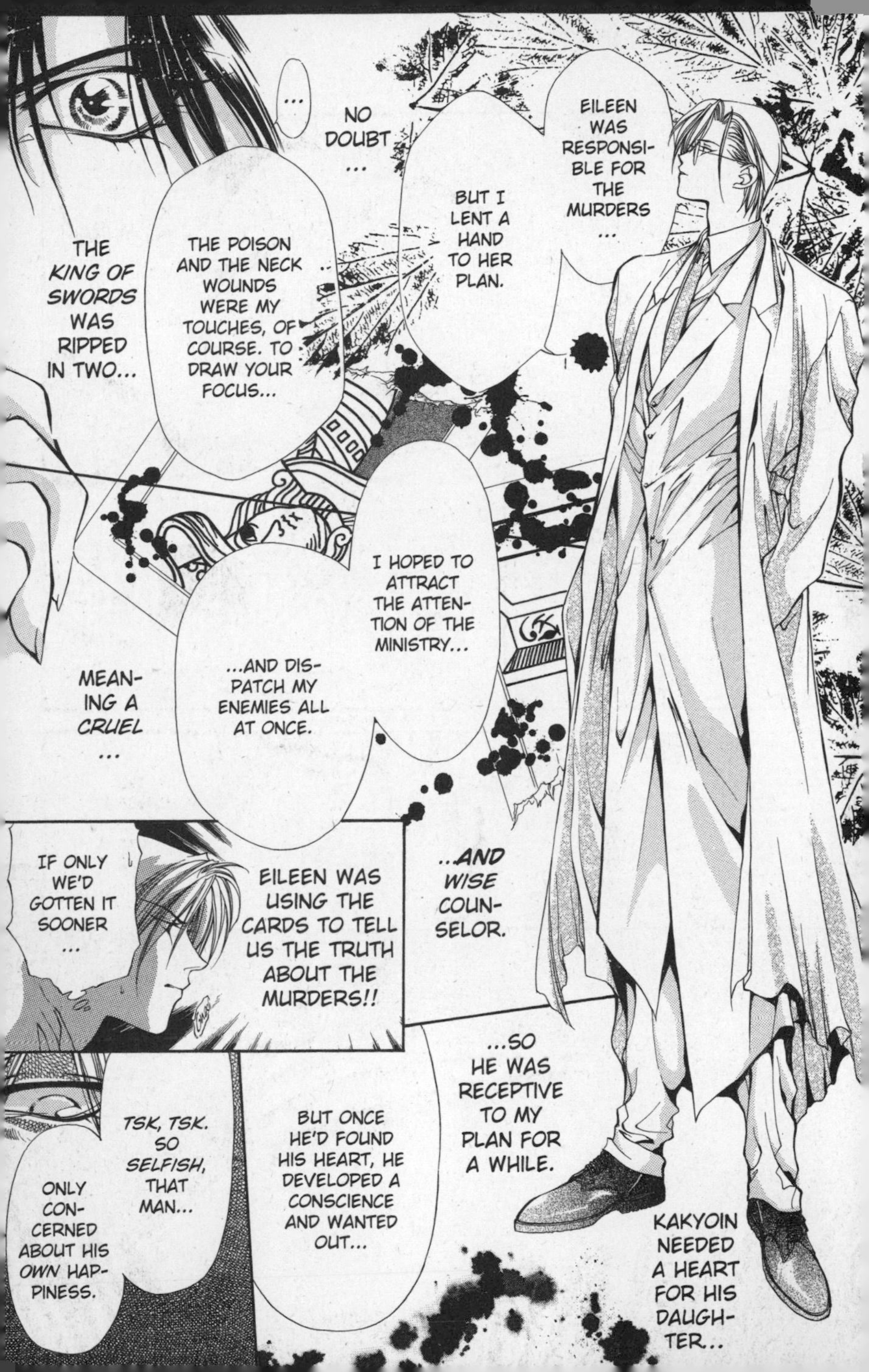
EILEEN WAS RESPONSIBLE FOR THE MURDERS...
BUT I LENT A HAND TO HER PLAN.
NO DOUBT...
...
THE POISON AND THE NECK WOUNDS WERE MY TOUCHES, OF COURSE. TO DRAW YOUR FOCUS...
THE *KING OF SWORDS* WAS RIPPED IN TWO...
I HOPED TO ATTRACT THE ATTENTION OF THE MINISTRY...
...AND DISPATCH MY ENEMIES ALL AT ONCE.
MEANING A *CRUEL*...
...*AND WISE* COUNSELOR.
EILEEN WAS USING THE CARDS TO TELL US THE TRUTH ABOUT THE MURDERS!!
IF ONLY WE'D GOTTEN IT SOONER...
KAKYOIN NEEDED A HEART FOR HIS DAUGHTER...
...SO HE WAS RECEPTIVE TO MY PLAN FOR A WHILE.
BUT ONCE HE'D FOUND HIS HEART, HE DEVELOPED A CONSCIENCE AND WANTED OUT...
TSK, TSK. SO *SELFISH,* THAT MAN...
ONLY CONCERNED ABOUT HIS *OWN* HAPPINESS.

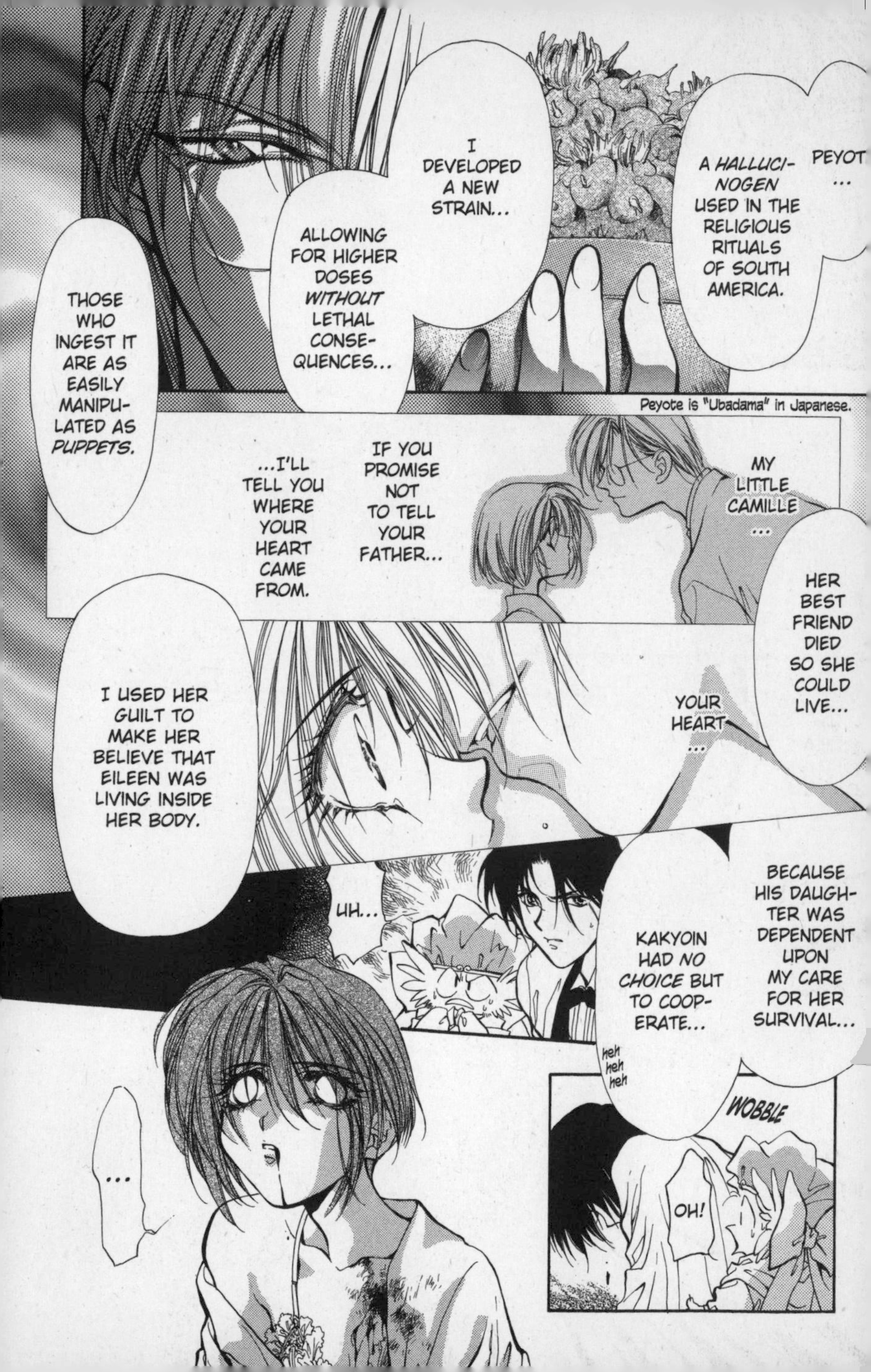
PEYOT ...
A HALLUCINOGEN USED IN THE RELIGIOUS RITUALS OF SOUTH AMERICA.
I DEVELOPED A NEW STRAIN...
ALLOWING FOR HIGHER DOSES *WITHOUT* LETHAL CONSEQUENCES...
THOSE WHO INGEST IT ARE AS EASILY MANIPULATED AS *PUPPETS.*
MY LITTLE CAMILLE ...
IF YOU PROMISE NOT TO TELL YOUR FATHER...
...I'LL TELL YOU WHERE YOUR HEART CAME FROM.
HER BEST FRIEND DIED SO SHE COULD LIVE...
YOUR HEART ...
I USED HER GUILT TO MAKE HER BELIEVE THAT EILEEN WAS LIVING INSIDE HER BODY.
BECAUSE HIS DAUGHTER WAS DEPENDENT UPON MY CARE FOR HER SURVIVAL...
KAKYOIN HAD *NO CHOICE* BUT TO COOPERATE...
UH...
heh heh heh
WOBBLE
OH!
...
Peyote is "Ubadama" in Japanese.

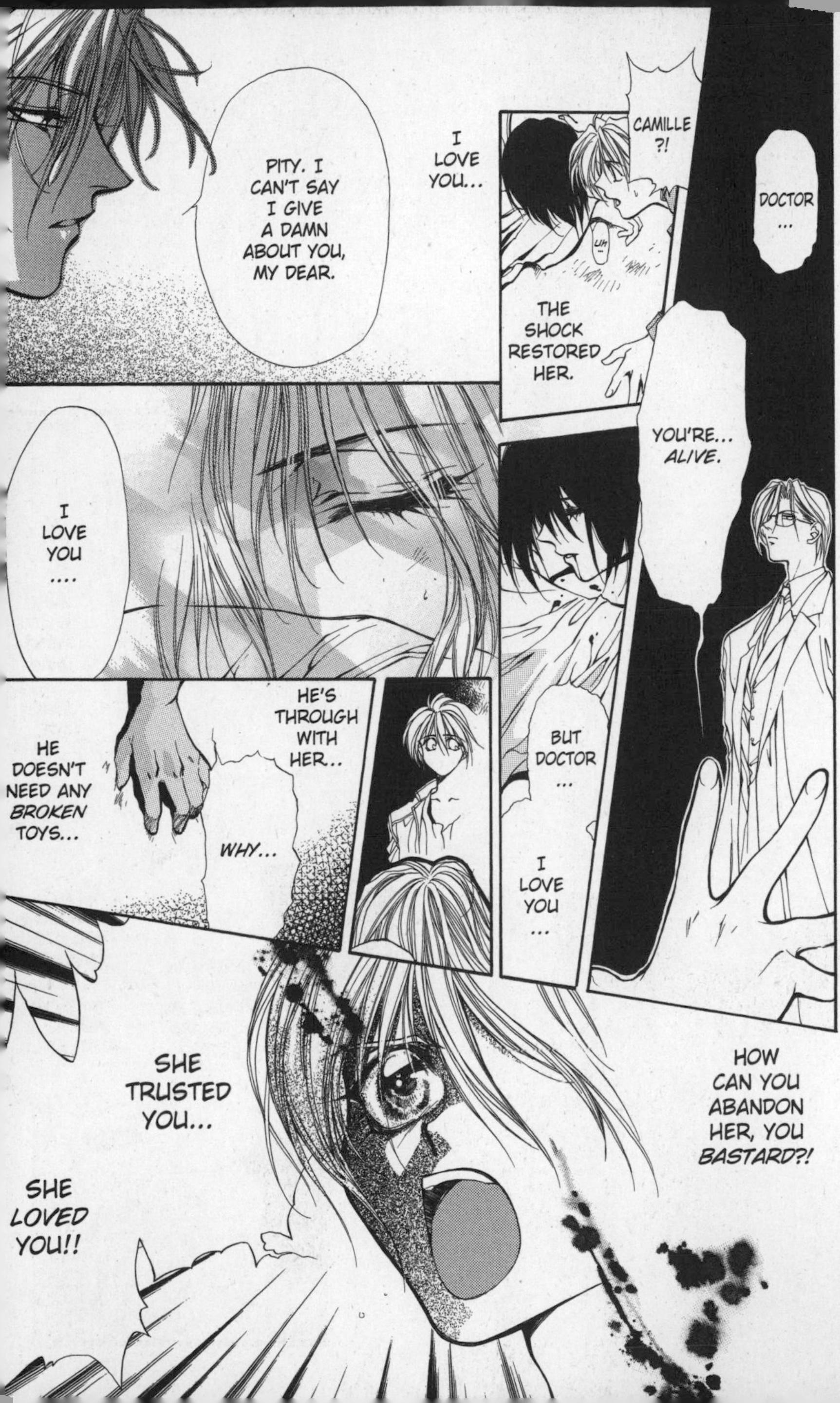
DOCTOR ...
YOU'RE... ALIVE.
CAMILLE ?!
UH
THE SHOCK RESTORED HER.
BUT DOCTOR ...
I LOVE YOU ...
I LOVE YOU...
PITY. I CAN'T SAY I GIVE A DAMN ABOUT YOU, MY DEAR.
I LOVE YOU ....
HE'S THROUGH WITH HER..
WHY...
HE DOESN'T NEED ANY *BROKEN* TOYS...
HOW CAN YOU ABANDON HER, YOU *BASTARD?!*
SHE TRUSTED YOU...
SHE *LOVED* YOU!!

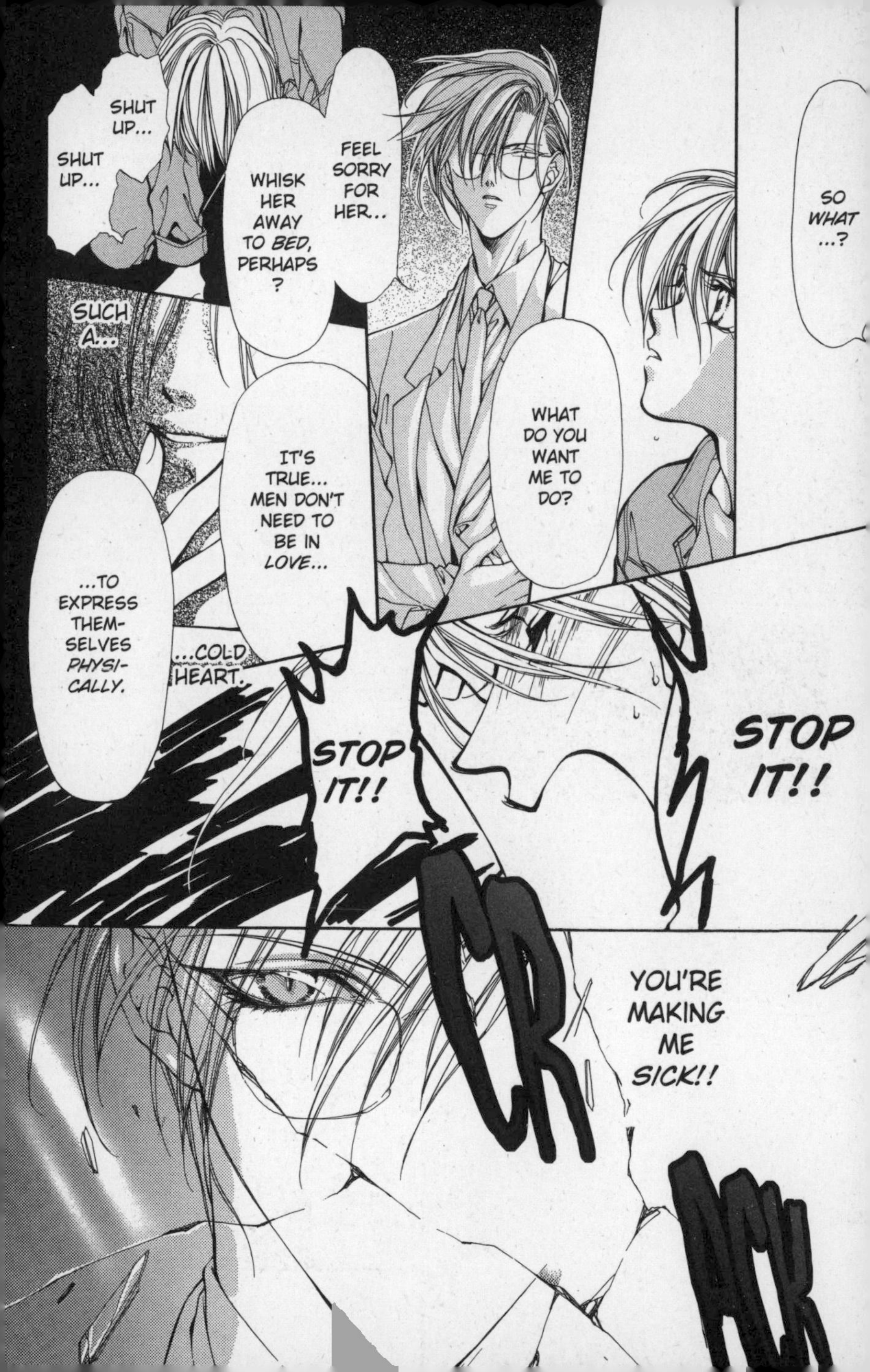
SO WHAT ...?
FEEL SORRY FOR HER...
WHISK HER AWAY TO *BED*, PERHAPS ?
SHUT UP...
SHUT UP...
WHAT DO YOU WANT ME TO DO?
IT'S TRUE... MEN DON'T NEED TO BE IN *LOVE*...
...TO EXPRESS THEM-SELVES *PHYSI-CALLY.*
SUCH A...
...COLD HEART.
STOP IT!!
STOP IT!!
YOU'RE MAKING ME *SICK!!*
CRACK

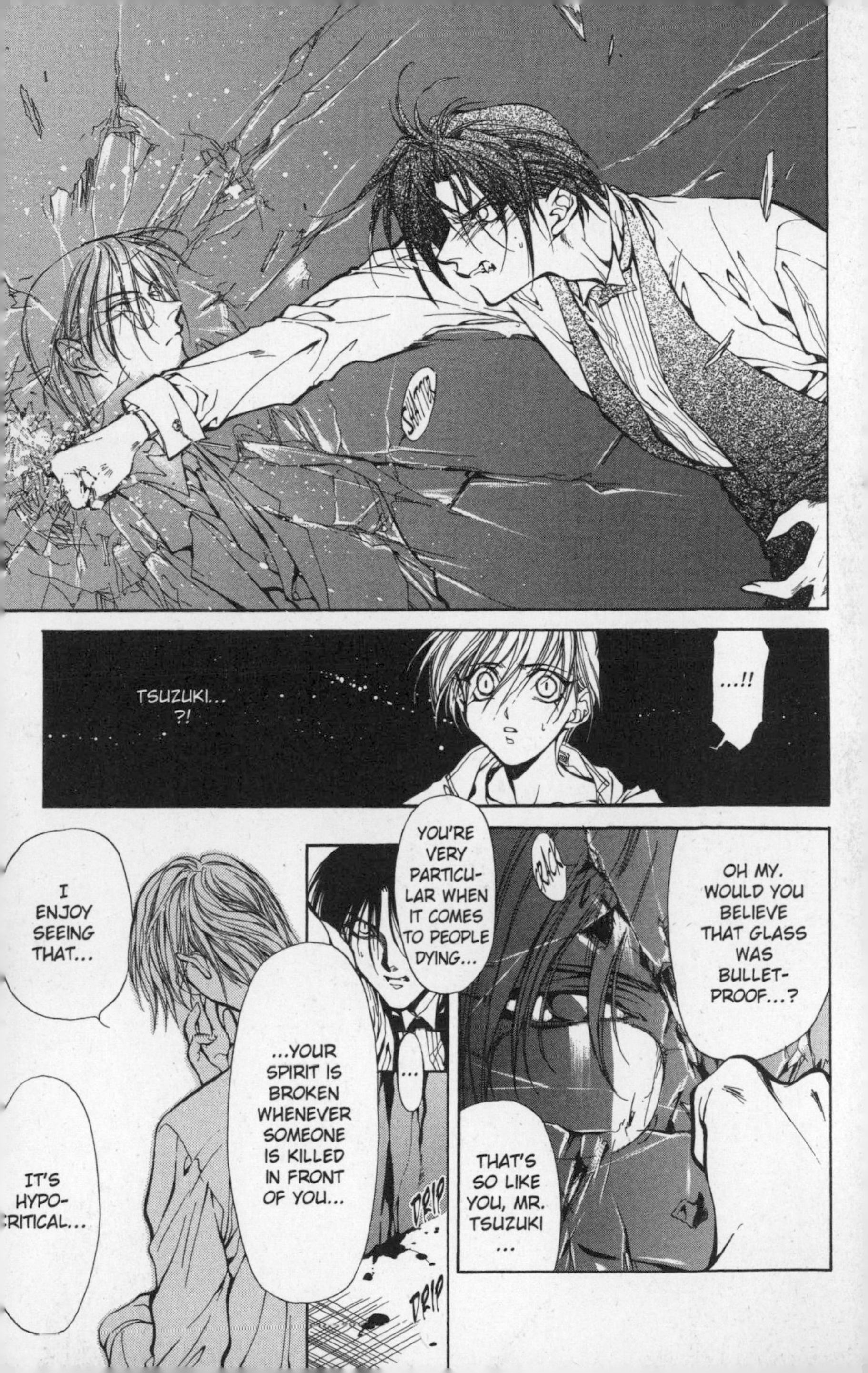
SHATTER
...!!
TSUZUKI... ?!
OH MY. WOULD YOU BELIEVE THAT GLASS WAS BULLET-PROOF...?
CRACK
THAT'S SO LIKE YOU, MR. TSUZUKI ...
DRIP
DRIP
YOU'RE VERY PARTICU-LAR WHEN IT COMES TO PEOPLE DYING...
...
...YOUR SPIRIT IS BROKEN WHENEVER SOMEONE IS KILLED IN FRONT OF YOU...
I ENJOY SEEING THAT...
IT'S HYPO-CRITICAL...

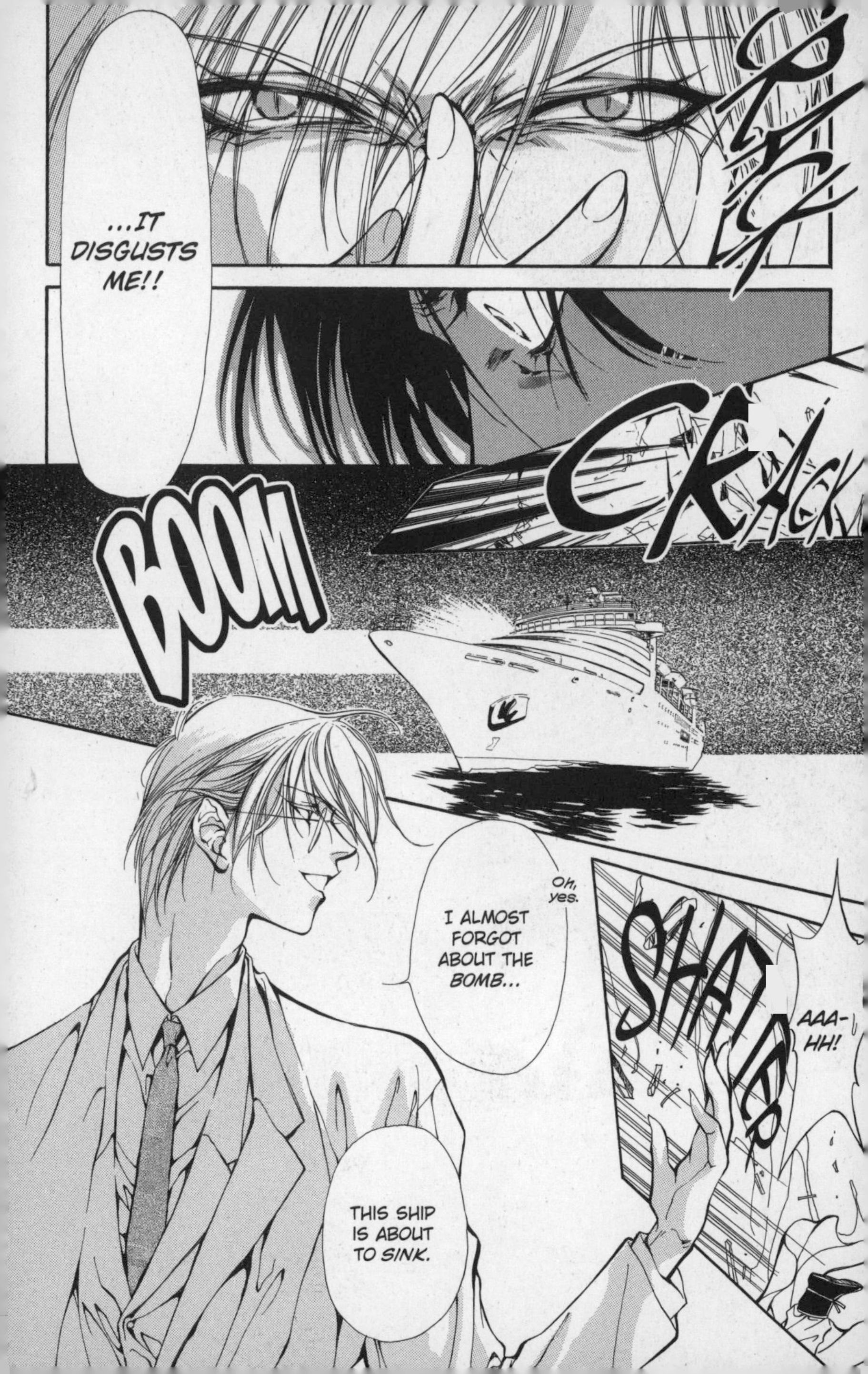
...IT DISGUSTS ME!!
CRACK
BOOM
SHATTER
AAA-HH!
Oh, yes.
I ALMOST FORGOT ABOUT THE BOMB...
THIS SHIP IS ABOUT TO SINK.

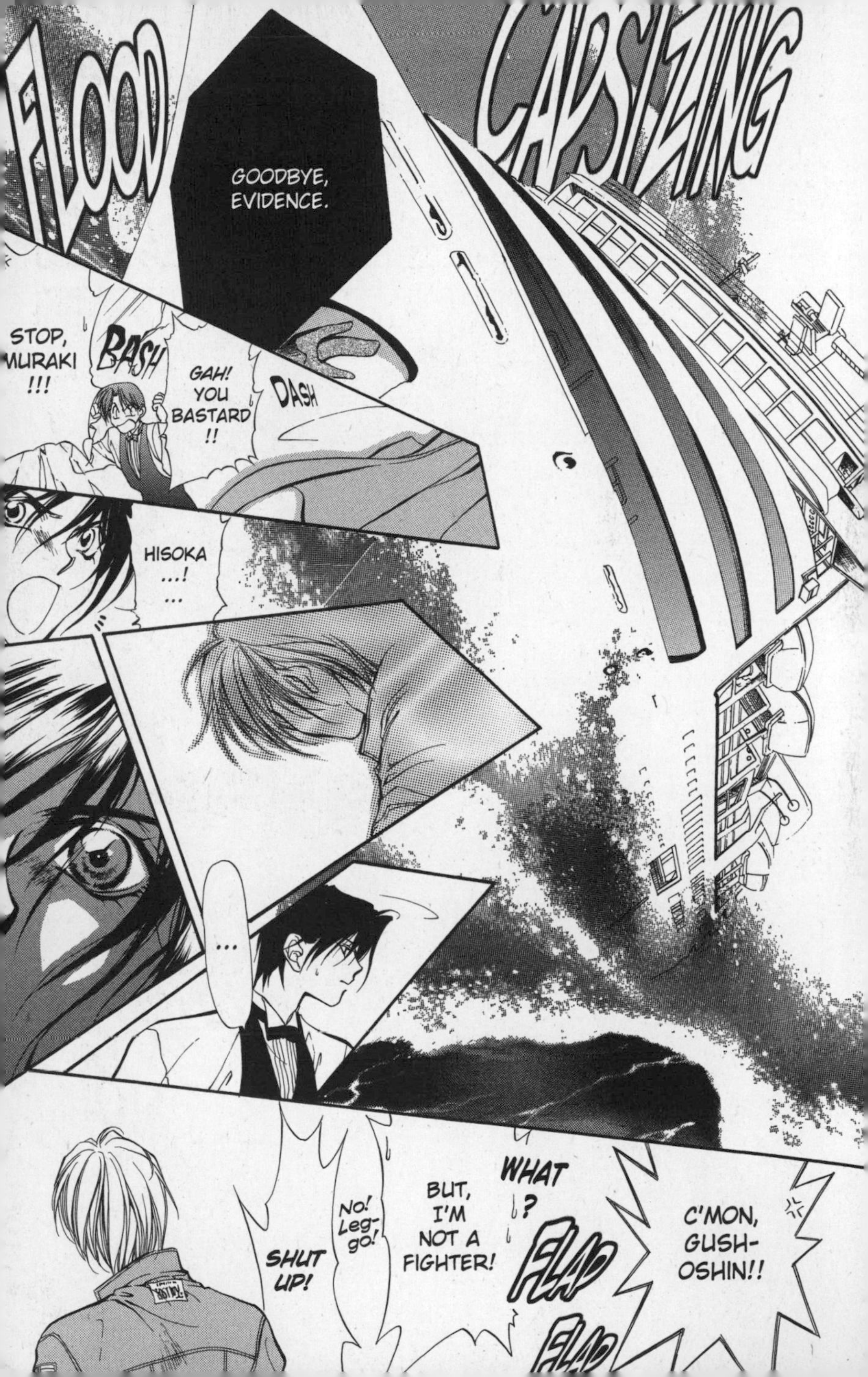
CAPSIZING
GOODBYE, EVIDENCE.
FLOOD
DASH
GAH! YOU BASTARD!!
BASH
STOP, MURAKI!!!
HISOKA ...! ...
...
C'MON, GUSH-OSHIN!!
FLAP
FLAP
WHAT?
BUT, I'M NOT A FIGHTER!
No! Leg-go!
SHUT UP!

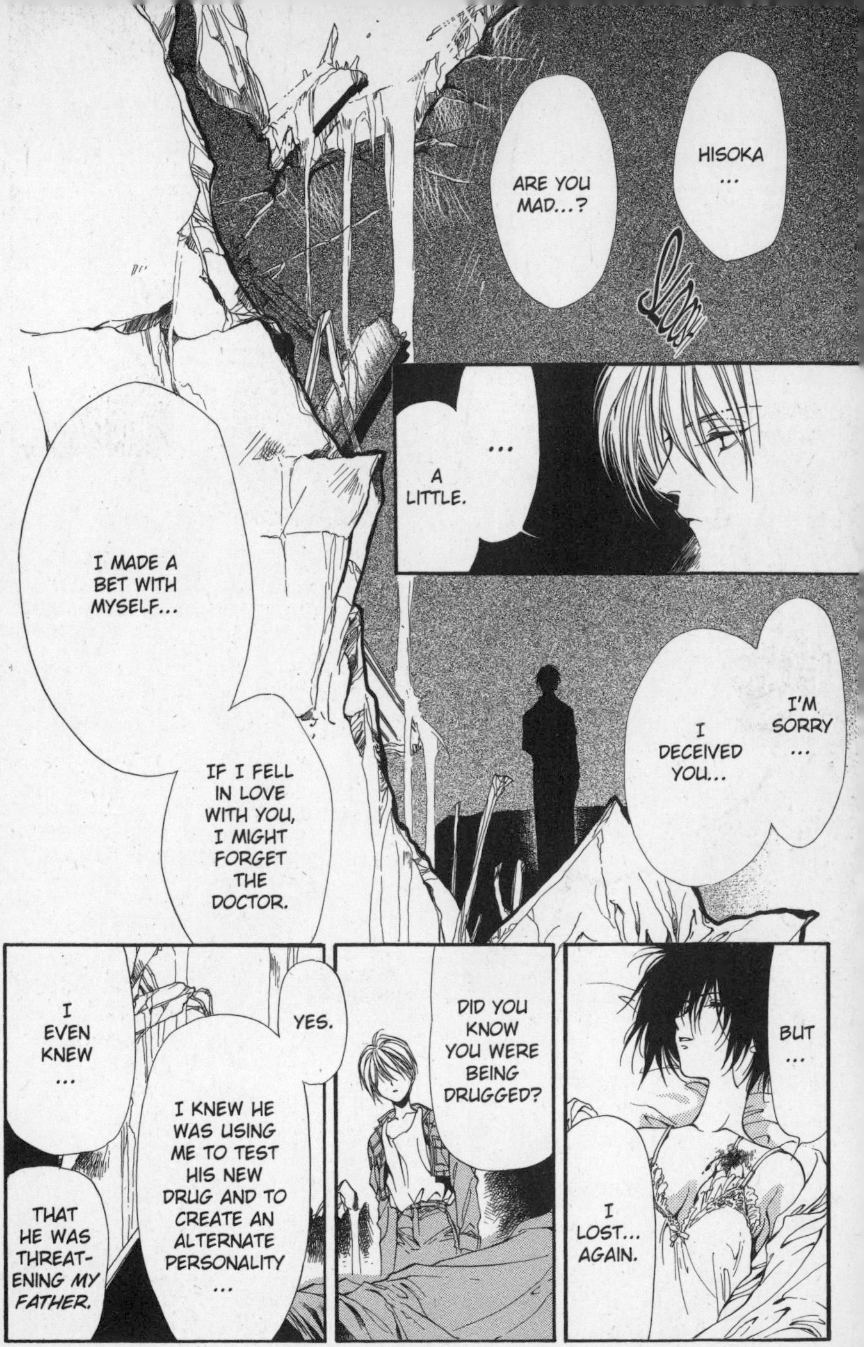
HISOKA ...
ARE YOU MAD...?
...
A LITTLE.
I'M SORRY ...
I DECEIVED YOU...
I MADE A BET WITH MYSELF...
IF I FELL IN LOVE WITH YOU, I MIGHT FORGET THE DOCTOR.
BUT ...
I LOST... AGAIN.
DID YOU KNOW YOU WERE BEING DRUGGED?
YES.
I EVEN KNEW ...
I KNEW HE WAS USING ME TO TEST HIS NEW DRUG AND TO CREATE AN ALTERNATE PERSONALITY ...
THAT HE WAS THREAT-ENING MY FATHER.

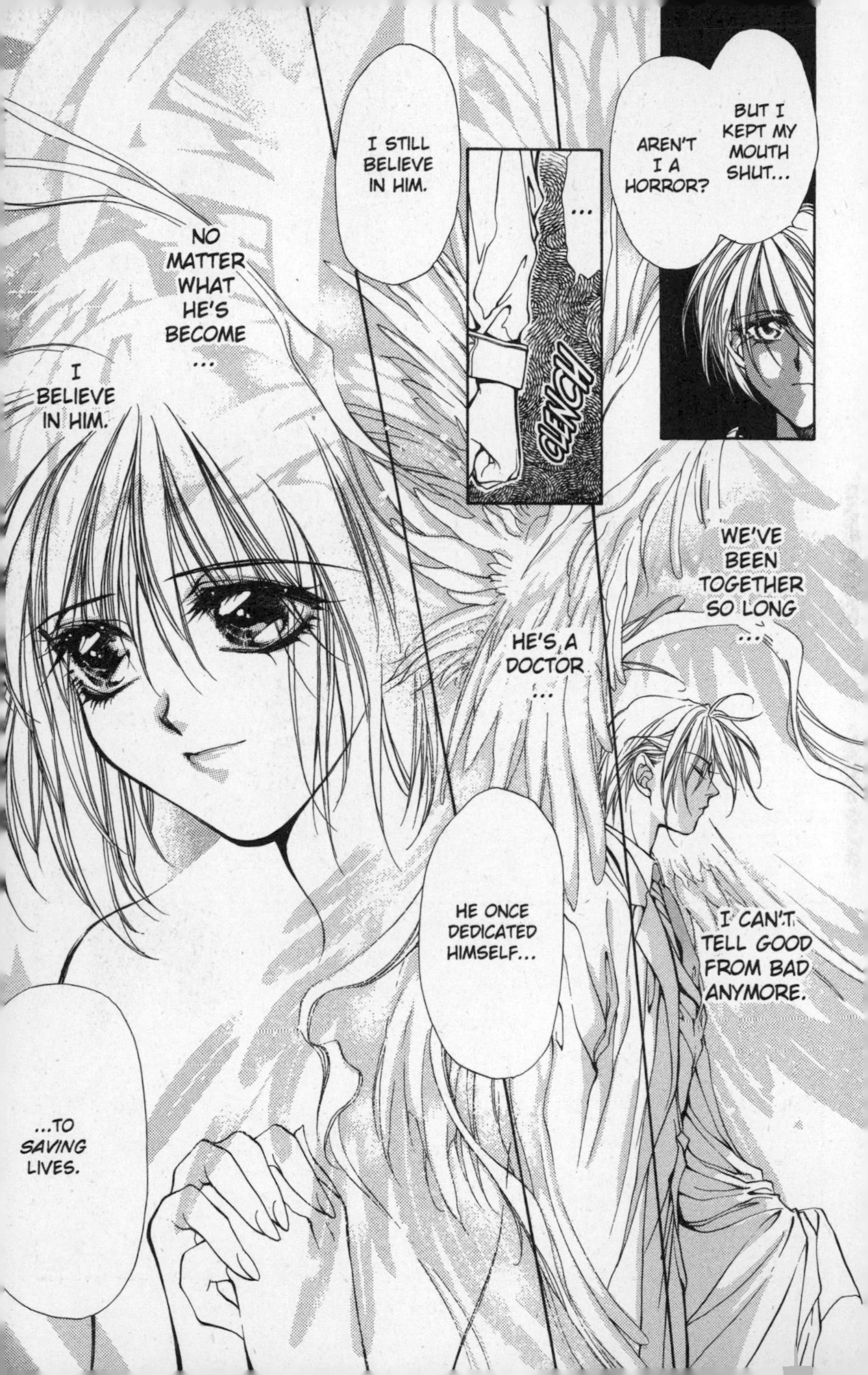
BUT I KEPT MY MOUTH SHUT...
AREN'T I A HORROR?
...
CLENCH
I STILL BELIEVE IN HIM.
NO MATTER WHAT HE'S BECOME ...
I BELIEVE IN HIM.
WE'VE BEEN TOGETHER SO LONG ...
HE'S A DOCTOR ...
I CAN'T TELL GOOD FROM BAD ANYMORE.
HE ONCE DEDICATED HIMSELF...
...TO SAVING LIVES.

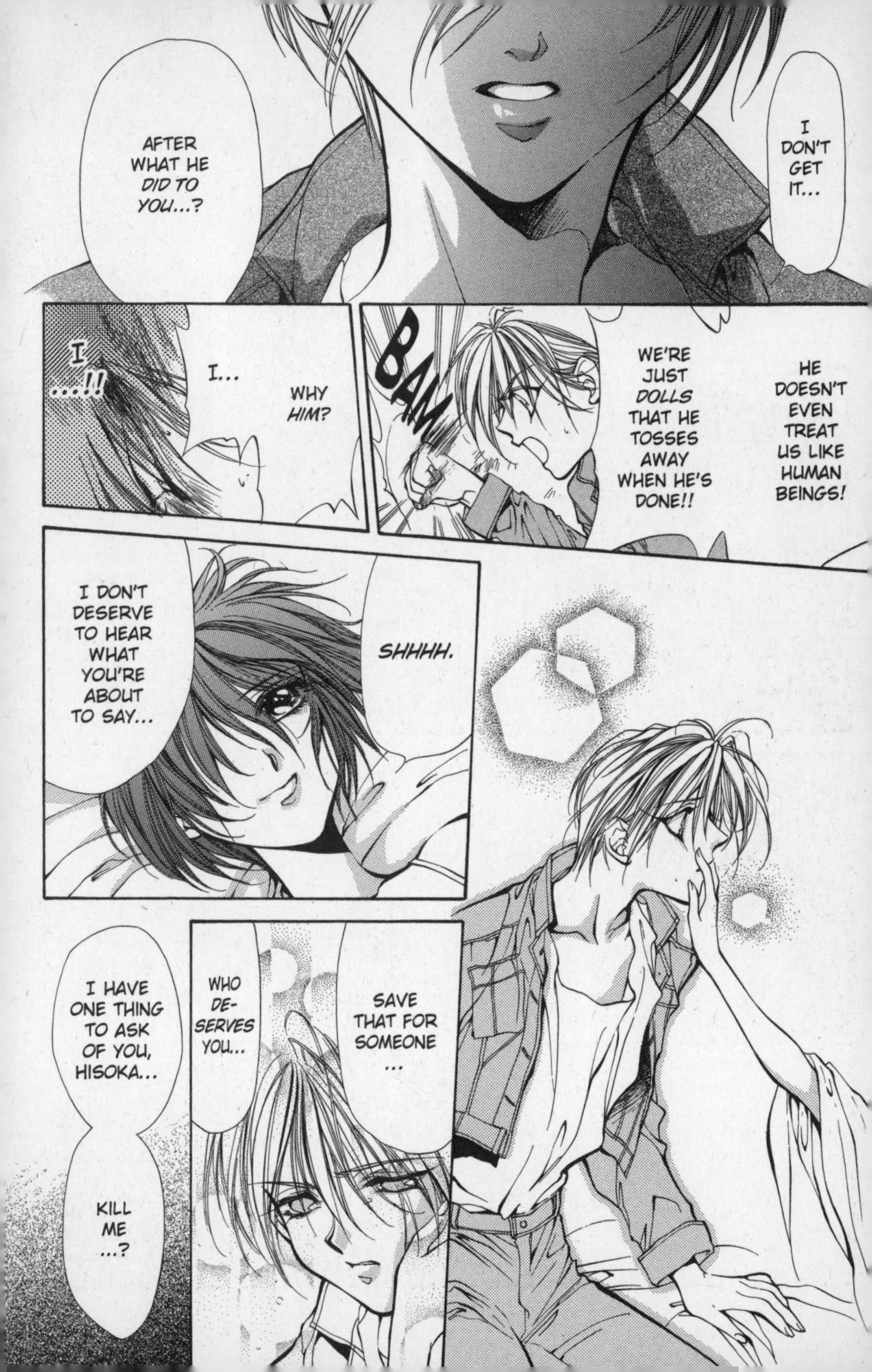
I DON'T GET IT...
AFTER WHAT HE DID TO YOU...?
HE DOESN'T EVEN TREAT US LIKE HUMAN BEINGS!
WE'RE JUST DOLLS THAT HE TOSSES AWAY WHEN HE'S DONE!!
BAM
WHY HIM?
I...
I ...!!
SHHHH.
I DON'T DESERVE TO HEAR WHAT YOU'RE ABOUT TO SAY...
SAVE THAT FOR SOMEONE ...
WHO DE- SERVES YOU...
I HAVE ONE THING TO ASK OF YOU, HISOKA...
KILL ME ...?

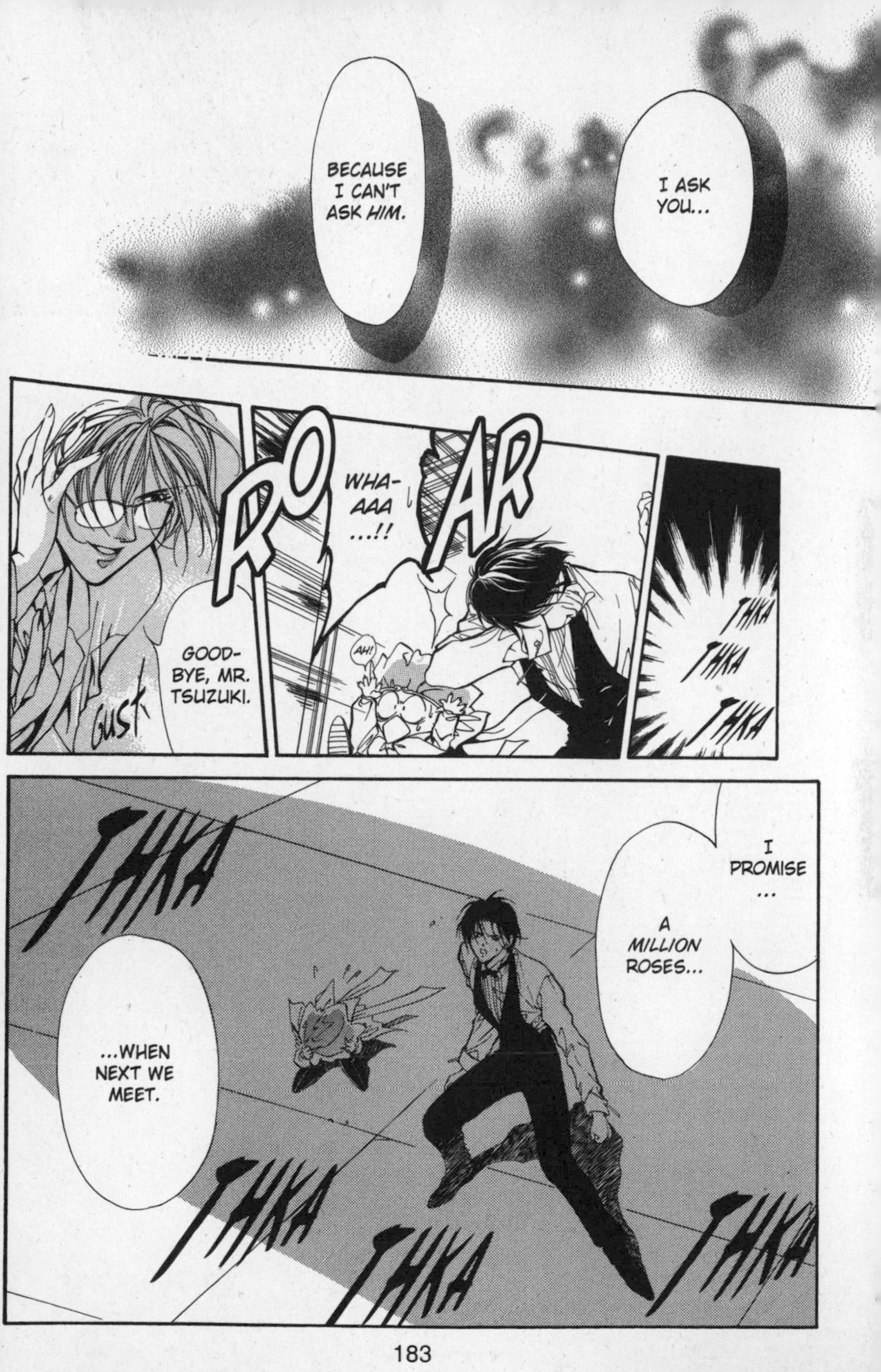
I ASK YOU...
BECAUSE I CAN'T ASK HIM.
THKA THKA THKA
ROAR
WHA-AAA...!!
AH!
GOOD-BYE, MR. TSUZUKI.
GUST
I PROMISE...
A MILLION ROSES...
...WHEN NEXT WE MEET.
THKA
THKA
THKA
THKA

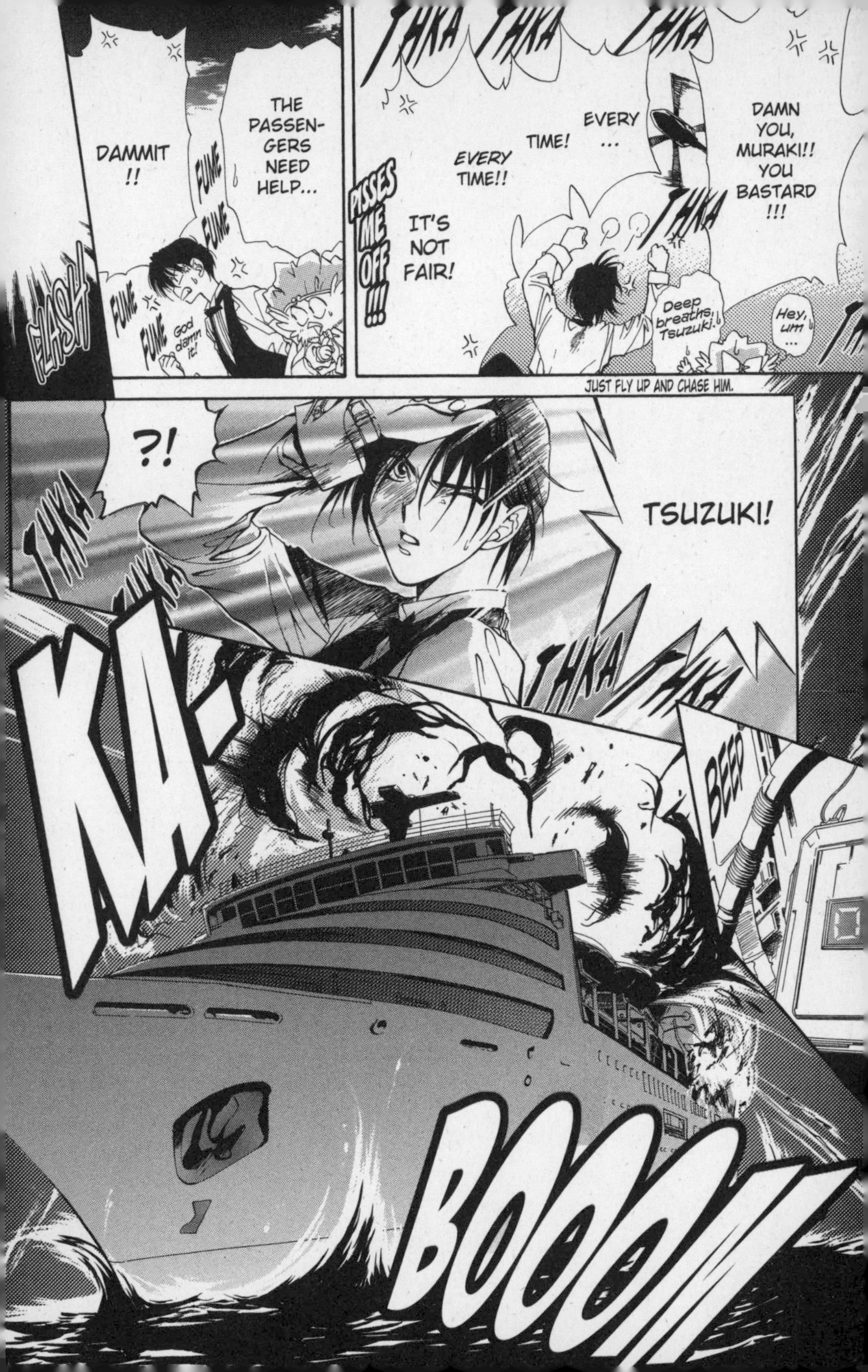
THKA THKA THKA
DAMN YOU, MURAKI!! YOU BASTARD!!!
THKA
Hey, um ...
Deep breaths, Tsuzuki.
EVERY ...
TIME!
EVERY TIME!!
IT'S NOT FAIR!
PISSES ME OFF!!!
THE PASSENGERS NEED HELP...
FUME FUME
DAMMIT !!
God damn it!
FUME FUME
FLASH
JUST FLY UP AND CHASE HIM.
TSUZUKI!
?!
THKA
THKA THKA
BEEP
KA-
BOOOM

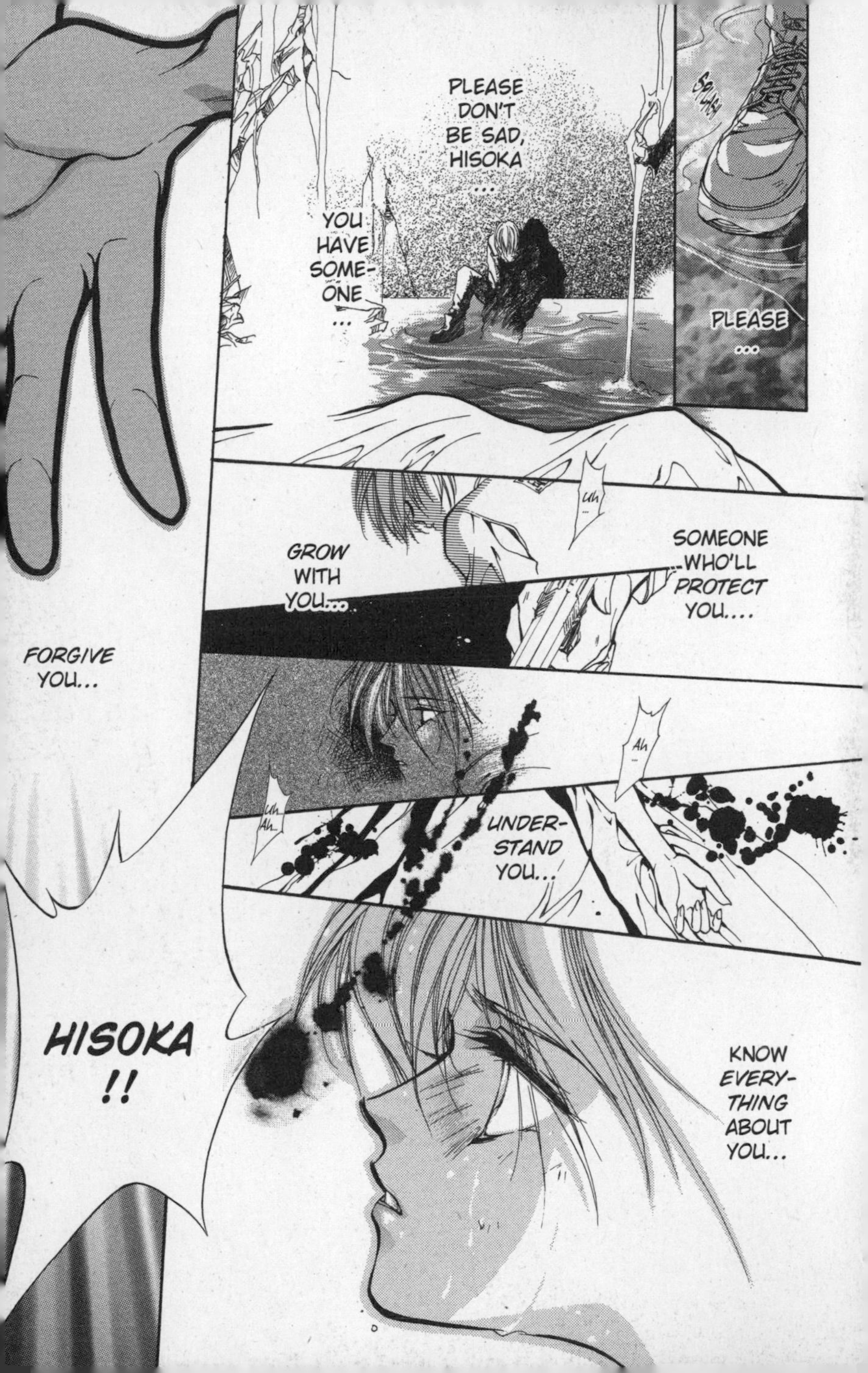
PLEASE ...
PLEASE DON'T BE SAD, HISOKA ...
YOU HAVE SOME-ONE ...
Uh ...
SOMEONE WHO'LL PROTECT YOU....
GROW WITH YOU...
FORGIVE YOU...
Ah ...
Uh Ah...
UNDER-STAND YOU...
KNOW EVERY-THING ABOUT YOU...
HISOKA !!

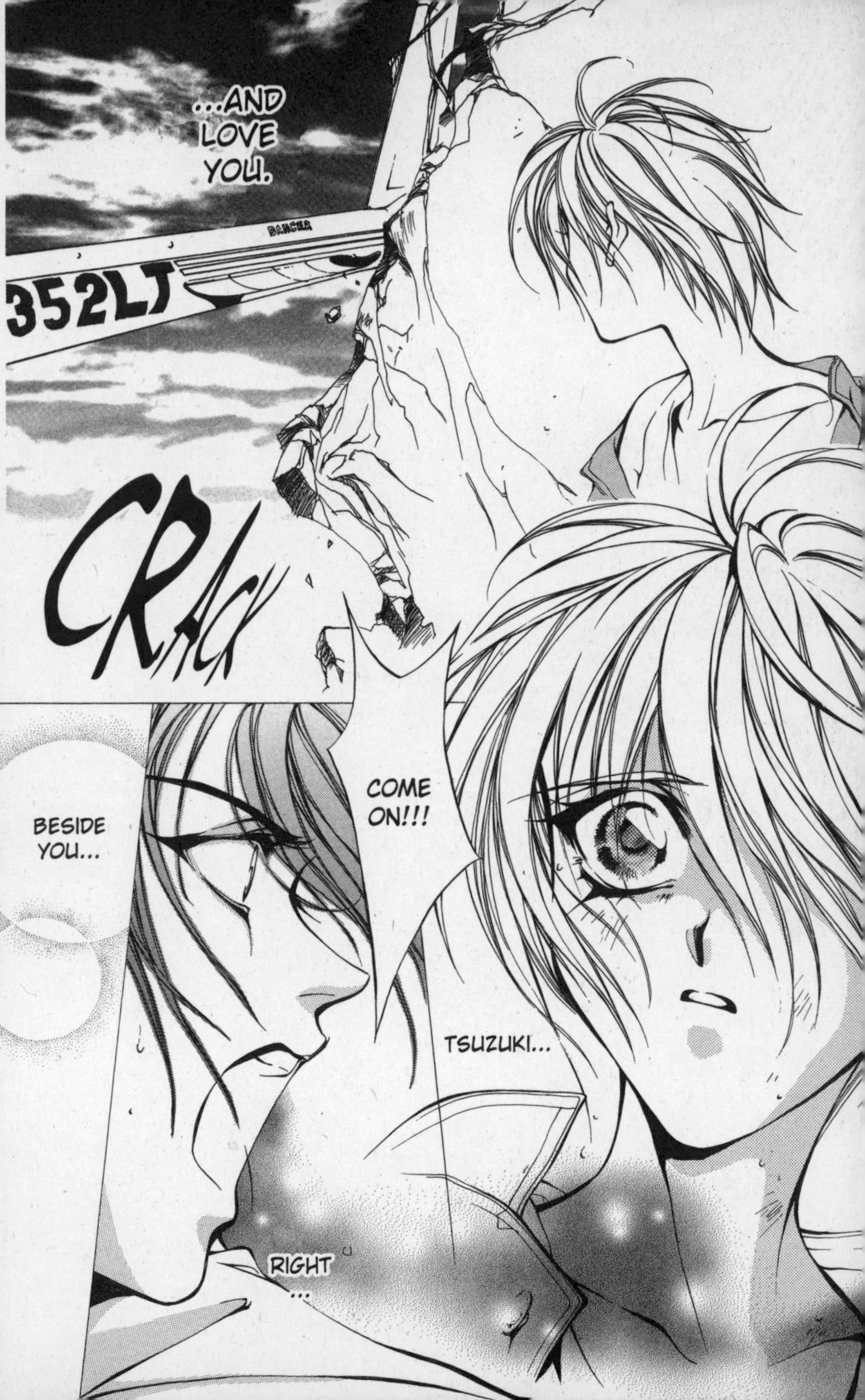
...AND LOVE YOU.
DANCER
352LJ
CRACK
COME ON!!!
TSUZUKI...
RIGHT ...
BESIDE YOU...

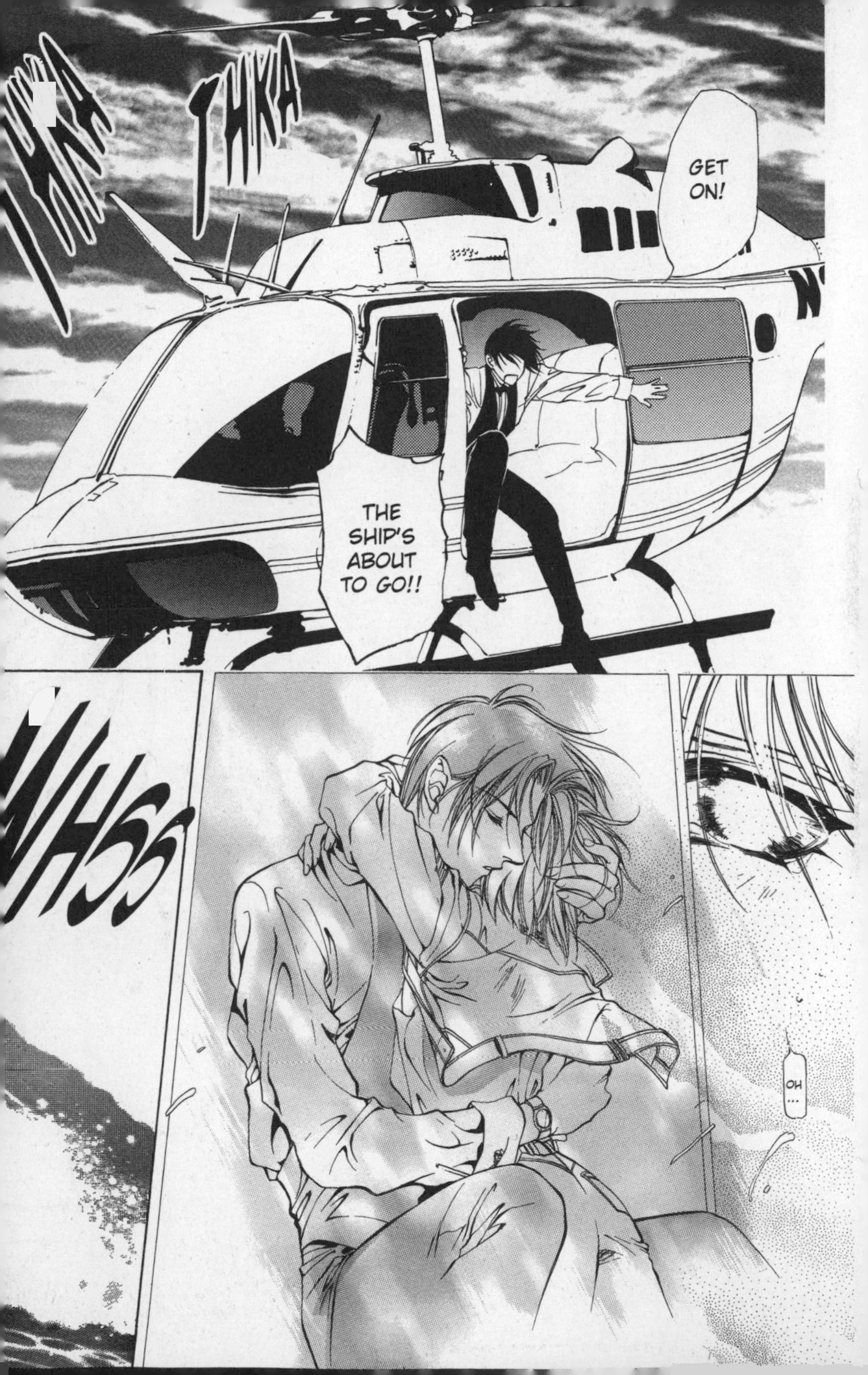
GET ON!
THKA
THKA
THE SHIP'S ABOUT TO GO!!
OH...
WHSS

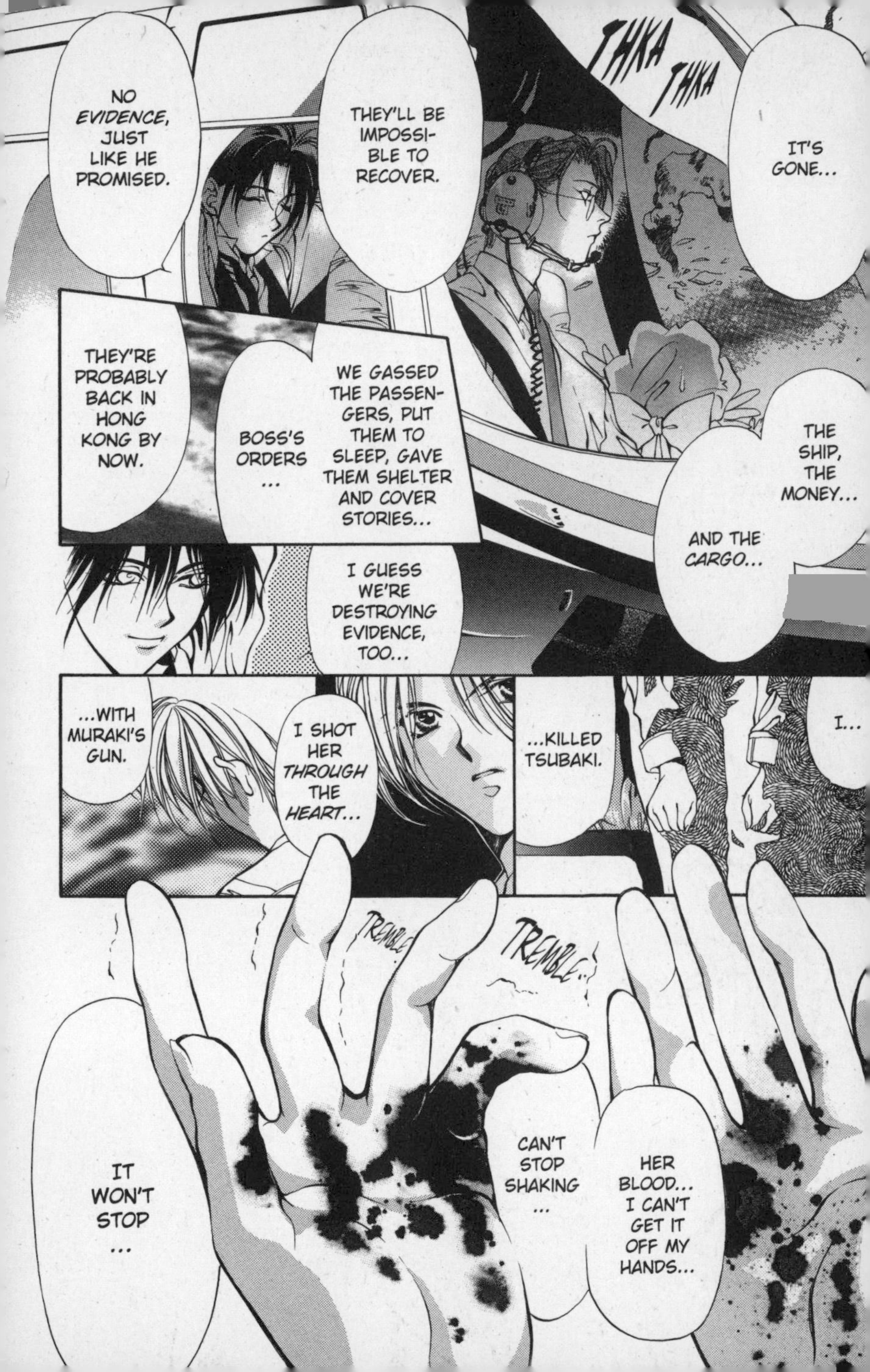
THKA THKA
IT'S GONE...
THEY'LL BE IMPOSSI-BLE TO RECOVER.
NO *EVIDENCE,* JUST LIKE HE PROMISED.
THE SHIP, THE MONEY...
AND THE *CARGO...*
WE GASSED THE PASSEN-GERS, PUT THEM TO SLEEP, GAVE THEM SHELTER AND COVER STORIES...
BOSS'S ORDERS ...
THEY'RE PROBABLY BACK IN HONG KONG BY NOW.
I GUESS WE'RE DESTROYING EVIDENCE, TOO...
I...
...KILLED TSUBAKI.
I SHOT HER *THROUGH* THE *HEART...*
...WITH MURAKI'S GUN.
TREMBLE
TREMBLE...
HER BLOOD... I CAN'T GET IT OFF MY HANDS...
CAN'T STOP SHAKING ...
IT WON'T STOP ...

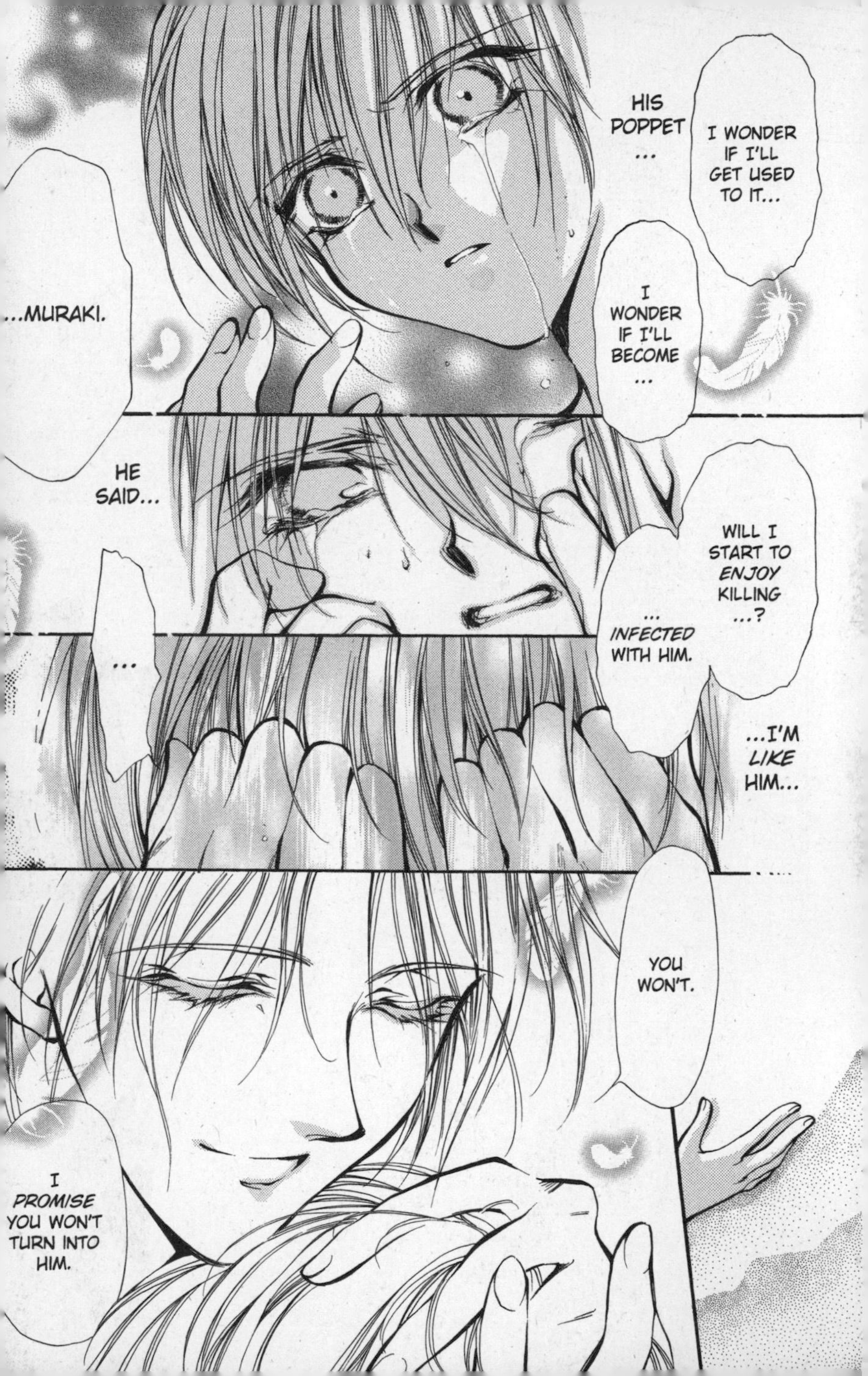
I WONDER IF I'LL GET USED TO IT...
HIS POPPET...
I WONDER IF I'LL BECOME...
...MURAKI.
WILL I START TO *ENJOY* KILLING...?
...*INFECTED* WITH HIM.
HE SAID...
...I'M *LIKE* HIM...
...
YOU WON'T.
I *PROMISE* YOU WON'T TURN INTO HIM.

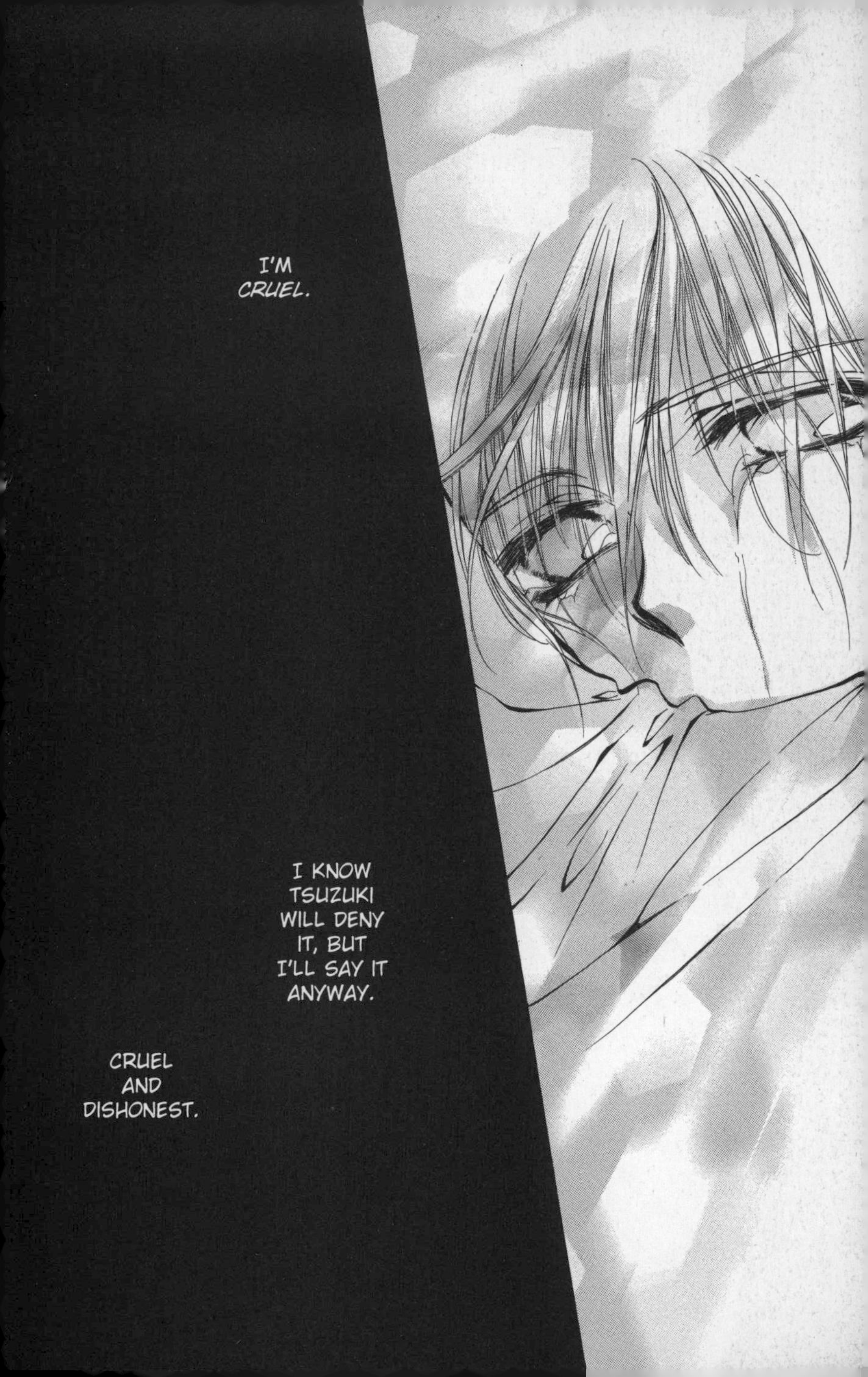
I'M CRUEL.
I KNOW TSUZUKI WILL DENY IT, BUT I'LL SAY IT ANYWAY.
CRUEL AND DISHONEST.

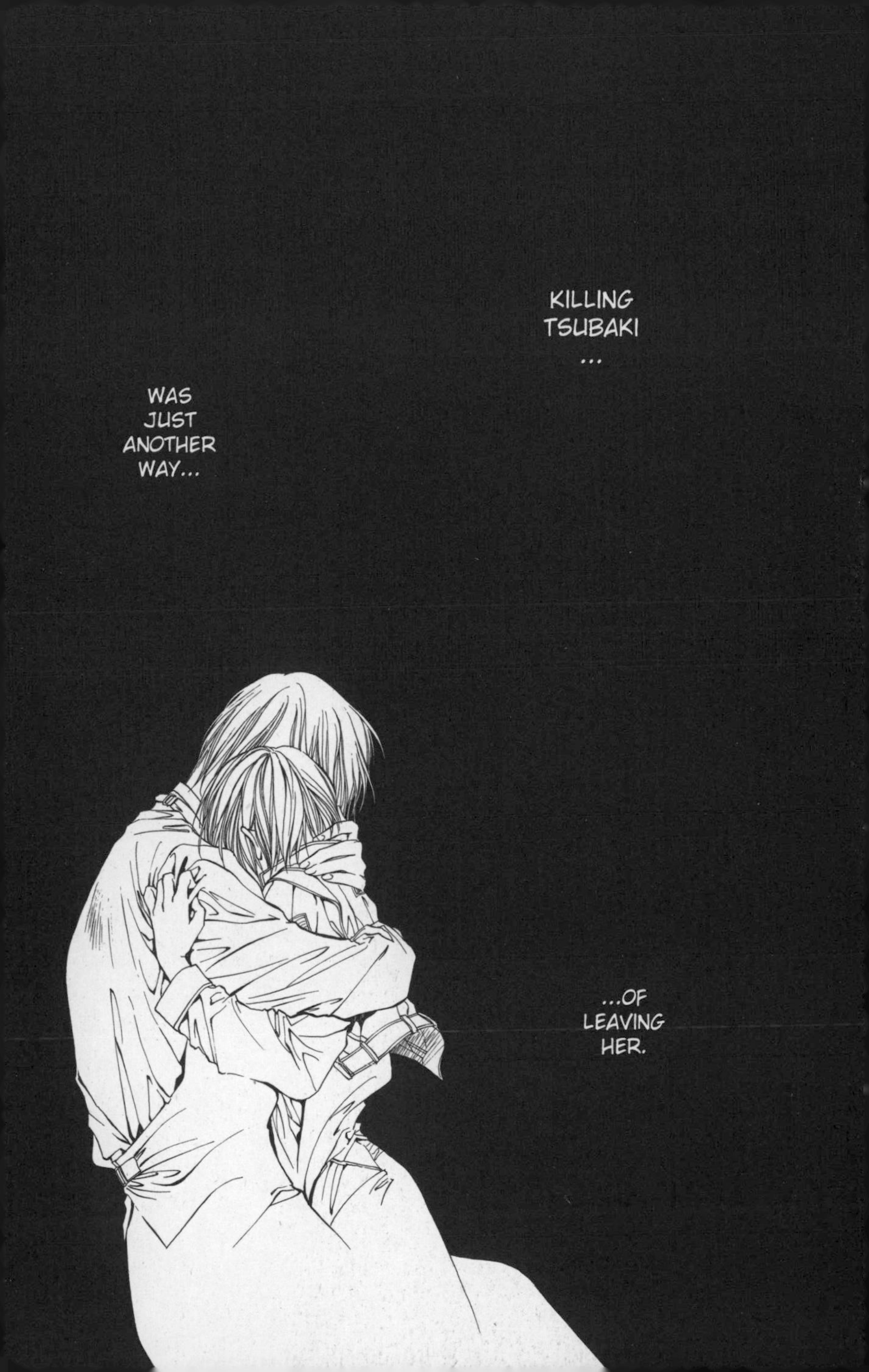
KILLING TSUBAKI ...
WAS JUST ANOTHER WAY...
...OF LEAVING HER.

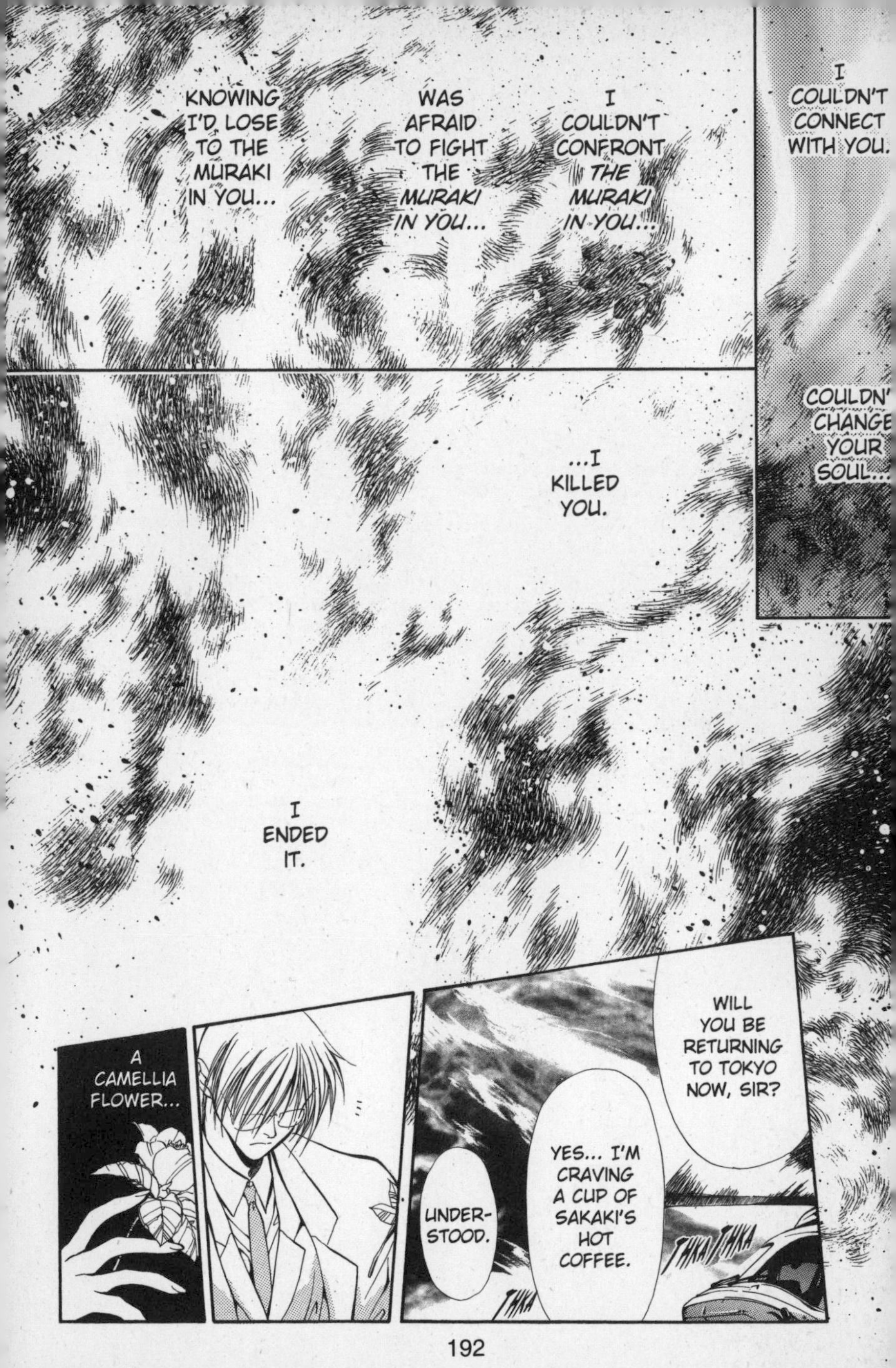
I COULDN'T CONNECT WITH YOU.
COULDN' CHANGE YOUR SOUL...
I COULDN'T CONFRONT THE MURAKI IN YOU...
WAS AFRAID TO FIGHT THE MURAKI IN YOU...
KNOWING I'D LOSE TO THE MURAKI IN YOU...
...I KILLED YOU.
I ENDED IT.
WILL YOU BE RETURNING TO TOKYO NOW, SIR?
YES... I'M CRAVING A CUP OF SAKAKI'S HOT COFFEE.
THKA THKA
THKA
UNDER-STOOD.
A CAMELLIA FLOWER...

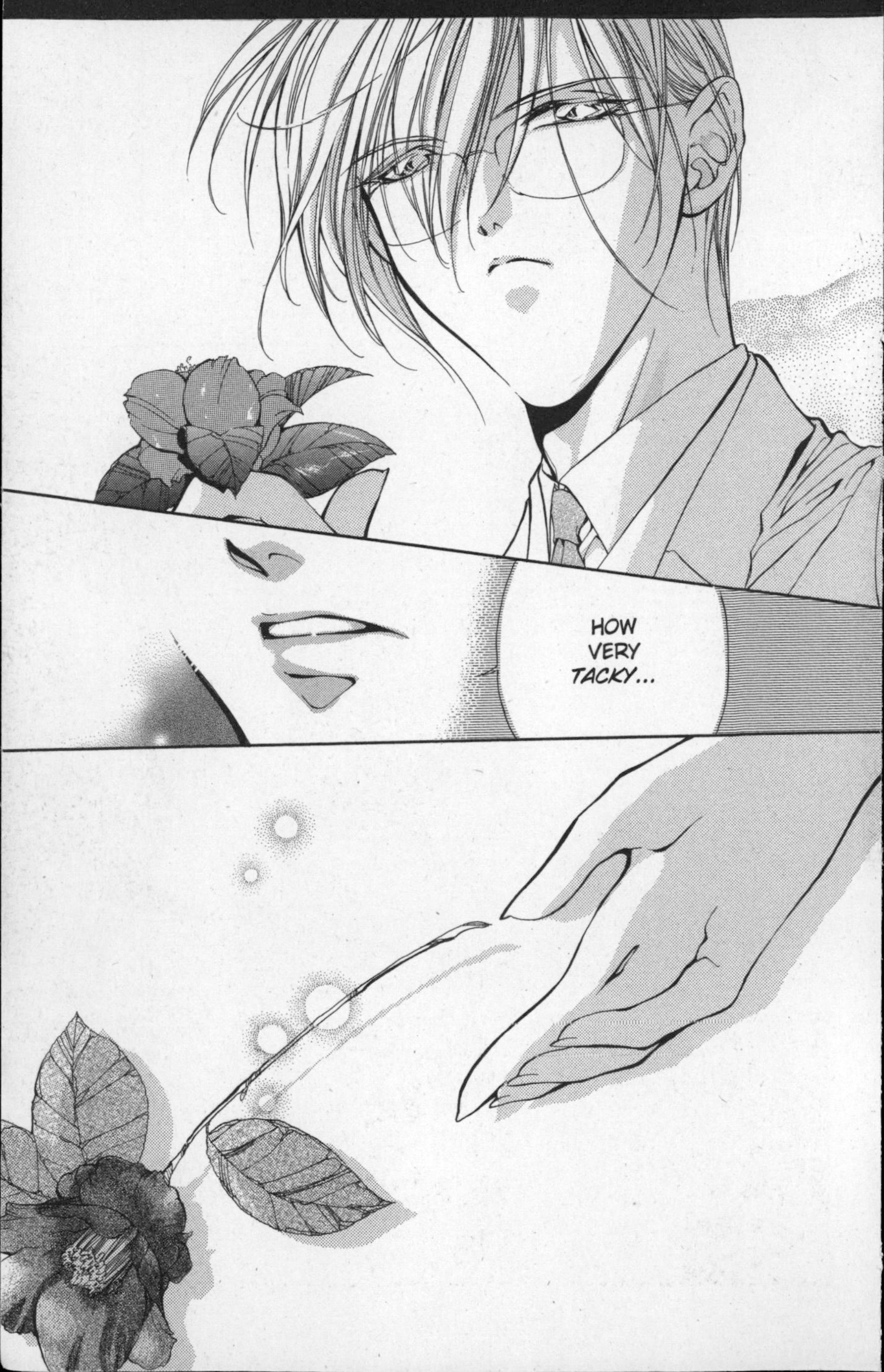
HOW VERY TACKY...

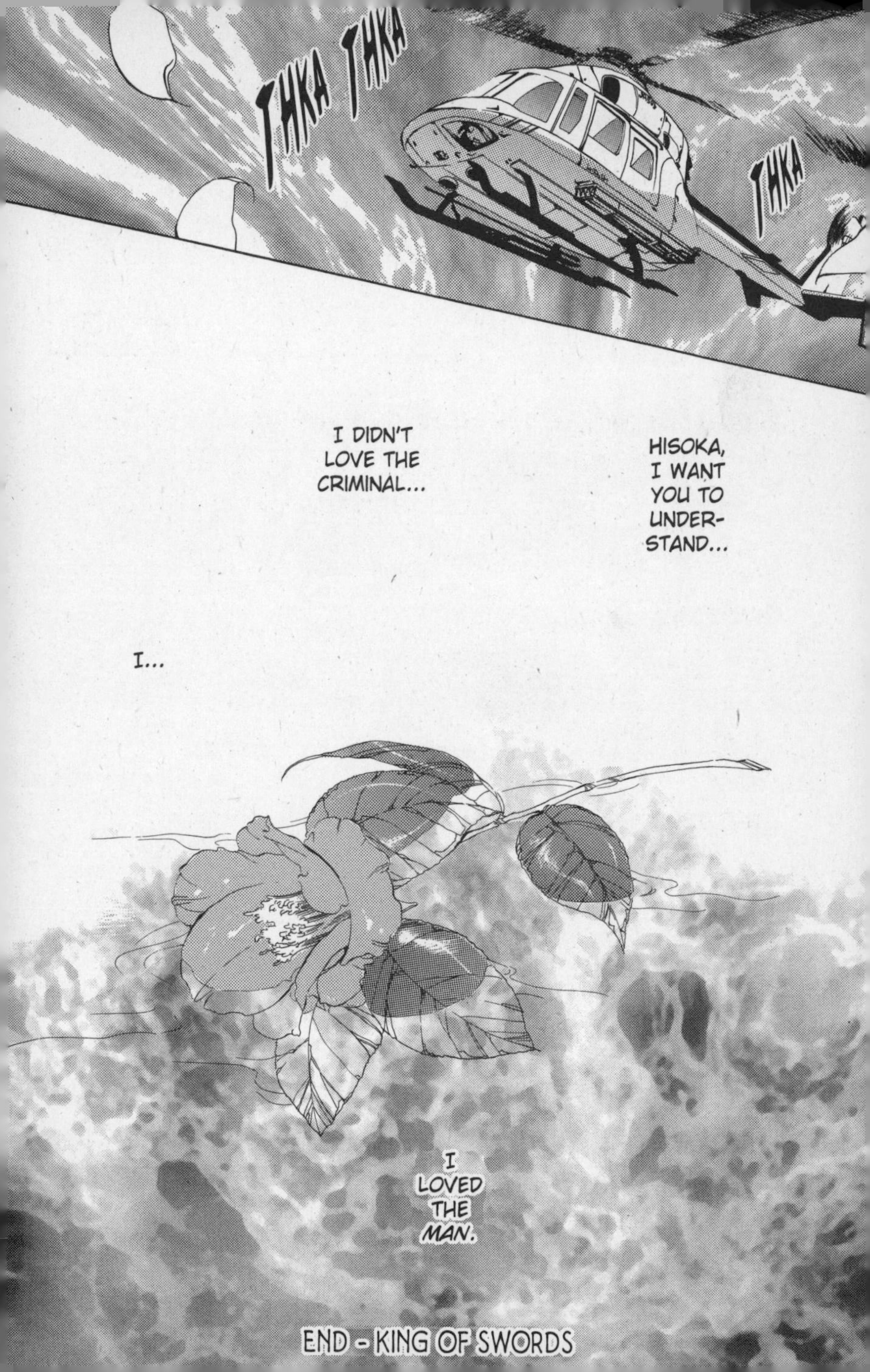
THKA
THKA THKA
HISOKA, I WANT YOU TO UNDER-STAND...
I DIDN'T LOVE THE CRIMINAL...
I...
I LOVED THE *MAN.*
END - KING OF SWORDS

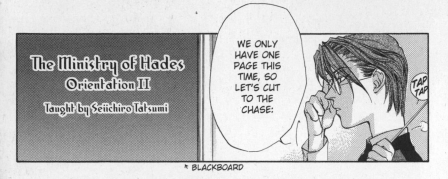

TAP TAP
WE ONLY HAVE ONE PAGE THIS TIME, SO LET'S CUT TO THE CHASE:
The Ministry of Hades
Orientation II
Taught by Seiichiro Tatsumi

↖ BLACKBOARD

WHERE DO THE EMPLOYEES OF THE SUMMONS DEPARTMENT LIVE?

ALL 18 OF THE EMPLOYEES ARE GIVEN MINISTRY HOUSING, BUT THEY'RE FREE TO CHOOSE TO LIVE ELSEWHERE. MR. TSUZUKI LIVES IN ANOTHER APARTMENT. MR. WATARI SPENDS THE BULK OF HIS TIME IN A RENTED RESEARCH LAB AND SELDOM GOES HOME, EVEN TO SLEEP. THEY ALL RESIDE WITHIN THE CITY LIMITS OF TOKYO, HOWEVER...

DOES PURGATORY HAVE SEASONS?

YES. THE FOUR SEASONS AREN'T AS CLEARLY DIFFERENTIATED AS IN THE MORTAL WORLD (THE TEMPERATURE DOESN'T VARY MUCH), BUT VEGETATION STILL OBSERVES GROWING SEASONS. (DUE TO THE RECENT CLIMATE CHANGE IN THE LIVING WORLD, SUMMER TEMPERATURES HAVE SKYROCKETED!)

CAN EVERYBODY USE MAGIC FROM THE BEGINNING?

KUROSAKI, WHO WAS BORN WITH HIS POWER, IS AN EXCEPTION. MOST PEOPLE BEGIN STUDYING MAGIC AFTER BECOMING SHINIGAMI. THE SHINIGAMI DETERMINE WHICH SORT OF MAGIC THEY'LL FOCUS THEIR STUDIES ON, AND THEY'RE TRAINED BY SPECIALISTS IN THAT AREA. THEY ALSO USE BOOKS FOR SELF-STUDY.

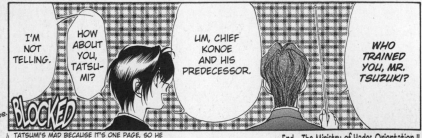

WHO TRAINED YOU, MR. TSUZUKI?
UM, CHIEF KONOE AND HIS PREDECESSOR.
HOW ABOUT YOU, TATSUMI?
I'M NOT TELLING.
BLOCKED
I see.

TATSUMI'S MAD BECAUSE IT'S ONE PAGE, SO HE DOESN'T GET PAID MUCH FOR HIS LECTURE.

End - The Ministry of Hades Orientation II

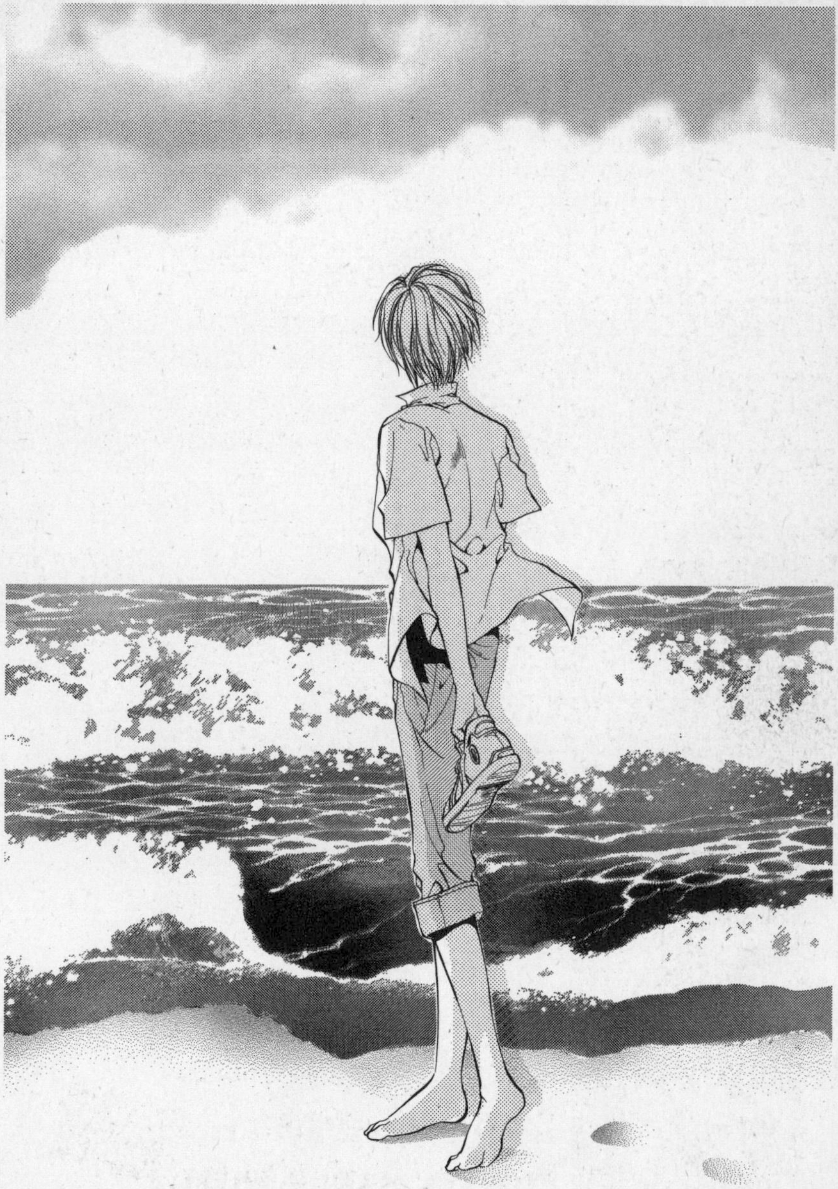

The Power of a Kiss

Soon after her first kiss, Yuri is pulled into a puddle and transported to an ancient Middle Eastern village. Surrounded by strange people speaking a language she can't understand, Yuri has no idea how to get back home and is soon embroiled in the politics and romance of the ancient Middle East. If a kiss helped get Yuri into this mess, can a kiss get her out?

shōjo
RED RIVER

1 story and art by **Chie Shinohara**

RED RIVER™

Start your graphic novel collection today!

ONLY $9.95!

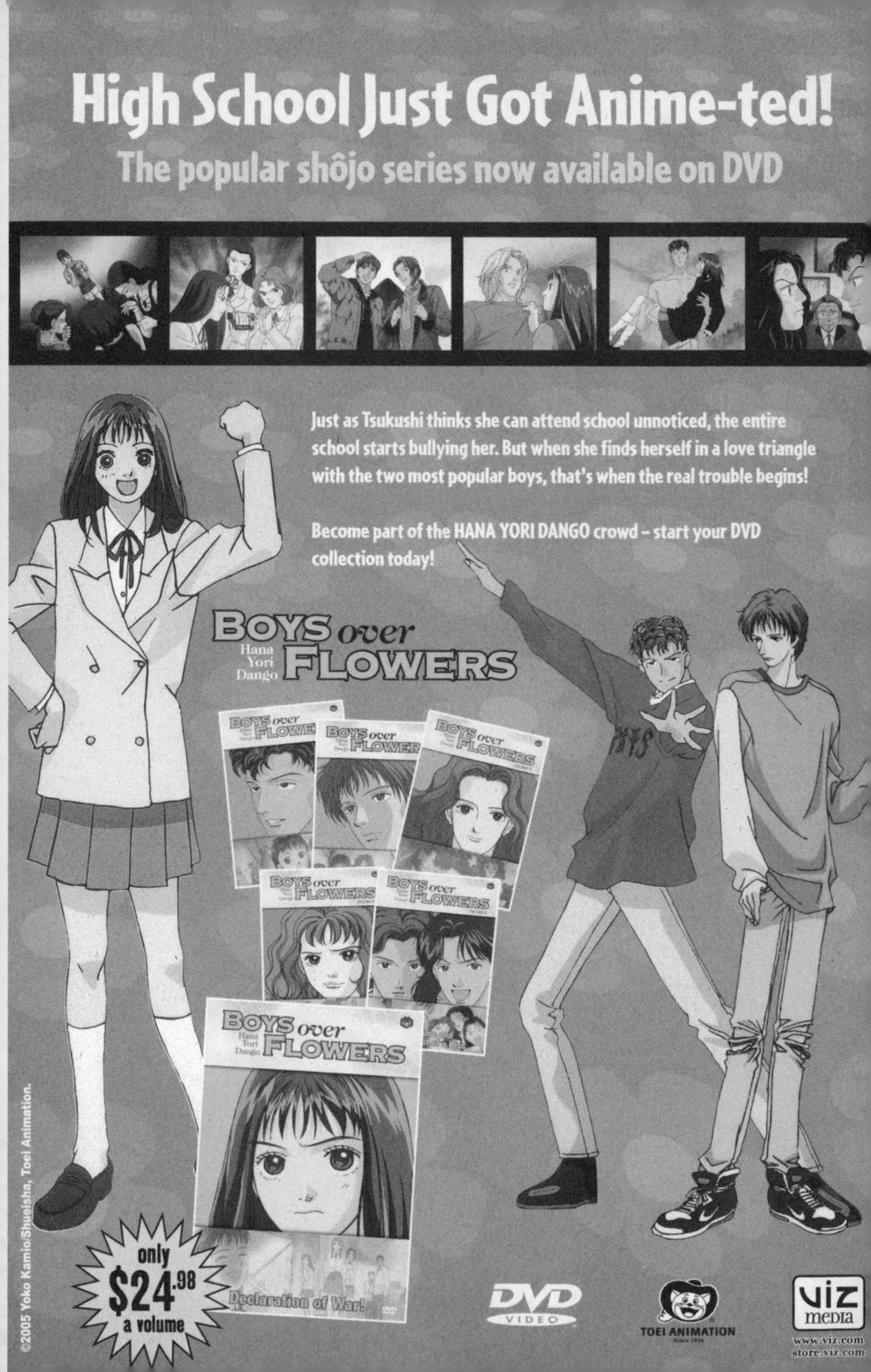
High School Just Got Anime-ted!
The popular shôjo series now available on DVD
Just as Tsukushi thinks she can attend school unnoticed, the entire school starts bullying her. But when she finds herself in a love triangle with the two most popular boys, that's when the real trouble begins!
Become part of the HANA YORI DANGO crowd – start your DVD collection today!
BOYS over FLOWERS
Hana Yori Dango
Declaration of War!
only $24.98 a volume
DVD VIDEO
TOEI ANIMATION
VIZ media
www.viz.com
store.viz.com
©2005 Yoko Kamio/Shueisha, Toei Animation.

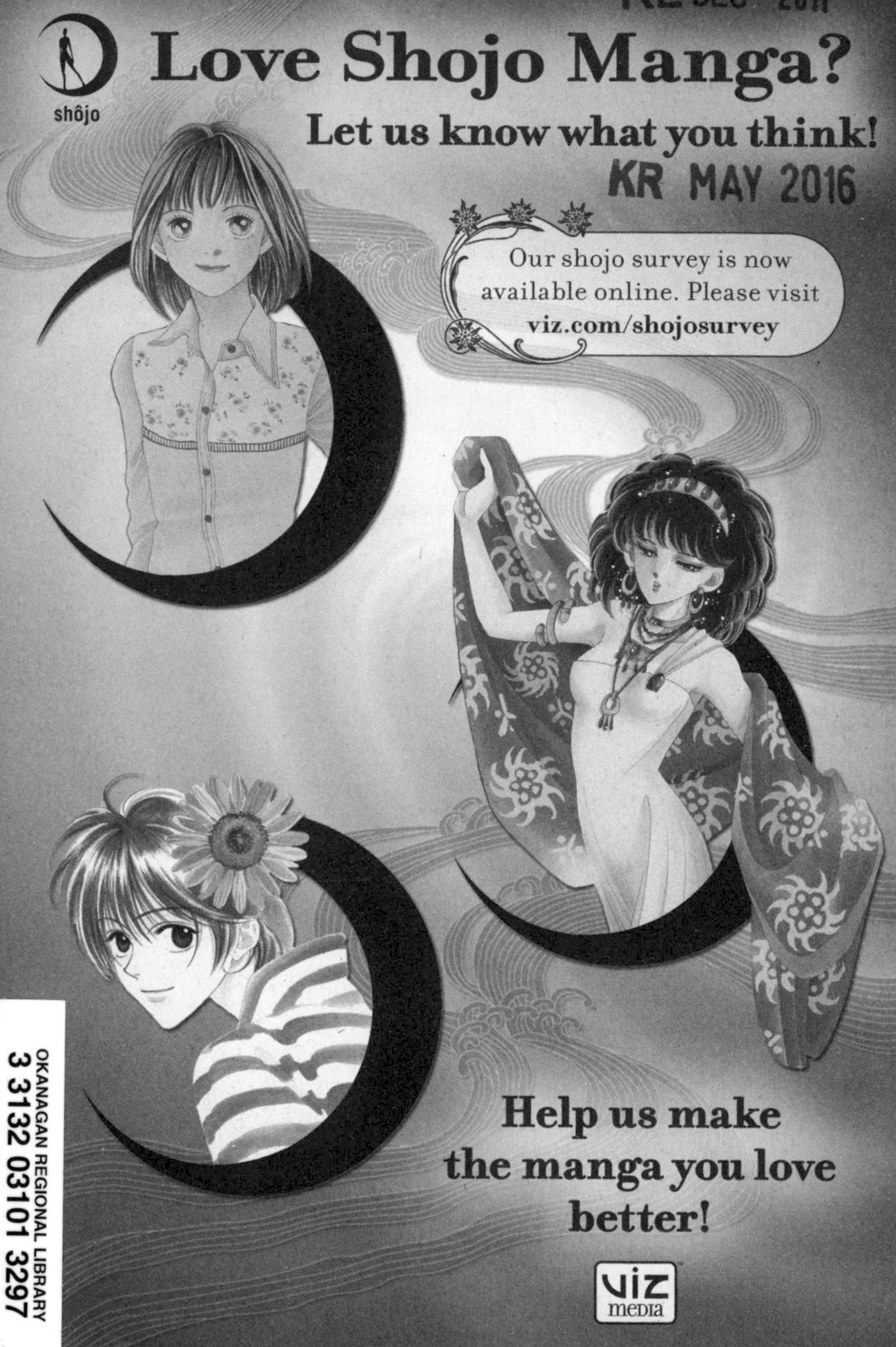